AF793061

Consent Matters

Consent Matters

ROBERT E. GOODIN

OXFORD
UNIVERSITY PRESS

OXFORD
UNIVERSITY PRESS

Great Clarendon Street, Oxford, OX2 6DP,
United Kingdom

Oxford University Press is a department of the University of Oxford.
It furthers the University's objective of excellence in research, scholarship,
and education by publishing worldwide. Oxford is a registered trade mark of
Oxford University Press in the UK and in certain other countries

© Robert E. Goodin 2024

The moral rights of the author have been asserted

All rights reserved. No part of this publication may be reproduced, stored in
a retrieval system, or transmitted, in any form or by any means, without the
prior permission in writing of Oxford University Press, or as expressly permitted
by law, by licence or under terms agreed with the appropriate reprographics
rights organization. Enquiries concerning reproduction outside the scope of the
above should be sent to the Rights Department, Oxford University Press, at the
address above

You must not circulate this work in any other form
and you must impose this same condition on any acquirer

Published in the United States of America by Oxford University Press
198 Madison Avenue, New York, NY 10016, United States of America

British Library Cataloguing in Publication Data
Data available

Library of Congress Control Number: 2023945524

ISBN 978-0-19-288902-7

DOI: 10.1093/oso/9780192889027.001.0001

Printed and bound in the UK by
Clays Ltd, Elcograf S.p.A.

Links to third party websites are provided by Oxford in good faith and
for information only. Oxford disclaims any responsibility for the materials
contained in any third party website referenced in this work.

MIX
Paper | Supporting responsible forestry
FSC® C018072
FSC
www.fsc.org

Contents

Analytic Table of Contents

II. CONSENT IN OPERATION

III. SPECIAL CASES

Preface

Torbjörn Tännsjö prefaced his book *Conservatism for Our Times* by saying that readers might find it odd that a card-carrying communist would write a book about conservatism (although as he wryly observed the Swedish Communist Party is a very *old* party).[1] Many will see a similar irony in a confirmed consequentialist such as myself writing a book about consent. According to conventional dichotomies, after all, consent is the exclusive domain of the opposite deontological way of thinking about morality.

Doubtless readers will find many things to disagree with in the analyses of consent to come. But not many, if any, of those disagreements will stem from disagreements over those ethical fundamentals. In this book, my main aim is simply to *describe* the existing social practice of seeking and giving, receiving and acting upon consent. My analyses will extend and elaborate upon the old Natural Lawyers (Pufendorf is a particularly rich source on this subject). But I doubt that anything I say would have surprised them, except perhaps in its detail and perhaps its systematicity. My analyses will also be broadly faithful to contemporary legal approaches to consent, particularly in contract and tort law—in broad outline at least if not in fine detail, since of course the law addresses rather different problems than morality and requires slightly different instruments for its somewhat differing purposes.

For followers of Leo Strauss, committed as they are to searching for hidden meanings in classic texts, it is absolutely essential to have highly accurate translations of the texts to work on.[2] So too for me to do political philosophy as I think it should be done, it is important to have a descriptively accurate account of the social practices that I am trying to theorize. My job in theorizing them is to provide a principled rationale for the practices (and to suggest some reforms of those practices based on those principles). But insofar as the ultimate goal is to provide a normatively rich explanation of the practice, I have to start from a clean, non-theory-laden account of that which I am trying to explain.

The task of social philosophy, as a great many of us see it, is to reach a reflective equilibrium between considered judgments in particular cases and general theories. Conjuring up artificial examples, elaborated at length, is nowadays the standard way of playing that game. But I think it is philosophically dangerous. Those artificially crafted examples often have theories baked into them; they are

[1] Tännsjö 1990, preface.

[2] As John Pocock emphasized to me in a memorable seminar that we conducted together long ago.

prejudicially tailored to bolster some theory over its rivals; they are crazy, atypical to the point that your intuitive responses to them cannot be trusted. I railed against the use of crazy cases in one of my earliest books, some forty years ago; and I continue to resile from them.[3]

Instead, I think that our explanandum should not be our intuitive responses to particular (particularly peculiar) cases so much as existing social practices that we think to be worthy. Those practices are governed by conventions that are common knowledge across the community, thus narrowing the scope for idiosyncratic responses to the prompts of crazy cases. Some of those conventions are semi-formally codified, as in the common law that judges have built up through confrontation with a great many particular cases over the years.[4] Those common law practices are themselves partially theorized by the judges, sometimes in ways responding to peculiarities of the legal setting but sometimes in ways that also speak to broader moral concerns.

The ultimate task of a social philosopher advocating a broader theoretical position such as my consequentialism is to show how those worthy practices can be seen as reflections of that broader theoretical position, suitably adapted to the circumstances to which it is being applied. In this book, I begin that task by attempting to weave together disparate strands of common law and commonsense morality into a comprehensive analysis of the social practice of consent, faithful to the social practice without (yet) being bent to fit into some overarching moral theory. What this book offers is thus more of a 'middle-range theory' than a new 'grand theory' of consent.[5]

Thus, in describing the social practice of consenting I shall be at pains not to 'bake in' my consequentialist predilections. Some of the features of that practice that I identify certainly do resonate with consequentialism. One is the social nature of consent and the role of socially conventional indicators in betokening it. Another is how others' reliance upon your tokens of consent provides a *pro tanto* reason for you to honour the consent that you conventionally (even if unintentionally) signalled. But I genuinely think that those features would have to loom large in any honest description of the social practice of consent as we know it.

[3] Goodin 1982, pp. 8–12. When I use examples to illustrate, and evoke, points I make in this book, I shall be at pains to choose common garden rather than crazy contrived ones.

[4] I explicitly made similar use of common law materials in Goodin (1976, ch. 7) and implicitly in much of my subsequent work (e.g., Goodin 1985b; 1988; 1995; Lepora and Goodin 2013).

[5] In the spirit of Merton (1949), who contrasted 'middle-range theories' in sociology to grand theories such as functionalism. My analyses will be middle-range in a similar sense: I aim to provide an analysis of the morality of consent that generalizes up from the many particular settings in which consent might be sought or given, but that stops short of grand moral theories like consequentialism or deontology. My analysis is also somewhere in the middle of the range between descriptive and prescriptive, describing prescriptions we often make at the same time as trying to excavate good normative reasons for making them and prescribing marginal reforms to existing practice based on them.

Given this book's aspiration to 'map existing social practice', it is inevitable (indeed, desirable) that it should start by covering common, familiar ground. Chapter 2 is largely, if hardly exclusively, devoted to setting out systematically 'what we already know' about consent. Systematizing the conventional wisdom is both a modest service in its own right and also, importantly, lays the groundwork for the more novel explorations in subsequent chapters. Those later chapters theorize various aspects of existing practices of consent and offer prescriptions for how those practices ought best proceed, based upon those theorizations. Yet even those later chapters do not aspire to provide a wholly new 'grand theory' of consent; instead, they merely weave together in a more systematic way those often neglected aspects of our existing social practice of consent.

As will be evident just from the table of contents, and all the more so over the course of the book, my interest in consent ranges across a wide array of substantive applications. Unlike much recent work on consent, this book is not narrowly fixated on sex. Only one of its eleven chapters specifically concerns sexual consent, and even then in very particular circumstances chosen to illuminate more general points about consent rather than to guide everyday sexual encounters. Consent to sexual relations is of course one very important application, and any general analysis must 'get it right' when it comes to that topic. Consent to sex is nevertheless a very *special* case. Throughout the book when offering some general conclusions about consent I find myself saying, time and again, 'sexual consent may be different for the following reasons...'. Treating sexual consent as the paradigm case of consent would thus seriously distort the overall contours of a general theory of consent. In adopting an insistently broader focus I hope to avoid that all-too-common fate.[6]

****

This book arose most immediately from conversations with a pair of friends and sometime coauthors who found themselves wrestling with very different aspects of consent. Chiara Lepora had just come off a stint as a detention doctor for the International Committee of the Red Cross in Algeria and Palestine and was still worrying how to secure meaningful consent to artificial feeding from hunger-striking patients she had been caring for there.[7] Ana Tanasoca was questioning whether politicians could secure valid consent in democratic elections on the basis of lies—which was a vexed question indeed in the backwash of Trump and Brexit.[8] I am grateful to both of them for many long and useful discussions, not only of

[6] Bolinger (2019, pp. 179–80) alludes to such risks when writing, 'Much of the philosophical and legal attention given to this question [concerning the nature of consent] focuses on a few high-stakes contexts: consent to sex, to medical procedures, or to legally binding contracts... [B]ut there are also more mundane cases, such as agreeing to swap seats on a flight, inviting someone onto your property, or purchasing a coffee.... [A] good account of consent should be serviceable in these domains as well.'

[7] For the fruit of her reflections, see Lepora (2021).

[8] Tanasoca (2022).

their own particular topics (which fed heavily into the corresponding chapters of the book), but also well beyond.

Those conversations rekindled my interest in consent as grounds for political obligation. I had come of age academically during the Vietnam War, after all. Against that background, it always struck me as odd that Rawls should proclaim 'justice' rather than 'political obligation' as the first question for political philosophy. I had a chance to explore the latter issues with John Plamenatz, the author of the first really analytical book on those topics, during his time as replacement-supervisor of my Oxford DPhil. My work since then has hewn more closely to the interests of my principal supervisors, Brian Barry and Jim Mirrlees. While not regretting that for a moment, I am nonetheless pleased to revisit the problems that attracted me to political philosophy in the first instance.

This book is also, in various respects, a lagged response to my year as visiting Senior Research Fellow in the Department of Bioethics of the US National Institutes of Health. There, Alan Wertheimer and I renewed and intensified our on-going but previously intermittent conversations on these topics (and many others) over weekly dinners and far more frequent seminars. During that year, Chiara Lepora, Frank Miller, Annette Rid, Dave Wendler and many others also contributed to my thinking on these topics, even if they may not necessarily want to take ownership of all of the results. Conversations in the corners of two conferences at Fondation Brocher in Geneva with Chiara Lepora and the fascinating coterie gathered there also contributed, in various deep-background ways, to this book.

During the writing itself, I have profited from frequent discussions with Christian Barry and Nic Southwood. Garrett Cullity and Ana Tanasoca provided not only invaluable conversational inputs but also helpful written comments on the manuscript as a whole. So too did the publisher's readers at a later stage.

This is my second *On the Beach* book, written in (almost) COVID19-free Canberra with Australia's drawbridges firmly up, while the plague raged across the rest of the world. We sorely missed the many academic visitors who would ordinarily have spent their summers with us. Still, having quiet time to pursue big projects was nice, too.

PART I
THE NATURE OF CONSENT

1
Introduction

Consent matters, sometimes hugely.[1] Why? For many reasons—and for all practical purposes, there is no need to choose among the various different grounds provided by different philosophical traditions. Suffice it to say that we all have a life to live, and we need exclusive control over some centrally important aspects of our lives to do so in any genuine, authentic manner.[2] But we also lead our lives alongside others, with whom we sometimes wish to share or to whom we sometimes wish to cede some of that control.[3] Consent enables us to allow selected others into our own protected spheres in that way.[4]

What is consent, and how does it work? We tend to think we have a pretty good grasp on that. Lord knows we should—it has been discussed for so long, not only among philosophers and lawyers but also among practical people of all sorts. But while there are a great many discussions of this aspect or that of consent, there remains a crying need for a systematic account of the practice in the round.

We need not only to know what consent is, conceptually.[5] We also need to know how something can be taken for consent, perhaps wrongly, and with what consequences.[6] We need to know not only how consent, when present, operates to change the moral landscape. We also need to know how consent comes into and passes out of being, and what moral norms govern the seeking out of consent and the revoking of it.[7] We need to appreciate how contextually sensitive norms governing consent can be in diverse settings, ranging from sexual relations to prison hospitals to voting booths.[8]

[1] Other times, far less so—and sometimes hardly at all. I will return to that point in Chapter 11. But it is important to get a clear grasp on how precisely consent is supposed to work, particularly for those cases where it matters more (sometimes much more). To avoid distracting from that task, which is the main aim of this book, I reserve such deflationary thoughts for the Epilogue.

[2] Recalling Thomas Rainborough's famous remark at the 29 October 1647 Putney Debate: 'For really I think that the poorest he that is in England hath a life to live, as the greatest he; and therefore truly, sir, I think it clear, that every man that is to live under a government ought first by his own consent to put himself under that government; and I do think that the poorest man in England is not at all bound in a strict sense to that government that he hath not had a voice to put himself under...' (Woodhouse 1938, p. 53). For a similar analysis of the role of consent see: Shiffrin 2008, pp. 501–2; Tadros 2016, pp. 3, 222; Bolinger 2019, p. 185; Dougherty 2021a, p. 58.

[3] This is what Owens (2011; 2012, ch. 7) calls a 'permissive interest'.

[4] That 'protected sphere' is delineated in terms of 'rights'; I shall use those terms interchangeably. Those are the 'centrally important aspects of life' just mentioned. Whether those aspects of life are centrally important because we have rights over them, or whether we have rights over them because they are centrally important, is an issue that I bracket for the purposes of this book.

[5] On which see Chapter 2.

[6] On which, see Chapters 3–4.

[7] On which, see Chapters 6–7.

[8] On which, see Chapters 8–10.

Consent Matters. Robert E. Goodin, Oxford University Press. © Robert E. Goodin 2024.
DOI: 10.1093/oso/9780192889027.003.0001

Many specific points, both large and small, will emerge over the course of this book. Here I shall foreshadow some of the most central, recurring themes to be elaborated over the course of the chapters that follow. The discussion in this chapter and those that follow will be replete with many suggestions for how we should think about consent in new ways. But given the book's 'middle-range theory' aspirations, I shall resist any temptation to impose any big unifying 'grand theory' tying all of these themes together. A necessary step before that can be done is mapping existing social practices of consent, thereby providing a set of observations that any larger theory of consent needs to accommodate. In the terminology of Rawls's 'reflective equilibrium', the aim of this book is to provide 'considered judgments' that need to stand in reflective equilibrium with any larger theory.[9]

This introductory chapter serves various functions. One, as just stated, is to preview arguments to be elaborated in subsequent chapters (Section 1.3 is particularly like that). But this introductory chapter also serves to provide essential background for the discussions to follow. That can sometimes be done briefly, as in establishing that there is a presumption that consent has not been given unless there is good evidence that it has (in Section 1.1) and that the moral importance of consent is variable (in Section 1.5). But sometimes those background discussions need to be more elaborate, as when correcting current understandings of the ontology and social function of consent (in Section 1.2) and in showing the importantly different ways in which consent might be false (insincere) and how best morally to respond to each (in Section 1.4).

Finally, by way of methodological preliminaries, let me add a few disclaimers that apply across the book as a whole:

- Firstly, when discussing what it takes for consent to serve its *social function*, I shall be looking for conclusions that are 'generally' true rather than 'necessarily' so. A single, isolated, atypical counterexample will not defeat those sorts of generalizations in the same way that it would conceptual or ontological claims of a stronger sort.
- Secondly, to simplify the exposition I usually omit the qualifier '*pro tanto*'. But that qualifier ought always be understood as applying (unless otherwise explicitly stated) to all of the worked examples that I discuss.[10] Whenever I say that consent makes something 'permissible', that should always be read as '*pro tanto* permissible'.[11] Whether it is permissible all things considered is

[9] Rawls 1971, § 9. See also: Sidgwick 1874/1907, bk. 3, ch 13; Singer 1974; Daniels 1996; 2016; Tersman 2018.

[10] Renzo (2022, p. 49) employs a similar 'blanket *pro tanto*' proviso.

[11] As will be obvious throughout this chapter, and as will be discussed explicitly in Section 2.1 below, I am following the near-consensus among philosophers that to give consent to someone is to give her

a separate question—there may be other reasons making it impermissible that would not be removed by consent.[12]

- Thirdly, I often refer to examples or principles drawn from the law or (less often) medical ethics. I do not intend those as appeals to authority in any way. On the contrary, I treat those sources merely as repositories of settled moral judgments of the communities in question—they are data, not dicta. Likewise, I often draw upon the wisdom of philosophers of old, but I do so with no intention of either invoking their authority or of contributing to the history of ideas. I mine those old texts for good ideas, nothing more.

1.1 The Presumption of Non-consent, and What It Takes to Overcome It

Let us begin with the basics. If someone else's consent is required for it to be morally permissible for you to do something to or with them, then you must presume that you do not have their consent unless you have good grounds for believing that you do. Otherwise, the requirement of consent would be meaningless (or anyway pragmatically pointless).

How strong that presumption is, and how much and how weighty the evidence must be in order to overcome it, will vary with the importance of the protected sphere that you would be violating if you acted without consent.[13] There can be two ways of fleshing out 'how important': how important to the particular person whose sphere you would be invading, or how important to people in general in our society. My proposal would be that in any particular case we should take whichever is the more demanding of those two standards. If I happen to know that you take far more pride in your car than most people do, then I must be all the more certain that I really do have your consent to borrow it than I would have to be before borrowing someone else's car. If on the other hand I happen to know that you take far less pride in your car than average, that should not entitle me to be more cavalier than I would ordinarily be permitted to be about your consent to let me borrow it.[14] You can be casual about that—I cannot.

permission to do something that she would not otherwise be permitted to do to or with me. Westen (2004) characterizes consent as 'acquiescence' instead of 'permission' (the *Oxford English Dictionary* includes both in its definition 1a of 'consent (n.)'). But if 'acquiescence' is something different from 'permission', it is hard to see how consent understood in that way can be 'morally transformative' and hence an exercise of a 'moral power' at all; Manson (2018, p. 70) remarks similarly concerning the relationship between 'agreement' and permissive consent.

[12] As Tadros (2022, p. 449) puts it, 'Most consent-sensitive duties are not exclusively consent-sensitive.'

[13] Note well: the issue here is not 'how important it is to get the consent', nor is it 'how likely is it that the person will give consent'; it is instead 'how certain are you that you really have the consent'.

[14] My conclusion here converges with Dougherty's (2021a, p. 159): '[O]ur society's conventions . . . permit a guest to leaf through the books on their host's shelves. However, . . . if it is common knowledge

People purporting to act with others' consent must take 'due care' to ensure that they really have it.[15] How much care is 'due' depends again upon just how important is the protected sphere they would be violating if acting without consent.[16] 'Due diligence' does not necessarily require you to find out absolutely everything you possibly could that bears on the question. It only requires you to make such further enquires as are 'reasonable'—appropriate in the circumstances, defined in terms of the stakes involved.[17] Where something very important is at stake—bodily integrity, for example—due diligence can be highly demanding. Surgeons must go to considerable lengths to ensure that they genuinely have informed consent from their patients, and sexual partners likewise.[18] In other cases, where the stakes are far lower, the diligence that is due can be far less demanding.[19]

1.2 What Constitutes Consent

From a moral point of view, it is often thought that consent is first and foremost (if perhaps not exclusively) a mental attitude, a 'consenting state of mind'.[20] From a social point of view, however, consent is first and foremost an interpersonal

between Ashley and Taylor that Ashley has a neurosis about other people reading their books, then the available reliable evidence does not support interpreting Ashley's consent as covering Taylor reading their books.'

[15] This is a special case of the more general 'duty of care' found in tort law (ALI 1979, § 7).

[16] Epistemologists sometimes worry about 'moral or pragmatic encroachment': what you are justified in believing to be true should not, they say, be affected by what would be morally desirable or pragmatically convenient to be true. Guerrero (2021) addresses this worry at length as regards varying standards of what counts as adequate evidence of consent. But while what beliefs we are justified in *holding* should not be sensitive to such considerations, perhaps, what we are justified in *doing* by way of acting on those beliefs certainly should be. The 'standard of proof' being higher in criminal cases than in civil ones—'beyond a reasonable doubt' rather than merely 'more likely than not'—is just one very familiar application of that principle (Dougherty 2015, pp. 252–3).

[17] For the tort rule, see ALI (1979, § 7). As applied to consent see: Dougherty 2015, pp. 227, 252–3; 2018, p. 101; 2021a, chs. 5, 9; Guerrero 2021, pp. 368–77. In fleshing out 'reasonableness' in terms of 'size of stakes', I am going beyond Dougherty (2021a, p. 150) who proclaims 'that it is impossible to define reasonableness in this context' and hence leaves it as 'a primitive notion' in his analysis.

[18] Lackey 2021.

[19] Dougherty (2021a, p. 144) imposes a similar principle of 'due diligence' in this connection, writing that the 'duty of due diligence is a duty to *adequately* investigate what someone meant to cover with their consent'. In fleshing that out, he goes on to say similarly to me: 'It would matter whether the consent is "low-stakes" consent, such as consent to minor uses of each other's property, or "high-stakes" consent, such as invasive medical surgery'. In any case, he says (as I do above), 'Often, adequate investigation is not equivalent to maximal investigation'.

[20] 'Signs' of consent 'argue the will' of the consent-giver (Hobbes 1651, ch. 14) or 'express the inward purpose of [the consent-giver's] mind' (Pufendorf 1672/1710: bk. 3, ch. 6, sec 15, para. 2). (Both of them thought that consent also required that those signs actually be given, however, making them 'Hybrid' theorists in the terminology below.) The *Restatement of the Law of Torts (Second)* declares: 'Consent is willingness in fact for conduct to occur. It may be manifested by action or inaction and need not be communicated to the actor' (ALI 1979, § 892(1)).

communication, an indication to others of what they have your permission to do or not to do.[21]

I think both perspectives contain important kernels of the truth and therefore ought to be combined. Consent is a social practice with moral importance. It therefore requires both mental and communicative elements. I shall argue that it does so, purely on functionalist grounds (Section 1.2.2). Consent is supposed to serve two distinct, interconnected functions, one moral and the other social—and each of those elements must be present for it to fulfil both of those functions.

Other philosophers have reached similar conclusions ostensibly on purely ontological grounds. But those discussions are flawed. They get the ontology of consent wrong—both as regards the internal mental element (Section 1.2.1.1) and the external behavioural element (Section 1.2.1.2) that is ontologically required for consent.

Correcting those misunderstanding of the ontology of consent correctly will assist at many points over the course of the book. But its importance in the immediate context lies in showing why a social functionalist element is needed to supplement a purely ontological account of consent. Of course, I do not deny ontological necessities, properly understood. The internal and external elements that I shall specify in Sections 1.2.1.1 and 1.2.1.2 are indeed necessary and sufficient for consent to exist at all. But something additional, over and above those ontological requisites, is needed in order for consent to serve its *social function*.

Specifically, while communication of consent is not ontologically required for the sheer existence of consent (Section 1.2.1.2), it most definitely *is* required for consent to successfully discharge its social function. That communicative requirement is what my social functionalist account of consent adds to the purely ontological requirements (Section 1.2.2). Adding that communicative requirement is what makes my social functionalist account superior to a purely ontological one as an account of consent as a *social* practice.

1.2.1 Ontological Requirements

Debates rage over the ontology of consent.[22] Attitudinalists say that consent is fundamentally just a state of mind (whether or not it is ever communicated to anyone).[23] Communicationists say that, on the contrary, consent is fundamentally just socially signalling that you are of such a state of mind (whether or not you

[21] Henceforth whenever I say in such contexts 'to do', that should be taken as including 'or not do'.

[22] This section includes brief excerpts from Goodin (2023), which provides further elaboration of the arguments set out here.

[23] See, e.g., Hurd 1996; Westen 2004, pp. 4–5; Alexander 2014; Alexander, Hurd and Westen 2016; and Guerrero 2021. For Attitudinalists, all that is required to render the conduct of others non-culpable

actually are).[24] The standard Hybrid view combines those two, holding that a consenting state of mind and communication of consent are individually necessary and jointly sufficient for consent to exist.[25] Those three alternatives are said to exhaust all the ontological options.[26]

There is widespread (if not universal agreement) that the Hybrid view is the correct one. But since that view just represents a combination of the other two, we can get a grip on what elements are ontologically necessary for consent by examining each of those other two views separately. Accordingly, I shall first critically assess the Attitudinalist account to see exactly what mental element is ontologically necessary for consent—which I show to be a 'mental *act* of consent' rather than the 'consenting state of mind' that is ordinarily supposed (Section 1.2.1.1). Then I shall critically assess the Communicationist account to see exactly what external, behavioural element is ontologially necessary for consent—which I show to be a 'performative act of consent' rather than a declarative act of communication as is ordinarily supposed (Section 1.2.1.2). I shall go on to argue in Section 1.2.2, however, that communication is *socially* required for consent to serve its social function, even if it is not ontologically required.

1.2.1.1 The Internal Ontological Element: A Mental Act, Not a State of Mind

Ontologists standardly identify the mental element that is necessary for consent as a 'mental attitude' which they describe as a 'consenting state of mind'. But those phrases are misleading in one important respect, and they are flat-out wrong in another.

Here is how those familiar formulations can be misleading. They suggest that signs of consent 'express the inward purpose of [the consent-giver's] mind'.[27]

is a 'justified belief'—which might be variously acquired—that the person whose consent they require is of a consenting state of mind (Guerrero 2021). Attitudinalists see communication as merely serving an epistemological function, enabling others to know the consenting party's state of mind. Describing a position that he himself rejects, Austin (1979, p. 236) traces all the way back to Euripides a 'classic' view, *a propos* the related notion of 'promises', that 'the utterance is simply the outward and visible (that is, verbal) sign of the performance of some inward spiritual act of promising'.

[24] As Wertheimer (2000, p. 567) says, 'One does not consent to be married by having the mental state of wanting or intending to be married. One does not consent to be married until one does something, like saying "I do."' Saunders (2012b, p. 71) likewise argues 'that consenting is an action, rather than a mental attitude. It is not simply that the action is necessary and the mental attitude insufficient. It is also that the action is sufficient and [the] mental attitude unnecessary. Someone who has performed the relevant consent action... cannot escape their obligation simply by saying that they did not mean to give their consent. Their intentions are irrelevant to what they in fact did.' See similarly: Austin 1962, p. 10; 1979, p. 236; Plamenatz 1968, p. 168; Simmons 1976, p. 276; Feinberg 1986a, p. 183; den Hartogh 2011, p. 301; and Bolinger 2019.

[25] Kleinig 1982, pp. 93–6; 2010, pp. 10–13; Wertheimer 2000, p. 566; 2003, ch. 7; Miller and Wertheimer 2010, p. 85; Dougherty 2015, pp. 227, 229; 2021a, p. 2; Guerrero 2021, p. 349.

[26] Husak (2006, p. 274) explicitly makes that claim, while it is at least implicit in the work of many others (e.g., Wertheimer 2000, p. 566; 2003, ch. 7; Kleinig 2010; Miller and Wertheimer 2010, p. 84).

[27] The phrase is Pufendorf's (1672/1710, bk. 3, ch. 6, sec 15, para. 2). But similar formulations are ubiquitous.

But it might be wrongly inferred from that that consent-givers must necessarily have some sort of 'pro-attitude' toward that to which they consent and that they necessarily wish for the consented-to eventuality actually to occur.[28] But there is no necessity in that at all.[29] I can consent to my children going on a trip that involves a dangerous sport, whitewater rafting for example, hoping all the while that they never go anywhere near the water. Or again: in olden times when a father's consent was required for his daughter to marry, a father could consent to what he took to be a bad marriage, hoping all the while that his daughter does not go through with it.[30]

The familiar formulations are also flat-out wrong to describe the mental element that is ontologically required for consent as some sort of diffuse 'attitude' or 'state of mind'. As I shall now proceed at greater length to show why that view is incorrect and why the mental element that is actually required for consent should instead be seen to be an internal, intrapersonal *mental act of consent.*[31] The 'mental act of consent' described in this section will be what is being referred to whenever I subsequently employ phrases like 'mentally consent', 'the mental element of consent' or even (occasionally) more colloquial but technically incorrect phrases like 'consenting state of mind' or 'mental attitude of consent'.

To see why consent requires a mental act and not merely an attitude or state of mind, focus on the question of *when* a consenting state of mind must be present. Attitudinalists clearly insist that consent-givers must be of a consenting state of mind at the time they *gave* the consent. But they must surely also require that

[28] In Guerrero's (2021) formulation, 'an agent, *A*, consents to some state of affairs, *SA*, only if *A* has an attitude (implicit or explicit) of affirmative endorsement toward *SA*'. Hurd (1996) endorses a similar specification of the intention required for consent. Hurd justifies that by analogy to the sort of *mens rea* required for liability under tort or criminal law; but it would not be at all surprising if more by way of intent were to be required for incurring tort or criminal liability than for consenting, which involves merely a limited waiver of certain of one's rights.

[29] Arguing against Hurd's (1996) claim suggesting that there is, Alexander (2014, p. 108) offers these examples: 'I can consent to your crossing my property or driving my car without wanting you to do it and indeed hoping that you will not.' See similarly Tadros (2016, pp. 209–10).

[30] Or one could say to a houseguest, '"I do wish you would stay", when in fact he wishes him to be gone.' Plamenatz (1968, p. 168) says of that example, 'There is no denying that he... consents to his guest's staying, however keen he may be to get rid of him.' See similarly: Owens 2008, p. 737; 2012, pp. 172–6; Tadros 2016, pp. 209–10. Similarly, the lack of a pro-attitude toward the consented-to eventuality does not invalidate that consent: it is no defence against bigamy for someone to say, 'I had mental reservations when I said "I do" at my first marriage!' Langille and Ripstein (1996, p. 72) say similarly in the context of contract law: 'Suppose you and I make an agreement, and as I sign it I say secretly to myself, "I don't mean it; the contract is not binding." That fact is irrelevant to whether or not we have a contract.'

[31] There are occasional (but only scant) intimations of this view in the extant literature. Hobbes (1651, ch. 14) and Pufendorf (1672/1710, bk. 3, ch. 6, sec. 16, para. 1), for example, refer to the internal aspect of consent as 'an act of the will'; but they offer no further elaboration. Tadros (2016, p. 205) similarly says, again without further elaboration: 'Some mental phenomena are states of mind: intentions, beliefs, desires, and so on. But we also perform mental actions—forming intentions and beliefs, deciding, choosing, and so on. Those who think that consent can be given without outward behaviour thus... may believe that it is a mental action, similar to the action of deciding or choosing.' Other recent writers refer to the internal aspect of consent as a 'mental choice' (Ferzan 2016, pp. 402–3) or an 'exercise of the will' (Hurd 1996, pp. 138, 121) but then immediately proceed to conflate those with a 'subjective mental state', from which I am here sharply distinguishing a 'mental act'.

consent-givers be of a consenting state of mind at the time the consent is *acted upon*.[32] Otherwise someone who had initially consented to sexual intercourse, but who had changed their mind before it commenced, would nevertheless be deemed to consent to the now-unwanted sex acts.[33]

But consider this counterexample. Suppose that my son asked for my consent to his using my car to go to midnight mass. I gladly consented to that, knowing that I would be soundly asleep by then and would have no need for the car. By the time my son acts on my consent, however, I am indeed soundly asleep. Not being conscious (in any way remotely bearing on consent, anyway), I am not of any state of mind whatsoever—certainly not of a 'consenting state of mind'—at the time he drives off. Does that mean that he took the car without my consent? Of course not. From that it follows that an occurrent consenting state of mind at the time the consent is acted upon is not always necessary for consent.[34]

At this point Attitudinalists might fall back on a dispositional gambit.[35] They might say, 'Sure, you were asleep: you were not, just then, of a "consenting state of mind"; but you were nonetheless *disposed* to consent, and that is sufficient!' 'Disposed' refers to a conditional, as in 'the glass is disposed to break if dropped on the bare concrete floor'. In the phrase 'disposed to consent', the conditional in question is presumably something like 'disposed to consent if asked' (or 'if the occasion arises', or some such).[36]

But that makes dispositional consent a species hypothetical consent, with all of its known perils.[37] Saying hypothetically that you '*would* consent if asked' is not to say you actually *do* consent—not until you have actually been asked and you have actually consented.[38] Likewise with dispositional consent, understood as a conditional of a similar sort. Saying that you are 'disposed to consent if asked' is not to

[32] As Dougherty (2021a, p. 28) insists, 'In order for consent to make an action permissible, the consent-giver must still *be consenting* to the action at the time the action takes place.' That would also be the upshot of Hurd's (1996) analogy to the criminal law, where *mens rea* must be present at the time the *actus reus* was committed.

[33] Although Attitudinalists go on to say that if that change of mind is not communicated, the unconsented-to sex constitutes 'nonculpable wrongdoing' (Alexander, Hurd and Westen 2016, p. 657).

[34] Dougherty (2021a, p. 29) offers a case where the parent has forgotten that he previously consented and he is now unwilling for the teenager to borrow the car. Dougherty argues that in that case the teenager does not have the parent's consent to borrow the car. But in that case it is the parent's 'current unwillingness' that should lead the Attitudinalist to say that consent is no longer present. In my case the slumbering parent, being unconscious, is at the time neither willing nor unwilling for the son to borrow the car. Yet, I argue, on account of the parent's previous (and unrevoked) *act* of consenting, the son takes the car with the parent's consent.

[35] As are, e.g., Dworkin (1986, p. 12) and Feinberg (1986a, pp. 173–4); cf. Malm (1996, pp. 149–50) and Tadros (2022, pp. 453–7).

Dougherty (2021a, p. 29), following Hurd (1996, pp. 126–38), says that 'an advocate of the [Attitudinal] view should identify consent with an intention'. But that would run into the same problem as with the sleeping consenter example immediately above—when you are unconscious you have no occurrent intentions.

[36] Simmons 1976, p. 286. [37] I say more about that below in Ssection 2.2.2 below.

[38] Dworkin (1975, pp. 17–18) had himself said as much, ironically enough; see similarly Waldron (1993, p. 55).

say you actually consent—at least not until you have actually been asked and you have actually consented (if only mentally, perhaps, on the purely Attitudinalist account).[39]

Here is another way of making the same point. Attitudinalists, recall, think that the existence of consent does not depend in any way upon its being communicated. Nevertheless, they must nonetheless surely agree that consent *can* be communicated. So what, for Attitudinalists, would count as communicating consent?

Suppose, *arguendo*, that Attitudinalists are correct that (i) being of a 'disposed to consent if asked' state of mind is what it is to mentally consent and (ii) mentally consenting is sufficient for consent. If so, then my reporting to someone else that fact *in precisely those words*—'I am disposed to consent if asked'—should count conclusively as communicating my consent.

Surely it does not, however. If you say to someone, 'I am disposed to consent to your using my toilet', you have not (yet) given your consent to their using your toilet. You have merely announced that you are inclined to do so.[40] Likewise if you say, 'I intend to consent to your using my toilet', consent has not yet been given.[41] 'Intending to φ' is not φ-ing.[42] 'Do it, then!' is the appropriate response from your interlocutor with the bursting bladder.

That point generalizes, making trouble for the Attitudinalist analysis regardless of how the requisite state of mind is fleshed out. If Attitudinalists were correct that the necessary-and-sufficient mental element of consent is a state of mind, then your reporting that you are 'of a mind to consent to φ' should surely count as a fully adequate report of precisely that which is supposed to be mentally required for the existence of consent?

Yet clearly it is not.[43] You can be of a mind to do something without having yet done it.[44] Merely having a 'consenting state of mind' (understood as an attitude,

[39] Tadros (2022, p. 462) says, *a propos* the sexual consent case (but I think it generalizes way beyond that case): 'The disposition to consent is almost never enough alone. The rights and duties of others are sensitive to a person's actual decisions about those rights and duties in the domain of sex, not merely what they value, desire, or would respond to. That is a crucial feature of sexual autonomy'—and I would argue, autonomy quite generally (what Enoch [2017; 2022] calls 'sovereignty').

[40] To be 'disposed' in the relevant sense just is to be 'inclined', according to the *Oxford English Dictionary* (q.v. 'disposed (adj.)', def. 4a).

[41] As is Hurd's (1996, pp. 126–38) and Dougherty's (2021a, pp. 29–30) way of understanding the requisite mental attitude associated with consent.

[42] This argument is inspired by the distinction drawn by Grotius (1625/1901, bk. 2, ch. 11, secs. 2–4), Hobbes (1651, ch. 14) and Pufendorf (1672/1710, bk. 3, ch. 5, sec. 8) between 'I promise to give you my car tomorrow' and 'I will tomorrow promise to give you my car'. See further Section 2.2.2 below.

[43] Unless 'of a mind' is taken to constitute a report that 'I have performed the mental act of consenting', discussed below. But that would be non-standard usage. The *Oxford English Dictionary* (qv. 'mind (n)', defs. 10a, 11a) reports that 'to be of a mind' means 'to be disposed' or 'to intend'—that, rather than 'to have decided'.

[44] In elaborating her analogy between *mens rea* in the criminal law and the attitudinal aspect of consent, Hurd (1996, p. 138) talks at one point of an '*exercise* of will'. But *mens rea* is a manner of

inclination, intention or disposition) is thus clearly not sufficient for the existence of consent.

I agree that *some* mental element is required for the existence of consent. Attitudinalists are right about that. They are simply wrong about what that necessary mental element must be. It is not a mere a state of mind. It is, instead, an *act* (even if only a mental act) of giving consent.

An act (mental or otherwise) must be done intentionally, in order to be an 'act' at all.[45] To do something intentionally is *to do* something; and it is to do something *deliberately* and with some specific *intention*.[46] That is as true of internal, mental acts as it is of external, physical acts. To perform a mental act is to decide, resolve or settle something mentally; it is to put to an end (at least for now) internal deliberation on that matter.[47] And it is to do so with some particular intention in mind—in the case of 'permissive consent', the intention to give the consent-receiver permission to do something that would be wrong for him to do without permission.

That mental act of consenting is an act of *commitment*. Once it is done, it remains in force until it is undone. Insofar as consent can be revoked at all (more on which in Chapter 7), it can be revoked only by another act of the same form by which it was done in the first place. You must deliberately perform the act (if only a mental act) of changing your mind, with the intention of revoking the consent that you had previously given (if only in your own mind). Other lesser sorts of changes in your 'state of mind'—simply forgetting, losing focus, falling asleep or whatever—are not sufficient to cancel a prior act of consent, even if that prior act occurred only in your own mind.[48]

A mental act is a 'resolution'. It is the product of a deliberation that is at least *pro tem* veridical. As such, it is presumptively conclusive in a way that mere 'states of mind' (understood to include mere attitudes or dispositions or inclinations) are not. An act of consent being an act of commitment means that once you have so acted—once you have consented, even just mentally—that act has continuing consequences. Your act of consent has changed the normative situation of yourself

'being'—a state of (mental) affairs—whereas an *exercise* of will is a 'doing'. It is a different 'doing' from the *actus reus* of committing the crime itself, to be sure. The 'exercise of will' in question—the mental act of 'deciding to commit the crime'—is nonetheless a 'doing'.

[45] That is what distinguishes them from 'other events' (Davidson 1980).

[46] I say more about what that intention must be in Section 1.3.2 below.

[47] Elaborating upon what it is for consent to be 'an act of the will', Hobbes (1651, ch. 14) adds: 'that is to say, an act, and the last act, of deliberation'. In an earlier passage, he had said that deliberation 'is a putting an end to the liberty we had of doing or omitting according to our own appetite or aversion' (ch. 6).

[48] Dougherty (2021a, pp. 28–9) offers the example of forgetting. He generalizes that to 'moving on mentally' to other topics, once having made a decision to consent. If the necessary mental element of consent is equated with the mental act of deciding, then consent exists only at the moment of that decision. Once you have mentally moved on to other topics, the 'deciding state of mind' associated with that decision has passed—and if the necessary mental element of consent is equated with that 'deciding state of mind', so too has consent passed out of existence.

and others in respect of the consented-to action.[49] So even if your 'consenting state of mind' has passed, the act of consent (the commitment, and its continuing consequences) endures. It does so, until and unless through some subsequent act (even if only a mental one) you deliberately revoke it.[50]

That explains why, in my earlier example, my son drives my car to midnight mass with my consent. True, at the time he drove off I was sleeping and hence not of any (much less a 'consenting') state of mind at all. But that is neither here nor there to the question of whether I consented. What is crucial is that I had performed the mental act of consenting while I was awake, and that unrevoked commitment persisted even while I was sleeping. Hence my son drove off with my consent even while I was asleep.

1.2.1.2 The External Ontological Element: Performative, Not (Necessarily) Communicative

Having established what internal mental element is ontologically required for consent, let me now turn to the external behavioural element. That is standardly said to be an element of communication. Sometimes commentators forthrightly label it as such.[51] Other commentators speak of it as the 'behavioural' or 'performative' element of consent—but when doing so, they almost invariably go on to equate that straightaway with a communicative element.[52] Equating them is a mistake, however. As I shall here show, the 'performative' and the 'communicative' acts of consent are in principle separable acts. And at least sometimes they are actually separate acts in practice, as well.

The distinction between performative and communicative acts of consent is going to prove important in separating out the ontological requirements from the social functions of consent in the discussion of Section 1.2.2 below. The external element that is *ontologically required* for consent is the 'performative act' of consent—not, as is standardly said, the communication of consent. And whereas communication depends for its success upon uptake on the part of the hearer, the performative act of consent can be successfully completed without any uptake

[49] All by itself, on the Attitudinalist account; together with something else, on the Hybrid account.

[50] In these terms, 'continuing consent' throughout sexual encounters means just that (1) each constituent activity within those encounters requires a positive consenting act; and (2) that consent can be withdrawn at any time during those activities.

[51] As in Dougherty (2021a, pt. 2), for example.

[52] Dougherty (2015, p. 229, emphasis added) says, for example: 'the "performative view" denies that a mere intention can be sufficient, countering that valid consent also requires *communication*'. Guerrero (2021, p. 349, emphasis added) similarly defines what he calls the 'performative/behavioral' view as holding that 'consent requires the right mental attitude *plus* some *communicative* performance regarding that attitude'. Brett (1998) allows that the 'performance' need not be verbal (it could instead involve things like gestures) but he nonetheless insists that the performance must be communicative behaviour of some sort or another. See similarly: Wertheimer 1996, pp. 94–5; 2000, pp. 94–5; 2003, ch. 7; Westen 2004, pp. 89–93; Husak, 2006, p. 274; Kleinig 2010, pp. 9–10; den Hartogh 2011; Owens 2012, p. 128; Alexander 2014, pp. 103–4; Tadros 2016, pp. 205–6; and Bolinger 2019, p. 182.

of it.[53] 'Communication' on the part of the consent-giver, or 'uptake' on the part of the intended-consent-receiver, is thus irrelevant to the *ontological* question of whether consent has been given. The performative act of consent is the only external act that matters *ontologically*.[54]

But as I shall go on to argue in Section 1.2.2 below, even if neither communication nor successful uptake is ontologically required for the existence of consent, both are *socially required* in order for consent to serve its function in shaping the behaviour of those who have been given it. No one's actions can be guided by things that they do not know about. That is simply to say that ontological necessity and social functionality come apart. Whether 'consent exists' and whether it is 'doing the job socially cut out for it' are two separate questions. And for consent to serve the social function cut out for it, something more (i.e., a communication requirement) must be added to what is ontologically necessary for it to exist at all.

That is why and how the argument of this section is going to matter, in the larger structure of the book. But now let me get on with the analysis of what external element is ontologically required for consent. First I shall offer a few examples showing how the external performative act of giving consent can come apart from the declarative act of communicating it. Having motivated the distinction through those examples, I shall then go on to offer some analysis of what the ontologically-necessary external 'performative' act of consent is and how it can differ from a declarative act of communication.

For purposes of this discussion, I shall assume, *arguendo*, that some external act is indeed ontologically necessary for the existence of consent.[55] My question, here, will simply be what *form* of external act that may be. Is what is ontologically

[53] That fact derails, for example, attempts to vindicate the possibility of retrospective consent through an argument, akin to Liberto's (2018) concerning promises, that if uptake is required to 'complete consent' then the subsequent uptake can have a 'backward' reach and subsequently turn something into 'consent' that was not 'consent' at the time the it was acted upon.

[54] That is (in effect, if not in their words) the upshot of arguments that others have given for thinking that successful uptake of communication of consent is not necessary for the existence of consent. While I endorse the same conclusion, I do not endorse the arguments that those others have given. Tadros' (2016, p. 206) argument is as follows: '[S]uppose that *X* owes *Y* a consent-sensitive duty not to *v*. *Y* attempts to communicate her consent to *X* to *v*, but mumbles. X is not quite sure what *Y* has said, but thinks that she has indicated that she has consented to *X v*-ing. X thinks that *Y* has consented, but is unsure. But if *X* is unsure about whether *Y* has consented, it must be true or false that *Y* has consented—there is something, *Y*'s consent, about which *X* is unsure. Hence, *Y*'s consent must be independent of whether *X* knows that *Y* has consented. Successful communication of consent is not required for consent.' Tadros' argument here, however, is like saying that the fact 'I am unsure whether what I saw at the bottom of my garden was a unicorn' proves that unicorns exist. It proves no such thing. At most, it merely implies that I think (perhaps wrongly, of course) that unicorns might exist. Dougherty's (2021a, pp. 79–81) argument is also flawed, albeit in a different way (Goodin 2023).

[55] Note that this assumption is consistent with the Hybrid view that some internal mental act is also required (i.e., they might be individually necessary and jointly sufficient). But to simplify the exposition this section will focus exclusively upon the question of exactly what external act is required. When employing locutions like 'that is the external act that is crucial', I shall merely mean 'among all the possible external acts that might thought to be crucial, that is the one that is'; I do not mean by that to deny that some internal mental act might also be crucial.

required an *act of communication*, or is it an external *performative act* of some other sort?

No doubt consent *can be* communicated. And no doubt when people do consent to something, they usually communicate that fact to the persons concerned. Indeed, in order for consent to play its *social role*, it *had better be* communicated, as I shall go on to argue in Section 1.2.2 below. Nothing I shall say here denies any of that. My question in this section is purely an ontological one: must consent necessarily be communicated in order for it to exist at all? My argument will be that it does not. Instead, an external 'performative' act is what is ontologically required for consent.

Of course, an act of communication can sometimes serve both declarative and performative functions (as when you say 'I do' at your wedding, for example). My argument *contra* Communicationists (and Hybrid theorists incorporating their claim) will be that: (1) the external performative act is what is ontologically required for the existence of consent; and (2) when communicative acts do what is ontologically required for consent, that is because they take this performative form and are not merely declarative acts of communication.

Even if they often occur together, the performative act of consent and the further external declarative act of communicating it can sometimes come apart. That is to say, they can sometimes be separate acts. Here is one example. Under the Royal Assent Act 1967, when the British king signs letters patent consenting to an enactment of Parliament becoming law, his signing is the external act that *constitutes* consent.[56] His consent is *communicated* only subsequently, and separately, by those letters patent being read out by the presiding officers in the two Houses of Parliament.[57]

For another example, take the case of consent to surgery. My physician has recommended surgery and gave me a consent form to sign and bring to the hospital on the day. As I am being prepared for surgery, the surgeon asks me, 'Have you consented to this surgery?' I reply, 'Yes, I left my signed consent form in a sealed envelope on the receptionist's desk.' I consented to the surgery when I signed the consent form at home, before leaving for the hospital. I communicated my consent when replying to the surgeon's query (and perhaps also when dropping the sealed envelope on the receptionist's desk, even if she has not yet seen it).

What was the status of my consent to surgery as I drove to the hospital, the signed consent form safely tucked away in my breast pocket? Surely it is that I had

[56] Or perhaps his affixing the Great Seal to the document.

[57] UK Parliament 1967. For those who worry that the Royal Assent is not really consent, substitute the example of the King's Consent which must be obtained before the enactment of legislation touching on the royal prerogative (the King's personal property): that is obtained in the same way and is communicated to Parliament only subsequently, as part of the Third Reading of the Bill (UK Cabinet Office 2017, § 3.17).

already consented, not just internally (mentally) but also externally. I had committed the crucial external performative act of consenting when I signed the form. I had not yet performed the *further* external act of communicating my consent to anyone—that came only after I arrived at the hospital. But both of the ontologically crucial acts of consenting (the internal mental one and the external one of signing the form) had been performed well ahead of those further external acts of communicating it.[58]

Some may make much of the fact that I could have changed my mind and torn up the form at any time before handing the form to the hospital receptionist.[59] But so too, even after turning in the signed form, could I revoke my consent any time before the anaesthetist rendered me unconscious.[60] The fact that I can still change my mind and revoke my consent does not mean that consent has not been given. Quite the contrary, if consent had not already been given there would be nothing to 'revoke'.[61]

Thus, insofar as some external act is ontologically required for consent, that act must be a 'performative' one and not merely a 'declarative' act of communication. The distinction is a familiar one from the theory of speech acts;[62] and it is common for consenting to be referred to as a speech act.[63] But even when the external act that ontologically constitutes consent takes the form of speech, in order for that to be an act of consent at all it must be more than a *mere* act of communication. It must *do* something rather than merely saying something.[64] Specifically, the external act of consent must constitute making a commitment to others.

For an act to be genuinely 'performative', it must be performed in just the right way in just the right circumstances. This fact about performatives has been

[58] Liberto (2018, pp. 17–19, 22–3) discusses a similar case of a letter-in-the-post and comes to the opposite conclusion regarding the cognate case of a promise, viz., that the promissory obligation does not exist until the letter has been delivered and read and the promise accepted by the promisee. Perhaps Liberto is being misled here by the fact that, in the very special case of contract law, it takes acceptance of an offer for a contract to have been concluded (ALI 1981, § 36 (1)(c)). But simple promises work differently. Acceptance of the promise is not conceptually required, in order for a promise to have been made. Indeed, the very language we use in spurning a promise belies that fact. We 'reject' an offer, but we 'release' someone from their promise. The verb 'release' clearly indicates there is something already in existence to release the promisor from.

[59] In Liberto's (2018, p. 18) letter-in-the-post example, she points out that you could always intercept it before it was delivered. She thinks that that would prevent the promise contained in the letter from ever having been made; I think it would amount to revoking a promise made when you signed the letter.

[60] Kleinig 2010, p. 9. AMC 2016, § 3.12.5.

[61] On the revocability of consent in general, see: Owens 2011, p. 407; 2012, p. 165; Dougherty 2014, p. 38; 2021a, p. 56, 120.

[62] Austin 1962; 1979; Searle 1965; 1969. It is clear from context that this is what Raz (1986, p. 81) is referring to when saying that 'the core use of "consent" is its use in the performative sense'.

[63] Brett 1998; Cowart 2004; Kukla 2018; Bolinger 2019, p. 182. Cf. Alexander 2014, p. 101. Of course, not all 'performatives' take the form of speech (as the 'signings' in my earlier examples clearly show). Neither does any old verbalization necessarily constitute a performative, which is what I shall now go on to demonstrate.

[64] That is to say, in Austin's (1962) terms, it must have illocutionary as well as locutionary force.

familiar from long before Austin taught us *How to Do Things with Words*. Blackstone's eighteenth-century *Commentaries on the Laws of England*, for example, described marriage as 'a civil contract' formed by the consent of both parties, if but only if the parties concluded the contract 'in the proper forms and solemnities required by law'.[65]

Pure speech—words by themselves—do not constitute any determinate performative.[66] Context matters. Uttering the words, 'I do', sometimes constitutes consenting to marriage. But those same words might in other circumstances constitute swearing an oath ('Do you solemnly swear that the testimony you are about to give . . . ?') or merely ordering a beer ('Do you want a glass of Theakston's Old Peculier?'). Yet other times, the same words might be purely declarative and not performative at all ('Do you think it is going to rain?').

Those strictures apply with particular force to communications of consent. Simply uttering the words 'I consent' does not necessarily suffice to constitute the external act of consent. Communicating (perfectly truly) that you have performed the internal mental act specified in Section 1.2.1.1 might, depending on circumstances, count as purely declarative—it might not be genuinely performative, in the way that is ontologically required of an external act of consent. In such cases (I shall give examples shortly), saying to someone else, 'I have mentally consented to your φ-ing', is a mere report, not an external performative act that confers consent.

Here are some examples where saying you consent and doing it can come apart. Under Australia's Marriage Act of 1961, a minor's parents must consent to the child's marriage. But their just saying to the child beforehand, 'We consent to your marriage', does not count as consent (at least under the terms of that law). Legally, what constitutes their consent is instead their signing an affidavit and presenting it to the judge who must approve the marriage.[67] Likewise when you are buying a house, your saying to the vendor, 'I consent to purchase the house at that price', often counts legally for naught until you have actually signed the contract.[68]

Saying certain words can sometimes literally constitute consent, but only when the words are said in the appropriate circumstances to the right person. The English Marriage Act of 1753 stipulated that, in order to be legally valid. a marriage had to be performed by a minister in a parish church or chapel of the

[65] Austin 1962; Blackstone 1765, bk. 1, ch. 15, p. 421.

[66] 'Saying the words "please come to dinner" need not involve inviting you to dinner: I might be joking', as Tadros (2016, p. 205) observes.

[67] Marriage Act of 1961, sec. 13(1), *Commonwealth Consolidated Acts*; available at <http://www5.austlii.edu.au/au/legis/cth/consol_act/ma196185/>.

[68] At contract law, 'A manifestation of willingness to enter into a bargain is not an offer if the person to whom it is addressed knows or has reason to know that the person making it does not intend to conclude a bargain until he has made a further manifestation of assent' (ALI 1981, § 26).

Church of England.[69] Saying 'I do' anywhere else, even as part of the same ceremony, simply did not legally count as consent to marriage. Likewise, saying 'I do' as part of a marriage ceremony in a stage play does not count as consent to marriage, even if the celebrant in the play is in real life a minister authorized to perform marriages. Or again, it is sometimes argued that consent to sexual relations must be given directly to the person concerned—saying to Y, 'I consent to having sex with X', does not constitute consenting to have sex with X.[70]

Like the internal mental act of consent described in Section 1.2.1.1, the ontologically-required external act of consent also involves making a commitment. The internal mental act of consent, however, is more of a commitment to oneself, albeit one concerning others. The external performative act of consent makes that internal commitment externally manifest. It does more than merely making the internal commitment externally accessible. however. The external performative act of consent amounts to doing what, by your internal act of consent, you had resolved to do. It amounts to the actual *giving* of consent, even if the fact it has been given has not yet been communicated to those to whom it has been given.

One way of seeing the difference between performative acts of consent and acts communicating consent is to focus upon whether uptake on the part of others is necessary for the acts to have been successfully performed. You have not communicated successfully unless the other person has heard and understood what you intended to convey. That is why speech acts are said to lack performative force without uptake on the part of hearers.[71] But that is a special feature of speech, not a fact about performances in general. Playing Rachmaninoff's *Third Concerto* perfectly constitutes a successful performance even if there is no audience.[72] The existence of an audience, much less an appreciative audience, is in no way necessary for the performance of that notoriously difficult piece to be a wholly successful performance.[73] The same is true of performances that constitute exercises of normative powers. You relinquish your rights in your gold watch and vest those rights in your son at the moment you sign an official document gifting it to him, whether or not your son yet realizes that he is its new owner.

[69] Marriage Act of 1753, 26 Geo. II, c. 33. [70] Lackey 2021.

[71] Austin 1962; 1971; Searle 1969; McDonald 2021.

[72] Some might say that the performer hearing it is enough to satisfy the uptake condition. But suppose the performer is deaf. Just as Beethoven could compose stunning music despite being deaf, we could well imagine someone might perform music perfectly despite being deaf.

[73] In one sense of the term anyway. The *Oxford English Dictionary* (qv. 'performance' (n)) acknowledges one sense in which a performance is something that is done 'in front of an audience' (def. 4c); but its first and most general definition contains no such stipulation, saying a performance is merely 'the accomplishment or carrying out of something commanded or undertaken' (def. 1a).

1.2.2 The Social Functionalist Account

Even if there is no *ontological* necessity for consent to be communicated, there is a crying *social* need for it to be communicated. That is simply to say that the ontological requirements for consent to exist must be supplemented by a further social requirement that it be communicated, in order for consent to serve its social role in guiding other people's behaviour.

I thus propose a social functionalist account of consent.[74] My thought is just this. Consent is supposed to play two distinct roles, one moral and the other social. Let me now say something about each of those roles, in turn.

Morally, consent is transformative. It renders morally permissible actions that would otherwise have been morally impermissible.[75] The point of consent, morally, is (as I said at the beginning of this chapter) to serve people's autonomy interests. In order for it to do so, people's consenting must itself be an expression (indeed, I have argued 'an exercise') of their will. That is why, given the moral function that it is supposed to serve, consent must involve some internal mental element.[76] The specific internal mental element is, as analyzed in Section 1.2.1.1 above, a 'mental act of consent'. Furthermore, that internal mental act of consent must morally (as well as socially) be made manifest—it must be given external expression in a performative act of the sort described in Section 1.2.1.2.

Connected to its moral role, consent also plays a social role. Consent is supposed to be action-guiding, or anyway option-delimiting.[77] Consent is supposed to help delineate the set of options from among which agents choose their actions. To serve that function, others obviously need to know whether or not they have your consent. That is why, in order to serve its social function, consent must not only be manifested through some external performative act (as in Section 1.2.1.2).[78] It must also somehow be made known to others. Following long-standing usage, I will refer to that as a requirement that consent

[74] Bolinger (2019, pp. 184ff.) similarly adopts a functionalist approach. Although Bolinger focuses primarily on a risk-managing function that is different from either of the two upon which I focus, she sees the communicative function as an important part of risk management—'[a]n uncommunicated internal attitude is not equal to this task', she writes (p. 186).

[75] In Hurd's (1996, p. 123) oft-quoted words: 'consent turns a trespass into a dinner party; a battery into a handshake; a theft into a gift; an invasion of privacy into an intimate moment; a commercial appropriation of name and likeness into a biography'.

[76] Hurd 1996, pp. 121, 124–5. See similarly: Alexander 2014; Alexander, Hurd and Westen 2016; Ferzan 2016, p. 397; and Guerrero 2021.

[77] That is to say, when *X* consents for *Y* to φ, *X* is not instructing or even necessarily encouraging *Y* to φ. *X* is not guiding *Y* to φ. *X* is merely permitting *Y* to φ. In other words, *X*'s consent merely adds φ to the set of options for action available to *Y*. For discussion of related issues, see Owens (2011, pp. 407–8; 2012, pp. 172–6) and Renzo (2022, pp. 59 ff.).

[78] Indeed, the autonomy interests of consent-receivers might require that they be informed that they have received consent, so there may be a moral aspect as well as a social aspect to the communication requirement (Miller and Wertheimer 2010; Renzo 2022). I do not deny this possibility; when referring to the communication requirement as a 'social' one and the internal mental requirement as the 'moral' one, I do so purely for expository convenience.

be 'communicated' to the others.[79] As I shall explain in Chapter 3, however, there are various ways other than explicit verbal communication for that requirement to be met.

Those two functional requisites lead to a Hybrid view of consent as follows:

- The ontologically-required internal mental component is *morally necessary* in order for a person to consent. When the mental element is present I shall say that he 'mentally consents'. That is what is meant when saying more colloquially (as I sometimes do below) that a person 'really' or 'genuinely' or 'actually' consents.[80]
- The ontologically-required external performative element is also necessary *morally*, as an external manifestation of that internal mental act of consent. That external performative act of consent is also necessary as a first, if incomplete, step toward doing what is *socially* necessary in making the fact that someone has mentally consented externally accessible. It is a first step, because an external performative act is at least in-principle accessible to others in a way that a person's internal mental actions are not. It is an incomplete step, because the ontologically-necessary performative act can be performed without anyone else knowing about it.
- A further communicative element is therefore ordinarily *socially necessary* in order for others to *be successfully given* consent.[81] When a person has, through socially conventional means, indicated to others that he consents, I shall say that he 'socially consents' or 'communicates consent' or 'conventionally signals consent'. And when I speak of that giving of consent as being 'socially successful', I refer by that to successful 'uptake' on the part the intended consent-receiver (i.e., the consent-receiver has understood the consent-giver's signals as indicating consent).
- All of those elements, taken together, are jointly sufficient for the existence of socially functional consent. The reason, on my functionalist account, is

[79] As Pufendorf (1672/1710, bk. 3, ch. 6, sec 16, para. 1) said long ago, 'signs of consent are absolutely necessary... in as much as the bare act of the will can have no effect amongst men, unless manifested and declared by some external tokens'. When philosophers speak of something 'tokening' consent, they almost invariably mean 'give a sign' which communicates that consent to others (*Oxford English Dictionary*, q.v. 'token (v.)', def. 1). Thus when Wertheimer (2003, p. 152, emphasis added) says that someone consents 'only when she performs some token of consent' he goes on to say in the very next sentence: 'Roughly speaking there are three ways by which [a person] can *communicate* consent...'

[80] Thus, when saying someone 'really/genuinely/actually consents', I am referring to their mentally consenting (their mentally performing an act of consent), and that alone. Whether the consent is morally 'valid' and ought therefore to be respected depends on further considerations—whether it was given free of force and fraud and by someone competent to give it.

[81] 'Ordinarily', because consent can sometimes be inferred from 'the nature of the business' (Section 3.2.2) or presumed on the basis of on-going relationships (Section 3.3.3), although both are predicated upon previous communications of various sorts. Note that sometimes the situation is such that people can communicate consent by silence (Sections 3.2, 3.3.4 and 3.3.5).

simply that the presence of those suffices for consent to serve the twin moral and social functions that consent is supposed to serve. I call the first of the elements 'morally necessary' and the second 'socially necessary' as reminders of why, functionally, each of those elements is required.

Reflecting upon the dual functions served by social practices of consent thus leads to substantively the same Hybrid conclusions as has already been advocated by others on ontological grounds, viz., that both a mental element and a communicative element are required for consent. But while the Hybrid structure of the conclusion may be the same, the functionalist grounds that I offer for it are importantly different.

1.3 Elements of Consent

With those fundamentals out of the way, let me now turn to preview the more operational aspects of consent that will preoccupy me over the course of the book. I shall begin by introducing the key elements of consent transactions, under three headings: indicators of consent (Section 1.3.1), intentions of consent-givers (Section 1.3.2) and interests of consent-receivers (Section 1.3.3).

1.3.1 Indicators of Consent

The mechanisms by which we communicate consent depend largely on context and conventions. Chapter 3 systematically explores all the types of things that might count as indicators of consent. Other examples arise, time and again, over the course of the rest of the book, further fleshing out the taxonomy introduced there.

Particular conventions for communicating consent obviously vary from community to community. Standing back from the particulars, however, there are a couple of things than can be said more generally:

- Some of those conventions will concern what signs *actively* signal consent (like verbalizing it or nodding your head). Others will concern what can conventionally be taken as a *passive* sign of consent (like remaining silent when the meeting's chairperson says, 'Any objections?').
- Some of those conventions will concern who bears the onus of speaking up. Typically that will be those who consent, but sometimes it is those who refuse consent. Occasionally that specification is a matter of formal enactment (as when countries adopt opt-in or opt-out rules for consenting to organ donations). More often, it is a matter of mere social conventions that people can reasonably be expected to know or at least to have surmised.

When consent-giving goes wrong, and mistakes are made as to whether or not consent has actually been given, much is going to turn not only on what conventions were in play in the circumstances but also on what each of the participants knew (or could and should have known) about what will conventionally be taken as indicators of consent in the circumstances.[82] I shall discuss those issues in Section 1.4 and then again, more fully, in Chapter 4.

1.3.2 Intentions of Consent-givers

In Section 1.2.1, I argued that consent requires 'acts' of various sorts. Ontologically, it requires an internal 'mental act of consent' and an external 'performative act of consent'. And to be socially functional, consent further requires an 'act of communication'. Those acts of consent, like all acts, must be intentional.[83] But what, exactly, must be the intention in question?

1.3.2.1 Two Alternative Intentions

There are two possible ways of fleshing out the intentions that might be associated with those various acts of consent.[84] One is that the consent-giver intends to permit the object of consent. The other is that the consent-giver intends to induce beliefs about his intending to permit the object of consent.[85] Suppose *X* consents to *Y*'s φ-ing. On the first reading, that would mean that *X* intends to *permit* (or waive his rights against[86]) *Y*'s φ-ing. On the second reading, it would mean only that *X* intends *Y* to *understand* that *X* is saying that he intends that.[87]

[82] 'Indicators', 'signals' and 'tokens' of consent will all be used interchangeably throughout.

[83] Faden and Beauchamp (1986, chs. 7–8) for example define consent as 'autonomous authorization' and include 'intentional' as a necessary condition for an autonomous act. (I argue in Section 6.2.3 that 'authorization' is inapt as a characterization of consent, but their analysis of what is required for an autonomous act is untouched by those criticisms.)

[84] There are of course various other things that one *might* be intending when consenting. One might be 'intending for the consented-to eventuality to occur'. But that is first cousin to the attitude of wishing for the consented-to eventuality to occur, which Section 1.2.1.1 has already shown not to be ontologically necessary for consent; hence I discuss that possibility no further here.

[85] Bolinger (2019, p. 183, italics in original) canvasses this possibility, without endorsing it, when commenting that 'a necessary condition for consent' may be '*intent to communicate consent*'. Bolinger (2019, pp. 194–5) also observes, quite correctly, that others might infer that you do without you doing those things with the intention of communicating consent. Indeed, those might be 'conventional signs of consent', which by reason of those conventions others are entitled to interpret in that way. Cases of consent being falsely signalled in wholly innocent error (discussed immediately below and in Section 4.6) are like that.

[86] I take those to be equivalent, as discussed further in Section 2.1. Simons' (2019, p. 10) headline claims that 'actual consent is not equivalent to waiver of a right', but all that his discussion under that heading actually shows is that the consent-giver 'need not know or intend' that 'this is indeed the legal (or moral) significance and effect of consent'.

[87] Many philosophers of language are Intentionalists who analyze illocutionary speech acts (of which 'I hereby consent to...' is obviously one) centrally in terms of the speaker's intention (Grice

Commentators on consent usually focus primarily on the first sort of intention, intending to permit the object of consent.[88] That, after all, is what is required in order for ontologically necessary acts of consent to constitute genuine consent and to be morally transformative. But in paradigm cases of consenting, *X* intends both things. In performing the two ontologically-necessary acts of consenting, *X* intends to permit what he consents to, *viz.*, permitting *Y* to do φ. And in socially communicating consent, *X* intends for *Y* to understand his communication of consent in that way.

There can, however, be cases where the latter intention is present but the first is absent. Performing acts of consent with the genuine intention of giving permission is no doubt morally superior to giving others to understand that you give them permission when mentally you do not. But there are various different ways in which the latter can happen, and those differences genuinely matter both for how we should assess and how we should respond to those different cases. I will say more about that in Section 1.4 and Chapter 4.

1.3.2.2 The Scope of Consent

In taking the first approach to intention and saying that the consent-giver must intend to permit the object of that consent, questions remain as to what, exactly, is within the 'scope' of that consent.[89] To what, exactly (or to what *all*, exactly), did the person consent when consenting? There is usually a clear core of what was consented to, but there is often an unclear surrounding penumbra.

One set of such cases, discussed in Section 3.4 below, arises when consenting to one thing might logically (or even just pragmatically) commit you to consenting to what is implied by that to which you actually consented. So, for example, when consenting to rent me a room in your house, you are pragmatically committed to consenting to me using such doors and corridors in your house as are required for me to access the room you have consented for me to use. Is that within the 'scope of the consent' you have given me? If by 'scope of consent' we mean your intention, narrowly construed, it may not have been. When consenting to rent me the room, you may not have been thinking at all about the nuisance of me traipsing through the shared passageways in your house at all hours. (That

1957; Strawson 1964/1971). For them, the 'intention' in question is to produce a certain conative state in the hearer. That intention for the hearer to believe that the speaker has consented is, of course, completely separate from any intention on the part of the speaker actually to consent or actually to do or permit what is indicated in the communication of his 'consent'. Conventionalist philosophers of language such as Searle (1965) deny that. For a good overview of this controversy with applications to consent see Cowart (2004).

[88] Attitudinalists of the sort discussed in Section 1.2 focus on that intention (almost) exclusively. Hybrid theorists are less committed by the logic of their analysis to do so, but in practice they often tend to do so anyway.

[89] Manson 2018; Dougherty 2021a; Tadros 2022.

form of 'rentor's remorse' is actually quite common: just ask anyone who has taken in a lodger!)

Still, it pragmatically follows from consenting to rent me the room that I must use the necessary passageways to reach it. We simply do not (yet) have teleporting technology whereby I could otherwise access it. You could and should have known that when consenting to rent me the room. Hence, having consented to renting me the room you are arguably bound, by that consent, to permit me to use the passageways required in order to reach it. That is a normative implication of your consenting to rent me the room—it is *normatively* within the 'scope of your consent'—even if it was not within the scope of what you consciously intended when consenting.

Maybe you did not 'actually consent to it' in the standard way, if you never thought of it. But you did 'actually consent' to something that 'implicitly included it'. So you can be said to have 'actually implicitly consented to it'. I argue in Section 3.4.3 below that it can, in that way, be seen as a subspecies (or anyway a close cousin) of genuine consent.[90]

Similar things can be said about the filling in of 'gaps' in people's consent, discussed in Section 5.2.4. When two people consent to a contract, they thereby explicitly consent to those things literally contained in the clauses of the contract. But contracts are invariably incomplete and fail to provide for every possible contingency that might arise under them. There are rules and principles that courts use for filling in those details, where contracting parties have not. Contracting parties could and should have known such rules and principles exist for that purpose, and they could and should have made alternative provision in the contract itself if they did not want to have those rules and principles applied to them. If through sheer inadvertence they fail to do so, we cannot say that they genuinely consent to having those rules and principles applied to them. But because they could and should have known that they would be, unless they made alternative provisions, we may once again quite properly treat them 'as if they consented' to those rules and principles being applied. And the same may be true, if only perhaps to a lesser extent, of the social norms that are conventionally used to fill in gaps in people's consent in non-legal contexts.[91]

[90] I introduce there a separate and more precise term—'derivative quasi-consent'—for this phenomenon. But that is synonymous with what I here call 'actually implicitly consented'. I shall use the two terms interchangeably.

[91] Treating him 'as if he consented', based on what he could and should have known about the legal rules and principles or the social conventions, deftly avoids Tadros' (2022, p. 434) counterexample. Tadros muddies that case by further stipulating that the seeming-consent-receiver is knowingly taking advantage of the seeming-consent-giver's ignorance on that score—a matter I deal with in Section 4.5 below.

1.3.3 The Reliance Interests of Consent-receivers

When you make any kind of assertion, you are inviting others to rely upon the truth of what you assert to be true. When you promise something to someone else, you are inviting him to rely on your promise. Likewise, when you give someone else your consent for him to do something, you are inviting him to rely upon your consent in organizing his subsequent affairs.

Others reasonably rely upon you to permit them to do what you have consented to them doing. That provides consent-givers with at least a *pro tanto* reason for not revoking consent, once given.[92] Even when they have not 'really' consented (because they do not mentally consent), others reasonably rely upon the putative consent-giver being morally debarred from preventing them from doing what they reasonably regard the putative consent-giver as having consented to them doing, on the basis of extant social conventions that the putative consent-giver could and should have known.[93] Those other people often make irreversible investments and incur unrecoverable costs in the process.

When I need your consent to something, I would ordinarily seek that consent ahead of making those investments and incurring such costs so as to ensure that they will not be in vain. Having obtained your consent, I invoke it in an effort to forestall that from happening. And should you change your mind and attempt to revoke your previously-given consent, the losses that I would suffer from that happening is what gives me legitimate grounds for complaint.

That is not necessarily to say people may never revoke their consent once it has been given, any more than it is to say that they must give their consent every time it is requested. Someone from whom consent is being sought is always formally at liberty to refuse his consent, in the first instance (although he might be criticizable on other moral grounds for doing so). But once consent has been given, the consent-giver is not morally at *complete* liberty to withdraw it. A consent-receiver's interests in being able to rely on what has been consented to are *pro tanto* reasons against the consent-giver revoking it. But those are no more than *pro tanto* reasons; and on the balance of reasons, all things considered, it may be permissible for him on any particular occasion to revoke his consent. Nevertheless, once consent has been given, the consent-receiver's reliance

[92] See Section 7.3. That *pro tanto* reason certainly is not conclusive and may not even be particularly strong. Furthermore, the person revoking her consent is simply reasserting her rights that had been waived by her previous consent—so all the *pro tanto* reasons we have for conferring such rights upon people in the first place then come back into play and must be set against the *pro tanto* reasons for not disappointing the consent-receiver's reliance interests when the consent is revoked.

[93] This is the case of 'culpably negligent false consent' discussed in Section 1.4. But I hasten to add that the 'others' reliance' point being developed here applied equally to all the other cases of 'false consent' discussed there, as well as to cases of 'genuine consent' (as will become apparent in Chapter 7's discussion of revoking consent).

interests always weigh in the balance—heavily in some cases, less so in others, of course.

Those interests on the part of the consent-receiver are further elaborated in Section 2.4 and Chapter 4, and they will make frequent reappearances throughout the book. They loom particularly large in Chapter 7's discussion of revoking consent.

1.4 Consent-like Transactions, and Their Consequences

We know from Section 1.2 above what is required for genuine consent to exist and to be socially functional. Three elements are required: (a) a mental act of consent, combined with (b) a performative act of consent, combined with (c) an act of communicating that consent.

Not all seemingly consent-giving transactions are 'genuine' by those standards, however. Sometimes you have the mental element (and perhaps even the performative one) without the communicative one. I mentally consent but simply do not say so—which gives rise to the inconvenience of others then having no way of knowing that I consent.[94] Or you can have the communicative element without the mental one—in which case others are being misinformed when I communicate my consent to them.[95] My communication conveys that I mentally consent, when actually I do not.

The latter sorts of cases will form the focus of my discussion in this section. I call those generically cases of 'false consent'. The defining feature of 'false consent' is simply that consent is communicated without it being mentally present. And the consent is 'false' insofar as that missing mental element is ontologically necessary for genuine consent.[96]

The standard ontologically-driven accounts of consent overlook the varying importance of the differing modes of false consent that I shall here be discussing. Indeed, they define the phenomenon away altogether. Either they say that 'false

[94] That is Bolinger's (2019, pp. 187–8) problem of 'moral opacity', which I shall further discuss in Section 4.6.3.2. There can be flukey cases in which *Y* secretly mentally consents to *X*'s doing something that would be wrong without *Y*'s consent. But since *X* did not know he had *Y*'s consent when he did that thing, *X* nevertheless acted culpably in doing it (Alexander 2014)—although the exact nature of the wrong *X* has committed may have to be described a little differently than in the case in which *X* did not even have *Y*'s secret mental consent to do it.

[95] You can also perform the external performative act of consent without having performed the internal mental act of consent, and if that fact is communicated to others it will be misleading in the same way. But unless it is communicated to them it will not mislead them. So in the discussion that follows, I will focus on cases of false communication alone.

[96] Of course, Communicationists would disagree: for them, communicating consent is sufficient and no internal mental element is ontologically required (Saunders 2012b, p. 71; Bolinger 2019, pp. 204–7). I have however given reasons for thinking that an internal mental act of consent is ontologically required (in Section 1.2.1.1 above); and I shall demonstrate further shortcomings of the Communicationist position in the present connection (in Section 1.4.2 below).

consent' is not 'false'—that is the upshot of Communicationist theories that say communicating consent is sufficient in itself for consent. Or else they say that 'false consent' is not 'consent'—that is the upshot of Attitudinalist or Hybrid theories that say mentally intending consent is necessary for consent. My social functionalist account of consent avoids both traps in saying that mentally consenting is indeed a necessary condition of consent (so 'false consent' is indeed 'false') but that socially communicating consent is what makes consent socially efficacious (and so communicating consent, even falsely, is socially speaking at least 'consent-like').

1.4.1 A Taxonomy of False Consent

There are three possible ways in which such false consent might occur. It is important to distinguish among them because they embody differing degrees of fault and blameworthiness and, because of that, differing consequences should attach to each.[97]

The first case of false consent is that of *deliberate fraud*.[98] There, you send a signal that conventionally betokens consent, knowing that it does so and fully intending for receivers of that signal to understand it as doing so, even though mentally you do not intend to permit that to which you purport to consent.[99] In the case of deliberately fraudulent consent, the sender of the false signal of consent is intentionally misrepresenting himself as mentally consenting when he does not. He is intentionally misleading others with his deliberately false signal of consent.

The second case of false consent is one of *culpable negligence*. There, you send a signal that conventionally betokens consent, without intending to do so.[100] But you were negligent in thus signalling. You might have been negligent in that, despite knowing the conventions, you sent those signals in reckless disregard of how others would understand and act upon them. That is to say, you were negligent in sending the signals of consent that you did. You did not take due care with the signals that you sent, and your negligence is 'culpable' for that reason. Alternatively, you might have been negligent in not knowing how your signal would be interpreted by others, when you could and should have known. That amounts to 'culpable ignorance'.[101] What makes your ignorance 'culpable' is

[97] As will be elaborated in Section 1.4.3.

[98] This is the case most commonly being referred to when others speak of 'insincere consent'; see further Section 2.3.1 below.

[99] That is to say, the signaller of consent in this case has the second but not the first sort of intention discussed in Section 1.3.2.1.

[100] In either of the senses in Section 1.3.2.1: you neither intended to permit the things to which your signal suggested that you consented, nor did you intend others to understand your signal to be understood in that way.

[101] Smith 1983.

precisely that you could and should have known. In subsequent discussions, I shall use the term 'culpable negligence' to cover both of those cases, unless otherwise specified.

The third case of false consent is one of *innocent error*. There, you send a signal that conventionally betokens consent, but you do so purely by mistake. It is a mistake, in the sense that you did not intend to give permission to the other to do the thing to which you seemed to be consenting. It is also a mistake, in the sense that you did not know that the other would understand your signal as betokening such consent. Your false signal is 'wholly innocent error', just so long as you neither knew nor could-and-should-have-known the convention in question, and hence how others would interpret your signal.

I call all of those cases of 'consent-like transactions'. They are not genuine consent—but merely consent-like—because they are missing the mental element of consent that is ontologically necessary for genuine consent. But they are indeed consent-like, insofar as consent *seems* to have been given. In the first case, that of deliberately fraudulent consent, the giving of consent is precisely what the false consent-giver himself purported to be doing. In the other two cases, that consent had been given is what others reasonably understood from the conventional signals of consent that were sent (culpably negligently in the one case, in innocent error in the other). In all three cases, consent has to all external appearances been given, even though the internal facts of the matter were otherwise, that is, the putative consent-giver did not mentally consent in the way ontologically required for genuine consent.

1.4.2 'As If Consenting': An Overview

In all of those circumstances, we are justified in treating the person in some sense 'as if he consented'.[102] In none of those cases is that because he 'really consented'. Absent the mental component, clearly he did not. Instead, we are justified in treating him in more-or-less the same way as we would have been justified in treating him had he actually consented.

I say '*in some sense* "as if he consented"', and I talk of treating him 'in *more-or-less* the same way' as if he had, because the details are going to differ among the

[102] As Tadros (2022, pp. 436) says, this simply goes to show that 'consent is not the only way of altering rights and duties—creating the [misleading] impression of consent might be another way'. My 'as if he consented' is broadly the same as Renzo's (2022) 'defective consent' and Miller and Wertheimer's (2010) 'moral transformation without valid consent'. The same moral transformation occurs as would have occurred had he consented (i.e., what had been impermissible becomes permissible), but through some mechanism other than the giving of valid consent (e.g., giving signals by which the other reasonably believed that consent had been given). Reiman (2013) uses 'as if they consented' in the same way as I do, to mean 'with the same effect as if they consented' (the 'moral equivalent of consent', in his terms), although he grounds his as if consent differently than I do.

three different types of false consent taxonomized above. I shall go on to detail those differences in Section 1.4.3 below. But let me first provide an overview of the broad strategy to be deployed.

The general idea is simply that false-signallers of consent should somehow be held responsible for the consequences of their seeming consent. There is widespread sentiment that that should be done.[103] Various ways have been suggested. Some commentators suggest appealing to notions of promissory estoppel, saying that a sort of quasi-contract arose when the false consenter induced others to rely on his false signals.[104] Other commentators see it as a matter of simple fairness that you should not lead people on and then let them down[105]—certainly you should not do so knowingly or recklessly, anyway, and even when you do so purely through some innocent error you might still owe them at least something in recompense.

I am sympathetic to those familiar approaches. But others sometimes baulk at them. It is generally agreed that 'promissory estoppel' can indeed be morally transformative and create new obligations (in a different way than consent, perhaps)—at least when the commitment was made intentionally. But some query whether the same sort of moral transformation can occur unintentionally.[106] And if it cannot, then the promissory estoppel approach clearly cannot cover cases of false consent through innocent error, or perhaps even through culpable negligence.[107] As regards the 'fairness' rationale, many people resist locutions such as 'a duty of fair play' on the grounds that they threaten to reduce morality to a game and moral requirements to rules internal to a practice we are entirely at liberty to opt out of.[108]

For anyone who is unpersuaded by those other formulations, let me offer another.[109] That is simply to say that: (1) there has been a mistake about whether

[103] Bolinger (2019, p. 193–8) does not employ the 'as if' phrase; indeed, she specifically eschews it. Still, she is referring to much same thing as I mean by treating people 'as if consenting' when she talks of people in these situations 'being held responsible for moral costs resulting from their behavior' (p. 193).

[104] On 'estoppel' see: ALI 1981, § 90; Fuller and Perdue 1936; Raz 1981, p. 123, n. 11; Dworkin 1988, p. 89; Green 1988, pp. 164–5, 171–2; and Simmons 1993, p. 70, n. 21. On 'quasi-contracts' see Singer (1973, pp. 47–59).

[105] See, e.g., Singer 1973, p. 55; Miller and Wertheimer 2010. This aspect of 'fairness' is different from, but related to, Hart (1955, p. 185) and Rawls's (1971, § 18, p. 112) notion of reciprocal forbearances in a joint enterprise, discussed in Section 3.5 below.

Perhaps those two propositions are, at root, the same, the latter being nothing more than a lay translation of the former's lawyerly language; nothing turns on that question for the purposes of this book.

[106] McDonald (2021, pp. 3517–22), for example, argues that it cannot.

[107] As regards the latter, however, note that the *Restatement of the Law of Contracts* refers to 'a promise which the promisor *should reasonably expect* to induce action or forbearance on the part of the promisee or a third party' (ALI 1981, § 90, emphasis added). That suggests that promissory estoppel can indeed extend to cases of culpably negligent false consent.

[108] Compare, for example: Rawls 1955; 1967; Scanlon 1990; 1998, ch. 7; Kolodny and Wallace 2003. See also Hare (1964) and Midgley (1974) responding to Searle's (1964) treatment of promising as a 'game'.

[109] Although it may be essentially the same thought, once again, merely differently expressed.

someone consents; (2) it is only fair (evoking a different aspect of fairness than before[110]) that those who have signalled consent falsely should bear at least some of the burdens of that mistake; (3) how much of the burden they should bear depends upon how culpable they were in falsely signalling consent; but (4) even if their false signal of consent was in wholly innocent error, they should nonetheless bear an equitable share of the costs that their error occasioned.

In the next section I will go on to say more about the differing degrees of culpability involved in the different types of false consent and how remedies should be tailored to reflect them. First, however, let me highlight how my more nuanced account contrasts with the sledge-hammer approach of the prominent purely ontological theories of consent discussed in Section 1.2.1 above.

As pointed out above, Communicationists, Attitudinalists and Hybrid theorists all simply define away the problem of false consent. Attitudinalists and Hybrid theorists say simply that 'it cannot be consent' if the ontologically necessary mental element is missing. (Maybe they would still say that 'false consent' is nonetheless a lie and lying should be always punished, but not for any consent-specific reason.) For Communicationists, 'false consent' is no problem because for them consent is consent just so long as it is communicated, no matter whether the communication is true or false, sincere or insincere. For Communicationists, simply by saying that he consents a person has thereby waived the rights, whether or not he mentally intended any such thing. But for the Communicationist, the same would be true of anyone who reports consenting—whether truly or falsely, whether deliberately fraudulently or culpably negligently or in innocent error. Communicationists are blind, in that way, to gradations of blameworthiness that can be involved in falsely consenting. Saying as Communicationists do that 'communicating consent is *ipso facto* consent' leaves fault out of the equation altogether. Yet that is something we should surely take centrally into account in trying to decide the appropriate treatment for people who falsely report consenting in the various different ways taxonomized in Section 1.4.1. And that is something I shall do when, in the next section, tailoring the consequences of those different types of false consent to the varying degrees of faultiness.

1.4.3 Tailoring Consequences

Having sketched the general strategy for attaching consequences to false consent, let me now proceed to elaborate the details. Those will, as foreshadowed, differ depending upon the type of false consent involved. The reason for the differences is just the different degrees of culpability involved in each type of false consent.

110 Superficially different, at least: both might be rooted in the same underlying concept of fairness.

1.4.3.1 Genuine Consent Waives Rights

To set the scene, let us start with the contrasting case of genuine consent. That, recall, is the case where: (1) the consent-giver has performed both of the ontologically-required acts of consent (the internal act of consent and the external performative act of consent), intending thereby to grant the permission specified in the consent; and (2) the consent-giver has communicated truthfully to the consent-receiver that the consent has been given, intending for the consent-receiver to understand therefrom that the permission specified in the consent has been given.

Genuine consent can be given in all manner of different ways, to be discussed more fully in Chapter 3. It can be given explicitly or tacitly. Tacit consent can be inferred or presumed. As foreshadowed in Section 1.3.2.2 and elaborated in Chapter 3, something akin to genuine consent can also be inferred for things that are logically or pragmatically implied in other things to which genuine consent of those various other forms has been given.

In all those cases, the upshot is the same: the consent-giver gives the consent-receiver permission to do something that would otherwise be impermissible. That is simply the consequence of genuine consent. In cases of genuine consent, the consent-giver *waives his right* against the consent-receiver doing that for which consent has been given.

1.4.3.2 Deliberatively Fraudulent Consent Forfeits Rights

Whereas genuine consent waives rights, deliberately fraudulent consent causes the purported consent-giver to *forfeit* the rights that he has through his fraudulent consent purported to waive.[111]

The practical upshot is the same in both cases. Both must, *ceteris paribus*, permit the (seeming) consent-receiver to do what has (albeit, in the case of the deliberately fraudulent 'consent'-giver, only seemingly) consented to permit. In that respect, the 'as if consenting' label is particularly appropriate for this case.

The result is the same, but the rationale is different. In the genuine consenter, the justification is that he genuinely granted that permission. In the case of the deliberately fraudulent consenter, what justifies requiring him to permit that which to which he purported to consent is that he sent signals he knew—and intended—that others would understand to be granting them permission to do that to which he purported to consent. He wrongfully misled others, and

[111] Rights forfeiture is most commonly discussed as a punishment for breach of the law (Blackstone 1765, bk. 2, chs. 18, 27; Wellman 2012) or as justification for inflicting defensive harm (Renzo 2017). But it sometimes occurs in consequence of failing to meet certain legal conditions as well.

intentionally so.[112] Others are fully entitled in the circumstances to act on his purported consent, and the deliberately fraudulent consent-giver has no grounds for complaint when they do so.

People who deliberately fraudulently signal consent intentionally mislead others into believing, and acting to their cost on the belief, that they intend to permit something which they have no intention of permitting. Such people should be held fully responsible for such misbehaviour; and the right way to do that is to require them to permit what they fraudulently or negligently reported that they intended to permit.

In order to accomplish that, however, there is no need to go nearly so far as Communicationists and say that such people have 'really consented' (on the Communicationist account, because any communication of consent is fully sufficient in itself for the existence of consent).[113] The same practical upshot can be achieved by saying, as I do, that people who deliberately fraudulently communicate consent forfeit the rights that they falsely purport to waive. They no longer have those rights, not because they actually waived them (as Communicationists would have it), but instead because, in fraudulently communicating consent, they forfeited those rights. That resolution has the advantage pointed out in Section 1.4.2 of preserving the possibility (that the Communicationist approach would foreclose) of treating less blameworthy cases of false consent differently and more leniently—and of course it does not come at the cost (as the Communicationist approach does) of denying that consent requires mental consent in any way whatsoever.

1.4.3.3 Culpably Negligent Consent Fully Encumbers Rights

Culpably negligent false consent still involves fault, albeit to a lesser degree. In such cases one person is still misleading another about his intention to consent to something. But he does so inadvertently rather than, as in the previous case, deliberately. He simply does not realize how the other would interpret the signals he is sending about his consent. Still, he was negligent—careless—in sending the signals he sent. And he was culpably so, insofar as he could and should have known how the other would interpret his signals. Hence it is worse than a case of false consent in wholly innocent error. The culpably negligent false consenter is at fault. He has done something wrong. His behaviour is not nearly so egregiously

[112] The deliberately fraudulent consenter thus acts with the second (but not the first) intention discussed in Section 1.3.2.1.

[113] Bolinger (2019, p. 189), for example, says (*a propos* promising, but she immediately then proceeds to apply the same principle to consenting): 'to keep insincerity from undermining safe reliance for recipients, the facts recipients *can* track (communicative behaviors) must be sufficient for determining whether a promise has been made; promissory *intent* can't be strictly necessary for promissory obligation'.

wrong as that of the false consenter who deliberately fraudulently misled others, to be sure. But it is still wrong.

The culpably negligent false consenter should therefore still bear some relatively serious consequences for his bad behaviour, but he should bear less severe consequences than the deliberately fraudulent false consenter. Instead of forfeiting the rights that he purported to waive (as in the case of the latter), those rights should merely be *encumbered* for the culpably negligent false consenter. But they should be *fully* encumbered, in the sense that the culpably negligent false consenter should be responsible for *all* of the reasonable costs that the putative consent-receiver incurred when acting in reasonable reliance upon the purported consent of the culpably negligent false consenter.

A culpably negligent false consenter *X* still has the right against *Y* φ-ing that *X* culpably negligently seemed to have waived. The culpably negligent false consenter does not forfeit that right entirely, as does the deliberately fraudulent false consenter. But because of his culpable negligence in giving false consent, that right is 'encumbered'. When exercising that right, *X* must pay *Y* compensation for *Y*'s reasonable costs in relying on *X*'s culpable negligent signals that *Y* reasonably understood as granting *X*'s permission for *Y* to φ. And when exercising his right against *Y* φ-ing, *X* owes Y *full* compensation for *all* of those costs. That is what it means to say that the right of the culpably negligent false consenter is 'fully encumbered'.

To foreshadow: I am going to suggest that same standard should apply in cases where consent that has genuinely been given is being revoked. I shall argue in Chapter 7 that a consent-giver should ordinarily be permitted to revoke his consent—but when he does, he should ordinarily be required to fully compensate the consent-receiver for costs reasonably incurred in reliance on the consent that is now being revoked. The culpably negligent false consenter must do the same, when standing on rights that he seemed to have waived. That is the sense in which we treat the culpably negligent false consenter 'as if he consented': when asserting the rights that he seemed to have waived through his false consent, we treat him 'as if he is revoking consent'.

The aim of compensation in the case of the culpably negligent false consenter is the same as in the case of the person revoking consent. In both cases, the aim is to restore the (putative) consent-receiver to the same position as she would have enjoyed had the (putative) consent never been (purportedly) given. This is a familiar approach in various branches of the law. It mirrors contract law's use of 'reliance interests' in compensating for breach of contract.[114] And tort law uses a similar standard to assess damages recoverable for 'negligent misrepresentation' in cases involving the 'tort of deceit'.[115]

[114] See Sections 2.2.5 and 7.3.2.2 below.

[115] ALI 1979, §§ 531, 549(2), 552B, comment a.

Being culpably negligent in reporting false consent is not as bad as doing so deliberately fraudulently. The consequences that I propose for the first sort of behaviour are less severe, accordingly. In the former case, I merely demand that the culpably negligent false consenter compensate putative consent-receivers for their full costs in relying on the false consent; that is much less draconian than insisting that deliberately false consenters forfeit the rights in question and actually permit what they purportedly consented to let the other person do.[116] Victims of culpably negligent false consent do not get to do what they seemed to have consent to do, as do victims of deliberately fraudulent consent.[117] They are merely entitled to full reimbursement for the costs they reasonably incurred on the basis of their reasonable belief that they were going to be able to do what they seemed to have consent to do.

1.4.3.4 Consent in Innocent Error Partially Encumbers Rights

In cases where the false communication of consent was instead in wholly innocent error, we should take a yet more lenient approach. Instead of requiring the false consenter to permit the putative consent-receiver actually to do what he purported to consent to her doing (as in the case of deliberately fraudulent consent), or even just requiring the false consenter to bear all of the putative consent-receiver's reasonable costs in relying on his purported consent (as in the case of culpably negligent consent), in the case of false consent resulting from a wholly innocent error we should merely require that those costs should be shared between the seeming consent-giver and the seeming consent-receiver in an equitable manner.

Assuming neither of them was in any way at fault in the situation, there is no reason that either of them should bear all the costs arising from the error. What would be an equitable division of the costs just depends, in that case, upon the stakes and financial capabilities of each of the parties involved.[118]

In the case of false consent through innocent error, just as in the case of culpably negligent consent, false consenter *X* retains the right against *Y* φ-ing that *X*'s false consent seemed to have waived. But when exercising that right, *X* owes *Y* at least *partial* compensation for *Y*'s reasonable costs in relying on *X*'s false

[116] Similarly in tort law cases involving the 'tort of deceit', the extent of damages recoverable is less (just out-of-pocket expenses) in cases of merely 'negligent misrepresentation', and it is more (the full 'benefit-of-the-bargain') in cases of 'fraudulent misrepresentation in a business transaction' (ALI 1979, §§ 531, 549(2), 552B, comment a).

[117] The latter protects a person's 'expectation interest' rather than merely her 'reliance interests', in the terminology of contract law discussed in Sections 2.2.5 and 7.3.2.2 below. Contract law protects the former interests when it orders 'strict performance' of contractual obligations—akin to my requiring the deliberately fraudulent false consenter to permit the putative consent-receiver to do what the false consent purported to permit her to do.

[118] This will be discussed more fully in Sections 4.6 and 4.7 below.

signals that seemed to give *Y X*'s permission to φ. That is why I say *X*'s right is only '*partially* encumbered' in cases where *X*'s false consent was in wholly innocent error.

Having falsely consented, even just in innocent error, *X* must share in some equitable manner the reasonable costs that *Y* incurred in relying on *X*'s seeming consent. But *only* those consent-related costs need be shared on account of the false consent in innocent error. And the reason that those costs should be shared is that, however innocently, *X* nonetheless sent signals that *Y* reasonably took to betoken *X*'s consent. Those two factors combine to make this, too, an instance of treating the false (albeit innocent) consenter 'as if he consented'.

1.4.3.5 Second-best Approximations

What I have outlined above are what should ideally be the consequences of each type of false consent. But sometimes in practice it is simply infeasible to tailor the consequences as precisely as those remedies prescribe.

Such problems will presumably rarely, if ever, arise in dealing with deliberately fraudulent false consenters. The ideal prescription in Section 1.4.3.2 above is for those people to be treated as having forfeited the rights that they purported to waive through their seeming consent. Doing just that will presumably always be possible. Anyway, it will always be possible wherever genuine consent is practically possible, because the consequence is the same in both cases, viz., requiring the (seeming) consent-giver to permit the (seeming) consent-receiver to do what has (seemingly) been consented to.

Practical problems seem more likely to arise in implementing the more nuanced treatments prescribed above for people who have falsely consented as a result of culpable negligence or innocent error. The ideal treatment prescribed above involves, in each case, requiring the false consenters to compensate seeming consent-receivers for some or all of the costs that they have incurred in reasonably relying on those people's false signals of consent.[119] Sometimes the costs that others have incurred are in principle uncompensatable.[120] Other times, it is simply impractical to assess and compensate people for the costs that they have incurred in relying upon someone else's false consent.

Let me anticipate here a recurring example that will figure at many places in Chapter 4 and occasionally later. That is the case of someone unintentionally signalling a bid at an auction, not knowing that his action (scratching his head) is a conventional signal of a bid in that auction house. Maybe he could and should have known that fact, and he was culpably negligent in sending that false signal of

[119] Compensating them for *some* of those costs, in the case of innocent error (Section 1.4.3.4) and for *all* of those costs in the case of culpable negligence (Section 1.4.3.3).

[120] Such cases are discussed in Section 7.3.2.5 below.

consent; maybe there was no way he could have known that that was the convention in that auction house, and he sent the false signal of a bid in wholly innocent error. Either way, the ideal prescriptions in Sections 1.4.3.3 and 1.4.3.4 above would require the inadvertent bidder to pay some compensation to those who have incurred costs in consequence of his false signal of consent. But who exactly might those people be, and how exactly might that be done?

Suppose the other bidders dispersed immediately after the auctioneer's hammer fell on the inadvertent bidder's bid, and it is impossible to reopen the bidding once the inadvertent bidder's mistake has been discovered. Further suppose that, for some reason, the item cannot simply be re-auctioned on some subsequent occasion.

In those circumstances, the options would seem to narrow to just two. Either (1) we could excuse the inadvertent bidder from his seeming consent to buy the item at the price to which he seemingly agreed; or else (2) we could require the inadvertent bidder to purchase the item at the price to which he seemingly agreed. Option 2 treats the inadvertent bidder more harshly than he ideally deserves; in effect, it treats him as if his consent had been deliberately fraudulent, when it was not in the cases here in view. But Option 1 treats the seller more harshly than she ideally deserves; the sale falls through, through no fault of her own. But in the circumstances as described, the ideally prescribed treatment is unavailable and those are the only two options.

Option 1 may well be the more appropriate second-best treatment in the case of false consent through innocent error (since it was after all 'innocent'), whereas Option 2 may well be the more appropriate second-best treatment in the case of false consent through culpable negligence (since it was after all 'culpable'). It is important to recognize, however, that those treatments are purely 'second-best'—we are driven to them simply by the impossibility or impracticality of implementing the first-best ideal treatments as prescribed above. It is equally important to recognize, though, that the ideal prescriptions offered above *can* sometimes prove to be infeasible or impractical, thus driving us to some such second-best alternatives.

1.5 Moral Transformations and Other Normative Implications

In discussions of 'consent', the headline normative claim is that 'consent is morally transformative'. Specifically, consent renders something permissible that would otherwise be impermissible. That occurs when, and because, in consenting the consent-giver waives a right that he previously had against the consent-receiver doing the now consented-to thing.[121] Shifts between those fundamental

[121] That is variously characterized as: waiving one's right to object to one's legal boundary being crossed (Alexander 2014); 'generat[ing] a permission that allows another to do a wrong act' (Hurd

deontic categories—right and wrong, permissible and impermissible—are what are referred to as 'moral transformations'.

Such categorical shifts are not the only thing that is morally going on in these situations, however. Within the categories, there often can be degrees of 'rightness' or 'wrongness'. We encountered that in Section 1.1: it is more or less wrong to mistakenly suppose that you have someone else's consent, when you do not, depending on that person's stakes in the matter. We encountered that once again in the discussion of 'false consenting' immediately above. A genuine moral transformation (forfeiting of rights) does occur in one of those cases (that of deliberately fraudulent consent). But in the other two cases, no moral transformation has occurred: false consenters of the other two types retain their rights; they merely (by reason of their falsely consenting) incur greater or lesser morally mandated costs in exercising them, and it would be more-or-less wrong for them to exercise their rights without paying that morally mandated compensation.

Likewise on the consent-receiver's side, it might be more-or-less wrong to act on a permission even when it has genuinely been given. Consider cases where consent has been given reluctantly, as foreshadowed in Section 1.2.1.1 and discussed more fully in Section 6.3 below. *Ex hypothesi*, the consent was given voluntarily, knowingly and by a fully competent person—the consent is genuinely valid, according to all of those standard validity conditions. Still, for one reason or another the consent-giver gave consent hoping that the consent-receiver would not make use of it. That fact constitutes a morally cognizable reason against the consent-receiver making use of the consent she has been given. It is not a conclusive reason, to be sure. It is nevertheless a reason to consider alongside all other reasons for and against her so acting. Whether or not the consent-receiver should act on the consent she has genuinely been given once again depends, inter alia, upon their relative stakes in the matter.[122]

The same sort of balancing comes into play in deciding whether someone who has given consent can revoke it, at what cost and with what compensation to the person from whom it is being revoked. There are some situations in which consent, once given, may not be revoked, as Chapter 7 will show. But in a great many cases, consent can be revoked, and whether or not it should be just depends on whether the one party has more at stake in revoking it than the other has in not having it revoked. That consideration is indirectly captured by the rule I propose in Section 7.3.2.4 that the party revoking consent should compensate the party

1996, p. 108); or releasing the consent-receiver from a duty that she otherwise owed to the consent-giver not to perform the consented-to act (Dougherty 2018, p. 2). I take all those to be equivalent expressions.

[122] Although there can of course be morally strong *pro tanto* reasons for the consent-receiver acting on the consent that have nothing to do with her own interests. Consider for example the case of a patient consenting to desperately needed surgery but who is frightened of surgery and hopes the doctor does not act on that consent. The doctor has a morally strong reason, rooted in the patient's interests rather than her own, to perform the surgery notwithstanding the patient's fear of surgery.

from which consent is revoked for costs he reasonably incurred in reasonably relying on the now-revoked consent. Such balancing figures even more directly in the rule I propose in Section 7.3.2.5 for cases in which compensation is impossible.

'More-or-less rightness' can also be found at work in cases of 'ineffectual consent'. Suppose that someone who is incompetent to give valid consent (because on strong pain medication for example) asking you to do something (such as perform surgery on him) that, were he competent, would require his consent. Section 8.5 argues that, if what is being asked for is what you should do anyway to someone who is incapable of giving consent, the fact that he asks for it is all the more reason for you to do that. *Ex hypothesi*, he is incompetent and hence incapable of giving valid consent. He may phrase his request in terms of 'consent', but the 'moral transformation' that would come with valid consent is lacking. Still, the rightfulness of your performing surgery is increased by his asking for you to do it, even if no full-blown 'moral transformation' can have occurred. Preferences, wishes and desires count for something, morally, even if they are those of someone who is not fully competent to consent.[123]

[123] Such cases would be classed as ones involving 'assent' rather than 'consent' in the specialized terminology of medical ethics discussed in Section 2.1. Tadros (2016, pp. 215–16) draws a different distinction, between 'consent' and 'advice', where 'advice' is not an exercise of any normative power but rather merely the provision of information about what the advice-giver thinks is in her 'best interests'. Expressions of one's 'wishes' can, in principle, be shoehorned into that model as 'information about what one wants'. But that sort of information provides reasons for others' action that are very different ('because she wants it') than those derived from information about her 'best interests' ('because it is good for her') or even about her 'own perceptions of her best interests' ('because she thinks it is good for her').

2
Consenting, Assenting and Promising

Having foreshadowed the main claims of the book in the previous chapter, I shall now sketch the general contours of consent as it is generally understood. This chapter does so by comparing and contrasting consenting with the most similar other normative power, promising. The next chapter does so by surveying modes of consent—the many ways in which consent is given, operationally. Over the course of these two chapters I will stake out some novel claims and take positions on some seriously contentions issues. But these two chapters are intended primarily as 'service' chapters, laying the groundwork for more innovative discussions to follow in later chapters, rather than as themselves offering any major innovations.

2.1 Assenting

Working toward a definition of 'consent', Faden and Beauchamp begin with the notion of 'assent'.[1] As they observe, 'to assent is to agree or acquiesce in an opinion or to comply with an arrangement'.[2] That, they say, 'strikes close to what occurs in giving . . . consent'. Close but, as they go on to say, not spot-on.[3] The consent-giver does not merely agree with something, he agrees *to* something—specifically, to give permission to someone, here and now, to do (or not do) something.[4] In the language of Section 1.2.1 above, he assents to a commitment. That makes 'consent'

[1] Faden and Beauchamp 1986, p. 278; see similarly Bolinger 2019, p. 180.

[2] Faden and Beauchamp 1986, p. 278.

[3] Faden and Beauchamp (1986, pp. 278ff.) say that consent involves assent plus 'authorization'. On why 'authorization' is not quite the right concept here, and 'permission' is, see Section 6.2.3 below. Ferzan and Westen (2017, p. 762) similarly define 'consent' in an 'assent plus' fashion—although the 'plus' that they would add ('sufficient conditions of knowledge, capacity, and freedom') does not so much distinguish consent from mere assent as distinguish valid from invalid consent. In this, they are apparently just reflecting debates among the American Law Institute membership on revising the *Restatement of Torts* (Simons 2019, p. 10)—which just goes to show you should never delegate linguistic legislation to a committee (except perhaps the Académie Française).

[4] The *Oxford English Dictionary* for example defines 'consent' as 'voluntary agreement to or acquiescence in what another proposes or desires; compliance, concurrence, *permission*' (q.v. 'consent (n.)', def. 1a, emphasis added).

Consent Matters. Robert E. Goodin, Oxford University Press. © Robert E. Goodin 2024.
DOI: 10.1093/oso/9780192889027.003.0002

a subspecies of 'assent'[5]—in common parlance, anyway, if not in the specialist discourse of medical ethics.[6]

'Consent' is sometimes used loosely to include all manner of other things.[7] But here I shall follow the practice of philosophers in taking, as the core notion, 'permissive consent'.[8] Such consent is morally transformative in a very particular way.[9] By consenting permissively, the consent-giver gives the consent-receiver moral permission to do something that, without the consent-giver's permission,

[5] The *Oxford English Dictionary* draws a sharp but different distinction between 'assent' and 'consent'. It defines 'assent' as 'agreement with a statement, an abstract proposition, or a proposal that does not concern *oneself*'—and it goes on to say that the latter is how 'assent' is 'distinguished from consent' in 'ordinary modern use' (q.v. 'assent (n.)', def. 5, emphasis added). But on that point the dictionary is surely just plain wrong. I can most certainly assent to the proposition that 'I consent to your φ-ing to/with/against me'.

[6] In specialist medical ethics, 'assent' is a term reserved for describing the 'positive endorsement' that is secured from children or others who nearly but do not quite have the capability to give valid consent. See, e.g.: Wendler 2006; Alderson 2012; and the 'Common Rule' in the *US Code of Federal Regulations* (US DHHS 1983, Title 45, § 46.406.a).

[7] Partridge 1971; cf. Green 1988, pp. 158–60. As Kleinig (1982, p. 93) puts it, '"consent" often functions as a kind of [conceptual] carry-all'. Simmons (1976, p. 275) offers the odd example of the locution 'Mr. Smiley has graciously consented to speak at the award dinner' (see similarly Plamenatz 1938/1968, p. 10). Some treat consent as a *form* of promising, from which I sharply distinguish it below: but while you can consent to a promise, just as you can consent to a marriage, that does not mean that consent *is* a promise or a marriage (cf. Ruben 1972; Simmons 1976, p. 275; Weale 1978; Kleinig 1982, pp. 114).

[8] See, e.g.: Manson 2016, pp. 3318–19; 2018; Dougherty 2021a, pp. 10–11. Note that that phrase refers to the *effect*, the normative consequence, of giving consent (it gives someone permission), not necessarily to the agent's intentions (leaving open the possibility that he can give consent unintentionally) nor the mode of giving consent (the agent can give consent indirectly or implicitly by giving a directive that implies consent [Dougherty 2021a, ch. 9]). Although the term 'permissive consent' is of relatively recent coinage, the idea has long prevailed. Simmons (1976, p. 275) for example writes, 'In Locke's discussion in his *Second Treatise*, we can distinguish (although Locke himself does not) three sorts of acts which for him count as acts of consent. First, there are promises; second, there are written contracts; and third, there are acts of consent which are essentially authorizations of the actions of others. My own inclination is to say that of the three, only the third sort of it is a genuine act of consent.' Similarly, Hart (1955, p. 184) speaks of rights being 'accorded by a person consenting or authorizing another to interfere in matters which but for his consent or authorization he would be free to determine for himself'. Plamenatz (1938/1968, pp. 9–10) before him wrote, 'The giving of consent is essentially the granting of permission, and there cannot be action by permission unless the right of the agent to act depends for its existence upon the granting of permission'. In the postscript to the second edition, however, Plamenatz (1938/1968, p. 167) revised that, saying: 'To give permission is to consent but to consent is not always to give permission, though it is always to do or to take part in doing something which the doer knows, or is presumed to know, creates in another a right he would not otherwise have' (p. 167); the latter he subsequently calls 'consenting to someone's authority' (p. 171). I shall argue in Section 6.2.3 however that 'authorization' is actually different from 'consent'.

[9] The 'morally transformative' language was introduced by Hurd (1996) and is now ubiquitous (e.g., Kleinig 2010), but of course the thought itself is much older. Note that Hurd herself used the 'morally transformative' terminology to apply only to a different sort of case: where one person's consent gives another person literally a 'right' to do what was consented to, rather than merely a 'permission' (and for her a 'stained' one at that). However, I would dispute that consent ever gives someone literally a right. In Hurd's example of how 'consent turns a trespass into a dinner party', when I invite someone to dinner, I give them permission to enter my home that evening, not a right to do so; and it would not be wrong (a violation of any right that they now have) for me to withdraw that permission and order them to leave.

would have been morally impermissible.[10] More specifically, by consenting in that way the consent-giver waives—narrowly, in respect of that particular consented-to act and that particular consent-receiver and on that particular occasion[11]—rights that the consent-giver had (or excusing the consent-receiver from duties that she had toward him) that would otherwise have stood in the way of giving effect to that proposal.[12] (Here and in my subsequent discussions, I take 'giving permission' and 'waiving his rights' as equivalent and shall use the terms interchangeably.[13]) In the paradigm case, the consent-giver waives rights that he has against the consent-receiver that the latter not interfere with him or his interests in certain ways.[14]

This chapter will be devoted to comparing and contrasting two normative powers, consenting and promising. The aim of that exercise is to help clarify the nature of consent itself. In tracing differences between those two normative powers, I shall not be arguing that either is morally more important than the other on account of those differences. (Those differences may or may not matter, morally.) Similarly, in identifying similarities between them I shall not necessarily be arguing that the moral grounds for those features are the same in both cases. (They may or may not be.) The aim of this book is to elucidate the nature of consent; and in that context the contrast case of promising is of interest only insofar as it assists in that quest, rather than in its own right.

[10] This is the standard formulation, and I will stick to it in the text of this book. Strictly speaking, however, the act need not be 'otherwise morally impermissible *all things considered*' (Green 1988, p. 163). What consent does is merely remove what would otherwise have figured as a *pro tanto* reason for considering it to be impermissible.

[11] 'That' in all those cases meaning 'that which is specified in giving the consent'. Strictly speaking each 'that' should read 'those', since the specification itself may of course stipulate consent is given to a number of people or in respect of a number of acts or a number of occasions.

[12] When consenting one should be taken to be waiving the minimum set of rights (or excusing the minimum set of duties) needed to accomplish the object of the consent.

[13] Simons (2019, p. 10) tries to drive a wedge between them, saying, 'the person who exercises the power to consent need not know or intend that, by doing so, he is extinguishing a legal right he would otherwise have or is thereby releasing the actor from his duty'. But he acknowledges the legal upshot is precisely that, whatever the consent-giver's intentions. And morally that is as it should be, since the consent-giver could and should have known that would be the consequence of giving permission. (I would put the point more strongly: he could and should have known the meaning of the word 'permission', which necessarily entails that.) At the very least, that gives us grounds for treating the consent-giver in the same way 'as if' he waived his legal right when granting the permission, to revert to the trope introduced in Section 1.4.2.

There may be a better argument for distinguishing between 'granting permission' and 'waiving a right' to be found in terms of the revocability of each of those actions. I shall return to discuss that in Section 2.2.4 below.

[14] Hurd (1996, p. 123) writes, most bizarrely, 'consent defeats any rights on the part of others (including the person consenting) that the actor not do the wrong act'. Surely she should have said 'specifically' rather than 'including'. If Joseph's act would wrong both Jack and Jill, then the fact that Jack has consented to it does not negate Jill's right that the act not be done.

2.2 Consenting and Promising

Both consenting and promising can be seen as subspecies of assenting.[15] They are alike insofar as both involve assent *plus* a commitment.[16] They differ in what form that commitment takes.[17] Consent involves the consent-giver committing to *waiving a right* he had against the consent-receiver's interfering with the consent-giver's interests in certain specified respects. A promise involves the promise-giver committing to *incurring a duty* to do whatever the promise-giver has promised the promise-receiver.[18]

2.2.1 Both Must Be Future-oriented

Consent and promises are also alike in both being future-oriented. Promises concern what the promise-giver will do in the future. Consent concerns what the consent-receiver will be permitted to do in the future.[19]

You cannot genuinely 'promise' to do something in the past. Perhaps you can say, in an extended usage, 'I *promise* you that I locked the door as we left!'[20] But that is not a promise in the morally transformative sense here under discussion; it is just an emphatic way of saying, 'I *assure* you that I did it!'[21] Morally, you cannot incur now a duty to have done something in the past. That would be a duty

[15] Other recent commentators who have fruitfully illuminated the notion of consent by tracing its similarities and differences to promises include Brett (1998, pp. 74–80), Owens (2011; 2012) and Dougherty (2015).

[16] Watson (2004, pp. 61–5) makes this point specifically about 'promising'; it applies equally to 'consenting'. The *Oxford English Dictionary*, too, defines a 'promise' in just these terms: as 'a declaration or assurance made to another person (usually with respect to the future), stating a commitment to give, do, or refrain from doing a specified thing or act, or guaranteeing that a specified thing will or will not happen' (q.v. 'promise (n.)', def. 2a).

[17] Simmons (1993, p. 69, n. 29; see similarly Raz 1986, pp. 82–4) is therefore right to resist the attempt by some commentators (Weale 1978, pp. 66–7; Den Hartogh 1989, p. 214) to view consent as a subspecies of promising.

[18] In Feinberg's (1986a, p. 178) succinctly puts it, 'The immediate effect of promises is to create obligations in the speaker; the immediate effect of acts of consent is to cancel obligations to [*sic.*, he means "of"] the one addressed.'

[19] Or, for a more precise (albeit more cumbersome) parallel with promising: 'consent concerns what the consent-giver will no longer have any moral right to object to the consent-receiver's doing in the future, *viz.*, what the consent-giver has consented to the consent-receiver's doing'.

Depending upon the content of the proposition consented to (see further Section 6.2.3), the commitment may sometimes involve the consent-giver incurring a duty as well, as when I consent to your exercising political authority over me. But while it may be 'the characteristic result of consent to the state's authority [is] the acquisition of an obligation on the part of the consenter', Green (1988, p. 162) emphasizes that 'this is not an essential feature of consent in general'. Indeed, what we speak of as 'consenting' in that connection might be better seen as 'promising'—although talk of 'political consent' is too well entrenched to try to replace it with something more accurate, at this late date.

[20] The *Oxford English Dictionary* (q.v. 'promise (v.)', def. 3a) recognizes the usage of 'promise' as an 'assurance of a statement relating to the present or the past'.

[21] Or, in Liberto's (2018, p. 22) terms, I 'guarantee' I did it.

that it would have been impossible for you to have discharged, supposing that 'discharging your duty' means 'intentionally doing what your duty requires just because it is your duty'—which it wasn't, at the time you would have had to do what the newly-incurred promissory duty requires you to have done. You might, for some other reason, have done then what is now required of you by the new promissory duty; you might, for some other reason, have been morally required to do it; but you could not have done it at the time *because* it was required by a promissory duty that did not exist at the time.

The same is true of consent. Insofar as the social function of consent is to inform another agent's subsequent moral choices (as argued it is, in Section 1.2.1 above), it follows that consent must refer to the other's *prospective* actions and choices.[22] It would be pragmatically pointless, in prospective action-guiding terms, to consent to things that cannot now be done or undone.[23] Action can only be 'guided' (by consent or anything else) in advance, not in arrears.[24] The same argument is standardly given for thinking that law, insofar as it aspires to be action guiding, must always be prospective and never retrospective.[25]

The more fundamental point, however, is a logical one. To consent is to give permission for something to occur, and 'permitting' is by its nature forward-looking.[26] One cannot be said to 'permit' something after it has already happened.[27] That would be simply incoherent.[28] After the fact, you can 'forgive' or

[22] Dougherty 2015, p. 231. This social function can be construed instrumentally or normatively—in the latter case, as an aspect of an agent's autonomy in forging normative relations with others (Healey 2015).

[23] In ancient Rome, a site was made religious by burying a dead body on it. Roman law stipulated that 'the land of a third party may be used for burial if its owner consents'; and 'the site . . . become[s] religious even if his *approval is given after the burial*' (Justinian 535, bk. 2, ch. 1, sec. 9, emphasis added). But note well, under that provision what the owner's subsequent consent does is to 'make the site become religious', an event which occurs only when (not before) the consent is given.

[24] As Renzo (2022, p. 59) says, 'we cannot give or revoke consent to conduct that happened in the past, for that would make it impossible for consentees to even try and respect our autonomous agency by responding to our consent'.

[25] Fuller 1969, pp. 51–62.

[26] Not necessarily very far forward—you can say 'I consent to your ø-ing here and now', which properly explicated means that you are consenting to my φ-ing immediately after you have said it (rather than literally simultaneously with your saying it).

[27] To 'permit' is 'to allow the occurrence of (an action, etc.); to allow (something) be carried out or to take place' (*Oxford English Dictionary*, q.v. 'to permit', def. 2).

[28] Chwang (2009, pp. 121–2) defends the coherence of 'subsequent consent' by claiming that 'the part of it that generates moral force is the exact same as for prior consent—the attitude of not minding'. But, firstly, I deny that an 'attitude of not minding' is either necessary or sufficient for morally transformative prior consent. It is certainly conceptually possible for me to consent perfectly validly to something that I would prefer not to happen. And it is certainly possible for me not to mind something without consenting to it. When Rhett Butler says to Scarlet O'Hara, 'Frankly my dear, I don't give a damn!', he is expressing indifference to what she does with the rest of her life, not consent. Secondly, even if *arguendo* that attitude is constitutive of consent, I would argue (for reasons given in the text) that it can be morally transformative only if it is present at the time the consented-to act occurs; if it is not, then the actor committed a wrong at the time of acting, even by that standard. At most, all that showing that the moral importance of both prior and subsequent consent derive from the same source ('the attitude of not minding') might show is that *ex ante* consent and *ex post* forgiveness

'excuse' a wrong that another has done to you.[29] A pardon may expunge the official record of his wrongdoing. After the fact, you can be compensated for the effects of the wrong that has been done to you. After the fact, he can apologize for having wronged you. But nothing that you do or anyone else does can retrospectively change the fact that what he did to you was wrong at the time he did it.[30] If what he did was something that was wrong to do without your permission, which he did not have at the time of doing it, then he committed a wrong. And you cannot retrospectively, through consenting, make permissible after-the-fact an act that was impermissible at the time it was performed.[31]

My anticipation of what you will do in the future can and does shape my current actions of course.[32] So, in the present case, if I anticipate that you will subsequently forgive my currently unconsented-to actions, my anticipation of your forgiveness can indeed guide my current actions in undertaking it. The question is simply what is the proper label for that future act of yours. I just called it 'forgiveness'. Others might prefer 'endorsement'.[33] My quarrel is merely with those who insist upon labelling it 'retrospective consent', as if it were actually a form of genuine consent.

Not everything that is morally permissible is so by purely virtue of consent. That is one very particular way of making things all right, permissible; but it is far from the only way. I can be grateful for what you did, even though I did not

have equal moral weight and for the same reason—but that does not show that both are necessarily forms of consent, any more than showing that fraud and assault are both morally sourced in respect for persons shows that they are the same crimes.

[29] Van Der Veer 1979, p. 639; see more generally Murphy and Hampton (1988). Forgiving or excusing could be construed as 'waiving your right to redress or apology', but in a *forward-looking* way (Warmke 2016; Bennett 2018). The Statute of Westminster II of 1285 made it a crime to 'ravish a woman... where she neither assented before nor after' (13 Edw. I, St. 2, ch. 34). Some say the latter constitutes a defence of 'subsequent consent' (Westen 2004, p. 254; Witmer-Rich 2011, p. 392); but it can equally well be seen as 'forgiveness' having the same legal effect.

[30] As Van Der Veer (1986, p. 69) is right to query 'how subsequent consent is supposed to "reach back in time"... and legitimize the past act'. Simons (2006a, p. 614) offers a similar rebuttal to Westen's (2004, pp. 256–7) defence of retrospective consent: 'Understanding consent in this tenseless sense, as "what *S* wants *A* to have done to her", simply papers over the problem. *S* can now be glad that *A* did something that she earlier opposed, but I don't think she can "want" or "choose" something that she cannot influence, i.e., *A*'s past conduct.'

[31] For example, 'case law is unanimous in holding consent given at any time subsequent to the act of intercourse will not prevent the act from being a rape' (California Court of Appeals 1985, p. 241). Westen (2004, pp. 254 ff.) thinks it can in cases of long-term partners; but the case law he cites does not bear that interpretation (Witmer-Rich 2011, p. 393), and in any case I think there is a better explanation of such cases (see Section 3.3.3).

[32] That is the central insight of 'rational expectations' economics (Kantor 1979).

[33] That is what was involved in Dworkin's (1972, p. 119) brief remark that seems to have launched the small 'retrospective consent' bubble: 'Parental paternalism may be thought of as a wager by the parent on the child's subsequent recognition of the wisdom of his restrictions. There is an emphasis on what could be called future-oriented consent—on what the child will come to welcome rather than on what he does welcome.' I agree with all of that, except calling the child's 'prospective future endorsement' any form of 'consent', which Dworkin says nothing to justify. In any case, note that the parental interventions Dworkin has in view do not clearly constitute 'wrongs' that it would take the child's consent to render permissible.

endorse it at the time; and my later gratitude can retrospectively justify your earlier action. I can forgive you a wrong that you have previously done to me, and my forgiveness can retrospectively rebalance the current moral ledger even if it does not undo the historical one. But forgiving is a way of dealing with the fact, rather than erasing the fact, that what you did was wrong at the time you did it, in a way that it would not have been if I had actually consented to it at the time you did it.

If retrospective consent were really consent—if it really had the power to go back and transform the moral status of acts in the past—there would be no need for you to do anything beyond saying, after the fact, 'I hereby consent to what you did'. Saying in addition to that, 'I forgive you for it', would then be redundant. Retrospectively consenting would have retrospectively rendered your past action permissible, and there would be no wrong left to forgive. So retrospectively consenting to something and retrospectively forgiving it would be alternative courses of action. We hear people forgiving one another all the time. For my own part, anyway, I have never heard anyone say to another that they retrospectively consent to something that the other person has already done. Of course it is possible that everyone but everyone has simply been overlooking one good moral option that is genuinely available to them. But a more reasonable interpretation, I would suggest (for reasons I have given) is that retrospective consent is simply an oxymoron.

Like hypothetical consent ('you would have agreed')—to which I turn next—'retrospective consent', the fact that 'you will or did retrospectively agree', might be morally relevant in all sorts of *other* ways.[34] It may constitute evidence that it was 'good' that I did that wrong thing to you.[35] But your subsequent agreement does not constitute consent. It does make it 'all right'—permissible—for me to do something that was morally impermissible for me to do to you without your consent, which I did not have at the time I actually did it.[36]

2.2.2 Both Can Be Conditional, Neither Purely Hypothetical

Both promising and consenting can be conditional in form. For an example of the former: 'I promise you can use my car to go to the concert if you get back in time to go.' For an example of the latter: 'I consent to sell you my car if you pay me $20,000 in exchange.'

[34] Carter 1977; Van Der Veer 1979; cf. Chwang 2009; Witmer-Rich 2011, pp. 391–7.

[35] Westen 2004, p. 263. Witmer-Rich 2011, pp. 395–6.

[36] Contrast 'informed consent' requirements governing medical treatment of conscious and competent patients and the very different standards governing emergency treatment of comatose patients (US DHHS 1991, § 46.116.f), which are sometimes given 'subsequent consent' rationales.

Notice however that with respect both to promising and consenting, conditionals can operate in two importantly different ways.[37] Those are illustrated in the two examples just given. In the first case I have promised you, *here and now*, that you can use my car. True, the promise does not become practically relevant unless the condition ('you get back in time') is met. But whether or not I have actually made the promise does not depend on the condition being met. In the second case I do not consent to selling you my car *until, and unless*, you hand over the money. The very giving of my consent is itself conditional on that. Although I have illustrated the first by reference to promises and the second by reference to consent, conditionals can in fact function either way with respect to both promising and consenting.

To put the point slightly more formally, conditions attaching to promising or consenting might be given either an 'internalist' or an 'externalist' reading. On the first reading, the 'if' condition is 'internal' to the proposition being promised/consented to ('I promise/consent [to φ if γ]'). On the second reading, the 'if' condition is 'external' to the proposition being promised/consented to ('If γ [I promise/consent to φ]').[38]

The difference made by that difference is just this. If the conditional promise/consent is internalist in form, the promise/consent has been made at the moment the utterance has been made, even before the condition comes to be satisfied. If it is externalist in form, the promise/consent will not have actually been made until the condition arises. To put the point in other words, to promise/consent in an externalist way is to say 'I *will*' promise/consent, whereas doing so in an internalist way is to say 'I *do*'. Or to put the point in still other words, an externally conditional promise/consent is not *yet* a promise/consent—it is not one, until the specified conditions arise.[39]

Hypothetically consenting/promising is externally conditional in just an analogous way. To say you hypothetically consent/promise is to say you *would* consent/promise under certain conditions, where those are contrary-to-fact conditionals.[40]

[37] This corresponds to a very old distinction—going back to Grotius (1625, bk. 2, ch. 11, secs. 2–4), Hobbes (1651, ch. 14) and Pufendorf (1672/1710, bk. 3, ch. 5, sec. 8)—between (a) 'I promise to give you this tomorrow' (in which case it has not yet been given to you) and (b) 'I give you this and I will deliver it tomorrow' (in which case it has been given today, and mere delivery is all that is pending).

[38] Gilbert (1993) makes the distinction by reference to promises. Chadha (2021, pp. 346–7) applies it to consent.

[39] This distinction will become important in Section 11.3.

[40] Stark (2000, p. 315) rightly remarks: '*Hypothetical* consent is not to be confused with *actual* consent about hypothetical circumstances. For instance, if one agrees to drive a friend to the airport if the friend's car is still in the shop, one actually consents though she consents to do something that, at the time of her consent, is a hypothetical scenario.' In the terminology introduced above, the driving-the-friend-to-the-airport example is an instance of the condition being internal to the proposition being consented to. In contrasting hypothetical consent to that, Stark is implicitly saying that that refers to counterfactual conditions that are external to the proposition being consented to—in which case, as I have said, consent does not become actual until the conditions in question are satisfied.

That is to say, in case of hypothetical consenting/promising, you have not consented to or promised anything (as yet).[41]

Furthermore, in the case of hypothetical consent extra 'wriggle room' is provided by the subjunctive 'would'. With an externally conditional promise/consent of the ordinary form, 'If γ [I promise/consent to φ]', your promise/consent to φ is automatically triggered by the presence of the condition γ. But externally conditional promise/consent that is hypothetical in form says, merely, 'If γ [I *would* promise/consent to φ]'. To say 'I would' is also to say 'I have not yet'.

This has been much discussed in connection with consent to incurring political obligations to obey the law, of course. I will return to discuss that more fully in Chapter 10. But to avoid getting prematurely bogged down in that sprawling literature, let us focus for now on a simpler, cleaner example.

Take the case of a physician confronted with a badly injured accident victim in urgent need of medical treatment. The patient is comatose and incapable of giving consent; he had no advance directive giving or refusing consent for the particular treatment that he now urgently requires; there are no family members or other credible surrogate decision-makers available to give consent on his behalf. Physicians in such circumstances proceed to treat him on the basis of what they (in the US especially) call 'presumed consent'—by which they mean treatment to which (to the best of their knowledge) the patient hypothetically would consent if he were conscious and able to give consent.[42]

But to say a person 'would' consent under some contrary-to-fact conditions—even if it is absolutely true that he would, and even if the physician had very good grounds for believing that he would—is different from saying that the person 'does consent', here and now. At the moment at which the surgeon's knife slices into his injured body, the patient has not consented to that surgery. The fact that the patient would consent subsequently does not change the fact that, at the time of the surgery, he has not consented—and as I have argued in Section 2.2.1, consent cannot be backward-looking, it can only be forward-looking. The surgeon operated without the patient's consent, even if there were the best grounds in the world for the surgeon's thinking that the patient would subsequently (or perhaps just counterfactually) consent.

In defence of hypothetical consent, some say that it respects the autonomy of a person by reflecting the will of that person.[43] That, they say, is why hypothetical

[41] As Simmons (1976, pp. 286–7, emphasis added) says, it being the case that 'if he had been asked to ... he would have consented ... is closely related to genuine consent in some way *without in fact being consent*'.

[42] Eyal 2019. Or sometimes they say they are treating him in that way on the grounds that their best guess is that he will, retrospectively, consent to that treatment once he becomes able to do so. But as I have argued in the previous section, retrospective consent is no kind of consent at all.

[43] Enoch (2017, pp. 23–36) phrases it in terms of respecting a person's 'deep commitments'. In Kuflik's (2010, p. 140, italics omitted) formulation, 'hypothetical consent is a reasonable way of extending respect for someone's right to decide what will happen in and to his or her own body, even in circumstances in which that person's capacity for decision making cannot be concurrently

consent amounts morally to more than merely a gesture toward the 'good reasons' that she would have for consenting.[44] What makes her 'reasons for hypothetically consenting' a morally interesting subset of all possible reasons is that they are '*her* reasons'. There is a moral difference between subjective and objective, internal and external reasons; and respecting her subjective reasons has a special moral importance, deriving from the obligation to 'respect her' tout court.[45] I agree with all that, but I would argue that its moral importance is better captured by the notion of 'respecting her wishes' rather than by any talk of hypothetical consent.[46] Remember, issues of consent arise only where the putative consent-giver has rights that can be waived by consenting. Not all of a person's wishes necessarily concern things over which she has any rights, yet those wishes still deserve at least some respect.

Maybe rights deserve even more respect. But, remember, with rights an important part of what we should respect is her *choice* in those matters over which she has a right to choose—and in cases of merely *hypothetical* consent, she has not (yet) made any choice for us to respect. Hypothetical consent theorists can talk about what she 'would chose' in those cases. But the whole point of rights is that it is for her (not hypothetical consent theorists on her behalf) to make the choice. For them to pretend that they are 'respecting her rights' by choosing as they think (even if rightly) that she would have done is like selling her house for her at a price they think she would have agreed to. Unless they are her authorized agents in the matter (and hypothetical consent theorists are nothing of the sort) selling her house out from under her, even at a price she truly would have agreed to, is no way of respecting her rights in the property.

In any case, the pretence that hypothetical consent respect 'her will' is strained. 'To will', remember, is an active verb. To say that consent is an '*exercise* of the will' simply serves to emphasize that consent requires an *act* of consent.[47] Unactualized—merely hypothetical—consent can at most merely track 'reasons for a person to consent'.[48] Sometimes hypothetical consent theorists counterfactualize those reasons, too, as reasons that people 'would under idealized circumstances'

exercised'. One problem with that formulation is that hypothetical consent is invoked not only in cases where the person 'cannot currently decide' but also in cases where the person merely 'has not' done so. A larger problem is that that is a purely symbolic exercise: 'respecting someone's right to decide' usually means abiding by the person's decision, i.e., letting the person's actual decision determine the outcome; but in the case of hypothetical consent the person has not decided anything, so there is no possibility of letting the person's own decision be determinative.

[44] Thomson (1990, pp. 185ff.) and Waldron (1993, p. 53) propose the reduction. Kuflik (2010, pp. 135–40) and Enoch (2017, pp. 9–21) resist it.

[45] Williams 1981, 101–13; see further Williams 1973, pp. 108–17; 1981, pp. 1–19.

[46] I say more about 'respecting wishes' as a substitute for consent in Sections 8.5, 11.2 and 11.3 below.

[47] The 'exercise of will' description is Hobbes' (1651, ch. 14) and Pufendorf's (1672/1710, bk. 3, ch. 6, sec. 16, para. 1). See further Section 1.2.1.1 above.

[48] As Waldron (1993, p. 55) puts it, 'when we move from asking people what they accept to asking what they *would* accept under certain conditions, we shift our emphasis away from the will and focus on the *reasons* that people might have for exercising their will in one way rather than another'.

(or sometimes just 'could in some possible world') harbour.[49] But even if they are reasons that the person actually currently harbours, such reasons merely provide an explanation (or more precisely, a prediction) of why the person would or will consent.[50] Until and unless the person actually acts on those reasons, the person has not yet consented. That is why so many of us think that hypothetical consent is 'no kind of consent at all'.[51]

We may (most of us certainly do) think that the surgeon should nonetheless proceed with life-saving surgery in such a case, even if the comatose patient is incapable of consenting to it.[52] Provisions are written into tort law permitting just that.[53] And we may also think that the surgeon should desist from surgery if the comatose patient has left standing instructions against surgery in such circumstances—that is, if the patient has performed an act of commitment refusing consent, an act that has standing effect until revoked (just like the consent I gave my son to borrow the car while I was asleep in Section 1.2.1.1).[54]

Thus, what the surgeon should do in the operating theatre is not in question. I completely agree with the substantive conclusions that the hypothetical consent device is being used to achieve. My argument is merely that we do not need that device to achieve them. There is no need to appeal to hypotheticals to pretend you have consent from the comatose patient when you do not—there are plenty of other considerations, besides consent, can sometimes justify giving them medical treatment. And there is no need to trade in hypotheticals to justify non-treatment of a patient who has actually previously given standing instructions from the patient refusing consent to such treatment.[55]

[49] On the 'idealization' version see Enoch (2017, pp. 21–3) and sources sited therein. On the 'possible world' version see Waldron (1993, p. 53) who shows it can be persuasive negatively if not positively ('showing that something *could not be* consented to is a way of showing that it *has not been* consented to').

[50] The 'explanation' language is Enoch's (2017, pp. 17–21), borrowed from the 'special sciences': there it is indeed appropriate; there, something exists and we want to explain it. But that language is question-begging as applied to hypothetical consent: it implies that that already exists, when it does not. That is why I say that, in the latter case, what the reasons are providing is better termed a 'prediction' than an 'explanation'.

[51] Recall Dworkin's (1975, p. 18) classic example of a poker game: just as he was about to rake in his winnings, the other player notices that the deck was one card short and petitions to replay the hand saying, 'Surely if asked before the hand was dealt you would have agreed that we must play with a full deck'; to that, Dworkin envisages the utterly telling reply, 'Yes, and it's a very good thing you didn't ask!' (anyway, that was the way he put it when I first heard him deliver that paper in Oxford in 1972, although the published version omits that telling phrase). On hypothetical consent more generally, see: Thomson 1990, pp. 185 ff.; Brudney 1991; Waldron 1993, pp. 46–50, 55; Stark 2000; Simmons 1993, pp. 78–9; Kuflik 2010; Enoch 2017; and Simons 2019, pp. 16–19.

[52] As Dworkin (1988, p. 117) writes, 'It is sometimes said of emergency cases that the patient has "implicitly" or "tacitly" agreed to the treatment, and hence there is no violation of autonomy. This way of talking is misleading.... In fact, neither explicitly nor implicitly has any agreement taken place; if there is no loss of autonomy in these situations by not getting consent it is because autonomy has already been lost and not because the patient has really consented.'

[53] ALI 1979, § 892D.

[54] For further discussion of 'advance medical directives' see Sections 8.4, 8.5 and 11.2 below.

[55] I discuss such cases further in Chapter 8 and Section 11.2.

2.2.3 Consenting is Self-executory, Promising Not

The commitments involved in consenting and promising also differ in their force. In the case of consent, the commitment is self-executory. By the sheer act of consenting, you bring about the very waiver that that act of consent commits you to making. In the case of a promise, in contrast, the commitment is not self-executory. Instead, the commitment is to do something further in the future—viz., whatever the promise commits you to doing.[56]

Some may suppose that that distinction is more apparent than real. Here is how that reasoning might go. In both cases, the *moral transformation* in view occurs at the moment the consent or promise is given; in the former case the waiver is made, in the latter case the obligation is incurred, at that very instant. Furthermore, in both cases there is *something further* you must subsequently do to honour the terms of that moral transformation. That is most obvious in the case of promising, which explicitly commits you to doing something further in the future. But, the argument in view claims, something similar is true of consenting as well: to honour the terms of the consent he has given, the consent-giver must abstain from interfering with the consent-receiver's doing what the former's consent has given the latter permission to do.

I dispute that last claim, however. I agree that, in order to discharge the commitment contained in a promise, something further must indeed be done—the promised goods must be delivered, or whatever. But with consent, in contrast, for the commitment contained in the consent to be completely discharged you do not need do anything more than merely give your consent. What consenting has committed you to doing is merely waiving your right against the other's interference; and by the very act of your giving consent to him, that has been accomplished.

Some might say that consenting commits you to more than that.[57] Granting consent, they might insist, also involves assuming some sort of special obligation not to interfere with the consent-receiver's acting upon the permission thus granted.[58] There are some cases in which that might seem plausible. For example,

[56] How to handle 'conditional consent'—of which 'advance directives' for medical treatment are a prime example (Section 11.2)—depends on whether, in the terminology of Section 2.2.2, the 'condition' in question is 'internal' or 'external' to the proposition being consented to. If it is external, then you have waived the right in question here and now, even if the waiver will only take effect later when and if the stipulated condition arises; externally conditional consent thus is indeed self-executory in the way described in the text. But if the condition is internal to the proposition being consented to, then it looks more like a promise to consent and thereby waive your rights at some later date (when the stipulated conditions arise).

[57] Hobbes (1651, ch. 14), for example, thought that 'when a man has... abandoned or granted away his right, then he is... obliged or bound not to hinder those to whom such right is granted or abandoned from the benefit of it'.

[58] In Simmons' (1976, p. 276) words, granting consent 'involves the assuming of a special obligation not to interfere with the right accorded'. But that is a clear mistake: granting consent confers 'liberties'

if I have consented to loan you my car to get to an important appointment tomorrow, it seems like it would be wrong of me to leave the car locked in a garage to which you do not have a key.[59] But there are other cases in which a 'special obligation not to interfere' with the consent-receivers' doing what I consented to him doing is not remotely plausible. When participating in a boxing match, for example, I consent to you hitting me. It does not remotely follow from that fact, however, that I must let down my guard so as not to interfere with you hitting me.[60]

What is going on in the former sorts of cases where a special obligation not to interfere seems to be present is, I submit, consent plus something else. At the same time as consenting, the consent-giver *also* makes (explicitly or implicitly) a promise not to interfere with the consent-receiver doing what the consent-giver has consented to him doing. Those would be two separate acts, however; they are not part and parcel of the same act.[61] *X*'s consent does not, in and of itself, create any 'special obligation not to interfere'. The example of the boxing match demonstrates that fact. On its own, consent merely creates a situation in which *X* now has 'no-right' (whereas he previously did have a 'right') against *Y*'s interfering with him by φ-ing—in the boxing match example, against *Y*'s hitting him.[62]

or 'permissions', not 'rights' (Westen 2004, pp. 32, 91). And from that mistake follows the mistaken proposition that I here want to challenge: while duties do indeed correlate with rights, liberties or permissions do not correlate with any duties. Simmons (1976, p. 275–6) blunts the force of his error by going on to emphasize that any such obligation is secondary to the main purpose of *X*'s consent, which is to 'authorize' *Y* to *a* (but see Section 6.2.3 below on the distinction between consenting and authorizing). Cf. Weale 1978; Kleinig 1982, p. 113.

59 If I do that, it might be said that I 'consented in bad faith'. But note that I nonetheless consented. If you managed to gain access to my garage and drive off with my car at the agreed hour, you have committed no wrong against me, as you would have done had I not consented to your taking my car. See further Sections 1.4 and 2.3.1.

60 Some may say that, in consenting to a boxing match, I am merely consenting to you *trying* to hit me, and keeping up my guard does not interfere with you trying (merely with you succeeding). But if all I have consented to is you trying, then when you actually succeed and hit me you have committed an assault upon me to which I have not consented. Every boxer who has been hit (perfectly within the rules of boxing) would in that case have a tort action against his opponent. That is not the case, so that cannot be the correct construal of what boxers have consented to in agreeing to the match.

61 Except perhaps in very special cases where what is consented to conceptually entails a promise of that sort. Raz (1981, p. 120; 1986, p. 82) nominates this as an example: 'to consent to be governed by another is to promise to obey him'. (Or as Raz [1981, p. 121; 1986, p. 83] later puts it: 'consent to a political authority is the same as a promise to obey it. It is the undertaking of an obligation'.) But even there the connection is not quite analytic: 'to consent to be governed' is to consent for him to give me legitimate orders; but I can consent to that, and admit the legitimacy of his orders, without necessarily promising to obey them. That is to say, I may treat them as content-independent *pro tanto* reasons to do what is ordered; but I may reserve the right to decide for myself what, all things considered, I ought to do. Maybe Raz would insist that that would be an 'insincere' form of consent; but we must preserve conceptual space for the possibility of insincere consenting (Section 2.3.1), or anyway for the possibility of 'false consent' carrying some of the same consequences as genuine consent (Section 1.4).

62 A 'no-right' in Hohfeld's (1923) sense.

X may also have a 'general duty' not to interfere with *Y*'s φ-ing, without some special (e.g., rights- or permission-based) warrant.[63] But if so, that was not created by his consent. Instead, it existed antecedently, albeit conditional in form: 'every *X* has a duty not to interfere with every other *Y*, unless *X* has a right or permission to do so'. When *X* consents to *Y*'s φ-ing and thus waives his right against *Y*'s φ-ing, that annuls *X*'s right to interfere with *Y*'s φ-ing; and that in turn cancels the 'unless' clause, thus causing the general duty to come to apply unconditionally to *X* in respect of *Y*. On that reading, *X*'s duty not to interfere with *Y*'s φ-ing does not arise from any 'special obligation' attendant on *X*'s consenting; instead it is merely a 'no-right' created by *X*'s consenting, conjoined with that pre-existing 'general duty'. On this analysis, *X*'s refraining from interfering with *Y*'s φ-ing would not be 'honouring the terms of the consent' in any strong sense at all. Instead it would merely be abiding by a wholly separate general duty not to interfere without some special (e.g., rights-based) warrant.

2.2.4 Promises Cannot Be Revoked, Consent Can (Sometimes)

Historically, the giving of consent and the making of promises have been much more thoroughly discussed than the revoking of them. Insofar as there is a traditional view on the matter, it would seem to be that one major difference between consent and promises is that the former can be revoked whereas the latter cannot be.[64]

Some recent writers have however tended to presuppose, with as little argument, that both can be revoked.[65] The temptation to think that revoking consent and revoking promises should be morally on a par presumably arises from the fact that both involve taking back something that you have previously given to another.[66]

[63] The proposition that everyone has a right that others not so interfere without some special warrant is the 'natural right' that Hart (1955) derives from the fact that special warrants are, and presumably need to be, issued at all.

[64] Owens (2012, p. 165) for example states plainly: 'you may rescind or revoke your consent' whereas 'there is no such thing as revoking a promise' (see similarly Scanlon 1998, p. 301; Shiffrin 2008, p. 501). That is not quite right. As Grotius (1625, bk. 2, ch. 11, sec. 16) says, 'a promise may be revoked, without the imputation of injustice . . . , before acceptance . . .'; and the same is true of 'offers' in contract law (ALI 1981, § 36 (1)(c)). Note well Grotius' phrasing however: he is saying (contrary to some more recent writers [Liberto 2018]) that a promise exists as soon as it has been made, even before it has been accepted. If the promisee then spurns his offer, the promisor is released from his promise; if the promisor retracts his promise before the promisee has responded, he has revoked his promise. But either way, there was a promise for the promisor to revoke or for the promisee to release him from, just as soon as the promisor completed the relevant performative of making the promise, as I argued in footnote 58 in Section 1.2.1.2 above. The same is true of consent: it has been given as soon as the consent-giver has performed the external act of consent, whether or not there has been uptake on the part of the consent-receiver (as I argue in Sections 1.2.1.2 and 2.3.1).

[65] Dougherty (2015) for example talks about how promises and consent alike can with due notice be unilaterally 'reversed or modified'. He declares, for example, 'Typically, when someone gives her consent, she can withdraw this consent later' (p. 234).

[66] Hobbes (1651, ch. 14) and Locke (1690, § 194) both offer verbiage to that effect, quoted in Section 7.1 below.

What that 'parity' argument would be overlooking is an important difference between what was given, in the two cases.

When *X* promises *Y* to φ, *X* gives *Y* a right to *X*'s φ-ing. On the 'choice' theory of rights, that means the choice of whether *X* φ-s or not is *Y*'s. *Y* can release *X* from his duty to φ, if he so chooses. But *X* cannot release himself—the choice is one for *Y* to make, not *X*.

When *X* consents to *Y*'s γ-ing, in contrast, *X* has merely given *Y* permission to γ, waiving any right *X* would have otherwise had to object to it. The moral upshot of *X*'s consenting is that *X* has no-right to object to *Y*'s γ-ing; it does not confer on *Y* a right to γ, merely a liberty to do so.[67] Whether and under what conditions it might be morally permissible for *X* to revoke his permission is the subject of Chapter 7. Just note, for now, that the compelling reason against revocation in the case of a promise—that *Y* literally has a right in the matter—is absent in the case of consent.[68] Taking away someone else's right is importantly different, morally, from merely retracting permission.

Note, too, that the standard slogan differentiating promises and consent in this regard—'promises cannot be revoked, consent can'—is systematically ambiguous. One reading of that slogan would be that 'promises can never be revoked, consent *always* can be'. Another reading of it would be, merely, that 'promises can never be revoked, consent *sometimes* can be'. Chapter 7 will offer reasons for thinking that the latter, more modest reading is the more appropriate one.

2.2.5 Differing Remedies for Breach

From the last difference between promises and consent follows another. That difference relates to the appropriate remedy for their breach: promised performances not being delivered in the one case; consented-to performances not being permitted (typically, by consent being revoked) in the other.

When *X* promises *Y* to φ, *X* makes a commitment to *Y* that *X* will φ.[69] In consequence, *Y* has a right against *X* that *X* φ.[70] By virtue of that right, *Y* has a

[67] In Hohfeld's (1923) terminology, a 'privilege' (Westen 2004, pp. 32, 91). But that phraseology makes it sound stronger than it is. For Hohfeld, to have a 'privilege' is just to have 'no duty not to' (or equivalently, the person vis-à-vis whom you have the privilege has 'no right that you not do it').

[68] Anyway, *Y* does not necessarily have a right in consequence of *X*'s consent, in the same way *Y* does in consequence of *X*'s promise. *Y* might of course have a right to γ on some other basis; in that case there would initially have been a conflict of rights (*Y*'s right to γ versus *X*'s right against *Y*'s γ-ing) that is resolved by *X*'s consent waiving *X*'s right against *Y*'s γ-ing. But that is not the standard sort of case in these discussions, as indicated by the ordinary characterization of what *X* consents to *Y*'s doing as something that would have been wrong for *Y* to do in the absence of *X*'s consent.

[69] Insofar as *X* is able to do so—'impossibility' is an excusing condition (ALI 1981, § 261).

[70] There are of course some things that cannot be the subject of morally binding promises. Promising to do something that is morally wrong is one such (Altham 1985). Some might say that promising to have or refrain from sexual relations is another. A better way of handling the sexual case,

claim against *X* that *X* φ—or, failing that, a claim that *X* provide compensation adequate to make *Y* as well off as *Y* would have been had *X* kept his promise to φ. In the language of contract law, *X* owes *Y* either 'specific performance' of φ or damage payments equivalent to *Y*'s 'expectation interest' in *X*'s φ-ing.[71]

Things are different with consent. When *X* consents to *Y*'s γ-ing, *X* merely waives X's rights against *Y's* γ-ing. That is to say, when consenting *X* merely commits to not standing in the way of *Y*'s γ-ing in one particular way, viz., by invoking rights against *Y*'s γ-ing that he waived when consenting to *Y*'s γ-ing. When *X* promised *Y* to φ, *X* was committing to make φ happen (to the best of his abilities). When *X* consented to *Y*'s γ-ing, *X* was not in the least committing to make *Y*'s γ-ing happen; *X* was merely committing to remove one particular obstacle to *Y*'s γ-ing, namely, *X*'s right against *Y*'s γ-ing.[72]

For that reason, when *X* does something that breaches his consent to *Y*'s γ-ing (such as revoking his consent to *Y*'s γ-ing), there is no need for *X* to pay *Y* compensation adequate to make *Y* as well off as he would have been if *Y* had successfully γ-ed. *X* need only pay *Y* compensation sufficient to make *Y* as well off as *Y* would have been had *X* never consented to *Y*'s γ-ing.[73] That is to say, *X* need only compensate *Y* for costs (both out-of-pocket costs and other opportunities *Y* has foregone[74]) that *Y* has incurred by acting in reliance on *X*'s consent to *Y*'s γ-ing. In the language of contract law, that amounts to damages adequate to compensate Y for his 'reliance interests' in *X*'s consent to *Y*'s γ-ing.[75]

Just as in certain cases we require specific performance of what has been promised, we might sometimes require the equivalent in the case of consent—that the consented-to act be permitted, rather than merely that compensation be paid to the disappointed consent-receiver. That might be particularly the case where the person had deliberately misrepresented himself as mentally consenting when communicating to the other that he consented. Deliberate misrepresentation of that sort might be seen as an egregious wrong of the sort that causes the

however, would be simply to say that the promise-receiver ought to refuse to accept the promise or else release the promise-giver from it (Liberto 2017)—just as I have argued (in Section 1.6) that consent-receivers sometimes ought not act upon the consent that they have received.

[71] On 'expectation interests' see ALI (1981, § 344); in tort law this is called 'benefit-of-the-bargain' (ALI 1979, § 549(2) and § 552B, comment b). On 'specific performance'—which is rarely ordered as a remedy for breach of contract—see ALI (1981, § 359). See further Section 7.3.2 below.

[72] In Hohfeld's (1923) terms, promises give rise to 'claim-rights' whereas consent gives rise merely to 'privileges' in those receiving them (Westen 2004, pp. 32, 91).

[73] 'Specific performance'—*X* permitting *Y* to γ, just as *X* had consented to *Y*'s doing—is required only in the special case described in Section 7.3.2.5. For an example of 'other opportunities forgone' for which *Y* should be compensated, consider the case of *X* consenting to *Y* using his car to get to a job interview and then not letting him do so, causing *Y* not to get the job that he would otherwise have gotten: supposing had *X* not made the promise *Y* would have taken the bus to the interview and gotten the job, *X* owes *Y* full compensation for the lost job (less the bus fare to get to the interview).

[74] Other, that is, than the benefits that *Y* would have accrued from actually γ-ing.

[75] ALI 1981, §§ 344, 349. In tort law they are referred to as 'pecuniary losses' or 'out-of-pocket losses' (ALI 1979, § 531 and § 552B, comment a). See further Section 7.3.2 below.

misrepresenter to forfeit the rights that he purported to have waived.[76] The person deliberately misrepresenting himself as consenting would then be morally required to permit the act to which he purported to consent—not because he has 'really consented' (he has not), but rather because his deliberate misrepresentation caused him to forfeit his rights against the other performing the act to which he purported to consent.

2.3 What Both Promising and Consenting Require

Despite those important differences, it is enlightening to note what promising and consenting share in respect of what is required to perform those sorts of acts. The first feature that they have in common is that they must be communicated. The second is that they are communicated in rule-governed, institutionally structured ways. Both are abundantly clear in the case of promising, and both come into sharper relief as regards consenting when it is analysed in tandem with promising.

2.3.1 Both Must Be Communicated

The verb 'to promise', in the sense relevant here, is a transitive verb with a two-place predicate. You make a promise *to* someone *to do* something.[77] So too with 'to consent', in the sense of 'permissive consent' under discussion here: you give your consent *to someone* for that person *to do something*. Morally, the function of both is to effect moral transformations, incurring an obligation in the former case and waiving rights in the latter. Socially, the function of both is to let others know what they can expect of you, in line with those moral commitments.[78]

There is, as I have already discussed, a longstanding controversy over whether or not the 'ontological essence' of consent is purely a state of mind, and communication is merely 'evidence' of that state of mind.[79] My position as set out in

[76] As argued in Section 1.4.3.2. Note that 'specific performance' goes beyond the ordinary legal remedy for the 'tort of deceit' as discussed in Section 1.4.3.3. The most that is ordered for 'fraudulent misrepresentation in a business transaction' are damages that protect the plaintiff's expectation interests and provide him with the benefit-of-the-bargain (ALI 1979, § 549(2)). Still, that is more than is ordered for 'negligent misrepresentation', where damages merely protect the plaintiff's reliance interests and reimburse him out-of-pocket expenses (ALI 1979, §§ 531, 552B). Note too that a tortfeasor is liable for damages inflicted by intentional torts, regardless of the harm that would have been done to his own interests in avoiding them, in a way the merely negligent tortfeasor is not (ALI 1979, §§ 550–552).

[77] *Oxford English Dictionary*, q.v. 'promise (v.)', def. 1.

[78] As Rawls (1971, § 52, pp. 347–9) says, 'promising is an act done with the public intention of deliberately incurring an obligation... [B]y uttering certain words... one becomes bound to do something, particularly when the action whereby one becomes bound is publicly performed with the very intention, which one wants others to recognize, of bringing about this obligation'.

[79] See for example Alexander (2014) and Dougherty (2021a, pt. 3).

Section 1.2 above is that, while a mental element (specifically, a mental act of consent) is necessary both ontologically and morally for consent, communicating it might be unnecessary ontologically but is nonetheless socially very necessary.[80]

As Pufendorf says, 'the bare acts of will can have no effect amongst men, unless manifested and declared by some external tokens' that are ' signs sufficient, to express the inward purpose of his mind'.[81] In the terminology of Section 1.2.2, that is to say it is 'socially necessary' that he not merely 'mentally consent' but also that he communicate his consent, in order for him to do what is socially necessary to *give* his consent to the other. If *Y* does something that is morally permissible only with *X*'s consent, and *Y* does not know that he has *X*'s consent to do it, then *Y* has 'acted wrongly' ('culpably')—and that remains true, even if *X* privately consents to *Y*'s doing it and so *Y* has not 'wronged' *X* in the process.[82] Socially, our concern is with whether or not someone has *acted* wrongly, not with the abstraction of whether someone was or was not wronged in ways no one else could ever have ascertained.

You can of course make insincere promises.[83] That is to say, *X* can promise *Y* to φ, without *X*'s having any intention of honouring that commitment and actually φ-ing.[84] Has *X* then really made a promise at all, or is an insincere promise just a 'pseudo-promise'? Debates have raged over this issue for centuries. Some insist that *X* must intend to φ in order for him to have promised to φ.[85] Others say that, while there is clearly something 'unhappy' or 'infelicitous' about an insincere promise, 'it is not like a misfire. We should not say that [the person] didn't in fact promise, but rather that [he] did promise but promised insincerely.'[86] This much, in any case, is clear and incontrovertible. Even when *X* has no intention of φ-ing, *X* must at the very least be intending for *Y* to understand *X* to be incurring a duty to φ when *X* insincerely 'promises' *Y* to φ.[87]

[80] Those who say that consent does not require communication (Alexander 2014; Alexander, Hurd and Westen 2016; Ferzan 2016)—or who say that consent does not require its 'successful uptake' (Tadros 2016, p. 206; Dougherty 2021a, ch. 6)—are all speaking of *ontological* necessities. In Section 1.2.1.2 above, I agree that neither is ontologically necessary. My claim (in Section 1.2.2 above) is merely that communication of consent is *socially* necessary, that is to say, necessary in order for consent to discharge its social function. All of the above commentators wholeheartedly agree that it is socially dysfunctional for consent not to be communicated.

[81] Pufendorf 1672/1710, bk. 3, ch. 6, sec. 16, para. 1 and sec. 15, para. 2.

[82] As even Alexander (2014) concedes.

[83] That is what Prichard (1940, p. 171) calls a promise 'made in ... bad faith'. Austin (1971, p. 14) calls such a promise 'hollow', adding: 'It is made, certainly; but still, there is an unhappiness' (see similarly: Austin 1962, p. 11; 1979, p. 236; Owens 2008).

[84] Plamenatz 1963, vol. 1, p. 240. Owens 2008.

[85] See, e.g., Pufendorf 1672/1710, bk. 3, ch. 6, sec. 15.

[86] Austin 1979, p. 236; see similarly Austin 1962, p. 11. Plamenatz (1963, vol. 1, p. 240) agrees: 'If you make a promise to someone with the intention of not keeping it, you are not the less bound by it because of your intention. If you make your promise voluntarily, and if you know what you are doing when you make it, your promise lays an obligation on you.'

[87] This is the promising analogue to my discussion of the 'intention to consent' in Section 1.3.2.1. When philosophers say that promising must be intentional, they might mean either (or both) of two

Something similar is true of consenting.[88] It too can be insincere. Consenting insincerely might take various forms.[89] *X* might consent to *Y*'s γ-ing in a way that *X* knows to be inefficacious (not using the prescribed form of words to effect consent, for example). Or *X* might consent to *Y*'s γ-ing fully intending to revoke that consent before *Y* can γ or in some way render it impossible for *Y* to take advantage of *X*'s consent to *Y*'s γ-ing.[90] Again, debates rage over the status of insincere consent: some say it is 'genuine consent';[91] others say it is merely 'pseudo-consent';[92] I argue that it is 'false consent', while nonetheless insisting that it has some of the same consequences as genuine consent.[93] But again, this much is clear. Even when *X* has no intention to give effective permission for *Y* to γ, *X* must be intending for *Y* to understand *X* to be giving *Y* permission to γ when *X* insincerely 'consents' to *Y*'s γ-ing.[94]

Particularly importantly for my purposes in this book, in order for promising or consenting to serve its social function, *X*'s promise or consent must be somehow communicated to *Y*.[95] Perhaps they need not always be communicated by *X* himself; in some cases, that can be done through an intermediary.[96] And for certain purposes, maybe it can be said that *X* has consented as soon as he has

things. One is that, when *X* promises *Y* that *X* will φ, *X* must 'intend to give *Y* a right that X φ-s'. The other is that, when *X* promises *Y* that *X* will φ, *X* must 'intend to communicate to *Y* that *X* gives *Y* a right that X φ-s'. These come apart in the case of insincere promising.

[88] As Simmons (1976, p. 276; see similarly 1993, p. 69) says, just 'as with promising, one can consent insincerely'. Plamenatz (1968, p. 168) offers the example of someone saying to a guest, '"I do wish you would stay", when in fact he wishes him to be gone. There is no denying that he... consents to his guest's staying, however keen he may be to get rid of him.' Green (1988, p. 163) offers another: 'If I sit down in a restaurant and order a meal, I consent to pay the listed price. This is so... even if my intention is to leave before paying.'

[89] All would be cases of what were called 'deliberately fraudulent false consent', as defined in Section 1.4. All involve 'intending to induce beliefs in others' but not 'intending the object of your consent', in the terminology of Section 1.3.2.1. That distinguishes deliberately fraudulent false consent from cases of *unintentionally* sending what are conventionally understood by others to be signs of consent, whether that is done in wholly innocent error or even culpably negligently (as defined in Section 1.4).

[90] Owens 2011, p. 407.

[91] E.g., Manson (2016, 3323–5) and Dougherty (2021a, ch. 7). This is the position of Communicationists more generally, as argued in Section 1.4 above.

[92] E.g., Siegler 1968, pp. 259–60. This is the position of Attitudinalists and Hybrid theorists more generally, as argued in Section 1.4 above.

[93] See Section 1.4 above.

[94] That is to say, at least *X* intends consent in the second sense discussed in Section 1.3.2.1. As I went on to argue in Section 1.4, that warrants us treating *X* 'as if he consented', even if actually he did not intend to do so in the first sense discussed in Section 1.3.2.1.

[95] 'Somehow' refers here, as in the same formulation in Section 1.2.2, to the various ways other than explicit verbal consent by which one person can come to know that another person consents that are canvassed in Chapter 3. Note that that does not require uptake by *Y* but merely that the communication is realistically accessible by *Y* (Dougherty 2021a, ch. 6)—although it must also be the case that (a) the communication is accessible somewhere that *Y* either knows or could and should have known to look for it (Dougherty 2021a, pp. 134–6) and (b) *Y* knows or could and should have known that consent might have been given or withheld and hence that he should look for it there.

[96] Dougherty 2021a, ch. 6. But perhaps that is not true in all cases: Lackey (2021) argues that consent to sexual relations, for example, must come directly from the person concerned and not through some intermediary.

communicated that to the intermediary, even before the intermediary has passed the message along to *Y*.[97]

It is typically said that being of a 'promising state of mind' is a necessary condition for 'having *really* promised'. But it would be absurd to say that *X*'s being of a 'promising state of mind' is in itself sufficient to constitute *X*'s *making* a promise to φ. Certainly, anyway, it hardly seems sufficient to constitute *X*'s making a promise *to Y*.[98] In order to make a promise to *Y* to φ, *X* must perform the 'act of promising' not only internally but also externally. And to make the act of promising socially efficacious, *X* must also communicate the promise to *Y*, either directly or indirectly.[99]

All the same can be said of consenting.[100] To consent is to 'give permission', and 'giving' is both an active and transitive verb. Merely being of a 'consenting state of mind' (even understanding that, as in Section 1.2.1.1, as having 'performed a mental act of consent') is not sufficient for *X* to *give* consent *to Y* for *Y* to γ. Giving consent requires communicating. Even if success in communicating (i.e., successful uptake on the part of the consent-receiver) is not *ontologically* necessary for consent to have been given, *socially* of course that is the whole point of the exercise.

One can of course communicate consent falsely, either through a deliberate intention to deceive or through innocent or not-so-innocent error.[101] Insofar as being of a standardly 'consenting state of mind' (i.e. having performed a 'mental act of consent') is an ontologically necessary condition of consenting, you cannot be said to be genuinely consenting when sending false signals of consent. But even if you have not 'mentally consented' you have 'socially consented'.[102] And as

[97] Although not just 'any old intermediary' will do for those purposes. On 'the difference between a bare messenger and a proper agent or proxy' in such situations, see Pufendorf (1672/1710, bk. 2, ch. 9, sec. 4).

[98] By analogy the analysis in Section 1.2.1.1, a 'promising state of mind' might perhaps be understood as 'having performed the mental act of commitment involved in promising'; and that mental act might be performed without ever telling anyone. But in that case, it is hard to see how *X* has made a promise to *Y*. Thus, for example, the father who stands over the newborn's crib and silently promises to stop drinking might *phrase* it, in his mind, as a 'promise to my baby'—but I would argue that it is really more a 'promise to himself, made for the sake of his baby' (or if he said it out loud, even out of the earshot of anyone except the sleeping newborn, perhaps a 'promise to the world at large, made for the sake of his baby').

[99] To see the importance of the mental as well as the social act of consent, notice if *X* merely says to *Y* (perfectly truthfully), 'I am minded to promise you that I will φ', *X* has not yet made *Y* any promise. As Hobbes (1651, ch. 14) says of promises of the form, 'tomorrow I will give', those words 'are a sign that I have not given yet and consequently that my right is not transferred but remains till I transfer it by some other act' (see likewise Pufendorf 1672/1710, bk. 3, ch. 5, sec. 8). Similarly in the law of contracts, 'A manifestation of willingness to enter into a bargain is not an offer if the person to whom it is addressed knows or has reason to know that the person making it does not intend to conclude a bargain until he has made a further manifestation of assent' (ALI 1981, § 26).

[100] See more generally the discussion in Sections 1.2.2 and 2.1 above.

[101] Chapter 4 will discuss both kinds of cases at greater length. Faden and Beauchamp (1986, pp. 277–87) worry, for example, that a patient might sign a 'consent' form without really understanding it—legally, they have consented, even if morally they have not.

[102] In the terms introduced in Section 1.2 above.

courts have regularly ruled in such cases, 'If the plaintiff's behavior was such as to indicate consent on her part, [the defendant] was justified in his act, whatever her unexpressed feelings may have been. In determining whether she consented, he could be guided only by her overt acts and . . . manifestations of her feelings'.[103]

One famous way of parsing that point is to say the following. If *X* acted in reliance on *Y*'s false sign of consent to do φ to *Y*, where φ is something that may not permissibly be done to *Y* without *Y*'s consent, *X* has committed a wrong against *Y*—but faultlessly so, given *Y*'s false signal of consent.[104]

But has *X* even committed a wrong, necessarily? Perhaps so, if *Y*'s misleading signal of consent was sent in completely innocent error. But consider the case in which *Y* deliberately sent a socially conventional signal knowing *X* would take it as betokening consent, when *Y* did not actually mentally consent. There, *Y* has committed a wrong against *X* in intentionally sending a false signal of consent. I have argued above that such deliberate fraud causes *Y* to forfeit the rights which his false consent purported to waive.[105] Even those who would not go as far as that 'rights forfeiture' claim might nonetheless agree that *Y*'s wrongdoing in making deliberately fraudulent reports of consent greatly mitigates (perhaps even cancels) the wrongness of *X*'s φ-ing without *Y*'s consent. At least in the case of deliberately fraudulent false consent on *Y*'s part, *X* has not merely an excuse but a *justification*—a complete justification on the 'forfeits/cancels' view, at least a strong partial justification on the 'greatly mitigates' view—for doing that thing which would otherwise be wrong (φ-ing without *Y*'s genuine consent).

That seems to me clearly the correct approach in the case of deliberately fraudulent signals of consent. Less draconian consequences seem more appropriate in cases of false signals growing out of either culpable negligence in triggering the conventions of consenting or culpable ignorance of what those conventions are.[106] Those are still faulty (culpable) performances, however, even if they are faulty to a lesser degree. And even if we are tempted to say, on account of that fact, that *X*'s wrong is merely excused rather than erased altogether, note well *why* it is excused—not on account of external, unavoidable circumstances but rather on account of *Y*'s wrongful (anyway, culpably faulty) performance.[107] And even in the case of *Y* sending a false signal of consent in wholly innocent error, it nonetheless was *his* error (however faultless it may have been) and *Y* owes *X* *something* in recompense.[108]

[103] Knowlton 1891, p. 272.

[104] The distinction is Alexander's (2014); many others, including e.g. Guerrero (2021), echo it.

[105] In Sections 1.4 and 2.2.4.

[106] What I describe, in Section 1.4.3.3, as the culpably negligent false consenter's right being 'fully encumbered'.

[107] Some would go so far as to say that, at least in certain circumstances, 'negligence is [a] . . . way . . . to forfeit a complaint against being harmed', more generally (Dougherty 2021a, p. 104). In Section 1.4.3 above, however, I reserve the 'rights forfeiture' remedy for cases of deliberate fraud, arguing that 'full compensation' is the more appropriate remedy for culpable negligence.

[108] See Section 1.4.3.4 above.

2.3.2 Rule-governed, Conventional or Institutionally-structured Communication

A second feature shared by both promising and giving consent is that both are communicated in a rule-governed, institutionally-structured manner. The paradigmatic case of both consenting and promising is saying so, in just those words. And of course the words of a language have the meaning that they do only through a set of social conventions.[109]

Perhaps you cannot promise without that very word or some close equivalent being used somewhere in the interaction, as I shall discuss in the next section.[110] But consenting certainly can be done tacitly, without the word (or indeed, any words) being used.[111] What are signs of tacit consent depends, likewise, upon what is taken to count as consent according to the conventions of the community in question. There is no 'brute fact' of the matter; the relevant facts of the matter are all 'institutional facts'.[112]

Something similar is utterly familiar and undisputed as regards promising. In order to make a promise you need to follow some socially-conventional script. There are 'institutionalized' rules of the 'promising game' that you must abide by if you are to succeed in making a promise.[113] So too, I would argue, with consenting. To successfully convey his consent to *Y*, *X* must communicate that consent to *Y* according to conventions that they both comprehend.

In calling these 'institutional' facts, philosophers may unwittingly be making them sound heavier-duty than they strictly need to be. 'Institution' conveys the impression of formal organization. All that is really required is a social convention that is well-entrenched and generally understood by the vast majority (if perhaps

[109] Lewis (1969), along with many before and since, make this basic point about language; Saunders (2012b, p. 71) notices its relevance for consent. In 'Of interpretation' of promises and contracts, Pufendorf (1672/1710, bk. 5, ch. 12, sec. 3) writes that 'words are to be understood generally in the most popular signification'. To underline the point, he proceeds to recount the following tale: 'When Tiberius had us'd a word, which was not Latin, Capito said that, in honour of the Emperor, it ought to pass current for the future, although no body before him had made use of it. But one Marcellus reply'd, that Caesar might, if he pleased, naturalize men, but words he could not.' Pufendorf goes on to acknowledge that, of course, 'terms of art' could be specified in the contract itself.

[110] What is a 'close equivalent' is itself socially conventional. Suppose you ask, 'Will you pick me up at 7?', and I reply, 'Yes.' Was that a promise or merely a 'statement of intention'? It depends on the social conventions surrounding 'will you?' in such situations.

[111] I give a fuller account of 'tacit consent' in Section 3.2 below.

[112] Anscombe 1958; Searle 1995.

[113] Searle 1964. As Rawls (1971, § 52, p. 344) glosses this conventional wisdom: 'promising is an action defined by a public system of rules. These rules are, as in the case of institutions generally, a set of constitutive conventions. Just as the rules of games do, they specify certain activities and define certain actions. In the case of promising, the basic rule is that governing the use of the words 'I promise to do X'. It reads roughly as follows: if one says the words 'I promise to do X' in the appropriate circumstances, one is to do X, unless certain excusing conditions. This rule we may think of as the rule of promising: it may be taken as representing the practice as a whole. It is not itself a moral principle but a constitutive convention.' As Rawls goes on to emphasize, we need a wholly separate and moralized 'principle of fidelity' to account for why one should actually do as promised.

not necessarily literally all) parties to such transactions.[114] Sometimes those are indeed formally institutionalized, as by the Académie Française's acts of linguistic legislation. But conventions need not be institutionalized as rigidly as that. General public knowledge of customary usage can be quite enough.[115]

How do practices get institutionalized in that looser way? Roughly speaking, that happens through practice and usage that is sufficiently recurring to become customary and thence normativized. That is how customary international law comes into force.[116] That is how social norms emerge.[117] Conventions about what constitutes a sign of consent emerge in much the same way. Rawls famously draws a sharp distinction between two kinds of rules, rules-of-thumb and rules-constituting-a-practice.[118] But the sharpness of the analytic distinction obscures the dynamic connecting them. Rules-of-thumb, if sufficiently shared in a community and recurringly applied there, *become* rules-constituting-a-practice.

2.3.3 Forms of Words

In ancient Rome, citizens made legally binding promises to one another by employing a prescribed pair of corresponding words. The promise-seeker would ask, '*Spondes?*' ('Do you solemnly promise?'). When the promise-giver replies, '*Spondeo*' ('I promise'), a legally binding 'obligation by words' would thereby have been created.[119]

Kleinig draws attention to the fact that, even in our own day, 'we rarely promise without using the words "I promise"'.[120] Consent, he notes, is interestingly

[114] See the discussion of 'signs of consent' in Green (1988, pp. 166–73). Bolinger (2019, p. 191 ff.) rightly argues that 'public knowledge', stopping short of Lewis' (1969, p. 78) more demanding 'common knowledge', is the correct standard here.

[115] Although 'general public knowledge' may be enough at the community level, genuinely mutual knowledge is needed among members of any given dyad in order for a consent transaction between them to be robustly socially successful. I say 'robustly' to rule out flukey cases like the following. Suppose *X* consents to *Y* φ-ing by nodding his head and giving a thumbs-up. But suppose that *X* thinks that consent is constituted by his nodding, whereas *Y* thinks it is constituted by the thumbs-up. Consent has been successfully given, in the sense *X* intended to give it and *Y* understood it to have been given, even though there was no mutual knowledge between them as to what constituted signs of consent. But that consent-giving was not robustly successful: if *X* had done all and only what he thought necessary and sufficient to constitute consent (i.e., nodded), *Y* would not have understood consent to have been given. This is a variation on Manson's (2016, pp. 3325–8) 'robust reason-changing' account of consent and of Renzo's (2022) requirement that the consent-receiver must be 'sensitive' to the mental state of the consent-giver.

[116] Goodin 2005. [117] Brennan et al. 2013, ch. 5. [118] Rawls 1955.

[119] Gaius 170/1988, bk. 3, § 92. The requirement of a specific form of words was revoked by Emperor Leo VI in the ninth century, in favour of a simple requirement 'that the parties understand each other's meaning and agree, whatever words they used' (Justinian 535, bk. 3, ch. 15, sec. 1, p. 107).

[120] Kleinig 1982, p. 114. Kleinig's point about promising might be better formulated as saying 'we rarely promise without the word "promise" being used, albeit not necessarily by the person making the promise'. When the priest asks the would-be bride 'Do you promise . . . ?' and she replies 'I do', she has made a promise without *herself* uttering the word. Or, again, Ruben (1972, p. 72) offers this fanciful example: 'Someone might say, quite arbitrarily, "All who promise . . . , stamp their feet and whistle

different: 'though it must be signified, is not usually, except in legal or quasi-legal contexts, given by means of the words "I (hereby) consent"'.[121] Why should that be so? After all, as I argued above, consent is self-executory in a way a promise is not. Should that not make us want to be all the more scrupulous in demanding a precise, explicit form of words in order to make sure that we genuinely had it?

Some may suppose that the answer to that question can be found in another difference noted earlier between consent and promise. As I have said, the former waives a right to others' non-interference whereas the latter imposes an obligation. Can that serve to explain why we ordinarily require (if we do) someone to say explicitly, 'I promise', whereas we do not necessarily require him to say explicitly 'I hereby consent'? It would do so only if we thought that imposing an obligation is morally more serious (perhaps because it infringes more on your protected sphere) than waiving a right against others' interference. That might sometimes be so, but surely it is not necessarily always the case. Sometimes the interference in view might be much more onerous than the obligation in view.

Still, maybe that proposal might be on broadly the right track. Notice that sometimes we *do* require consent to be given in explicit terms, particularly where something of great consequence is at stake.[122] As Kleinig observes, we typically require explicit consent in legal and quasi-legal contexts. Likewise, before patients undergo major invasive medical procedures, they are asked to sign a 'consent form' explicitly granting consent.[123] So too are human subjects before

'Dixie'!" Anyone in the circumstances who does stamp his feet and whistle "Dixie" has promised....'—again, without themselves uttering the word (but note that the person proposing that novel way of promising himself had to utter it). Even the above reformulation is not quite correct: Prichard (1940, p. 172) more correctly phrases the point by saying: 'promising requires the actual use of the word "promise" or else of some equivalent, such as "undertake", "agree", "give you my word", or "will" in "I *will*".' But Watson (2004, p. 57) approvingly quotes Pierce as saying, 'we promise much more frequently than we use this word (or something equivalent)'; and the *Restatement (Second) of the Law of Contracts* explicitly provides that, 'A promise may be stated in words either oral or written, *or may be inferred wholly or partly from conduct*' (ALI 1981, § 4, emphasis added).

[121] Kleinig 1982, p. 114; see similarly Guerrero 2021, p. 365. Alexander (2014, p. 103) likewise observes that 'there is no canonical form of words or action that count as consent'.

Note that the 'I *hereby* consent' formulation is a particularly strong one: the 'hereby' makes it emphatically 'performative' (Manson 2016, p. 3326, building on Austin 1962, p. 57). That, I suggest, is why that form of words *is* used in legal and quasi-legal and other particularly important contexts, where something of considerable consequence is typically at stake.

[122] Green (1988, p. 169) argues that 'the more central and important the interests which are at stake, the clearer will be the sign of consent that is required to effect them', giving this example: 'contracts to sell land must [legally] be made in writing; an oral agreement which is valid for many other purposes is not enough here'. Pufendorf (1672/1710, bk 3, ch. 5, sec. 11, para. 4) before him had similarly speculated that the *stipulatio*—the prescribed form of words required to make a legally binding promise among citizens of Rome—was required 'not because serious promises do not bind by the mere Law of Nature; but that the ceremony of these solemn forms might put men on considering thoroughly, whether it was expedient for them to enter into a promise which it would be impossible afterwards to revoke'. A similar function might be served by the legal requirement that, to be valid in the absence of 'consideration' for both parties, a contract be made 'under seal' (ALI 1981, § 95).

[123] Note that no one is asked to sign a consent form for the violation of bodily integrity involved in a routine medical examination or a minor injection: just presenting yourself at the doctor's surgery (Snyder 2012, p. 77) or holding out your arm to receive the injection (Knowlton 1891; Saunders 2012b, p. 70) is deemed to be a sufficient sign of consent in those cases.

participating in research. And while no precise form of words is yet prescribed for conveying one's consent to a sexual encounter, increasingly explicit avowals are increasingly coming to be expected.[124] As I said in Section 1.1, the higher the stakes the more certain you need to be that you *really* have the other person's consent; and these all seem to be cases where more demanding standards of ensuring consent are applied for precisely that reason.

Those cases hardly exhaust everything that we might suppose to be morally particularly serious, perhaps. But between them, those cases where a relatively precise form of words is required may cover a large proportion of what we consider morally the most important cases of consent. The cases that remain, where nothing remotely like 'I hereby consent' needs to be communicated for consent to occur, arguably are mostly of lesser moral seriousness.

A puzzle nonetheless remains on the other side, however. Surely some promises, owing to their content, are morally much less important than others. Yet we almost invariably require an explicit statement like 'I promise' in all of them for a promise to be deemed to have been made.

Why so? Maybe because the very act of promising is *itself* morally momentous. We thereby put our honour on the line.[125] We therefore need to make very certain that someone has performed that act by prescribing a precise form of words. And that is so, even if the content of the promise is of little moment for anyone involved.

'Honour' is easy to parody.[126] It can amount to little more than a code of in-group favouritism, as in 'honour among thieves' or the 'code of honour' among mafioso or slaveowners in the Antebellum South.[127] But on at least certain accounts of virtue ethics, 'honour' is a central moral virtue. And historically it has certainly played an important role in social relations.[128] Note, for example, how historically gambling 'debts of honour'—debts that are backed by no

[124] See, e.g., Dougherty 2015. [125] Rawls 1955, p. 15.

[126] Berkeley's (1732, Third Dialogue, sec. 2) *Alciphron* imagines the following dialogue against a free-thinker, Nicander, and Menecles, 'a Christian' like himself:

M. From what principle are you gentlemen virtuous?

N. From honour. We are men of honour.

M. May not a man of honour debauch another's wife, or get drunk, or sell a vote, or refuse to pay his debts, without lessening or tainting his honour?

N. He may have the vices and faults of a gentleman: but is obliged to pay debts of honour, that is, all such as are contracted by play.

M. Is not your man of honour always ready to resent affronts and engage in duels?

N. He is ready to demand and give gentleman's satisfaction upon all proper occasions.

M. It should seem, by this account, that to ruin tradesmen, break faith to one's own wife, corrupt another man's, take bribes, cheat the public, cut a man's throat for a word, are all points consistent with your principle of honour.

TV. It cannot be denied that we are men of gallantry, men of fire, men who know the world, and all that.

M. It seems therefore that honour among infidels is like honesty among pirates—something confined to themselves, and which the fraternity perhaps may find their account in, but every one else should be constantly on his guard against.

[127] Gambetta 1993. Wyatt-Brown 1982. [128] French 2002.

collateral, unenforceable in courts and rest on nothing but one's honour—were thought to be all the more morally compelling for that very fact. Or note how historically bankrupts were confined to debtors' prisons, not because that was a particularly good way to get their debts discharged, but more because it was dangerous for society to let such dishonourable people interact socially with innocent, trusting others. Or note how historically bankrupts were deprived of the vote, at least in part on the grounds that such dishonourable individuals cannot be trusted to vote honestly with an eye to the common good.

2.4 Inviting Reliance

Asserting, consenting and promising have one more thing in common that is going to prove important over the course of this book. All three, in different ways, constitute *invitations* to other people to *rely upon* what the speaker is saying.

When you assert something, you are not merely floating a possibility. You are vouching for its truth. That is why you need a 'warrant' for asserting something, in a way that you do not when you are merely 'suggesting' or 'supposing' something. Furthermore when asserting something, and thereby vouching for its truth, you are inviting others to trust your assurances that it is indeed true. You are inviting them to rely upon you in this respect. And one of the distinctive wrongs in lying is that it involves your betraying that trust which you have invited others to place in your assurances.[129]

Consenting and promising are subspecies not only of assenting but also of asserting. They are assertions that involve commitments—commitments that are themselves morally transformative. In promising, the promise-giver asserts that he is now morally under a duty that he did not used to be under to do the thing promised to or for the promise-receiver. In consenting, the consent-giver asserts that the consent-receiver is now morally permitted to do something that, without the consent-giver's consent, would have been morally impermissible.

In making those assertions, those giving a promise or consent invite those to whom they give it to rely on the truth of their claims that the moral landscape has indeed been transformed in those ways.[130] The promise-giver invites the promise-receiver to rely upon the fact that the promise-giver has incurred a duty (and one

[129] O'Neil 2012.

[130] Simmons (1993, p. 70, n. 31), following Raz (1986, p. 96), is insistent that the intention of the consent-giver must be to alter the moral landscape rather than to induce reliance (cf. Weale 1978, pp. 68–9). Simmons (1993, p. 70, n. 31) is right to say that, definitionally, 'Another's reliance is not necessary for me to have a consensual obligation'; to think that 'confuses one common consequence of consent . . . with its essence' (Raz 1986, p. 97). In giving his consent to others, however, a person is not merely informing the others that the moral landscape has been transformed—he is also inviting them to rely on that fact. The moral landscape remains altered whether or not they do so, of course. But the invitation stands.

that he will discharge) to do as he promised.[131] The consent-giver invites the consent-receiver to rely upon the fact that the consent-receiver now has permission to do whatever the consent-giver has consented for him to do.

Consenting and promising are thus assertions that typically create expectations in other people, expectations about what consenter-givers will permit and promise-givers will do.[132] Consent-receivers and promise-receivers, having been invited to trust the truth of those assertions, legitimately organize their affairs on the basis that those assertions are true.[133] They 'count on' them being true, and legitimately so given the invitations and assurances they have received in that regard from consent-givers and promise-givers.[134]

Just as lying would be a breach of trust, so too would failing to honour one's consent or promises be a breach of trust.[135] That is one strong other-regarding reason for consent-givers and promise-givers not to breach trust. And insofar as they do, consent-receivers or promise-receivers have a morally legitimate complaint and typically a claim for compensation in consequence of that breach of trust.[136]

[131] Scanlon 1998, ch. 7.

[132] They do so by creating expectations about what those people *should* do, in the first instance. But the very fact that those people have employed those moralized descriptions of their intentions, they also create expectations that those people *will* do as they should. Needless to say, those beliefs might be in error (more of which in Chapter 4); but they are legitimate, well-warranted expectations nevertheless.

[133] Weale 1978. Pritchard (1940/1968, pp. 171–2) is correct that it is not merely the fact that others *have* such expectations that create moral obligations to do as you promised, or (we might add) consented either. It is instead that fact that the promise-giver and consent-giver invited such expectations.

[134] As Pufendorf (1672/1710, bk. 3, ch. 5, sec. 10 and 11) said, 'Those promises by which we impower another to expect some particular and determinate service from us, ought most strictly be fulfill'd, because the other party building on our word has adjusted his affairs accordingly. . . . [I]f a man by breaking his promise, has caus'd the other party to suffer damage (who for instance, might depend perhaps on his word, and so neglect to provide for his own necessities) that in this case he should be bound to make good the loss sustain'd.'

[135] Southwood and Friedrich 2009.

[136] These are, in the language of the law, claims of 'estoppel' (Dworkin 1988, p. 89; Green 1988, pp. 164–5, 171–2) or 'quasi-contracts' (Singer 1973, pp. 47–59). See further Sections 5.1.1 and 7.3. In high-stakes situations (involving bodily integrity, e.g.: sex, surgery), consent may be revocable without payment of compensation as I note in Section 7.1 below.

PART II
CONSENT IN OPERATION

3
Modes of Consenting

What consent *is* is one thing. What it is, operationally, to *give* consent is another thing altogether. It is the latter issue with which this chapter is concerned. Its focus is on how consent-givers communicate that they mentally consent and how consent-receivers surmise that others mentally consent.[1] Of course, as I have already foreshadowed, those communications can be true or false, those surmises correct or incorrect—those matters will be the subject of further discussion in the next chapter.

3.1 Five Different Modes

How, exactly, does one go about giving one's consent to someone in respect of something? Generically, as I have said, this is done through an act or forbearance prescribed by some well-known and widely accepted social convention for doing just that. There are several different modes of socially consenting, however, which I shall now go on to elaborate.

The most straightforward way of giving your consent to someone in respect of something is to say so explicitly, in so many words.[2] That is what happens when you say 'I do' in response to the priest's question, 'Do you consent to take this man . . . ?' That is what happens when you sign a legal deed saying you consent to transfer your property to someone else.

The words must of course be said in the correct context (people uttering those words when performing a stage play do not end up consenting to marriage). They must be said by the right sort of person (people of insufficient age or sanity are incapable of consenting) and in the proper circumstances (people cannot genuinely consent when subject to force or fraud)—those are the standard conditions for consent to be 'valid'. To perform the social function that consent is supposed to perform, the words conveying consent must be spoken in a language

[1] As Bolinger (2019, p. 182) says, 'Theorists who focus more on the transactional nature of *giving* consent take OBSERVABILITY to be quite important and emphasize that the principal value of consent is in its role in facilitating certain interactions.'

[2] The *Oxford English Dictionary* defines 'explicit'—as applied to 'a declaration, indication, utterance, etc.'—as meaning 'distinctly expressing all that is meant; leaving nothing merely implied or suggested; express' (q.v. 'explicit (adj.)', def. 2a).

Consent Matters. Robert E. Goodin, Oxford University Press. © Robert E. Goodin 2024.
DOI: 10.1093/oso/9780192889027.003.0003

understood by both the consent-giver and the consent-receiver.[3] And so forth. Hence, even explicitly verbalized consent is not absolutely straightforward. But it is much more straightforward than the other modes of consenting that I shall be considering, so I shall not discuss it further here.

There are four other decreasingly straightforward modes of consenting that instead form the focus of my concern in this chapter.[4] The first is 'tacit consent'.[5] That occurs when someone does (or refrains from doing) something that in the circumstances he intends to be understood, and expects others to understand, as constituting consent. The second is 'presumed consent'. That occurs when the putative consent-receiver believes, for good agent-specific (or in one version, community-specific) reasons, that the putative consent-giver actually gives tacit consent. The third is 'implicit consent'.[6] That occurs when someone does something that logically or pragmatically commits him to consenting. The fourth—which I shall go on to argue does not actually belong on the list of 'modes of consenting' at all—is what I shall call 'ought-to consent'.[7] That occurs when there are normative reasons according to which a person ought to consent to something, even though he does not explicitly, tacitly or implicitly do so.

The terminology surrounding consent has been used in a great many ways over the years. It therefore behoves me to state at the outset how I propose to carve up the conceptual space.

- Contrary to common practice, I shall here take both explicit and tacit consent to be forms of 'express consent'.[8] That is to say, in both of those

[3] Hobbes 1651, ch. 14. Gaius (170/1988, bk. 3, § 93) says that promises can be legally binding 'even if they are put into Greek, . . . provided that they [the promise-giver and the promise-receiver both] understand Greek; conversely, even if Latin is used the obligations are valid between foreigners, provided they understand Latin'; see similarly Justinian (535, bk. 3, ch. 15, sec. 1).

[4] I have already argued (in Sections 1.2.1.1 and 2.2.2 above) that 'hypothetical consent' is no kind of consent at all, so not discuss it separately here—although I will sometimes find that some of the types I do discuss are flawed because they amount to no more than that. Medical ethicists fixated on 'advance consent directives' may be tempted to add 'consenting in advance' to this list, but as I have argued (in Section 2.2.1 above) *all* consent must be 'forward-looking' and hence 'advance'; I discuss other aspects of 'advance directives' in Sections 2.2.2, 8.4, 8.5 and 11.2.

[5] According to the *Oxford English Dictionary*, 'tacit' means 'unspoken, unvoiced; silent, emitting no sound; noiseless, wordless' (q.v. 'tacit (adj.)', def. 1a). It can also mean 'not openly expressed or stated, but implied; understood, inferred' (q.v. 'tacit (adj.)', def. 2), but that conflates 'tacit' with 'implicit'. In distinguishing the two, I shall take 'tacit' to mean 'indicated clearly but non-verbally', and 'implicit' to mean 'not clearly indicated but merely implied'.

[6] According to the *Oxford English Dictionary*, 'implicit' means 'implied though not plainly expressed; naturally or necessarily involved in, or capable of being inferred from, something else' (q.v. 'implicit (adj.)', def. 2a).

[7] Estlund (2005; 2008, ch. 7) calls this 'normative consent', but that is unhelpful nomenclature for distinguishing it from all the other modes of consenting, all of which have normative force. Another description might be 'obligatory consent'; but that would root the ought firmly in a theory of The Right, whereas calling it 'ought-to consent' leaves open the question of whether the 'ought' in question is rooted in a theory of The Right or The Good.

[8] 'Express' as defined by the *Oxford English Dictionary*'s definition: 'Of a meaning, purpose, stipulation, law, etc.: expressed and not merely implied; definitely formulated; definite, explicit. Of language, statements, indications: definite, unmistakable in import' (q.v. 'express (adj.)', def. 2).

cases the consent-giver expresses an intention for others to take him to be consenting.[9] In the case of explicit consent, he does so verbally (orally, in writing or through sign language[10]); in the case of tacit consent, he does so non-verbally but no less intentionally (in the case of presumed consent, that is what he is being presumed to have done). The difference that I see between explicit and tacit consent is merely the difference between for example shouting out 'aye' and raising your hand as ways of registering your vote in a meeting.[11]

- Whereas I regard both explicit and tacit consent as forms of 'express consent', neither presumed nor implicit consent are.[12] In the case of presumed consent, we assume (on more or less good grounds) that the person actually consents and simply has not given expression to that fact. In the case of implicit consent, consent is implied rather than expressed. What exactly is implied can vary. At one extreme, what is implied is that the implicit-consenter actually does tacitly consent—even though he has given no conventional signal of that, requiring us to infer his consent from some other considerations.[13] At the other extreme, what is implied is that the implicit-consenter must—is logically committed to—consent by virtue of other things to which he is committed. The latter case is most interesting because it is most clearly distinct from standard cases of tacit consent. I will argue that in that latter case we may properly treat someone 'as if he consented' to what is implied in that to which he actually consented.
- 'Ought-to consent' refers to the case in which the person is not consenting or committed to consenting in any of the above ways, but he morally ought to consent nonetheless. In that case, the person has not (yet) consented at all, any more than he has in the case of hypothetical consent.[14]

3.2 Tacit Consent

The notion of 'tacit consent' is today most familiar through Locke's talk of people consenting to the king's rule merely by walking on the king's highway.[15] But that

[9] Note well: what he intends is for *others to take him* to be consenting; but he may not be sincere in that (see Sections 1.4 and 2.3.1 above and Chapter 4 below).

[10] Here I am following Pallikkathayil (2020, p. 110).

[11] Simmons 1976, p. 279. Ruben (1972, p. 72) would say this is just explicit consent 'by alternative means' (see similarly Saunders 2012b, p. 70). In my terminology it is 'express consent by alternative means' to verbal consent, which I take to be the defining feature of 'explicit consent'.

[12] This distinction is what Pufendorf (1672, bk. 3, ch. 5, sec. 3) seems to have in mind when he speaks of 'consent, either express or presumptive'.

[13] This is what lawyers call 'implied-in-fact' consent. As the US Supreme Court (1923, p. 397) puts it, 'an agreement "implied in fact" [is] founded upon a meeting of minds, which although not embodied in an express contract, is inferred, as a fact, from conduct of the parties showing, in light of the surrounding circumstances, their tacit understanding'.

[14] Already discussed in Ssection 2.2.2.

[15] Locke 1690, sec. 119.

sort of argument dates all the way back to Plato's *Crito*.[16] And certainly it was very much in the air in Locke's own time. Grotius and Pufendorf had both explicitly discussed tacit consent before him.[17]

There can be no doubt that it is possible to give consent tacitly. Indeed, 'genuine instances of tacit consent, at least in nonpolitical contexts, are relatively frequent'.[18] The standard example is that of a meeting in which some proposal is on the table and the chairperson asks, 'Any objections?' Virtually every commentator agrees that 'one's silence may be a legitimate expression of consent'—at least 'presuming that one has heard [and understood] the call and been able [at not unreasonable cost] to make known any objection one has'.[19]

Doubts surrounding tacit consent concern not whether it is possible but instead whether the conditions making tacit consent valid actually obtain, either on some particular occasion or in certain whole domains of social interaction more generally. Some of those conditions are the same as required to make explicit consent valid. The consent must be voluntary, conscious and wilful, free of force or fraud.[20] It must be possible for the person tacitly consenting to have done otherwise,

[16] Plato (399 BCE/1961, 52d). Socrates imagines the laws asking, 'Are we or are we not speaking the truth when we say that you have undertaken, in deed if not in word, to live your life as a citizen in obedience to us?' Socrates then asks Crito, 'Are we not bound to admit it?'

[17] Grotius (1625/1901, bk. 3, ch. 24) devotes a short chapter to tacit consent and Pufendorf (1672/1710, bk. 3, ch. 6, sec. 2) a substantial section to it.

[18] Simmons 1979, p. 79.

[19] Kleinig 2010, p. 11. See similarly: ALI 1979, § 892, comment b; Simmons 1979, pp. 79–81; Wertheimer 1996, pp. 94–5; Saunders 2010, pp. 84–5; 2012b, p. 71.

In the context of a meeting where decisions are made by some voting rule other than unanimity, it may not be strictly correct to assume that everyone consented if no one objected. As Robert (1876/1951, p. 198) notes, silence 'does not necessarily mean that every member is in favor of the motion, but, that knowing it is useless to oppose it, or even to discuss it, the opposition simply acquiesces in the informality'. Where the consent of all is required for the motion to pass, silence can be taken as a sign that each has consented. The same is true where each person's consent is required for the rule enacted to apply to that person; in the formation of rules of customary international law, for example, 'persistent objectors' will not have the rules to which they objected applied to them (Green 2016).

Dougherty (2015, p. 230) objects saying that 'silence typically admits of multiple interpretations' (e.g., you 'may simply prefer that the meeting does not drag on any longer'), so silence cannot be taken to communicate consent uniquely (see similarly Lackey 2018). Pallikkathayil (2020, p. 109) replies that 'when silence is understood by all to communicate consent, it does not particularly matter if the primary reasons why one is silent are orthogonal to changing others' permissions, … one has indeed consented to the proposal.' That is clearly correct so long as communicating consent was at least *among* his reasons for remaining silent. Even if it was not, we may still want to hold him responsible for doing or allowing that which others understood him to have consented, not because in that case he 'really consented' but instead out of fairness to those he knowingly misled in that way (see further Section 1.4 and Chapter 4).

[20] Pufendorf (1672/1710, bk. 3, sec. 4, note d) illustrates the importance of consciousness and willfulness by recalling Suetonius' (121/1957, ch. 4, sec. 38) account of emperor Caligula auctioning off his superfluous gladiators: 'as the cryer was performing the sale, a gentleman … [was] happening to sleep upon one of the benches, [and] the emperor commanded the cryer to take notice of the worthy [gentleman] that nodded to the price proposed. And the business was so managed, that the poor gentleman had laid out ninety thousand sesterces before he knew a word of his bargain.'

at not unreasonable cost.[21] In the previous example, not objecting would not have counted as valid tacit consent if the chairperson had said, 'Anyone with an objection to my proposal will kindly so indicate by lopping off his arm at the elbow.'[22]

In addition, and particularly importantly, for your act or inaction to count as actually (as opposed to 'as if') giving tacit consent you must know that what you are doing or not doing will be taken as a token of tacit consent.[23] Otherwise you would be 'consenting' unintentionally—which is impossible, since consenting must be an intentional act.[24]

This point has long been a familiar one. Hobbes for example says that 'signs of contract are either express or by inference'. Express signs of consent must, he says, be 'words spoken with understanding of what they signify', and he says that the same must be true, *mutatis mutandis*, of tokens of tacit consent:

> Signs by inference are sometimes the consequence of words, sometimes the consequence of silence, sometimes the consequence of actions, sometimes the consequence of forbearing an action; and generally a sign of inference of any contract is whatsoever *sufficiently argues the will* of the contractor.[25]

Pufendorf gives a classic example, saying that 'consent . . . must be express'd by sufficient signs; and for this a bare nod will serve, if the thing offer'd . . . had been before requested'.[26]

For tacit consent to be given robustly socially successfully in any given instance, there must be 'mutual knowledge' between the tacit-consent-giver and the

[21] Hume 1760. As Pufendorf (1672/1710, bk. 3, ch. 6, sec. 1, emphasis added) says, 'there can be no better argument to hinder a man from complaining of this burden than to allege that he took it upon him by his own free will and consent, *when he had full power to refuse it*' (Pufendorf 1672/1710, bk. 3, ch. 6, sec. 1, emphasis added; see further secs. 9–14).

[22] Simmons 1979, p. 81.

[23] As foreshadowed in Section 1.4, under certain circumstances we may properly count you 'as if you consented' even if you lacked the mental element required to qualify as 'genuinely consenting'. Those issues will be taken up further in Chapter 4. Here I focus exclusively on what is required for actual (albeit tacit) consent.

[24] See Section 1.3.2. You might of course be doing something else intentionally, from which others wrongly infer that you are consenting—but if you did not intend your actions to be understood in that way you have not performed the external act of socially consenting (much less the mental act of consenting).

[25] Hobbes 1651, ch. 14, emphasis added. Grotius (1625, bk. 2, ch. 11, sec. 3) before him held that promising requires 'signs sufficient to indicate' the will of the promise-giver. Pufendorf (1672/1710, bk. 3, ch. 6, sec. 15, para. 2) concurs, saying that it requires 'signs sufficient to express the inward purpose of his mind'. Context can play an important part in this. 'If I tossed you my keys out of the blue, there would be no particular reason to take this action to communicate consent to borrow my car. I might be showing off my key chain or killing time with a game of catch. But with enough context [it can]. . . . Suppose that you have just been lamenting that since your car is in the shop it will take you considerably longer than usual to run your afternoon errands. And I [—a long-standing friend—] respond to your comments by tossing you my keys' (Pallikkathayil 2020, p. 112).

[26] Pufendorf 1672/1710, bk 3, ch. 6, sec. 15.

tacit-consent-receiver regarding what betokens tacit consent.[27] The consent-receiver has to know that, by that token, the consent-giver means to tacitly consent; the consent-giver has to know that the consent-receiver will understand that token to constitute tacit consent; each has to know that the other knows; and so on.[28]

How might that mutual knowledge arise? 'Custom and usage' is the standard mechanism.[29] As I have argued in Section 2.3.2, among a group of people frequently interacting with one another in a club or assembly or trade or society, customs grow up governing *inter alia* what will be taken to be tokens of consent. And members of the group know—or anyway can be presumed to know, because they could and should have known[30]—their own customary practices and usages.[31] On that basis, customary tokens of tacit consent can ground valid consent, at least among those who are (or can reasonably be expected to be) privy to the same customs and practices.[32]

Perhaps we can analyse 'consent by conversational implicature' in the same way.[33] When my son asks 'Can I borrow the car?' and I reply 'The key is on the counter', I have given him consent to borrow the car.[34] I did not say so in as many words. But that was the clear implication of what I did say. Similarly, a conversational implicature of my asking 'Can I walk with you?' is that I consent to your

[27] 'Robustly', for the reason given in Section 2.3.2 above. Some see this as an analytic claim (Healey 2015, p. 358), others as merely a strong empirical generalization (Dougherty 2015, p. 240) about the real world (if not one containing Renzo's [2022, pp. 60 ff.] fantastical mind-reading device).

[28] This poses particular problems for tacit consent to sexual relations. 'Differences in the extent to which men and women perceive their interaction to be sexually charged pose a problem for arriving at the same interpretation of behavior that might potentially communicate consent' (Pallikkathayil 2020, p. 113).

[29] There can of course be non-standard cases in which some particular idiosyncratic act—stamping your feet and whistling 'Dixie', for example (Ruben 1972, p. 72)—might be authoritatively stipulated by the chairperson of the meeting as what will be taken as consent among this particular group on this particular occasion.

[30] I discuss that standard briefly in Section 1.4.3.3 and more fully in Section 4.4.1 below. I will argue there that this grounds, not actual (albeit tacit) consent, but rather treating people 'as if they consented'. The practical consequences for them will turn out to be substantially the same, however; so it does no harm to defer fuller discussion of this wrinkle in the argument until the next chapter.

[31] In characteristically purple prose, Bentham (1776/1977, p. 92) declaims: 'how a custom . . . is to be known, is a question, which upon the supposition that it is the custom of the people in general, . . . seems neither very natural nor very material. How is it to be known? meaning by the people? Why, they know it, by the supposition; they even practice it, it is their custom. "How are the people to know what it is they do themselves?" God knows, unless they already know.'

[32] ALI 1979, § 892, comment b. This has long been the received wisdom. Grotius (1625/1901, bk. 3, ch. 24) says that 'tacit consent . . . is allowed [i.e., enabled] by custom'. Pufendorf (1672/1710, bk. 3, ch. 6, sec. 2, para. 1) speaks similarly of expressing 'our consent by the signs generally made use of in human commerce and transactions'.

[33] On conversational implicatures in general see Grice (1975). In the cases I shall discuss as ones of 'implicit consent' in Section 3.4 below, consent to one thing is implied in consent to another. In the cases under discussion here, that you consent at all is what is implied by what you have said.

[34] It was arguably (but far less clearly) the implicature of Henry II's asking, 'Who will rid me of this turbulent priest?', that one of the knights within earshot had the king's consent to kill Thomas à Becket (Plamenatz 1938/1968, p. 9).

walking with me.[35] Some would also say that my asking 'Can I have sex with you' carries the conversational implicature that I consent to your having sex with me—although that may be less clearcut.[36] If everyone concerned knows that that conversational implicature will be read into the request, then it is indeed the case that you have given your own consent in making the request for the other's consent.

3.2.1 Inferring Tacit Consent

When talking of signs of consent 'by inference', Hobbes lumps together many different forms of non-verbal consent. Consent by silence, in circumstances in which silence clearly betokens consent, is one of them.[37] But raising your hand, when the chairperson of a meeting says, 'All in favour raise their hands', is another. 'In many medical encounters, when the patient presents for evaluation and care, consent can be implied'—although in surgical settings, much more explicit consent to medical treatment is ordinarily sought.[38] According to the latest version of the American Law Institute's *Model Penal Code*, 'Consent [to sexual contact] ... may be ... inferred from behavior—both action and inaction—in the context of all the circumstances.'[39]

In all of those cases, we must infer what the putative consent-giver means (and what the putative consent-receiver will understand that person to mean) by displaying whatever is supposed to be a sign of consent. In a way, of course, the same is true of explicit verbal consent—there, too, we must infer what the speaker means by the utterance and what hearers will take it to mean. In the case of verbal consent that is generally straightforward, assuming everyone involved is a competent speaker of the language being employed. But even there issues of incorrect inference can arise. Imagine for example someone saying, 'Sure', his voice dripping with sarcasm.[40]

[35] Grotius (1625, bk. 2, ch. 11, § 13), speaking more generally, says 'a precedent [i.e., prior] request ... is the same as acceptance' of the thing requested once it is offered. Dougherty (2021a, pp. 2–3, 108–9) has recently rediscovered (without reference to Grotius) the point that you consent to *Y*'s φ-ing by requesting that *Y* φ.

[36] Pallikkathayill (2020, p. 110) maintains that it is a 'presupposition of a request to have sex is ... that one consents to having sex'. But 'presupposition' is too strong; you can request something without intending to use it. 'Conversational implicature' better captures what is going on in that case. Here is why I say this case is 'less clearcut': I may ask to have sex with you because I am on a power trip, or I am be being deliberately cruel, in seeking consent to sexual relations from someone with whom I do not myself intend to consent to having sex. In that case, I did not 'really consent' to having sex with the person whose consent I requested; the necessary mental intention is missing.

[37] For Plamenatz (1938/1968, p. 8) this is the paradigm case of 'tacit consent'.

[38] Snyder 2012, p. 77.

[39] Section 213.0(3)(b) (ALI 2016).

[40] Alexander 2014, p. 105. Lest it be thought a trivial example, just recall how regularly President Trump or his spokespeople insisted he was 'only joking', and 'did not really mean' what he had said, after he had said something outlandish to delight his most deplorable followers (Zoglin 2020).

The bases of the inference can vary. Nodding your head is, by convention, a sign of assent (and hence of consent, where consent is what is in question).[41] Raising your hand is a sign of consent by virtue of the chairperson's instructions. But custom, convention and instruction do not exhaust the bases upon which consent can be inferred. In the next section I will discuss others.

Just note, for now, that when we are inferring people's consent in any of these ways, we are inferring that they actually do consent, however tacitly. That is to say, we are inferring that they do indeed mean by their actions or forbearances to give non-verbal signals of their intention that others take them to be consenting.

3.2.2 The Nature of the Business

Sometimes people's actual, albeit tacit, consent can be inferred from the 'nature and circumstances of the business' in which they are voluntarily engaging.[42] Pufendorf offers this example, to which many others have returned:

> A guest sits down to a table at a public house [i.e., tavern]; and though he has not exchanged a word with the host about the price of his dinner, yet by the bare act of sitting down to eat, he is supposed to consent to the payment of his scot [i.e., account]; since all know that this is not a place where men are treated for nothing.[43]

Surely there is a lot of custom and convention at work in this example as well, however. By what signs is the guest to know this is a public house and not a soup kitchen, or that public houses do not serve food free of charge at that particular hour of the day?

A clearer case, perhaps, is that of the innkeeper. As Blackstone says, 'when a man professes the keeping of such inn or public house, he thereby gives a general

[41] In Western Europe, but not for example in Bulgaria where nodding your head means 'no' and shaking it from side-to-side means 'yes' (Andonova and Taylor 2012). Whereas gestures like that were once thought to be universals, it has come to be appreciated that many of them are conventional (Cooperrider 2019).

[42] Pufendorf 1672/1710, bk. 3, ch. 6, sec. 2, para. 1. Grotius (1625/1901, bk. 3, ch. 24) before him had said that 'there are other signs of consent besides words and letters: some of them indeed naturally rising out of the action itself'.

[43] Pufendorf (1672/1710, bk. 3, ch. 6, sec. 2, para. 4). Miller and Wertheimer (2010, p. 89) similarly remark, without attributing the observation to Pufendorf, that 'one can agree to pay for a meal simply by ordering it (even if one is not told the price)'. It is not clear whether Miller and Wertheimer think that it is implicit in the 'nature of the business' of restaurants that one consents to pay when ordering (as Pufendorf clearly believes) or whether that simply follows from social conventions. Saunders (2012b, p. 71) opts clearly for the latter; in reply Wilkinson (2012, p. 75) says, 'it is more accurate to see the case as one in which it is reasonable to treat patrons as if they have consented rather than have actually consented' (cf. Section 4.4.1 below). See similarly: Green 1988, p. 163; Dougherty 2015, p. 240.

license to any person to enter his doors'.[44] That is in the nature of keeping a *public* house. And when the keeper of it puts up signage indicating that it is indeed a public house, he surely knows that that is what he is doing in employing that conventional signage.

Others offer gambling as a prime example in which consent can be inferred from the nature of the business. Of gambling debts, it is said (in the words of Bishop Berkeley) that one is 'obliged to pay debts of honour, that is, all such as are *contracted by play*'.[45] For present purposes, let us read 'contracted' there as 'incurred' rather than 'agreed'.[46] On that reading, it is in the nature of 'play' that one implicitly consents to honour one's gambling debts. Once again, there probably must be some element of custom and convention at work. By what signs are players to know that they are playing for keeps rather than just for fun? Some may say that that is obvious from the fact that players are putting money (or IOUs denominated in money) on the table when laying their bets. But again perhaps it is not completely clear from the 'nature of the business' that the IOUs would necessarily be expected to be cashed in rather than forgiven at the end of an evening's entertainment.

An even better example of consent that can be inferred more purely from the nature of the business might be pari-mutuel betting. Of course even there you need some (probably conventional or customary) way of knowing that this is an instance of that. But once you know that fact, you can infer from the nature of the business that anyone laying a wager must sacrifice what he has staked if he loses the wager, for in pari-mutuel betting the only way the winner can be paid more than he wagered is from the pooled stakes forfeited by those who lost the wager. Since winners dividing the winnings from the pooled losses of the losers is the very essence of pari-mutuel betting, anyone knowingly engaging in the practice must by the nature of the practice consent to forfeiting their stakes if they lose.[47]

For another example, consider the business of getting to your middle-of-the-row seat in a crowded theatre. It is in the nature of the business that you will brush up against the knees of patrons already in adjacent seats as you shuffle toward your own seat, and others will brush up against your knees on the way to their seats. When you purchase a theatre ticket knowing all that, you consent to that minor physical contact inevitably involved in the theatre's patrons getting seated.[48]

[44] Blackstone 1765, bk. 3, ch. 12.

[45] Berkeley 1732, Third Dialogue, sec. 2, emphasis added. Pufendorf (1672/1710, bk. 5, ch. 9, sec. 6) similarly says that is in the nature of raffles that, 'by agreement, he whom fortune favours is to have the whole and the rest are to be at the loss of what they contributed'.

[46] I.e. the *Oxford English Dictionary*'s sense 6 rather than sense 1 of 'contract (v.)'.

[47] In similar vein, it might be said that people who use public goods provided by a state at some cost tacitly consent, by using those goods, to paying such taxes to that state that are required to pay for them (Valentine 2018, p. 519). But see Section 3.5 and Chapter 10 below.

[48] Westen 2004, p. 322. The Delaware Penal Code, section 451, states: 'Any person who enters the presence of other people consents to the normal physical contacts incident to such presence' (quoted, disapprovingly, by Valentine 2018, p. 511).

A much more dramatic version of the same might be consenting to known risks of injury when voluntarily participating in violent sporting activities, like boxing or ice hockey. It is in 'the nature of business' of boxing that you will get hit. The Queensberry Rules under which boxing matches are conducted permit that; indeed, the whole point of a boxing match is for boxers to hit one another, which is how they score points (or *in extremis* a knockout) in the match.[49] When consenting to fight a match, boxers consent to the risk of getting hit by their opponents.[50]

Sometimes 'the nature of the business' is established by pure stipulation. Conditions are posted for entry to an establishment, and everyone voluntarily entering the establishment tacitly consents to those conditions by the very act of their voluntarily entering.[51] Similarly, where there is a contest being conducted according to publicly known rules, the sheer fact of your 'entering [the] competition implies acceptance of the rules'.[52]

Other times, 'the nature of the business' is fixed by law. Take the case of the payment of physicians. In Roman and English common law, payments to physicians were construed as 'gratuities' and, as such, were not something that a patient was necessarily consenting to provide when seeking professional assistance from a physician (or hence for which physicians could sue). The Medical Act of 1858 reversed that presumption.[53] Thereafter, it was (by law) in the nature of the business of calling a physician to attend upon you that you consent to pay his fee.

When we are inferring people's consent from 'the nature of the business' in all such ways, what we are inferring (I would argue) is once again that they actually do consent, however tacitly.[54] Assuming they know the nature of the business in which they voluntarily engage, they must do so—that is the business in which they are consenting to engage. Of course we always need some grounds for assuming that they do actually know the nature of the business (or, more precisely, understand it in the same way that we do) in order to ground that inference; and the

[49] *Oxford English Dictionary*, q.v. 'boxing, n.', def. 2.

[50] Westen 2004, ch. 7. Enoch (2017, p. 15) says that in the case of participating in a boxing match consent is 'actual though perhaps implicit': in the terminology of this chapter his 'implicit' should be read as 'tacit'. In formally sanctioned boxing matches participants sign consent or waiver forms granting explicit consent to being hit (Dixon 2001b), but in informal matches consent might be merely tacit.

[51] Raz 1981, p. 121; 1986, pp. 83–4. Similarly, 'a prisoner's voluntarily made choice…to use a telephone he knows may be monitored implies his consent to be monitored'—and that is true 'even [if it is] a Hobson's choice', i.e., there is no unmonitored telephone available to the prisoner. Consent can be inferred, the US Tenth Circuit Court of Appeal held in that case, 'where awareness and a voluntary choice are present' (McConnell 2008, p. 894; cf. Valentine 2018).

[52] Saunders 2010, p. 84. See similarly Applbaum (1999, pp. 115–18).

[53] 21 & 22 Vict. c. 90, sec. 31. That that statute in effect reversed this presumption was confirmed in *Gibbon v. Budd (1863)* 2 H and C 92 at 97. For discussion see Stroud (1939, p. 769).

[54] As the US Tenth Circuit Court of Appeal emphasized, 'by this term [implied consent] we mean actual consent inferred from circumstances other than an express declaration, not constructive consent implied by operation of law' (McConnell 2008, p. 894; cf. Valentine 2018).

higher the stakes the higher the threshold of what grounds are good enough for that purpose.[55] But as long as we have good enough grounds for that assumption, given what is involved, the sheer fact they are engaged in a business that requires them to tacitly consent in such ways can itself be taken to signal their consent—unless of course they explicitly disavow that they are consenting.

3.3 Presumed Consent

Sometimes we 'presume' someone's consent. That is to say, we 'assume' or 'take for granted' that he has consented.[56] What, exactly, is going on in such cases? To foreshadow: my conclusion will be that consent can only be credibly presumed when we have good grounds for thinking that the person tacitly consents.[57]

3.3.1 Against Presumed Consent in General

Presumptions are sometimes assumptions that we believe are highly likely to be true.[58] That may seem to suggest that when saying 'we presume that he consents' we are simply saying we think it is highly likely that he actually does consent, albeit tacitly and without any clear sign of consent. But note well, we are *presuming* his tacit consent rather than inferring that from anything that he has said or done. Perhaps we are grounding our presumption on the simple fact that the vast majority of people in similar circumstances do actually consent.[59] But what is true of most people in similar circumstances does not necessarily warrant presuming the same of any particular person.[60]

Consider the judge instructing the jury that the defendant is to be presumed innocent until proven guilty. That presumption holds, both legally and morally, even if the vast majority of people brought before the court on the same charge are found guilty.[61] People are *entitled* to the presumption of innocence, even if very

[55] Among the high-stakes situations requiring particularly strong grounds are sexual encounters, as discussed in Section 1.1. Sometimes the stakes might be so high that inferring tacit consent from the nature of the business would never be permissible.

[56] The American College of Physicians' *Ethics Manual*, for example, says: 'In medical emergencies, consent to treatment necessary to maintain life or restore health is usually presumed unless it is known that the patient would refuse the intervention' (Snyder 2012, p. 77).

[57] For a spirited discussion of these issues see Enoch 2017. Sometimes we presume that someone has explicitly consented: for example, when I see a 'Sold' sign appear on my neighbour's lawn, I presume he has explicitly consented to sell his house. But I take it that those are less common cases, and in this discussion I shall take it that it is tacit consent that is being presumed.

[58] Ullmann-Margalit 1983, p. 157.

[59] Cantor 1996; Rid and Wendler 2014; Eyal 2019.

[60] As Saunders (2012a, p. 76) asks regarding consent to organ donation: 'Should we assume that, if 60% of people are in favour of donation, then a given individual has a 60% probability of wanting to donate? That seems absurd.' See similarly: ALI 2019, §16, comment d, p. 99; Simons 2019, p. 19.

[61] It would be a pretty poor prosecutor who loses more than half the cases he chooses to take to trial.

much more often than not that presumption is eventually rebutted.[62] Likewise in the case of consent, in any high-stakes situation people should surely be entitled to a strong presumption that they have not waived any important rights, in the absence of clear evidence that they have done so.[63]

Consider the sort of argument often heard in rape cases. The defendant often claims to have had good grounds for presuming the victim's consent, based on various other things that she had said or done. He will ask, rhetorically, 'What was she doing there at 3 o'clock in the morning? What did she think was going to happen? Why did she think he invited her back?... Women who put themselves in compromising positions shouldn't complain when they are compromised.'[64] One way of reading such aspersions is as claiming that the perpetrator had reasonable grounds for presuming that the victim consented.[65]

That claim would of course be vitiated if (as is typically the case) the victim did actually say 'No!' clearly and loudly before the rape occurred.[66] But imagine she failed to do so. Should being scantily clad late at night in a bad neighbourhood really constitute sufficient grounds for a presumption of consent to sexual intercourse? Surely not. Even if *some* women dressing in that way and walking in those neighbourhoods at those hours do intend that as a signal of consent to sexual relations (prostitutes, for example), not all women do so.[67] Again, all women should surely be entitled to the presumption that they have not waived their rights against sexual assault, in the absence of much more direct evidence than that indicating that they personally (and not just 'most women there at that hour dressed like that' generically) have waived their rights in that way.[68]

[62] Ullmann-Margalit 1983, p. 158.

[63] As set out in Section 1.1 above. Of course, proceeding without the other's consent can sometimes be the correct thing to do, all things considered, in both high-stakes situations (medical emergencies, e.g.) and low-stakes ones (borrowing a pen), as will be argued in Chapter 11.

[64] Estrich (1992, p.10) is describing this view without endorsing it. As she goes on to say, 'Interestingly, no one... would extend the assumption of risk approach to people who walk alone on dangerous streets at night and get mugged, or people who forget to lock their cars or leave the back windows of their houses wide open.'

[65] There are of course other ways of reading such claims. One, which few defendants are so bold as to offer, might be that what the rape victim did constitutes conventional signs of consent to sex. Another, perhaps even more consistent with the phrasing of the questions in the text, is that the rape victim voluntarily assumed the risks of others mistakenly taking her actions as signs of consent (for further discussion of which, in a non-rape context, see Section 4.4.2).

[66] As Estrich (1992, pp. 10–11) says, 'the real problem for assumption of risk adherents is the fact that even these foolish women [in the famous Palm Beach and Indianapolis cases she was discussing], if you credit their accounts, ultimately did say no. So granted she was foolish, granted she never should have been there in the first place, if she said no, why isn't he required to stop?'

[67] This points to a difference between what is 'common' and what is 'conventional', echoing Hart's (1961, pp. 9–13, 50–60) distinction between a 'habit' and a 'rule'.

[68] To those who say, 'Well, that is the socially conventional meaning of such behaviour in our society!', some such as Bolinger (2019) would respond, 'Well, there should be no such convention, it imposes unjust risks and burdens on those trying to avoid signaling any such intentions!' That may be true too. My point here is that strong rights (such as against unwanted sexual advances) cannot be overcome by weak presumptions (such as 'what most people mean by dressing in that way'),

3.3.2 The Positive Case for Presumed Consent: A False Start

Perhaps the most prominent recent invocation of the notion of 'presumed consent' comes in the latest *Restatement of the Law of Torts*. As I said at the very beginning of this book, the common law is often a good guide to settled moral judgments of the community;[69] and the American Law Institute's *Restatements of the Law* are ordinarily good guides to the content of the common law. But that is not so in this case, as the title of this subsection suggests.

The relevant section of the new *Restatement of the Law of Torts* reads as follows:

> Presumed consent exists if:
>
> (1) under prevailing social norms, the actor is justified in engaging in the conduct in the absence of the other person's actual or apparent consent, and
>
> (2) the actor has no reason to believe that the person would not have actually consented to the conduct if the actor had requested the person's consent'.[70]

The language of that rule is doubly misleading. First, when it says that the action in question is 'justified' prevailing by social norms, 'justified' does not mean 'legally justified' or even 'morally justified'. It does not mean 'justified' at all. It merely means 'is in accordance with social norms'. It is logically essential that the text be read in that way. Any stronger reading would render 'presumed consent' otiose. If 'justified' really meant 'legally justified' (all things considered), then on the new *Restatement*'s rule consent could be presumed only where the action would be independently justified anyway; and conversely, where the action was not independently justified already consent could not be presumed. So scrub 'justified'.

Scrub 'presumed consent', too. The new *Restatement* explicitly says that the cases it is talking of as 'presumed consent' are *not* ones where consent is being presumed actually to exist. The *Restatement* has a separate term for that: 'apparent consent'. The quoted rule about 'presumed consent' says explicitly that 'presumed consent exists ... in the *absence* of ... actual or apparent consent'.[71] Cleary, then, 'presumed consent' is not supposed to be a subset of 'apparent consent'. Translating back into ordinary English, the existence of the new *Restatement*'s 'presumed consent' does not mean that consent can be presumed to exist.

particularly when those presumptions are known not to be true of everyone and may therefore not be true of the person to whom you are applying them. You should explicitly seek consent even from a prostitute before having sex. (See also related remarks in Section 3.3.4 below).

[69] See the preface and the opening pages of Chapter 1. [70] ALI 2019, §16b.

[71] The Reporters acknowledge in a note that 'some courts use "presumed consent" to mean "implied consent" in the sense of either inferred actual consent or apparent consent', but they decline to follow the lead of those courts (ALI 2019, Reporters' Note, comment d, p. 110).

But what else could 'presumed consent' possibly mean? What, if not consent, could be being presumed? Maybe that rule is merely pointing towards actions that are presumably justified in the absence of consent (many actions are[72]) but saying that is a defeasible presumption which can be defeated by (actual or apparent) *refusal* of consent. On that account, however, an action which would be permissible without consent would be rendered impermissible by a refusal to consent. How can that be? If consent was not needed in the first place, how can its absence be a defeater?

Maybe the thought is just this. There are *pro tanto* reasons for thinking that the action would be permissible in the absence of consent. But refusing consent counts as an even stronger *pro tanto* reason for thinking that the action in question is impermissible. Still, why label the countervailing reason a 'refusal of consent'—as opposed to just a 'strong objection' of some more ordinary sort? It makes perfectly good sense that someone might have legitimate reasons to object strongly to an action for which his consent is not required. It is far more mysterious how someone's refusal of consent counts as a strong reason against an action for which his consent was not required in the first place.

Here is an alternative and more straightforward way of making sense of the *Restatement*'s new rule—although I hasten to add that it is clearly not the *Restatement*'s own. On this alternate reading, the fact that an action is in accordance with existing social norms would give rise to a presumption that the person actually does consent to that action; but that is a defeasible presumption, and it is defeated if the person clearly does not consent to it. Unless and until he clearly disavows consent, however, we are entitled to presume that he does consent. That account makes clear what role 'consent' is genuinely playing (consent is necessary to make the action permissible, and it can be legitimately presumed in these cases[73]). That account also explains how the explicit refusal of consent can make a genuine difference (it defeats the presumption of consent directly, and is not just *another pro tanto* reason of a wholly separate sort weighing in the balance).

I shall elaborate that approach in Section 3.3.5 below. Notice, however, that that approach is explicitly disavowed in the new *Restatement*. My suggested approach would, in effect, make the *Restatement*'s 'presumed consent' into a form of what it calls 'apparent consent'—consent that we are presuming actually (albeit inexplicitly) exists. But in specifying existence conditions for 'presumed consent', the

[72] One example is the rule on 'Emergency Action Without Consent': 'Conduct that injures another does not make the actor liable to the other, even though the other has not consented to it', if the stipulated conditions are satisfied (ALI 1979, § 892D). Another example is a 'privilege' to do something that would otherwise incur tort liability if it 'is necessary for the protection of some interest of the actor or of the public which is of such importance as to justify the harm caused or threatened by its exercise' (ALI 1979, § 10 (1) and (2); see further § 890).

[73] On grounds of 'silence on notice' (Section 3.3.4 and 3.3.5 below).

Restatement explicitly stipulates the complete absence of 'apparent consent'. So my proposal must be seen as a distinctly unfriendly amendment to the *Restatement*—as a genuine alternative, rather than any sort of sympathetic extrapolation.

The *Restatements of the Law* are ordinarily a good place to look for guidance as to what the common law holds and for hints as to what morally might stand behind those codes. In this instance, however, the new *Restatement* seems to me hopelessly muddled. Best to draw a veil over that muddle and launch an investigation wholly independently of it into what circumstances might genuinely warrant a presumption of consent.

3.3.3 On-going Consent

One set of circumstances in which consent may legitimately be presumed is in connection with on-going practices, where consent to the practice had clearly been given (either explicitly or tacitly) on an earlier occasion and no indications have been given that that consent has been withdrawn (even though the consent-giver could have done so without undue cost).[74] Then one may legitimately presume that consent previously given to practise still persists.[75]

Consent of that sort is what is involved in the 'implied in fact' doctrine in contract law. Those are cases in which, while there is no explicit agreement, the behaviour of the parties is such as to make it clear that there actually was tacit agreement.[76] A classic application is in labour law, when workers continue working for a firm after the expiration of their previous contract while a new contract is being negotiated. In such circumstances, courts recognize a contract implied-in-fact, under which the workers continue working on the same terms as in the previous (but now expired) contract until a new one is concluded.[77]

David Enoch offers another example: that of waking one's long-term sexual partner for sexual intercourse by provocative touching that, if done without her

[74] In the slightly different context of discussing rules governing how to interpret contracts, the *Restatement of the Law (Second), Contracts* says similarly: 'Where an agreement involves repeated occasions for performance by either party with knowledge of the nature of the performance and opportunity for objection to it by the other, any course of performance accepted or acquiesced in without objection is given great weight in the interpretation of the agreement' (ALI 1981, § 202(4)).

[75] Plamenatz (1938/1968, p. 24) gives this example: 'a man may at times be morally obliged to disobey a law to the enforcement of which he has consented in the past; but it does not follow that the fact of having consented to it in the past does not, other considerations apart, create a further obligation to obey it. In fact it is quite clear that consent does impose a special obligation of this kind upon the consenting party.'

[76] In the words of the leading US Supreme Court case: '[A]n agreement "implied in fact" [is] founded upon a meeting of minds, which, although not embodied in an express contract, is inferred, as a fact, from conduct of the parties showing, in the light of the surrounding circumstances, their tacit understanding' (*Baltimore & Ohio Railway v. United States*, 261 U.S. 592, 597 [1923]). See further Boyd (1991).

[77] Anon. 1946.

consent, would constitute a sexual offence. Being asleep, she did not consent to being touched in that way on that occasion (and, to make the case philosophically interesting, we also need to assume that she had not consented in advance to being touched in that way when sleeping[78]). But from the facts that she has been your long-term sexual partner, and she has never objected to such things in the past, might you not be entitled to presume your sleeping partner's consent in this case?[79]

Now, there are two ways of looking at an on-going activity. One is as a series of separate actions: however similar they may be to one another, and however interconnected they may be, they really are nonetheless discrete episodes. Another way of viewing an on-going activity is as a practice: seen that way, it is a single entity, albeit one comprised of a series of various actions that are similar or connected to one another.[80]

Looked at in the first way, each and every one of the discrete acts requires consent (if any of them do).[81] Looked at in the second way, it is the practice overall that requires consent rather than each of the discrete actions comprising it.[82] That consent to the practice should ordinarily be revokable.[83] But once given, that consent to the practice need not be continually renewed.[84]

On the 'practice' view, therefore, you consent at one moment in time (when first entering into the practice *qua* practice[85]), and your consent then remains in

[78] Wertheimer 2003, p. 156. Adding that assumption makes this case different from 'advance directives' granting consent to sexual encounters in case one develops dementia (Boni-Saenz 2016; Director 2019).

[79] Enoch 2017, pp. 26–7, fn. 41. See similarly Wertheimer 2003, pp. 155–7. Pallikkathayil (2020, p. 112) concurs, saying 'that much of the work must be done by the history of interactions between the parties'. Dougherty (2018, pp. 106–9) agrees that 'sexual encounters within the context of established long-term relationships' are different, but for him that is principally because such people are better able to interpret one another's words and deeds as they relate to consent to the sexual encounter. In discussing such cases, Westen (2004, pp. 254 ff.) supposes instead that '*A* has a defense of consent to a criminal charge of rape based on *S*'s subsequent ratification of what *A* did while she was asleep'; but Witmer-Rich (2011, p. 393) shows that none of the cases Westen cites in support of that proposition are actually on point. Another more plausible interpretation of this case is that, in intimate relationships, people do not 'stand on their rights' vis-à-vis one another—and rights are precisely what consent waives (Waldron 1988).

[80] The *Restatement of Torts* might be read as gesturing towards that when it says that 'to be effective, consent must be... to the particular conduct, or to substantially the same conduct' (ALI 1979, § 892A (2)(b)). See further Section 5.2.1 below.

[81] Viewing sexual encounters in this way, policies requiring 'affirmative consent to sex' insist that consent to sex on one occasion cannot be taken to imply consent on subsequent occasions (Pallikkathayil 2020, p. 114).

[82] The practice view incorporates Pallikkathayil's (2020, p. 114) 'Modifiable Consent Standard' according to which partners in an on-going sexual relationship 'could have a conversation in advance about what kinds of sexual contact they agree they will permit in the future while reserving the power to revoke consent at any time'.

[83] On which see Chapter 7.

[84] When Kleinig (2010, p. 9) says 'the initial act of consent will usually reflect an ongoing commitment', it is unclear whether he means that as a report on the mental state of the person giving consent or on what the person given consent is entitled to presume.

[85] I.e., on the first occasion the consenting parties conceived of it as an ongoing practice; there may have been earlier occasions which they had conceived of as merely 'episodic' at the time.

force until such time as you communicate your intention to revoke it. If you mentally revoke consent at some point, then you may not 'genuinely consent' thereafter. But from a social point of view, your revoking of consent, just like your giving of it, must be clearly communicated to the other person. Otherwise, the other is fully justified in presuming that your consent to the practice continues.[86] On the 'discrete episodes' view, in contrast, your consent must be regularly renewed with every new episode.

We are often told we should ask people to renew their consent to on-going activities. For example, the World Health Organisation says that, in the context of an on-going medical experiment, 'the investigator should once again seek informed consent from the subjects' from time to time.[87] London's Metropolitan Police's webpage on 'rape and sexual assault' advises people engaged in sexual intercourse not only to 'check [with the other that they consent] on each occasion you start any sexual conduct' but also to 'check with them each time you start a new type of sexual activity'.[88] Rousseau's suggestion that consent to the social compact be renewed at the beginning of each and every session of the legislature is in the same spirit.[89]

Clearly, however, it would be cumbersome (and perhaps counterproductive of the activities being consented to) for consent to have to be renewed literally *continuously*.[90] Notice that even Rousseau only suggested it be renewed at the *beginning of each legislative session*, not each minute or hour or day of that session. Similarly, the Metropolitan Police say only that when engaged in sexual intercourse you should 'check with [the other] on each occasion you *start any sexual conduct*' and 'check with them each time you *start a new type of sexual activity*'.[91]

[86] Some might try to assimilate consenting to surgery under general anesthesia to consenting to an ongoing practice, supposing you consent before the operation and your consent remains in force during the operation. But that must presuppose that the mental act of consent is (as I have argued in Section 1.2.1.1 that it must be) a mental act of commitment that endures until revoked by a mental act of a similar sort. If the mental element of consent were instead characterized, as Attitutionalists traditionally characterize it, as a 'consenting state of mind', someone who is unconscious lacks any occurrent 'state of mind' at all. See similarly Sections 8.4 and 11.2 below.

[87] CIOMS & WHO 2002, guideline 4. That is particularly so if 'new information ... [has] come to light, either from the study or from other sources, about the risks or benefits of products being tested or about alternatives to them'. See also US DHHS 1991, § 46.116.b.5.

[88] Metropolitan Police (2019), linking to the website of Consent Is Everything (2019).

[89] Assemblies 'ought always be opened with two propositions, which no one should be able to suppress, and which should pass separately by vote. The first: "Whether it pleases the sovereign [assembly] to maintain the present form of government." The second: "Whether it pleases the people to leave the administration to those at present entrusted with it"' (Rousseau 1762, bk. 3, ch. 18).

[90] As Miller and Wertheimer (2010, p. 93) say, 'We don't want insistence on autonomous authorization to undermine the object of choice. We don't insist on informational disclosure and written consent for sexual relations because, among other things, it would thoroughly distort the activity to which consent is being given.' See similarly: Schulhofer 1998, p. 272; Sender 2018; ALI 2019, §16, comment d, p. 100; Simons 2019, pp. 20–22, 30.

[91] Metropolitan Police (2019), linking to the website of Consent Is Everything (2019).

Now, it is unclear in which of the two ways I identified that WHO and the Met were thinking of the on-going activities in question.[92] Maybe they were thinking of them as 'discrete episodes', for each of which consent ideally should be sought (but in practice it is just too awkward to do that). Or maybe they were thinking of them as 'practices', for which consent once given should ideally not have to be renewed (but it is safer, in practice, to check from time to time that consent persists[93]).

The upshot of that ambiguity is more important than its resolution, however. The upshot is that, in practice, the distinction between the two ways of looking at consent to on-going activities might be a distinction without much practical difference. Even if on-going activities are a series of 'discrete episodes' each of which ideally requires consent, in practice we typically have to presume that consent carries over from one episode to the next for at least a few episodes in that series. And even if on-going activities are practices to which consent once given need not be renewed, it is typically prudent to get consent to the practice renewed from time to time.

The upshot of that upshot, in turn, is that whichever way we view on-going activities it is permissible in practice (if not, on the 'discrete episodes' view, in theory) to presume that consent previously given persists through at least a few subsequent episodes or iterations of that practice. But the presumption is a relatively weak one: even on the 'practice' view, one ought prudently check back from time to time.

We should not generally be permitted to presume the other's consent, as I have argued.[94] But the cases here in view are special in one crucial respect. Here, the practice is on-going, and those whose consent we are presuming have actually previously consented to that practice knowing it would be on-going. Furthermore, they did nothing, then or later, to indicate that that consent would not or did not continue, even though they clearly could have done so at not undue cost.[95]

The sheer fact that they have consented previously does not, in and of itself, constitute consent on the present occasion, to be sure. But if they have given consent to what they understood would be an on-going practice, and they have done nothing subsequently to indicate that they no longer consent (even though they could have done so without undue cost), the presumption that they actually do continue to consent is morally well warranted.

[92] And notice that neither WHO nor the Metropolitan Police specify any exception to their general rules for 'repeat players' (ones who have participated in many medical experiments in the past, or long-term sexual partners).

[93] Dougherty 2021a, ch. 9.

[94] In Sections 1.1 and 3.3.1 above.

[95] If in consenting on the previous occasion they had said 'just this once', then of course that gives no grounds for presuming that they consent on subsequent occasions—just the opposite.

3.3.4 Silence-on-Notice

Recall the case of the meeting where the chairperson asked, 'Any objections?' There, silence can rightly be taken as evidence of unspoken tacit consent, precisely because the chairperson's question put everyone in the room on notice that it would be taken in that way.[96] There, we can presume people's consent—we can 'take [it] as proved in the absence of evidence to the contrary'[97]—because people are on notice to that effect.[98] Something like that is, I would argue, what is going on in many cases of ostensibly 'presumed consent'. In an important way however that is a misnomer, since the chairperson's instruction has made 'remaining silent' literally a sign of consent.[99] Silence literally constitutes 'socially consenting' in such circumstances.

There are many other examples of that.[100] Take for example organ donor schemes. The law traditionally required people to 'opt-in' to such schemes by signing a form (or carrying a signed organ donor card in their wallet) explicitly consenting to donate their organs for transplantation into others in need of them when they die. Some jurisdictions have now enacted instead an 'opt-out' system, in which people are presumed to consent to donate their organs unless they sign a form indicating that they do not so consent.[101]

[96] As Simmons (1993, pp. 221–2) rightly says, '*Failing* to do something can only be a way of consenting when that inactivity is in response to a clear choice situation, only when inactivity is significant as indicating that a choice has been made...' More generally, 'silence respecting a circumstance, which would naturally and necessarily have been mentioned, may be fairly taken as a proof that it never existed' (Grotius 1625/1901, bk. 1, ch. 2, sec. 7)—and the chairperson's putting people on notice is just a special case of that.

[97] *Oxford English Dictionary*, q.v. 'presume (v.)', def. 3.

[98] If they are not 'on notice' then no such thing can be presumed. Suppose a friend emails asking three questions, 'Can I borrow your lawn mower? And your rake? And your car?'; and you reply, 'Sure, you can borrow my lawn mower and rake'. Your silence regarding your car certainly cannot be taken as consent to his borrowing it, unless he had added in his email, 'I will assume the answer to each is "yes" unless you say otherwise'.

[99] As Den Hartogh (2011, p. 289) says, 'if it is correct to say of someone under appropriate circumstances that he has given his tacit consent...no appeal to a presumption rule is needed'.

[100] One other is abandonment of property: when you know some piece of property of yours in in the possession of another, your silence in failing to reassert your ownership claims to it betokens your consent to relinquishing your rights to that property. As Grotius (1625/1910, bk. 1, ch. 4, secs. 5, 6) writes: 'if a person knows his property to be in the possession of another, and allows it to remain so for a length of time, without asserting his claim, unless there appear sufficient reasons for his silence, he is construed to have entirely abandoned all pretentions to the same.... But for silence to be taken as a valid presumption that property is deserted, two things are requisite: it must be a silence with a knowledge of the fact, and with a perfect freedom of will in the person concerned. For a silence founded in ignorance can have no weight; and where any other reason appears, the presumption of free consent must fail.'

[101] Healey 2006; these are standardly referred to as 'presumed consent' laws (see also, e.g., Kennedy et al. 1998). Laws that people operating a motor vehicle on public roadways thereby consent to blood alcohol testing work similarly for drivers who are conscious, and who may (in exercise of their Fourth Amendment rights) withdraw that 'implied consent'. But those laws work differently as regards unconscious drivers, who are deemed to consent to such testing even if there is clear evidence that they do not (Valentine 2018, pp. 505–7).

What such a law does, I suggest, is put people on notice that their silence on the matter will be taken as consent, in the same way as does the meeting chairperson's asking 'Any objections?'[102] Assuming the law is well publicized and that opting-out is not unreasonably burdensome, that provides good grounds for believing that people not opting-out do indeed tacitly consent to be organ donors.[103] Indeed, silence in that case is a way of their communicating their consent.[104]

As I have observed in Section 2.3.3 above, there may be some waivers of rights that are sufficiently morally important that we do not think tacit consent is enough and we think we ought to insist that the consent be made explicit. Perhaps opponents of opt-out organ donation schemes think that the sanctity of the human body, even after death, should be considered a case in point.[105] Proponents of 'only yes means yes' when it comes to consent for sexual relations are certainly of the view that 'consent by silence' is definitely not enough to signal consent to violations of bodily integrity, there.[106]

Notice that, even in the case of meetings, a chairperson can ordinarily ask 'Any objections?' and take silence to settle the matter only informally and on routine matters that are of little consequence.[107] After all, if even a single person objects, the chairperson must either drop the matter or take it to a formal vote.

That suggests that, while silence can sometimes be taken as consent in contexts where people are on clear notice that their silence will be interpreted in that way, that seems like a device that is and should be used only where the stakes are

[102] In Eyal's (2019) terms, the law thereby creates a well-publicized 'general convention [that] specifies that silence expresses consent'.

[103] Saunders (2012b) endorses this analysis in his later work on the topic. Earlier Saunders (2010, p. 85) had insisted that: 'Whether these conditions hold in the case of organ donation is unclear. First, people may be unaware that their silence will be taken as consent or of exactly what is involved in organ donation. Second, it is not necessarily costless for would-be objectors to opt out. Those who opt out may face social stigma unless privacy can be guaranteed, and even making a decision requires one to consider the uncomfortable fact of one's own mortality, which may be a cost that people should not be forced to bear.' As regards the first, that is simply an argument for better publicizing the law; as regards the latter, the test is not 'costless' but 'not unreasonably costly', and surely neither of those costs is unreasonable when it is a matter of saving someone else's life, as Saunders (2010, p. 86) had gone on to say even in his earlier article.

[104] Den Hartogh (2011) argues that 'presumed consent' of this sort cannot be real consent on the grounds that consent must be 'communicated'. I agree it must be communicated; my point is merely that it can in this way be communicated by silence.

[105] We ordinarily think it improper for a physician to take the silence of a conscious, competent patient to constitute consent to an invasive medical procedure (see Section 9.4). The reason that those who are prepared to accept silence as consent to organ donation in opt-out systems is, presumably, that they see a big moral distinction between cutting into a cadaver and cutting into a living person.

[106] Dougherty 2015. Sexual partners in an on-going relationship might, of course, have established a convention between themselves according to which (under certain circumstances perhaps) silence is to be taken as consent to sex—but that would be a case of consent that was either explicit or presumed on the basis of the on-going practice, rather than consent being presumed on the basis of 'silence on notice'.

[107] Robert (1876/1951, pp. 198, 203) thus writes: 'Business can be expedited greatly by avoiding the formality of motions and voting in routine business and on questions of little importance [by] the chair assuming general (unanimous) consent until someone objects.... The action thus taken is said to be done by general consent, or unanimous or silent consent.'

relatively low for the person whose consent is to be presumed from silence.[108] Where the stakes for potential consent-givers are substantial, silence—even on notice—will not and ordinarily probably should not suffice as a signal of consent.

3.3.5 Customary Consent on Notice

In Section 3.2 I observed that what counts as a signal of consent is purely conventional and just depends on customary usage. I now want to extend that claim to suggest that there can also be a convention within a community that people will be presumed to consent to certain actions unless they explicitly declare otherwise.[109] I foreshadowed this approach in Section 3.3.2, suggesting that this would be the best way to make sense of the role that social norms play in underwriting 'presumed consent' in the new *Restatement (Third) of the Law of Torts*. Let me now develop that argument more fully.

The previous—second—*Restatement of the Law of Torts* addressed this issue explicitly. It said that 'in determining whether conduct would be understood by a reasonable person as indicating consent, the customs of the community are to be taken into account'. It went on to offer this example:

> if it is the custom in wooded or rural areas to permit the public to go hunting on private land or to fish in private lakes or streams, anyone who goes hunting or fishing may reasonably assume, in the absence of a posted notice or other manifestation to the contrary, that there is the customary consent to his entry upon private land to hunt or fish.[110]

Against the background of those customary practices, not posting a 'No Hunting' sign on your fence would reasonably be taken as indicating your consent to people hunting on your property—just as remaining silent when the meeting chairperson asks 'Any objections?' is reasonably taken as indicating consent to the proposition on the table.

[108] And, as I said above, the costs of registering dissent are not unreasonably high. And, one might further add, the act presumably consented to by silence is not in itself immoral, even with one's consent—although that limitation is not peculiar to consent via 'silence on notice' but instead applies to consent of any form. See further: Bolinger 2019, pp. 192–3, 200–1; Dougherty 2021a, pp. 128–9.

[109] In this section I shall be talking about community-wide customs and conventions, rather than ones that have grown up among small sets of people in on-going relationships (such as long-standing lovers, in the case discussed in Section 3.3.3). The latter can often be more akin to (implicitly or explicitly) negotiated arrangements that themselves actually (implicitly or explicitly) *confer* continuing consent, rather than merely putting people on notice that consent will be presumed unless they explicitly say otherwise.

[110] ALI 1979, § 892, comment d. Parking in many cities is like this, permitted everywhere except where 'No Parking' signs explicitly indicate otherwise.

I call this 'custom on notice', to emphasize that it works in just the same way as 'silence on notice' in the previous section. What the custom does is to put people on notice that their inaction will be taken as a sign of their consent to customary practices whereby others infringe (if only marginally) on their rights. People are free not to consent. But if they want to do that, they must say so explicitly—by posting a sign saying, 'No Hunting!', in the above example.[111]

Inconsequential intrusions are subjects of customary-consent-on-notice in just this way. A pat on the back is a customary form of congratulations in the US, for example; consent can be presumed there for that, and anyone who does not want to be touched on the back there knows that they must say so. Touching the British monarch on the back is not customary, in contrast.[112] Touching anyone on the back in China is definitely contrary to customary consent there: you definitely need to ask for consent to do that, and even asking might well itself give offence.[113]

Presuming consent to customary practices avoids the need for cumbersome rituals of seeking specific consent for common and frequent sorts of encounters, to which few in that society would actually object. Presuming such consent thus eases the burden of seeking and giving consent in all manner of everyday interactions, such as bumping against one another in a crowded subway car.[114] People who do not want to give consent in the course of those interactions are on notice, by reason of customary practice, that they must say so explicitly.

Earlier I said that people should be entitled to the presumption that they have not waived any important rights, in the absence of clear evidence that they have done so.[115] But I also observed even earlier that we often make do with more gestural forms of consent in lesser matters, whereas we typically require much more explicit expressions of consent when 'something of great consequence is at stake'.[116] My suggestion-cum-speculation is that we ordinarily only presume that people consent to what is done to them on the basis of customary practices as regards relatively common and minor intrusions.[117] For any genuinely major intrusions we ought not presume consent on the basis of customary practice—in the absence of evidence that the person does consent, we instead presume that they do not.[118]

[111] There is an analogous practice in international law. 'Customary international law' is generally regarded as being based on the general consent of states to it. A norm of customary international law is binding on every state, unless it was a 'persistent objector' throughout the time that norm was emerging as a norm of customary international law (Green 2016).

[112] Although touching the Queen of Australia (one and the same person) on the back may be on its way to becoming so (BBC 2000).

[113] Limitations on asking for consent will be further discussed in Section 6.1.3.

[114] Simons 2006b, p. 1067 n. 20.

[115] In Sections 1.1 and 3.3.1 above.

[116] See Section 2.3.3 above.

[117] Or perhaps as regards more consequential intrusions in cases of 'dire emergency', if we want to include the permission of the surgeon to operate on the gravely injured comatose patient under this heading.

[118] The practice of genital cutting, customary in some places, might seem a counter-example. It certainly is a major intrusion on the bodily integrity of the person upon whom it is performed, and it is typically done without the consent of the person upon whom it is performed (typically, because they are

3.3.6 Shifting the Burden of Speaking Up

In these last three sets of cases—cases of 'customary consent on notice', 'silence on notice' or 'on-going practices to which you have previously consented'—we are entitled to presume that people consent because people actually have done or not done something that, in the context, conveys their consent. In the on-going practice, they actually consented at some point in the past to what they knew would be an on-going practice and they have not given notice of their intention to revoke that consent. In cases of 'silence on notice' and 'customary consent on notice', they have been put on notice that remaining silent is a way of consenting, and they have remained silent. We are entitled to presume that we have their consent because they have, in those ways, actually communicated it to us.[119]

In all of these cases that presumption of consent is a *defeasible* one. And all a person needs to do to defeat the presumption that he consents is to indicate that he does not. Taking previous consent to an on-going practice, or silence in the face of notice, as consent merely shifts the burden of speaking up. Ordinarily, a person who wants to give consent needs to speak up (or do something equivalent) to give positive indication of that fact. In cases where consent may be presumed, a person who wants not to give consent needs to speak up (or do something equivalent) to indicate that fact.

Why should we shift the presumption in that way? There may be reasons of policy for doing that (we will get more organs donated for transplant that way, for example). Or there may be simple reasons for practicality for doing that (having to seek permission from each person we bump up against on a crowded stairway during a fire alarm is simply impractical).

There are also reasons of a more principled sort, however. Making errors about whether or not someone else consents to something is morally costly.[120] Of course either way we set the presumption, people will be invited to speak up and correct the record if that presumption attributes false attitudes to them. But realistically, not all of them will speak up, and not all who do will be correctly understood. If the vast majority of people do in fact consent, then presuming that people in general consent unless they say otherwise will yield less errors of that sort than would presuming that people in general do not consent unless they say that they do.[121]

too young to give valid consent). Notice, however, that the genital cutting is typically performed either by or with the consent of close relatives of the victim who would ordinarily be treated as 'surrogate decision-makers' authorized to consent on behalf of the under-age victim.

[119] In my taxonomy, therefore, it would be more apt to say we are 'inferring their consent' rather than 'presuming' it—but the latter is the more common way of describing these cases so for expository convenience I will stick with that terminology here.

[120] 'Mistakes in consenting' will be discussed more fully in Chapter 4 below.

[121] For development of similar themes in different contests, see Goodin (1985a) and Green (1988, p. 170). Of course it is worse to make the error of wrongly supposing someone consents when actually they do not than it is to make the error of wrongly supposing someone does not consent

3.4 Implicit Consent

When inferring from something that someone has said or done that he tacitly consents to something, we are inferring something about the state of his mind.[122] When presuming that someone consents, we are presuming something similar about the state of his mind. With what I shall call 'implicit consent', we are doing something different to that. There, we are concluding from the nature of the situation that he is compelled (paradigmatically, logically compelled) to consent. In the former cases we are saying 'he actually does consent'; in the latter we are saying 'logically he must consent'. Those two are clearly different.[123]

Of course, often the person will see the logic of the situation, and he will proceed to do as logically he must and actually give his consent. When he does, implicit consent will have been converted into tacit or perhaps even explicit consent. And once that has happened, we have no further occasion for speaking of implicit consent in relation to that case at all.[124] Here, therefore, I shall be concerned instead with the case in which implicit consent remains no more than that—it remains merely implicit. I shall argue that, in the absence of actual consent, we can at most treat someone in that situation in the same way 'as if he consents'.[125]

3.4.1 Logically Implicit

The paradigmatic case of 'implicit consent' is one in which (i) X consents to Y's φ-ing and (ii) Y's φ-ing logically entails Y's γ-ing.

Sometimes that latter proposition might be true because of an identity relation between φ and γ.[126] So when I consent to your frying the fish, I implicitly consent to your cooking the fish, because frying is one form of cooking. Or, again, when

when actually they do. But if the base rate of 'actually consenting' is very high, there will be many more instances of the latter sort of error than the former; and even though each of them is less important, summed together they can be more important.

[122] Or at least what that person intends to communicate (perhaps falsely) about his state of mind; see Sections 1.3.2, 1.4 and 2.3.2 above on the difference. Remember, per Section 1.2.1.1, by 'state of mind' here and throughout I mean more precisely 'whether he has performed a mental act of consent'.

[123] Among the conditions that 'imply consent' Simmons (1976, pp. 286–7) includes cases in which 'an act... that... "commits" the actor to consenting. By this I mean that the act would be pointless or hopelessly stupid unless the actor was fully prepared to consent; the act commits the actor "rationally" to giving his consent.' But as Simmons goes on to say, this 'is closely related to genuine consent in some way without in fact being consent'.

[124] Except maybe to justify why he actually consented, if he is ever challenged to justify that.

[125] 'As if consent' is discussed in Sections 1.4, 4.3 and 4.4.1. In Section 3.4.3 below, I call consent that is logically or pragmatically implicit 'derivative quasi-consent' to distinguish it from the cases discussed in Section 1.4. But while the grounds for such treatment differ, the practical upshot is the same.

[126] Sometimes the identity is even clearer, as in Pallikkathayil's (2020, p. 110) example that when I 'ask you to move my car so I can avoid a parking ticket... [,] I consent to your moving my car'.

I consent to your walking across my land, I implicitly consent to your stepping on it, because walking just is a series of steppings.

Other times φ-ing might logically entail *Y*'s γ-ing because the one is a logically necessary condition of the other. Thus, when consenting for my ashes to be buried at sea I implicitly consent to my body being burned, because ashes by definition are the product of combustion.[127] And when consenting to invasive surgery I am, by definition, consenting to my bodily cavity being penetrated.[128]

Even if *Y*'s γ-ing is logically equivalent to or logically entailed by *Y*'s φ-ing, however, the fact remains that it is *Y*'s φ-ing—not *Y*'s γ-ing—to which *X* has consented. Consent is given 'under a description'.[129] Given the logical equivalence or entailment, by consenting to *Y*'s φ-ing *X* may well be *committed* to consenting to *Y*'s γ-ing. But being committed to doing it and actually doing it are two separate things.

3.4.2 Pragmatically Implicit

Pufendorf offers the following examples that have something of the same flavour:

> (1) A prince or magistrate, who by covenant gives leave to strangers to frequent his markets; is supposed to consent likewise, that they shall carry home the goods they purchase there.
> (2) In the same manner, he who lets out a chamber to hire is suppos'd to consent withal, that the lodger shall make use of such other parts of the house as he cannot be without; as of the doors, entries and the like; at least so far as to have free access to his apartment and free passage from it.[130]

While there is certainly a *pragmatic* absurdity in refusing the further consent in both of those cases, there is nothing *logically* absurd about doing so. One can imagine a sharp dealer consenting to the rental of a room without consenting to the renter's using the hallway required to access it—just as Portia ruled that Shylock's contract entitling him to a pound of Antonio's flesh did not entitle

[127] *Oxford English Dictionary*, q.v. 'ash (n2)', def. 1. [128] Valentine 2018, p. 512.

[129] Anscombe 1963, pp. 393–4. Her example is a blind man signing a piece of paper that his friend presents to him saying it is a petition for a reprieve for a convicted mutual friend, when in fact it was a property transfer. Her conclusion is: 'Under the description "signing the document presented by so and so" there was consent to what took place; under the description "signing a transfer of property" there was not.'

[130] Pufendorf 1672/1710, bk. 3, ch. 6, sec. 2, para. 6. Hobbes (1651, ch. 14) before him had written similarly: 'He that transfers any right transfers the means of enjoying it, as far as lies in his power. As he that sells land is understood to transfer the herbage and whatsoever grows upon it; nor can he that sells a mill turn away the stream that drives it.'

him to shed a drop of Antonio's blood, even though doing so is the only way in which Shylock can procure the pound of flesh due to him.[131]

Pleased though we may be with Portia's disposition of that case, in general we are morally disinclined to look favourably upon such sharp dealing. Pufendorf gives a couple of other examples where that would be the case:

> Thus a certain person deny'd positively that he had laid hands on a priest, for he had only cudgell'd and kick'd him. Thus Temures having articles with the garrison of Sebastia that no blood should be shed, nevertheless ordered all prisoners to be buried alive.[132]

Pufendorf quotes approvingly Cicero's judgment on such cases: 'deceit does not remove the guilt of perjury—it merely aggravates it'.[133]

Thus, even if *Y*'s γ-ing is only pragmatically implicit in *Y*'s φ-ing, *X*'s consenting to *Y*'s φ-ing can reasonably be taken to commit him to consenting to *Y*'s γ-ing. That would certainly be so if *Y*'s γ-ing is literally the only way for *Y* to φ; and it would arguably be so if *Y*'s γ-ing is much the most practicable or reasonable way for *Y* to φ. But again, being committed to doing something (here, consenting) and actually doing it are wholly separate matters.

3.4.3 What Morally Follows?

What morally follows from the conjunction of the facts that (i) *X* has consented to *Y*'s φ-ing and (ii) *Y*'s φ-ing logically (or even just pragmatically) entails *Y*'s γ-ing? Any of three possible conclusions might follow. In order of increasing strength:

- One conclusion might be that *X*, while he has not consented to *Y*'s γ-ing, *X* nonetheless *ought to permit Y* to γ because that is necessary for giving practical effect to his consent to *Y*'s φ-ing.
- Alternatively, and more strongly, we might say that *X*'s commitment (via his consent) to permitting *Y*'s φ-ing entails that *X* is thereby also *committed to permitting Y*'s γ-ing.
- We might reach an even stronger conclusion, yet again, by building on Kant's insight that 'whoever wills the end also wills... the indispensably necessary means to it...'[134] In the case at hand, *X*'s consenting to *Y*'s φ-ing means that *X* wills *Y*'s being permitted to φ; and *Y*'s φ-ing logically

[131] Shakespeare 1596, act 4, scene 1, lines 305–11.

[132] Pufendorf 1672/1710, bk. 5, ch. 12, para. 5.

[133] Cicero 44/1928, bk. 3, ch. 32, para. 113.

[134] Kant 1785/1991, 4: 417. Hobbes (1651, ch. 14) similarly holds that: 'He that transfers any right transfers the means of enjoying it, as far as lies in his power.'

> or pragmatically entails *Y*'s γ-ing means that the latter is a necessary means to the former. So from the Kantian maxim it follows that *X* also *wills Y*'s being permitted to γ.

Even that last and strongest argument—that '*X* wills *Y*'s being permitted to γ'—is not quite sufficient to allow us to conclude that *X* has genuinely consented to *Y*'s γ-ing. First, the necessary mental element may be missing. 'Willing', in the sense here in view, and mentally consenting (having performed a mental act of consent) may not be exactly the same. 'Willing', for example, may be merely 'wanting'; and wanting or wishing for something to be done is importantly different from requesting or consenting to it being done. Or again, if *X*'s mentally consenting means '*X* intends to permit that to which *X* consents', what *X* intends to permit is *Y*'s φ-ing (which is what *X* has consented to), not *Y*'s γ-ing.[135] Maybe, if the latter is a necessary means to the former, *X* should (prudentially) also intend to permit the latter; but whether or not he actually *does* so intend is a separate question. Second, and even more straightforwardly, the communicative element is necessarily missing: socially giving consent requires the consent-giver somehow to communicate his consent to the consent-receiver, and by definition that is a condition that no form of (merely) implicit consent can satisfy.

Still, all of those three implications in *some* way link 'what is implicit' to 'what is consented to'. Take for example the first and weakest conclusion—that '*X* ought to permit *Y* to γ *because* that is necessary for giving practical effect to his consent to *Y*'s φ-ing'. *X*'s consent (albeit to something else, *viz.*, *Y*'s φ-ing) is what *grounds* the proposition that *X* ought to permit *Y* to γ. The fact that *X* ought to permit *Y* to γ is in that way consent-based, even if *Y*'s γ-ing is not itself anything *X* consented to. The same can be said, *mutatis mutandis*, of each of the other two stronger conclusions set out above.

For that reason, I shall call these all cases of 'derivative quasi-consent', which I regard as a subspecies of 'as if consent'.[136] That is to say, *X* has not *actually* consented to *Y*'s γ-ing. Nevertheless, something like consent ('quasi-consent') is derived from the conjunction of the facts that: (i) X *has actually* consented to *Y*'s φ-ing; and (ii) X's 'consent' to *Y*'s γ-ing is *logically or pragmatically implicit* in X's consent to *Y*'s φ-ing. The quasi-consent in question is merely implicit rather than actual. But the implicit quasi-consent being derived from actual consent, rather than from some other non-consent considerations altogether, makes it more nearly a form of consent.[137]

[135] Bratman (1984, p. 401) gives a suite of examples suggesting that 'rational intention need not be transmitted along the lines of known, necessary constitutive means'.

[136] Introduced in Section 1.4.2 above.

[137] 'Derivative quasi-consent' differs in this way from 'ought-to consent', to be discussed Section 3.5 below. It also differs from quasi-contracts that are 'implied-in-law': there, the implication arises not from anything else the parties have agreed to but rather from freestanding principles of law.

Derivative quasi-consent thus has a tight enough connection with actual consent, I suggest, for us to treat cases of (merely) implicit consent in the same way once again as we treat actual consent.[138] That is to say, we are justified in treating a person as if he consented to (as if he actually granted permission for) whatever is logically or pragmatically implicit in that to which he actually consented. That is not because he actually consented to that which is merely implicit. It is merely to say that the one is so tightly connected (logically or pragmatically) to the other that we are justified in treating him in the same way as if he had. That is certainly the case, anyway, so long as the consent-giver could and should have known of that logical or pragmatic connection.

Of course, once the implicit has been made explicit, the consent-giver might want to revoke his consent to the thing that carries that implication. Suppose you consented to my using your truck to haul crates of $C_3H_5N_3O_9$, not realizing that that is the chemical formula for nitroglycerin. Or suppose you consent to your child being enrolled in the mission school, not realizing that it was so far away that that would necessarily mean the child would have to live away from home. You may well want to revoke your consent, once you realize that that was implicit in your consenting. Chapter 7 proposes criteria for governing when and why you should be allowed to revoke consent. In both of the above examples, those rules would probably ordinarily allow you to do so, because your stakes in the matter are so much greater than the consent-receiver's. In other cases, however, they may not.[139]

3.5 Ought-to Consent

In the case of implicit consent, one ought to consent to further things that are logically or pragmatically entailed by things to which he has already actually consented. In consenting to one thing, you implicitly commit to those others. That can be true whether or not you realize it or hence have occasion to ponder whether or not you actually consent to those further things to which your existing

[138] The same was as if he genuinely consented, or the same was 'as if he consented' in the sense of Section 1.4.2.

[139] Dougherty (2013; 2021, pp. 5–8, 164–7) argues that deception in obtaining actual consent renders that consent invalid if knowing the true facts would have been a 'deal-breaker' for the consent-giver. In the cases of implicit consent here under discussion similarly involve unknown deal-breaking considerations, but they are different in other morally important respects: specifically, there is in my cases (unlike Dougherty's) no deliberate deception on the part of the consent-receiver. Some might nevertheless be tempted by an analogue to Dougherty's rule in cases of implicit consent: i.e., *X*'s consenting to *Y*'s φ-ing is morally invalid if, had *X* realized that his consenting to *Y*'s γ-ing is implicit in his consenting to *Y*'s φ-ing, *X* would not have consented to *Y*'s φ-ing in the first place. Even those who do not agree to that stronger rule would nonetheless surely agree that, where *X* was *culpably ignorant* of what is implicit in his consenting to *Y*'s φ-ing, *X* should bear the costs of the mistake as set out in Section 1.4.3.3 and Chapter 4.

consent implicitly also binds you. In the case of what I shall call 'ought-to consent', the 'ought' in question is not logical or pragmatic but, instead, moral. You ought-to consent, not because it follows from anything else you have committed or consented to, but purely because it would be morally the right thing to do.

Now, of course, the same moral reasons for thinking that *X* ought-to consent to *Y*'s φ-ing might also, completely independently of that fact, suggest that (all things considered) *Y* ought be permitted to φ whether or not *X* consents.[140] But in cases like that, ought-to consent is morally redundant.[141] So let us focus instead on cases where ought-to consent might arguably be a moral difference maker.

For an example of something you ought-to consent to, take Hart's 'mutuality of restrictions' that Rawls subsequently adopted as his principle of 'fairness'.[142] Here is how Hart describes the principle:

> when a number of persons conduct any joint enterprise according to rules and thus restrict their liberty, those who have submitted to these restrictions when required have a right to a similar submission from those who have benefited by their submission.[143]

That is an intuitively appealing principle, but I will not here argue for it. Instead let me merely stipulate that it is a principle to which you morally ought-to consent.[144] It was on this sort of ground that Locke thought that people ought-to consent to a government if they enjoy its benefits (travelling on its highways, etc.).[145] And it is on this ground that many since have thought

140 Dire necessity cases are like that. Adapting an example from Feinberg (1978, p. 102), *Y* ought to be permitted to break into *X*'s mountain cabin to take shelter from a snowstorm, and *X* ought consent to *Y*'s doing so for the same moral reason—but *Y* ought be permitted to do so, with or without *X*'s consent.

141 Thomson (1990, pp. 188 ff.), I think rightly, says that 'consent' is then morally epiphenomenal; those other good- or right-making moral considerations are what is doing all the work. Estlund (2008, pp. 132–3) comes close to agreeing when he says that 'the advantage of [adding this "duty to consent"] step is that it is often easier to see that such a refusal to consent would be wrong' than it would be to see the moral force of those other considerations directly. See similarly: Rawls 1999, pp. 512–13; Kuflik 2010, pp. 155–7.

142 Saunders (2010) uses the example of a 'duty to consent to organ donation', but that is much more tendentious (Potts et al. 2010; Manson 2013).

143 Hart 1955, p. 185. Rawls 1971, § 18, p. 112.

144 Estlund (2008, pp. 132–3) himself appeals to this example. Westen (2004, p. 278) similarly justifies 'constructive consent'—imputing a person's consent to something to which he has not in any sense actually consented—by reference to the person's decision to 'take advantage of the benefits of a practice which depends upon the sharing of "personal sacrifices" and "concomitant burdens"' (as glossed by Valentine 2018, p. 514).

145 Locke 1690, § 119. Simmons (1976, pp. 287–8) shows that this 'implies consent' in an 'ought-to consent' rather than an 'actually consents' sense: 'none of Locke's "consent-implying enjoyments" is in fact a genuine consensual act. In analyzing any obligations which might arise from such enjoyments, we do not appeal to a principle of consent; rather, such obligations would arise, if at all, because of considerations of fairness or gratitude.'

that people have a moral duty to submit to such restrictions, regardless of whether they have consented to do so.[146]

Here once again, people might of course do as they ought and actually consent to that principle. Once they have actually consented, whether explicitly or tacitly, there is not much further role for the concept of ought-to consent. Again, maybe there is a little: maybe if someone is challenged to justify why he consented, 'I ought-to have done so!' would constitute a good reply. But once he has actually consented to what he ought-to consent to, it is his actual consent rather than ought-to consent that morally governs his actions. So let us confine our attention to cases of ought-to consent alone, since those are the only cases where it might do more moral work.

On the face of it, it would seem to be a plain fallacy to infer from the fact that someone ought-to consent the conclusion that they *ipso facto* do consent. To see this point more clearly, transpose the case from the moral to the legal realm. Imagine you apply for a planning permission to build a new house. Further suppose that the relevant statute is written in such a way that the planning minister is under a legal obligation to grant consent under certain conditions, which your application meets. But now suppose that the planning minister wrongly fails to grant consent. Would you be legally permitted to build the house anyway? Maybe. But one thing you clearly had better not argue, in taking that case to court, is that 'I *actually had* consent because the minister was legally required to grant it, even though he did not'.

Consider this analogy. The English Annulment Act of 1557 required that 'maidens' under age 16 obtain the consent of their parents to marry.[147] But the rule was that 'the consent of the mother or guardians, if unreasonably withheld, might be redressed and supplied by the judge . . .'.[148] There was no pretence that the mother or guardian consented when they did not. The rule was merely that if the judge held their refusal of consent to be unreasonable (i.e., they 'ought-to' have consented), the judge can substitute his own consent to the marriage with identical legal effect.

To consent, as I have said, is to assent to a commitment (or, more precisely, perform an 'act of' commitment).[149] Without the assent to the commitment, no consent has been given, and that remains true even if it ought to have been given.[150] A person has committed a wrong in not consenting when he ought to have done so, to be sure. But where his consent is required for another

[146] Simmons (1976, p. 291) argues for example that this is what can be salvaged from Locke's theory—and that it is just as strong a conclusion as would have emerged had Locke's detour through 'consent' been successful.

[147] Annulment Act of 1557, 4 & 5 Ph. & M. c. 8.

[148] Blackstone 1765, bk. 1, ch. 15, sec. 1, subsec. 3, p. 425.

[149] See Sections 1.2.1 and 2.1 above.

[150] The same is standardly said about hypothetical consent. The fact that you would have consented is morally neither here nor there, if you have not actually consented. See Section 2.2.2 above.

to be morally permitted to interfere with his rights in a certain way, wrongfully non-consenting is his prerogative.[151] He has 'a right to do wrong', in Waldron's famous phrase.[152] In any case, he certainly has a right to his rights, until and unless he actually waives them. Ought-to consent is no kind of consent at all.

Estlund pushes back against this seemingly irrefutable conclusion, insisting that 'nullity goes both ways'. Just as the giving of consent can be null and void under certain conditions (force, fraud, etc.), so too Estlund insists can the withholding of consent be null and void under certain conditions—conditions under which morally you ought-to consent. And for Estlund the moral upshot of nullifying non-consent is that consent is actually obtained.[153] As he puts it, 'when non-consent is disqualified, the authority condition is as it would have been if there had been *qualified* [i.e. valid] *consent*'.[154]

But can nullified non-consent ever be equivalent (even just functionally equivalent) to actual consent?[155] To see how that view simply must be incorrect, take a case of someone whose non-consent is nullified for some reason other than Estlund's. Suppose Sam refuses to consent to the police searching his house, but he is not mentally competent. Incompetence is one of the classic conditions that would nullify his consent, had Sam given it. If as Estlund insists 'nullity works both ways', the same conditions should nullify non-consent as well. So Sam's non-consent to the police search of his house would by Estlund's reasoning be null and void. But do we really think that, for that reason, the police should be taken actually to have Sam's *consent* to search his house? Maybe their searching his house would be the right thing to do, all (other) things considered.[156] But surely what makes it permissible is not anything remotely like 'Sam's consent': *ex hypothesi*, Sam is incompetent to consent. This is just a particularly striking case in which someone's non-consent being deemed invalid is most certainly *not*

[151] Maybe in some of Estlund's (2008, p. 127) cases—where 'you have a duty not always to say no'—what is really going on is that this condition is not met. Estlund thinks that your violating that duty nullifies your non-consent, with the effect that you have actually consented. A more plausible interpretation would be that, after your saying 'no' too many times, your consent is not required.

[152] Waldron's (1981) point is a much more general one about the nature of rights. If to have a right is to have a morally protected choice, and if one of the options is morally the correct option, then the choice that the right gives you includes the option of choosing wrongly.

[153] Estlund is simply wrong insofar as he is here claiming that negating non-consent necessarily yields consent. It merely establishes a condition where consent has neither been given nor withheld—the same condition as would have prevailed if the agent had simply remained silent on the matter. See further Section 9.3.2.

[154] Estlund 2008, p. 123, emphasis in original. Estlund cagily phrases the point in terms of 'as if'. But if 'authority condition' refers to it being 'permissible to do something that would have been impermissible without the person's consent', there is no 'as if' about it—you actually have the permission in question.

[155] I argue more fully it cannot in Section 9.3.2 below.

[156] In this example, it is something else than 'ought-to consent'—i.e., incompetence—that nullifies Sam's non-consent. But the larger point is simply that the double negative—nullified non-consent—is not sufficient to establish anything like consent, in Sam's case or Estlund's either.

tantamount to his consent being deemed to having been given. But various other examples along the same lines could be given.[157]

Estlund tries to motivate his case for treating the wrongful withholding of consent as null and void by recalling that there are some things we cannot do to people even with their consent.[158] Selling oneself into slavery is the standard example.[159] Your consent to being enslaved would simply not be morally transformative. Estlund wants to say that, just as there are some cases where giving consent is morally inert, so too are there cases where withholding it is likewise. But the real parity of reasoning would lead us instead to the observation that, just as there are some things that cannot be done to us even with our consent, so too are there other things that can be done to us without our consent. Withholding consent there would not be morally transformative, not because wrongly withholding it nullified your non-consent, but instead because your consent was not required in the first place in that situation.[160]

The most credible case for a conclusion in the neighbourhood of what Estlund is seeking with his notion of ought-to consent is, I think, along those lines. What the fact that 'you ought-to consent' is showing is that there are *pro tanto* moral reasons for what you ought to consent to being permitted. Of course there are also moral reasons, but on this account only *pro tanto* (rather than trumping rights-style) ones, for those things not being morally permitted without your consent.[161] When we say with Estlund that 'that to which you ought-to consent ought to be morally permitted even if you do not actually consent to it', what we are really saying is merely that the former *pro tanto* reasons outweigh the latter *pro tanto* reasons, all things considered.

That, anyway, seems to me the best way to make an Estlund-style ought-to consent argument work. But even on that reformulation, it will not always (or perhaps even often) work. There is no compelling reason to think that the former *pro tanto* reasons will always necessarily (or even often, contingently) outweigh the latter ones. And when they do not, then it will not be the case that that to which you ought-to consent ought morally to be permitted even if you do not actually consent.

[157] Suppose for example than Sean was staying in the house of a friend when the police came knocking. They asked for consent to search the property, but Sean refused on the grounds it was not his house and he had no authority to give consent. Assuming any consent he gave would indeed have been invalid, then so too by Estlund's standard is his non-consent. But is his non-consent being invalid tantamount to his having consented to the search? Surely not. He has no authority to consent to a search of someone else's property.

[158] Estlund 2008, pp. 122–3.

[159] Hobbes (1651, ch. 14) and Tadros (2016, ch. 14) offer others.

[160] Alternatively, your consent might be morally relevant but not completely determinative, and the same considerations that make it true that 'you should have consented' also make it true that doing that to you even without your consent is nonetheless the right thing to do 'all things considered'. This is Sreenivasan's (2009) 'riding roughshod' rejoinder to Estlund.

[161] This of course is contrary to ordinary views about consent, which see it as waiving rights that would have 'trumping' force were it not for the consent-based waiver. To foreshadow, however, I shall myself reject that view of rights in Section 11.1.

4
Mistakes in Consenting

Ideally, people say or signal what they mean, and they mean what they say or signal. But mistakes happen. People say or signal one thing while meaning another. People fail to appreciate what they need to do in order to communicate clearly to others that they do or do not consent. People misunderstand what others are trying to tell them about whether or not they consent to this or that.

This chapter is concerned with who should bear the burden of such mistakes concerning consent. In many discussions of consent mistakes might figure only marginally, if at all. On my account, they figure far more centrally.

As foreshadowed in Section 1.4, being treated 'as if you consented', in various ways, will be the cost of your doing something that you know or that you could and should have known others would take as an indicator of consent. Even if you did not mean to consent—even if you lacked the key mental element required for genuine consent—your deliberate fraud or culpable negligence in misleadingly communicating consent can justify your being treated 'as if you consented' even when you 'really' (mentally) did not.[1] And as I argued there, even falsely consenting in innocent error can carry some of the same consequences.

On the part of the putative consent-receiver, too, when something very important is at stake very high standards of 'due diligence' are required to ensure that you really do have the other's consent. Your negligence in failing to 'do due diligence' makes you liable to bear the burdens of any mistakes about others' consent that you make in consequence.

4.1 Types of Mistake About Consent

There are two distinct types of mistake that might be made concerning consent.[2] One regards the *factum* of consent—whether or not consent was actually given.

[1] 'Deliberate misleading' is of course a deliberate act, not a mistake, on the part of the person doing the misleading. But it leads to mistakes on the part of the person misled about whether she had the other's consent. For that reason, I discuss it under the rubric of 'mistakes in consenting'.

[2] Here I build on a similar distinction that is often made in discussions of forms of deception that can invalidate consent (Feinberg 1986b).

Consent Matters. Robert E. Goodin, Oxford University Press. © Robert E. Goodin 2024.
DOI: 10.1093/oso/9780192889027.003.0004

The other regards inducement—the reasons we or others have for giving or seeking consent.[3]

Within each of those basic types of mistake, there are subspecies. As regards the *factum*, putative consent-receiver *Y* may be mistaken about various things: about what putative consent-giver *X did* (e.g., *Y* thinks *X* signed the consent form, when in fact *X* did not); about the *conditions* under which *X* did it (e.g., *Y* thinks *X* gave consent voluntarily and free of force or fraud, when in fact *X* did not); or about what *X meant* by doing what he did (e.g., *Y* thinks *X* understood what he was doing as something that would confer consent, when in fact *X* did not). A mistake of any of those sorts may lead *Y* to believe that he has *X*'s consent, when actually he does not. Or putative consent-giver *X* may be mistaken about how what he does will be interpreted by putative consent-receiver *Y*. *X* may believe that *Y* will take *X*'s action as indicating *X*'s consent, when *Y* will not understand *X*'s action in that way; *X* will then be mistaken in believing that he has been socially successful in giving *Y* consent. Or *X* may believe that *Y* will not take *X*'s action as indicating *X*'s consent, when *Y* will understand *X*'s action in that way; *X* will then be mistaken in believing that he has not socially signalled consent, when he has.

Mistakes in the inducement might likewise arise on the part of both consent-giver *X* and consent-receiver *Y*. *X* might have erroneous beliefs about the circumstances or the consequences of his giving, or not giving, consent to *Y*; and *X* might mistakenly give consent to *Y* on the basis of those erroneous beliefs.[4] Consent-receiver *Y* might be mistaken about the consequences of performing the action for which he's seeking *X*'s consent. Such erroneous belief might lead *Y* to mistakenly seek *X*'s consent.

In this chapter I shall focus primarily on mistakes about the *factum*—mistakes about whether consent has indeed been conferred. Those seem to be the more grievous sorts of mistakes. Mistakes about the factum are *moral* mistakes. They lead you to make incorrect inferences about your moral relations with others. Mistakes about inducements are merely *prudential* mistakes. They merely lead you to make incorrect inferences about your own most preferred course of action. They do not lead you to inadvertently wrong anyone else by violating their rights without their permission, which in contrasting cases of mistakes about the *factum* you incorrectly believe you have.

Mistakes about inducements can of course lead you to consent, to your cost, to things to which you would not have consented had you not made those mistakes. And moral questions can be raised about how the costs of mistakes of that sort

[3] Actually, there is a third type of mistake that is possible: a mistake over whether the conditions required for validly consenting are met (conditions of competence, voluntariness, absence of deception and coercion).

[4] These are the sorts of mistakes that lie at the heart of Tadros' (2016, ch. 13) discussion of 'error and consent'.

should be allocated, as well.[5] Many of the same conclusions I shall reach here about mistakes concerning the *factum* also carry over to mistakes concerning the inducement as well, even if (purely to simplify the exposition) I couch my discussion purely in terms of the former.

4.2 Who Should Bear the Burden of Mistakes?

In Section 2.3.2 I argued that there must be mutual knowledge among both consent-giver and consent-receiver as to what each takes to be signs of consent in order for consent-giving to be robustly socially successful. If the consent-giver had no idea that what he is doing—scratching his head at an auction, for example—will be taken by others as consenting, then he has not actually consented to make a bid at the auction. Socially he consented, but mentally he did not. Likewise, if the consent-receiver had no idea that what the other person meant by clasping his hands together and bowing his head was to give consent to the proposal under discussion, then the hand-clasper has failed to be socially successful in communicating consent to the other.[6]

Both sorts of failures of mutual knowledge of what the other intends or understands as a sign of consent can be frustrating for people seeking to transform their moral relationships with one another. Someone trying and failing to give consent is trying to create a sort of moral intimacy—giving some particular other person permission to do things with and to him that others lack permission to do.[7] It is frustrating not to succeed in doing so because others mistake his intentions. But the other sort of misunderstanding is perhaps even more morally fraught. When others believe they have your consent to do something that, if done without your consent, would violate your rights—but they are mistaken in thinking they have your consent—they are likely to end up violating your rights. Accordingly, it is that latter sort of case upon which I shall particularly focus in this chapter.

The issue under discussion here is who should bear the burdens of mistakes about the *factum* of whether consent has or has not been given. Note well, however: we are talking here about *mistakes*. Someone thought that consent had been given, but that was a mistake—consent had not really been given.[8]

[5] That the consent-giver has based his consent on a mistake about inducements may, for example, be a reason for the consent-receiver not to act on the consent that he has been given (as foreshadowed in Section 1.5).

[6] He may mentally consent. But as I have argued, consent inherently has a social as well as mental dimension, and the latter is missing in this case (see Sections 1.2.2 and 2.3.1). The hand-clasper has failed to 'give'—convey—his consent to others who do not understand that 'I consent' is what he means by that gesture.

[7] Raz 1981, pp. 124–5.

[8] Of course people can also be mistaken about the scope of the consent given (Dougherty 2021a, ch. 1). For example I may correctly believe I have your consent to use your house while you are away but incorrect in the belief that I also have your consent to help myself to your best wine. When someone

So the question here is not whether or not the person mistakenly believed to have given consent *really* gave consent. Clearly he did not.[9] The question is who should bear the burdens arising from the mistaken belief that he had.

Of course if the mistake is discovered and corrected before any burdens have been borne, that issue does not arise.[10] It may be a truism that 'misleading another... leads to the obligation to correct the misconception', quite generally.[11] But that general truism would seem to apply with particular force where the mistake concerns one another's moral rights and duties. For the purposes of this discussion, however, I am going to focus on cases where the mistake was not corrected in time and, owing to the mistake, there are now some burdens that will have to be borne.[12]

Furthermore, I shall for the bulk of this chapter assume that there are only two options: either we can let the 'consent-giver' bear the burden (by permitting the person who mistakenly thought he had consent to do that which he thought he had consent to do); or else we can let the 'consent-receiver' bear the burden (by not permitting him to do that when he mistakenly thought he had consent to do).[13] As Section 1.4.3 has already shown, that forced choice elides various less draconian options that are often more appropriate; I shall return to them in the final section of this chapter. But for the bulk of the chapter I shall talk in terms of only those two most draconian remedies, purely to simplify the exposition.

4.3 Who Caused the Mistake to Be Made

One natural way to decide who should bear the burden of error is to ask 'whose' mistake it was. But there are various different ways of allocating 'ownership' of a mistake. One is to assign it to the person who caused the mistake to be made; that is the subject of this section. The other is to assign it to the person who made the

is 'partially mistaken' like that, then what Pufendorf (1672/1710, bk. 3, ch. 6, para. 3) says of promises would be true of consent as well ('if the promise were but in part occasion'd by an error, it may as to the rest of it remain valid').

[9] Or so I have argued in Section 1.2, and so shall I assume for the rest of my discussion.

[10] As Pufendorf (1672/1710, bk 3, ch. 6, sec 7, para. 1) says analogously about promises, so too with consent: 'If I am prevail'd with to enter into a pact or contract upon mistake, and I find this mistake out, before anything is done in order to the fulfilling of the agreement, it is but equitable, that I should have the liberty to retract'.

[11] Prichard 1940/1968, p. 170.

[12] By 'burdens' I refer to both out-of-pocket expenses and the costs of forgone opportunities predicated on the mistaken beliefs about consent having been given. But claims are limited to what it would take to make the people concerned as well off as they would have been if the mistake had not been made, not to make them as well off as they would have been if the mistaken beliefs had been true. See further the discussion of 'reliance interests' versus 'expectation interests' in sections 2.2.5 above and 7.3 below.

[13] Both are in 'scare quotes' because in the cases here in view consent was not really given or received, of course. I shall omit the scare quotes to unclutter the text on subsequent occasions; but they should always be understood as being implied throughout my discussion of mistakes about consent.

mistake; that is the subject of Section 4.4. Often those are one and the same person, of course. But sometimes they differ.

The clearest case of one person causing another to make a mistake about consent is by deliberately misleading him. If the misled party was the putative consent-giver, that would be akin to a case of consent obtained by fraud, which is standardly said to invalidate consent.[14] If the misled party was the putative consent-receiver, it would look more like a case of entrapment: the putative consent-receiver is misled into believing, and acting on the belief, that he has the putative consent-giver's consent when he does not. In either case, the person doing the deliberate misleading should clearly be the one to bear the full burdens of the ensuing errors.[15]

The same might be true of someone who, through his culpable negligence, misleads another into making a mistake about consent.[16] Suppose a friend, whom you know to be a landlubber unfamiliar with watery ways, asks if he can borrow your yacht for his honeymoon. You reply, 'It's in dry dock'. He understands your reply as granting consent and telling him where he can find the yacht; but you mean it as an explanation of why he cannot borrow the boat (because it is undergoing repairs). Any member of the yachting fraternity would have understood your reply in precisely the way you meant it. But you knew your friend was not wise in the ways of that world, and you should have realized that replying in nautical code might not communicate your meaning to him. At the very least, you should have prefaced your reply to him by saying clearly, '*No*, it's in dry dock'. It was negligent of you not to do so. Hence you are responsible for causing your friend to make a mistake about your consent, and you should be the one to bear any ensuing burdens arising from that mistake.[17]

Suppose, however, there was neither deliberate intent to mislead nor negligence in misleading. Suppose, instead, that the person who caused the mistake did so purely accidentally.[18] Then there is a less strong case for allocating the ensuring burdens to him. It was just plain bad luck that he ended up misleading someone. By the same token, however, it was (let us suppose) just plain bad luck that the other ended up being misled.

In that case, neither party is at fault and neither deserves (in any fault-based sense anyway) to bear the burdens of the error. But someone must. Now suppose,

[14] Grotius 1625, bk. 2, ch. 11, sec. 6. Pufendorf 1672/1710, bk. 3, ch. 6, sec. 8. ALI 1979, § 525. ALI 1981, §§ 162, 164.

[15] Indeed, a 'deliberately fraudulent false consent-giver' should be treated as having forfeited the rights he purported to be waiving (as argued in Section 1.4; see further Sections 1.5, 2.2.4 and 2.3.1).

[16] See Section 1.4 above.

[17] In cases of culpably negligent false consent, calibrated as the difference between how well off your friend is after discovering the error and how well off he would have been had you not been negligent in leading him to believe you consented to his using your yacht for his honeymoon. See Sections 1.4.3 and 2.2.5.

[18] Through 'wholly innocent error', in the terminology of Section 1.4.

as I shall for expository convenience throughout most of this chapter, that (a) the burdens cannot be divided between them and (b) one or the other of them must bear all the burdens.[19] Which of them should it be? I reserve discussion of such cases for Section 4.6 below.

4.4 Who Made the Mistake

Another plausible candidate for 'who owns the mistake?' is the person who made the mistake. It was 'his' mistake, after all. Assigning the mistake to him might therefore seem to be a 'natural default', in the absence of any reason for assigning it to anyone else.[20]

Over and above that, however, there may be special reasons for thinking that the person who made the mistake about consent ought to bear the ensuing burdens. The first, and probably much the most common, is that the person who made the mistake was guilty of culpable negligence, often in the form of culpable ignorance. A second, which might sometimes be applicable, is that the person who made the mistake 'voluntarily assumed the risk' of erring. A third might be that the person who made the mistake should be held 'strictly liable' for its consequences, owing perhaps to some very special features of the burdens that would be imposed by any error. I discuss each of these sorts of special reasons in turn in what follows.

4.4.1 Culpable Negligence and Culpable Ignorance

Culpable negligence is the first sort of special reason for holding the person making the mistake about consent responsible for bearing any burdens arising from it. To say that he was culpably negligent in making the mistake is to say that he made the mistake as a result of a lack of due care and attention. Pufendorf, for example, says that 'he that mistakes jest for earnest, ought to pay for his want of apprehension'.[21] He should have been paying more attention. It is only fair that he should therefore be the one to bear the burdens of his careless error.

In cases of mistakes about consent, the negligence often takes the form of culpable ignorance about what someone means, or others will take, to be a sign of consent. The person's ignorance is culpable, because he could and should have

[19] The latter is to say, 'assume that there is no system of insurance of social support that enables the costs of such mistakes to be shared more widely'.

[20] Calabresi (1970, p. 21) canvasses the related approach to allocating the costs of accidents more generally of 'placing . . . losses on those activities that, in some undefined sense, engender them'.

[21] Pufendorf (1672/1710, bk. 3, ch. 5, § 10), paraphrasing the long-forgotten jurist Connanus.

known the true facts about that.[22] That is to say, he could and should have known he needed to learn those facts, and he could and should have known there were ways for him to learn those facts (at not-disproportionate cost).

Consider the case of an auction, where bidders signal their consent to purchase the vase being auctioned at the price the auctioneer has called out.[23] Bloggs knew that he was new to this particular auction house and (let us suppose) he also knew that different auction houses have different customs governing how to signal a bid. In that case, Bloggs could and should have known that he was at risk of inadvertently signalling consent to making a bid with gestures that he did not intend to do that; and he could and should have asked someone 'what counts as a sign of making a bid in this auction house?' If he failed to find out what he could and should have done, and others relied to their detriment on his signalling his consent without intending it, then it is Bloggs who should bear the costs of the mistake.[24]

Note well, once again: this is not to say that Bloggs 'really consented' without intending to do so.[25] Without intention—not even the intention for others to understand you to be bidding—no consent has been given. But Bloggs has negligently failed to discover crucial facts that he could and should have discovered about what others would legitimately infer from his seemingly-consenting actions, and they have incurred costs in consequence. It is on account of his negligence, not on account of any consent on his part, that Bloggs should be required to bear those burdens.[26]

[22] ALI 1979, § 12; Smith 1983.

[23] We colloquially speak of the bidder 'consenting to purchase the item at the nominated price', just as we speak of parties negotiating a contract 'consenting to a contract being concluded on these terms' (see Section 7.3.2.1 below). Recalling the distinction drawn in Section 2.2 above, however, those might be better seen as cases of conditional promises: through those actions, you have incurred conditional duties (as in promising), not merely conditionally waived rights (as in consenting). But the same issues as regards mistakes and misunderstandings arise with both promising and consenting, and they are handled in the same way with both. Hence it does not matter to the analysis that follows whether we characterize bidding at an auction as 'consenting' or 'promising'.

[24] The law of contracts holds that: 'A mistaken party's fault in failing to know or discover the facts before making the contract does not bar him from . . . [relief], unless his fault amounts to a *failure to act in good faith and in accordance with reasonable standards of fair dealing*' (ALI 1981, § 157, emphasis added). Arguably, failing to find out something he could and should have known amounts to just that.

In the analysis of culpably negligent false consent in Section 1.4.3.3, I suggest that someone sending false signals of consent in that way should merely be responsible for compensating those who were misled for the reasonable costs that they incurred in consequence of reasonably relying on the false signals. But that ideal remedy may be unavailable in the special circumstances surrounding auctions and holding the false signaller to the bid he seemingly signalled, although theoretically excessive, may be the best remedy that is practically available (as Section 1.4.3.5 suggested can sometimes happen).

[25] Thus, I agree with Hurd (1996, p. 125) that 'negligent ignorance . . . does not . . . constitute consent'. But—as I shall go on to say in this paragraph—that is beside the point. The reason someone should be held responsible for the natural consequences of acting on that negligent ignorance has nothing to do with whether he 'really consented'.

[26] Cf. Carr (1990, p. 343), who argues that, by participating in a practice, an agent incurs an obligation of 'familiarizing herself with all the rules associated with' that practice; from that, he infers

Culpable ignorance presupposes, of course, that Bloggs could and should have known that there was something further he needed to know. If there was no way he could possibly have known that different gestures are taken to be signs of consent in different auction houses, or that this was one of them, then his ignorance would not have been culpable.[27] Or again, we cannot say he 'should' have found out what the local conventions were if there is no way in which he 'could' have done so. In that case the negligent-due-to-culpable-ignorance argument for allocating to Bloggs the burdens of his mistake about consent cannot get off the ground.

4.4.2 Voluntary Assumption of Risk of Errors about Consent

Another reason for holding the person who makes the mistake about consent responsible for bearing the ensuing burdens might be based on his 'voluntary assumption of the risk'.[28] Feinberg offers the example of '*A*... acting in a way that is moderately risky to *B* without *B*'s explicit permission...' Then, Feinberg concludes, '*A* assumes a moral risk himself'; and 'if *B*'s interests, contrary to *A*'s expectations, are set back, then... *B* has a grievance against him, and a claim for redress...'[29]

Suppose that the mistaken party knew that there was a non-negligible risk that he was mistaken as to what counts as a sign of the other's consent. And suppose he voluntarily proceeded with the interaction nonetheless.[30] (Think of the case of someone having what seems to be consensual sex with someone whom he knows

that 'by participating in [the practice, the agent] tacitly consents to [its rules] regardless of whether she is aware of all the rules...'. I agree there is some such obligation, but I disagree that tacit consent is involved. In my auction example, Bloggs may be duty bound to pay the price stipulated by the auctioneer for the vase (cf. footnote 24 in this section), not because he has tacitly consented to doing so, but rather because he acted in culpable ignorance of (in violation of his duty to find out) what others would take as signs of consent.

[27] Although arguably he should still bear some of the consequences of his error (see Sections 1.4.3.4 above and 4.6 and 4.7 below).

[28] In tort law, it is a defence available to someone who has been proven to have been negligent in causing harm to someone else that the latter 'voluntarily assumed the risk'. Here, obviously, I am adapting that rule for a quite different purpose. In recommending her 'Modifiable Consent Standard' whereby sexual partners would consent to certain kinds of sexual acts in the future without requiring explicit consent on each occasion, Pallikkathayil (2020, p. 114) describes that in 'assumption of risk' terms (as enabling 'people to determine for themselves how much unwanted sexual contact they are willing to risk in order to obtain experiences of intimacy that are not proceeded by affirmative behavior in the moment'). Bolinger (2019, pp. 186–8) similarly talks about consent-givers assuming the risk that they might not actually like what happens when consent-receivers act upon the consent that has been given (consented-to surgery having unanticipatable bad side-effects, for example).

[29] Feinberg 1986a, p. 173. Feinberg is here talking about a case in which *A* is so acting 'on the grounds that he had good evidence that *B* would be willing for him to do so, and would have explicitly signified his consent if *A* had only been in a position to ask for it'; but his point about the assumption of risk is wholly independent of that.

[30] Of course, were he acting under duress, it would not be a case of '*voluntary* assumption of risk' at all.

is an uncertain speaker of the language in which that consent was communicated.[31]) Then that party can be said to have 'voluntarily assumed the risk of being in error', and should bear any burdens arising from such an error.[32]

Again, however, this way of resolving the issue only arises when the mistaken party knew that there was a non-negligible risk of his being mistaken. If he had no way of knowing that there was any such risk, then he could not have assumed that risk voluntarily.

4.5 Knowingly Taking Advantage of Another's Mistake

Sometimes there is another relatively easy way of answering the question of who should bear the burden of mistakes about consent. Those are cases where one party knew the other party was acting on mistaken beliefs about what is intended as (or taken to be) a sign of consent, and the knowing party uses that knowledge to take unfair advantage of the mistaken party.[33] Then, I suggest, the knowing party should be the one to bear the burden of the mistake that he knew was being made.

Take the auction example again. Suppose that Bloggs had only very recently arrived from a country where the way—and the only way—to make a bid at an auction is to shout out in response to the auctioneer's question 'Do I hear two million?' the words 'Two million!' Further suppose the auctioneer knew Bloggs was under the impression that the same rules prevail here. That is to say, the auctioneer knew that Bloggs did not know that, according to the conventions prevailing in this auction room, scratching one's head in response to the auctioneer's question would also constitute a sign of consent.

When scratching his head at the auction, Bloggs thus inadvertently sends what under the rules governing that auction house constitutes a signal that he consents to purchasing the item at the price indicated. Bloggs has made a mistake about signs of consent. But if the auctioneer knew that Bloggs did not know that that would be taken as a sign of consent, it would be unfair to hold Bloggs to his inadvertent 'commitment'.[34]

[31] Or who is drunk, maybe (or maybe not) so drunk as to be incompetent to give valid sex (Dixon 2001a).

[32] This corresponds to the rule in the law of contracts that 'a party bears the risk of a mistake when... he is aware, at the time the contract is made, that he has only limited knowledge with respect to the facts to which the mistake relates but treats his limited knowledge as sufficient' (ALI 1981, § 154(b)).

[33] Both of the cases below are just an application of the rule of contract law according to which, 'where a mistake of one party at the time a contract was made as to a basic assumption on which he made the contract has a material effect on the agreed exchange of performances that is adverse to him, the contract is voidable by him if... the other party had reason to know of the mistake or his fault caused the mistake' (ALI 1981, § 153(b)). Economists are acutely sensitive to how 'asymmetrical information' distorts market outcomes (Arrow 1963; Akerlof 1970; Mirrlees 1971).

[34] It would constitute what lawyers in other contexts refer to as 'a failure to act in good faith and in accordance with reasonable standards of fair dealing' (ALI 1981, § 154).

Note well, once again: That is different from saying that 'Bloggs did not really consent'. That may be true, too. After all, Bloggs did not mentally consent, and that is a necessary condition of consenting.[35] But the argument from unfairness works differently to that. It says that when one party knows that the other is making a mistake about what counts as a sign of consent, it is unfair for the knowing party (the auctioneer in this case) to hold the unknowing party to it.

Now reverse the situation. Suppose that Bloggs knows fully well that the auctioneer will take the head-scratch as a sign of consent. But he does not really mean to consent by so doing. He is bidding insincerely. He has no intention of paying the price he seemingly agreed to by his head-scratch (although if no one else bids after him he may of course get trapped into doing so). Instead he is just in league with the owner of the property being auctioned, trying to drive up the price. The auctioneer, however, has no way of knowing that Bloggs did not by his head-scratching intend 'real consent' at all.

In that sort of case, it seems more reasonable to let the full burden of the auctioneer's mistake about Bloggs's sign of consent fall on Bloggs. Again, that outcome may be overdetermined: Bloggs should be penalized for his insincerity and perhaps twice over for his immorally conspiring.[36] But again, part of the reason that Bloggs should bear the burden of the auctioneer's mistake about his head-scratching constituting a sign of consent was the differential knowledge enjoyed by the two parties. Bloggs knew the auctioneer would make that mistake and he knew the auctioneer could not know he was making a mistake. In those circumstances, it seems only fair to hold Bloggs to the 'commitment' communicated by his head-scratching.

Again, note that that is not because Bloggs has 'genuinely consented'. Insofar as the necessary mental element is missing, Bloggs has not consented at all. Instead, my argument here is one grounded in fairness. Given that Bloggs deliberately misled others into believing that he consented, it is only fair to require Bloggs to bear the burdens of his deliberate fraud by requiring him to go through with the transaction to which he purportedly consented.

4.6 Mistakes Arising from Innocent Error

Many of the cases discussed in previous sections involved allocating costs for mistakes about consent on the basis of fault of some sort or another. Someone was

[35] As I say in Section 1.3.2, he must at the very least intend that others understand him to be consenting, which he does not in this case.

[36] Indeed, I have argued in Section 1.4.3.2 that the consequence of Bloggs' deliberate fraud is that he should be taken to have thereby forfeited the rights he purported to waive through his false consent.

at fault for sending misleading signals or for misunderstanding others' signals or for knowingly taking advantage of others' errors. And in those cases, the suggestion was that the person who was at fault should bear the burdens of the mistake about consent.

But of course there remains a large class of cases where mistakes about consent involve no fault (not even culpable negligence or culpable ignorance) on anyone's part. Such cases involve nothing more than an 'innocent error'—'innocent' in the sense that (i) the error was not known to the erring party and (ii) it was not the case that the error could and should have been known to the erring party. Who should bear the burden of mistakes about consent in cases like that is less clear than in previous cases where fault of some sort was involved.

Broadly speaking, there seem to be three possible approaches to such cases if we persist with the assumption—to be relaxed in Section 4.7—that the burden must be allocated entirely to one party or entirely to the other.[37] One is to make one party or the other strictly liable for the costs of the mistake. A second is to let the burdens of the mistake lie where they fall. A third is to allocate the burdens of the mistake to whichever party will find them least burdensome.

4.6.1 Letting Burdens Lie Where They Fall

One way of dealing with the burdens of mistakes is to do nothing about them, but rather just let the burdens lie where they fall. Someone has made a mistake about consent and someone (perhaps someone else, perhaps the same person) has suffered losses in consequence of the error. The proposal here in view is simply to let whomever suffers the losses bear those losses.

Outside the context of consent, letting costs lie where they fall is a common default rule for allocating costs. That is the received principle of tort law, where no party can be deemed to have been at fault for having acted wrongly or negligently. That is the received principle of burden (non)sharing in military alliances like NATO—whichever country provides the troops pays for them.[38] And letting the costs lie where they fall—letting each party pay their own legal costs, rather than awarding costs against the unsuccessful litigant—is commonly ordered by the judge at the end of a civil suit.[39]

[37] Recall, however, that that assumption is purely for expository convenience. Splitting the costs between them is actually the best solution in cases of innocent error, as argued in Sections 1.4.3.4 above and 4.7 below.

[38] Homan 2006. [39] New Zealand Ministry of Justice 2020.

4.6.2 Allocating Burdens to Those Who Find Them Least Burdensome

Another approach would be to let the burden fall on whomever would find it least burdensome.[40] Burdensomeness is a joint function of (a) how badly affected each party is affected by the mistake about consent and (b) the capacity of each for coping with those burdens.[41] That is the obvious consequentialist total-cost-minimization way of allocating the burden of mistakes regarding consent.

4.6.3 Strict Liability for Errors about Consent

A final—and generally less defensible—approach to allocating costs in the absence of fault is 'strict liability'. In tort law, liability is ordinarily grounded in either fault or negligence (which morally is just a lesser form of fault). But there is also provision in tort law for holding someone 'strictly liable' for harm that occurs as a result of his activities, even if he was in no way at fault for the harm and indeed even if he took every possible precaution to avoid it. In tort law, that is done only in very exceptional cases, as I elaborate immediately below. Morally, that is as it should be. Some very special reason needs to be given for why someone should bear all the costs for an unfortunate outcome for which he was not at fault, rather than (as I go on to suggest in Section 4.7) those costs being shared in some equitable fashion among everyone party to the unfortunate events.

In what follows, I shall canvass two possible ways in which strict liability might apply in mistaken-consent cases. We might hold those who mistakenly (but faultlessly) believe that they have received consent strictly liable for any burdens that ensue from their acting on those mistaken beliefs (Section 4.6.3.1). Alternatively, we might confer strict liability on those who (again, faultlessly) lead others to believe mistakenly that they have given them their consent (Section 4.6.3.2). To foreshadow, my conclusion will be that neither is a particularly commendable strategy morally, although there may be good pragmatic grounds for pursuing the latter policy.

4.6.3.1 Strict Liability for the Putative Consent-receiver

Even in cases of 'innocent error' where there is no fault on anyone's part it remains the case that rights are in play—specifically, the rights that a consent-giver is

[40] Or, to anticipate Section 4.7, to let the burden fall on people in proportion to how burdensome it would be for them, if the burden is divisible.

[41] This akin to the 'deep pockets' principle for allocating the costs of accidents more generally. See, e.g., Calabresi 1970, p. 21; MacCoun 1993.

thought to have waived in giving consent. Hence the deontologically correct approach might seem to be to allocate the burden of mistakes about consent to the (seeming) consent-receiver, on the grounds that, in acting on consent that they wrongly thought had been given, they are actually violating rights without permission.

In the cases here in view, however, they are violating rights *innocently*. They did not know they were doing that; on the contrary, they thought (and it was eminently reasonable for them to think) that they had gotten permission. Neither, *ex hypothesi*, could and should they have known that the signs they reasonably thought betokened consent did not actually convey that. Owing to mistakes about what constituted signs of consent, rights ended up being violated—but the mistakes were innocent errors for which no one is to blame. The absence of fault is precisely why there was a need to resort to notions of strict liability in such cases.

In tort law, strict liability is typically visited upon someone because he was engaging in 'ultra-hazardous activities' of one sort or another.[42] Here I shall be considering whether we can sometimes adapt that rule for purposes of deciding who should bear the burden of mistakes about consent. That is to say, might there be certain actions for which consent is required that are sufficiently 'special' that anyone undertaking them is on notice that they will be held 'strictly liable' if they end up performing those actions without the other's consent, despite the fact that they took every possible precaution to avoid mistakes in believing that they had the other's consent?[43]

Only a very limited set of activities seem sufficiently 'special' to warrant applying such an extraordinary liability rule in cases of consent. Violations of bodily integrity are perhaps the most prominent candidates. Such cases are frequently discussed, particularly in the wake of the #MeToo movement. No doubt it is true, and unexceptionable, that 'you must be very, very certain you have the other person's consent before engaging in sexual acts with them'.[44] Perhaps, some might suggest, we should go further and say that 'you will be strictly liable if it turns out that you have engaged in sexual acts with someone without their consent'.

[42] ALI 1934, § 520. The phrase was revised to 'abnormally dangerous' in the subsequent *Restatement*, which also stipulated that the activity in question is 'not a matter of common usage' (ALI 1979, § 520(d)); but Shavell (2019) argues persuasively that that limitation is widely unwarranted and, indeed, that it is regarded as such.

[43] Note that this is not just to say that some 'higher standard of care in verifying consent' applies. With strict liability, you are liable if it turns out you were wrong, regardless of how much care you took to avoid errors. But note, too, that there remains even with strict liability an evidentiary issue of whether or not you actually acted without the other's consent at the time you acted. Strict liability does not mean that you are liable in case the other retrospectively regretted and tried to withdraw consent.

[44] As argued in Section 1.1.

Notice, however, that bodily integrity is also at stake when a surgeon operates on a patient. There too, we ordinarily expect the surgeon to go to great lengths to get consent from the patient (provided she is conscious and competent) before cutting her open; and if she refuses consent we expect the surgeon not to cut the patient open, even if doing so would be manifestly in her best interests. But if an accident victim is comatose and incapable of giving consent (and there are no close relatives available capable of giving surrogate consent), surgeons operating upon her to save her life are *not* strictly liable for 'medical battery' even if the patient turns out to be someone who never would have consented to surgery.[45]

What is the difference between the accidental rapist and the unaware surgeon, beyond the general 'sex is special' arguments?[46] The key point of difference would seem to be that the surgeon, like members of the 'helping professions' more generally, occupies a special 'fiduciary' social role that enjoins him to do things in the best interests of those entrusted to his care.[47] Even the most attentive sexual partners, in contrast, are never guided exclusively by what is in the other's best interests without any regard whatsoever to their own needs and desires.[48]

That observation merely suggests that there are weaker grounds for holding the unaware surgeon strictly liable than the accidental rapist. It does not provide any positive argument for holding the accidental rapist strictly liable. Perhaps it merely serves to show that people engaged in sexual activities must have particularly good reasons for thinking that the other consents to those activities. What count as 'particularly good reasons' then needs to be spelt out, of course. But however stringent that standard may be, it structurally stops short of strict liability. If they had 'reasonable' beliefs ('reasonable' to a suitably high standard) that they had the other's consent, they would not be liable for the wrong they committed when acting on what turned out to be a mistaken belief.[49]

4.6.3.2 Strict Liability for the Putative Consent-giver

The second option is to visit strict liability for the burdens of mistakes about consent upon the putative consent-giver. I say 'putative', because in the cases in view he did not intend to give consent; and since the necessary mental element was missing, he did not genuinely give consent.[50] But I call him a 'putative

[45] Such cases are further discussed in Chapter 11 below. [46] Goldman 1977.

[47] Frankel 1983. I say more about 'fiduciary relationships' and the special responsibilities that come with them in Sections 6.2.3 and 8.4 below.

[48] I return to this point and elaborate it further in Section 8.4 below.

[49] Bolinger (2021) offers a parallel argument that 'reasonable' beliefs that they are under imminent threat of grievous harm can excuse people from wrongfully inflicting defensive harm on people they think are threatening them. Note that in both the case of mistaken consent and the case of mistaken self-defence it is, on my account, still wrong for people to have done what they did—what they did was excused, but not justified, by their reasonable albeit erroneous beliefs.

[50] See the discussion of the ontologically necessary elements of consent in Section 1.2.

consent-giver' because he has (innocently, inadvertently in the cases here in view) done something that conventionally constitutes a sign of consent. From the signals that he has sent, others quite reasonably (albeit incorrectly) infer that he has consented. The proposal here in view is that anyone who performs actions that conventionally signal consent should be strictly liable for any burdens that arise from his mistaken signals.

There are two arguments in favour of that approach. The weaker, in my view, is the argument from 'opacity'.[51] Other people's behaviour is observable, their mental life is not. If we want to enable people confidently do the sorts of things that require other people's consent, that consent had therefore better be predicated on those behavioural manifestations alone. If someone gave conventional signals of consent, then other people should be able to act in reliance on those without risk of subsequently discovering to their cost that 'he didn't really mean it'. That could be accomplished by making those who give conventional signs of consent strictly liable for any burdens from mistakes that arise from having done so.[52]

In assessing that argument, we need to decide which is more important: 'enabling people confidently doing the sorts of things that require other people's consent' or 'protecting people from having those sorts of things done to them without their consent'. In effect, making putative consent-givers strictly liable for their mistakes prioritizes the former over the latter.[53] But surely that gets things the wrong way around. Surely it is more important to protect a person's rights than to facilitate others' infringement of them. That is the whole point of ascribing rights to people in the first place.

It would be perfectly fair to assign the burdens of mistakes to people who have been negligent in employing conventional signs of consent (or negligent in not finding out what they are).[54] But remember, that is not what we are talking about,

[51] Both the term and the particular version of the argument outlined below owe to Bolinger (2019), although the basic idea is much older (see, e.g., Brett 1998). It should be noted that Bolinger herself stops well short of endorsing a strict liability approach, however: she specifies that '*B* receives a consent-based permission from *A* just if . . . *A* communicates that they consent . . . and [this] is *not undermined by B' s best available evidence*' that *A* did not thereby intend to consent (2019, p. 190, emphasis added); and Bolinger holds *A* responsible for burdens that *B* incurs from her employing conventional signs of consent only if it is 'public knowledge' what the signs of consent are, so 'agents can reasonably demand that those who do not wish to communicate consent avoid the behavior', thus making *B*'s employment of them 'negligent or reckless' (p. 192).

[52] We would also have to add a clause to the effect that there was no coercion inducing them to give those signs (Brett 1998), of course. But we could set an objective ('reasonable person') test of that rather than a subjective one ('were they in fear of serious injury?').

[53] Indeed, it comes perilously close to violating the presumption, outlined in Section 1.1, that you do not have another person's consent unless you have good grounds for thinking that you do. In the case here in view you have *some* grounds for thinking you do (he said it). But are those *good* grounds, in the absence of any reason to believe that he meant it or, indeed, in the presence of some reasons to believe that perhaps he did not?

[54] As argued in Sections 1.4.3.3 and 4.4.1 above.

here. Instead we are considering cases in which theirs was a completely innocent error, to which no fault attaches.

The stronger (but in the end still not compelling) argument for visiting strict liability on the putative consent-giver, in my view, is the argument from 'disingenuous denial'. As J.L. Austin says of the parallel practice of promising, 'if we slip into thinking that such utterances are reports, true or false, of the performance of inward... acts, we open a loophole to perjurers and welshers and bigamists and so on'.[55] That, Austin says, is why we must socially insist that 'your word is our bond'[56]—if you say you consent, then you will be socially treated as having consented, whatever your mental reservations. Otherwise people could invalidate consent to sales of property or to marriage simply by asserting, 'I did not really mean it when I said it.'[57]

Of course, people should ordinarily be allowed to revoke their consent if they want, provided they compensate others for their reasonable reliance upon their previous signs of consent.[58] But, the thought here in view goes, they should not be allowed to withdraw their consent willy-nilly, without compensation, simply by saying 'I never intended to consent'. The proffered reason why they should not be allowed to get away with that claim is that, even if what they say is true, there is no way for others to tell if it is true, either ahead of their own acting (the 'opacity' argument) or after the fact (the 'disingenuous denial' argument).

The 'disingenuous denial' argument for strict liability thus rests heavily on the 'opacity' argument. But even if the forward-looking version of the 'opacity' argument is true (which it probably is not in all cases), the backward-looking version required by the 'disingenuous denial' argument is quite certainly too strong to be true universally or even at all generally. If it were, the entire criminal code would be a dead letter, since a criminal conviction requires *mens rea* on the part of the defendant. If a person's intentions were always completely opaque to outside observers, even after the fact when the case comes to trial, the prosecution's burden of proof on that score could never be met.

While it would thus be a gross overstatement to claim people's intentions are always opaque to others, even after the fact, let us allow that sometimes they are. Sometimes when a person says 'I consented in innocent error' they are lying, and sometimes when they say that they are telling the truth—and sometimes outsiders have no way of telling which is which.

The ordinary way of approaching such situations would be to set a defeasible presumption one way or the other. Either presume that they are lying unless it can

[55] Austin 1979, p. 236; see similarly Austin 1962, p. 10. [56] Austin 1962, p. 10; 1979, p. 236.

[57] In his seventeenth-century *Table Talk*, John Selden (1689, ch. 77, sec. 2; 1934, p. 60) says something similar against claims that ignorance of the law should be a legal excuse: 'Ignorance of the Law excuses no Man; not that all Men know the Law, but because 'tis an excuse every man will plead, and no Man can tell how to confute him.'

[58] As argued in Chapter 7 below.

be demonstrated to the requisite degree of confidence that they are not; or else presume that they are telling the truth unless it can be demonstrated to the requisite degree of confidence that they are not. Proceeding in that way, the key question is which way to set the presumption and, secondarily, how strong the presumption should be.

There are various different ways of answering those questions. A highly principled way would be to say that the paramount consideration should be respecting people's rights. That in turn implies a presumption that people do not consent to others doing things that would violate their rights if done without their consent, unless there is strong evidence that they do consent. A more pragmatic way of answering those questions would turn on relative stakes or relative frequencies or a combination of both. How frequently are claims of consenting in innocent error actually true, as compared to how frequently they are false? Which is ordinarily worse, having your claim treated as false when it is really true, or having it treated as true when it is really false?[59] If (a) it is ordinarily much worse to treat true claims of having consented in innocent error as false and (b) true claims are far more common than false ones, then we should once again set a relatively strong presumption in favour of treating such claims as true.

The structural upshot is the same either way. A defeasible presumption is set. But being defeasible, the presumption can be overriden with sufficiently strong evidence. If the presumption is that claims of having consented in innocent error are true, sufficiently strong evidence in any given case that the claim is false will override that presumption. And if the presumption is that claims of having consented in innocent error are false, sufficiently strong evidence in any given case that the claim is true will override that presumption.

Imposing a rule of strict liability on putative consent-givers for the costs arising from their seeming consent would have the same effect as setting an *irrefutable* presumption that any claim of having consented in innocent error is false. Under a strict liability rule, putative consent-givers would be liable for the consequences of their seeming consent, whether given in innocent error or otherwise. Case-by-case assessments of the sort described above are ruled out by a blanket policy of strict liability.

That might be appropriate if we could be sure that all claims that consent had been given in innocent error were fraudulent. But in the cases here in view, *ex hypothesi* they are not—we are explicitly considering, here, only cases of innocent error. And in some cases it is going to be demonstrably true the seeming consent had indeed been communicated in innocent error. Take the case, for example, in which the putative consent-giver is new to the country and obviously has a

[59] In the former case the reference is ordinarily 'how bad is it for the putative consent-giver', whereas in the latter it is ordinarily to 'how bad is it for the putative consent-receiver', of course.

weak grasp of its language and other local conventions surrounding signals of consent—such a bad grasp that it is not even the case that we can reasonably say that he 'could and should have known' there were such conventions to be discovered.[60]

The arguments above suggest that the most reasonable way of setting the presumption is to treat claims that consent has been given in innocent error as true. But suppose that for some reason of policy or principle we want to give people reasonable reassurance that they can rely upon consent that they seem to have been given. In that case, it would seem preferable to adopt a defeasible presumption that consent conventionally communicated is binding (and that claims it was given in innocent error are defeasibly presumptively false), rather than to adopt a policy of strict liability which would in effect makes such a presumption absolutely binding. The defeasible presumption would be open to being defeated by a clear demonstration that the conventional signs of consent had been emitted in innocent error. The strict liability approach would admit of no such excuses or exceptions.

Innocent errors might not be all that common, and convincing evidence of them may be even less so. Still, the structural question is simply whether we should leave the door open to true claims that consent had been given in innocent error, however common or uncommon they may be. My response is that there is little to be lost and much to be gained by leaving that door open, in a way that the strict liability approach does not.

4.7 Burden Sharing

So far I have been speaking generically about 'bearing the burdens' of a mistake in consenting. Let me say, in concluding, a little more about what that might involve. And in so doing, let me relax the assumption—introduced in Section 4.2, purely in order to simplify the discussion—that the burdens of a mistake about consent must be borne wholly by one or the other of the two parties.

Suppose it is the seeming consent-giver who is allocated the burden of others mistakenly supposing he consented. There are two principal ways in which he might be asked to bear the burden.[61] One is, to borrow a term from contract law,

[60] 'Ignorance of law, within the meaning of the rule that ignorance of law will not excuse, is to be construed as meaning ignorance of the laws of one's own country or state, not laws of foreign countries or states, which are regarded as mistakes of fact' (*Marshall v. Coleman*, 58 NE 628, 637, 187 Ill. 556). A wide range of individuals (people under age 25, women, soldiers, peasants) were excused ignorance of the law in Roman times on the grounds that their status was such they had no reason to be expected to know what the law was (Keedy 1908, p. 80). People might be excused ignorance of consenting conventions on similar grounds.

[61] As already foreshadowed in Sections 1.4.3 and 2.2.5 above.

'specific performance'—permitting the other to do what he thought he had consent to do. The other is to compensate the other for the costs he has incurred in reasonably relying upon the consent that he thought that he had been given.[62]

If it is the seeming consent-receiver who is allocated the burden of mistakenly supposing that someone else has consented, there are two analogous ways in which he might be asked to bear the burden. First, and most obviously, he could be required not to do what he mistakenly thought that he had the other's consent to do. That is of course relevant only insofar as he has not yet done (or is still in the process of doing) it. Second, he could be required both to bear his own costs of things he has done in reliance upon the consent that he wrongly thought that he had, in addition to compensating the other for any damage the other suffered in consequence of his error.[63]

With compensation now in play as one possible remedy, however, the possibility of dividing the burden between perpetrators and victims of mistaken consent comes into view. In partialling out liability between them, all the same considerations as before apply. In cases where both parties were somewhat at fault, we can allocate liability to them in proportion to their relative faultiness, instead of allocating the whole burden to the one most at fault. In cases of innocent error, we can allocate the burdens equally or in proportion to the comparative costs each bore in consequence of the mistake or their comparative capacity for bearing those costs.[64]

[62] I will return to say more about both in Section 7.3, in connection with revoking consent. Contract law also allows damages on the basis of 'expectation interests' and 'restitution interests'. But I take it the latter are less relevant in cases involving unilateral consent than in cases involving bilateral exchanges of promises. Protecting 'expectation interests' may sometimes be an appropriate remedy for breach of promises and breach of contracts; and I have argued that it is likewise in cases of deliberately fraudulent false consent (Section 1.4.3.2). But protecting 'reliance interests' is more relevant in cases of merely culpably negligent false consent—and doing that only partially may be more appropriate in cases of false consent given in innocent error (Sections 1.4.3.3, 1.4.3.4 and 2.2.5).

[63] Not all such damages are capable of being compensated, of course. Section 7.3.2.5 proposes a method of handling those cases.

[64] Which is precisely what was suggested in Section 1.4.3.4, for cases of false consent through innocent error.

5
Consenting Without Knowing

Can you consent without knowing? Without knowing *that* what you are doing counts as consenting? Without knowing *to what* you are consenting? Textbook accounts would say 'no' to both.[1] But as I shall show in this chapter, there may arguably be ways in which you can consent without knowing to what you are consenting, exactly. Furthermore, there are cases in which you may properly be treated at least 'as if you consented' without knowing, in both respects; hence, claims in the neighbourhood of, and with the same practical upshot as, the target claims will prove to be true.

5.1 Consenting Without Knowing That You Are Consenting

'If *X* consents to *Y*'s doing φ, then *X* must realize that this is what he/she is doing' is ordinarily regarded as an utter commonplace, both legally and morally.[2] But is that commonplace necessarily true? Over the course of this section I shall be arguing that it is not. You can, unknowingly, consent—or anyway do something 'consent-like' that carries just the same consequences.[3]

5.1.1 False Signals and 'As If Consent'

Perhaps the most compelling reason for thinking that you cannot consent without knowing that that you are consenting is that consent must be intentional, and you cannot intend anything that is unknown to you.[4] You can, however, socially signal

[1] This basic point is of long standing; see, e.g., Pufendorf (1672/1710, bk. 3, ch. 6, sec. 4, para. 2). Simmons (1979, p. 70) tersely says, *a propos* both consenting and promising, 'One must know what one is doing in order to perform these sorts of acts.' Faden and Beauchamp (1986, p. 300) complain that the modern 'literature on informed consent' in medical and research ethics 'neglects almost altogether the fact that persons must understand not only *what* they are authorizing but, more basically, *that* they are authorizing'; and they go on to explain at length what each involves and why it is morally important (chs. 7–9).

[2] The formulation is Kleinig's (1982, p. 106) but similar statements are ubiquitous.

[3] In the phrasing, and on the argument, of Section 1.4.

[4] This formulation is neutral as between Section 1.3.2.1's two different things the consent-giver might intend, which I discuss further below. Simmons (1976, p. 276) alludes somewhat more tentatively to a close connection between intending and knowing when writing, 'consent must be given intentionally and (perhaps this is redundant) knowingly'.

Consent Matters. Robert E. Goodin, Oxford University Press. © Robert E. Goodin 2024.
DOI: 10.1093/oso/9780192889027.003.0005

consent without mentally intending it. That is to say, you can trigger the social conventions by which others will understand you to be consenting without your having performed the mental act of consenting.[5]

Sometimes you do that accidentally, through innocent error.[6] Sometimes you do that through culpable negligence.[7] I shall focus the bulk of the discussion in this section on the latter case, although much the same applies in the former as well.[8]

First, however, let me briefly discuss the even more dramatic case in which you socially signal consent, not accidentally or negligently, but deliberately fraudulently. That is the case in which you know fully well that what you are doing constitutes socially signalling consent, and you do that knowing fully well that you do not mentally consent.[9]

The case of deliberately fraudulently signalling consent does not itself constitute a case of 'consenting without knowing', of course. (*Ex hypothesi*, it was deliberate: you know precisely what you are doing in sending the false signals.) That case is of interest in the present context in that it shows most starkly that there can be (some sort of) 'consenting without intending'. That demonstration undermines, in turn, the most fundamental reason for thinking that there can never be any sort of 'consenting without knowing'.

Clearly, it is perfectly possible for me to signal consent insincerely—for me to communicate my consent to permitting something to be done without my having the slightest mental intention of actually permitting that thing to be done. I can socially signal my consent to an agreement without having any intention whatsoever of keeping my side of the bargain. So too can I socially signal my consent to your using my car, fully intending revoke that consent before you have a chance to use it.

Of course it is possible for me to send false signals of consent of that sort. No one would dispute that. And of course it would be wrong of me to do so.[10] No one would dispute that, either. But does my having done so count as having consented? Many would dispute that, and in the end I myself deny it. Nevertheless, here is an argument for thinking that socially signalling consent, even falsely, does indeed constitute consent. Focus on the distinctive reason why it would be wrong for me falsely to signal consent.[11] My falsely signalling consent, and then not carrying through with it, amounts to reneging on a commitment I made to you

[5] See Section 1.4 above. [6] See Sections 1.4 and 4.6 above.

[7] See Sections 1.4 and 4.4.1 above.

[8] False consent in innocent error just counts as 'as if consent' in a somewhat more attenuated sense, as Section 1.4 above has shown.

[9] See Sections 1.4 and 2.3.1 above.

[10] Of course, it would also be wrong not to permit something to which you sincerely consented (unless you first revoked your consent in the proper way, as specified in Chapter 7 below). But for the next few paragraphs I am going to be focusing on the case of 'deliberately fraudulently reporting consent' as set out in Section 1.4, above.

[11] In addition to the more generic reason it is wrong: i.e., I lied. In the end, that more generic reason, combined with the subject matter about which you lied (about consenting for me to do something that

when socially signalling my consent. But if consenting-without-intending-to-permit-the-thing-consented-to were deemed not to be any form of consent at all, then you would have no grounds for complaint when I renege—for if I have not given consent, I have not have made any commitment upon which I could renege.[12]

That consideration might seem to argue in favour of the second analysis of what intention is required for consenting canvassed in Section 1.3.2.1, according to which 'giving consent' requires merely that you intend for your signal to be understood by others as indicating that you are giving consent. Even in the case here in view, where you are insincerely signalling your consent to something that you have no intention of actually permitting, you nonetheless clearly intend for others to understand you to be giving them permissive consent.[13] And on the analysis here in view, that would be enough to qualify you as consenting.

Lacking as it does the necessary mental element, insincere consent cannot count ontologically as 'genuine consent'. But socially, at least, deliberately fraudulently reporting consent does nevertheless provide good grounds for treating the insincere consenter 'as if he consented'.[14] All the same practical consequences follow. In the case sketched above, that would include you having grounds for complaint if I renege on my seeming-consent—not because I have reneged on my genuine consent, but rather because I misled you as to whether I consented at all. Indeed, I have argued above that, by deliberately fraudulently reporting consent, the fraudster literally forfeits the rights which his faux-consent purported to waive.[15]

In any case, focusing exclusively upon the intentions of the speaker (the consent-giver) would ignore the important role of uptake on the part of hearer (the consent-receiver). I have argued that uptake is not *ontologically* necessary for consent to exist.[16] But in order for consent to serve its *social function*, consent must surely be communicated and the communication must be received as well as sent.[17] Socially, giving consent is inherently interpersonal, as its Latin root ('*com*', together with) implies.

if done without your consent would violate your rights), would on the analysis of Section 1.4.3.2 mean that you have forfeited your rights and may be treated 'as if you consented' to me doing the thing you pretended to consent to me doing.

[12] Alexander (2014) distinguishes between 'wrongdoing' (someone's actually crossing someone else's moral boundary without their consent) and 'culpability' (someone's believing they are crossing someone else's moral boundary without their consent). The person misled into believing he has consent, when he didn't, would on that account be engaged in wrongdoing of a non-culpable sort. But Alexander's framework provides no account of, or remedy for, the wrong done by the person who misled him. Holding the misleading 'consent-giver' to what he has misleadingly said, treating him 'as if he consented', would be one apt remedy.

[13] As argued in Section 2.3.1. [14] See Section 1.4.3.2. [15] In Sections 1.4.2 and 1.4.3.2.

[16] In Section 1.2.1.2. This matter is of course philosophically disputed: cf., e.g., Healey (2015, pp. 358 ff.) and Dougherty (2021a, ch. 6).

[17] See Section 1.2.2. Giving consent is granting a permission, and how can I have your permission without your having given it to me? Seeing consent as a 'permission' and not merely as a 'moral-transformer' makes it more like a 'promise', which Alexander, Hurd and Westen (2016) agree *does* require communication.

It is standardly said that for the giving of consent to serve this interpersonal permission-granting role, those receiving it—along with anyone policing whether those who need consent actually have it—must have been given some indication of the mental acts that have been performed by those giving it. In Hobbes' famous phrase, signs of consent to a contract are 'whatsoever sufficiently argues the *will of the contractor*'.[18]

At first brush, the emphasis there would seem to be on 'the will of the contractor'. Those were the words Hobbes himself italicized, after all. But note well that what Hobbes actually says is that signs of consent to a contract are 'whatsoever sufficiently *argues* the will of the contractor'. 'Argues' here means 'betokens', which is to say, provides external evidence to others that that is indeed the will of the contractor.[19]

Now, as I have said, the signs by which we betoken our consent are purely conventional.[20] Language itself is one set of conventions. So too are social understandings of what is communicated by nodding one's head or 'shaking on it'.[21] That opens up the possibility for someone with an imperfect grasp of the conventions accidentally to consent without intending to consent, by doing something that (unbeknownst to him) is conventionally taken to be a sign of consent in the context in question.

Let me therefore now shift the focus from the previous case of someone 'deliberately fraudulently reporting consent' to a case of someone employing the socially conventional signs of consent unintentionally but culpably negligently. This case is much closer to this section's target of someone 'consenting without knowing he is consenting'. *Ex hypothesi*, in the case of someone who conveyed conventional signals of consent unintentionally, he did not know that that is what he is doing. But because he did that culpably negligently (i.e., he could and should have known that that is how those conventional signals would be understood), he ought to be treated 'as if he consented', with some of the same material consequences as if he genuinely consented.[22] So he did what he did unknowingly, and what he did is the same as consenting in its consequences.[23]

[18] Hobbes 1651, ch. 14.

[19] *Oxford English Dictionary*, q.v. 'argue (v.)', def. 3. 'Betoken', in turn, means: 'To give evidence of, point to, indicate, show'; *Oxford English Dictionary*, q.v. 'betoken (v.)', def. 4a.

[20] On which see further Sections 2.3.2 and 3.2 above.

[21] Pufendorf 1672/1710, bk 3, ch. 6, sec 15.

[22] As argued in Sections 1.4.3.3 and 4.4.1 above. 'Some of', because the proper remedy in the case of culpable negligence is not that the false consenter must permit that to which he has seemingly consented (as in the case of genuine consent or deliberately fraudulent consent) but, instead, that he must fully compensate the putative consent-receiver for the costs that he incurred in relying on the false consent when the false consenter fails to permit what he seemingly consented to permit (cf. Sections 1.4.3.2 and 1.4.3.3). That is the same remedy that properly applies when a genuine consenter revokes consent (Section 7.3.2.4 below). Hence we can say that we are treating the culpably negligent false consenter 'as if he is revoking consent' when he refuses to permit that to which he has seemingly consented.

[23] The same as for revoking genuine consent, per the footnote immediately above.

Return to Chapter 4's case of scratching your head at an auction. When you scratched your head, everyone else in the auction room understood you to have consented to purchase the vase for the price the auctioneer had just indicated, even if you had no such intention and were just scratching an itch. Suppose that at least some of those present relied to their detriment on that understanding of what you had done.

Some may say that, because you lacked the relevant intention, you did not genuinely consent and you should not be bound to buy the vase for the price indicated. Hobbes, for example, says that signs of consent must be given 'with understanding of what they signify' in order for them to betoken consent.[24]

Concluding thusly, however, would be hard on all the others in the auction room, who had every reason to believe that your scratching your head did indeed betokene consent to make a bid and who relied to their detriment on the assumption that that was precisely what you had done.[25] Thinking along those lines, it is often said that you should be bound to buy the vase even though you had not genuinely consented to doing so.[26]

Certainly if you had made that gesture knowing fully well that it would induce those beliefs and expectations in others, then you could be said to be in a 'quasi-contractual' relation with something like 'promissory estoppel' binding you to honour the expectations you knowingly induced.[27] And that would be so whether or not you, in your heart of hearts, intended to consent by scratching your head. Knowing that others would take you to be consenting is sufficient, in and of itself, to make you bound *as if* you had consented, as I have already argued. You would be bound out of fairness to the others rather than by reason of your consent, to be sure. But you would be bound, all the same.[28]

In deciding how to adjudicate these conflicting claims of the maker of the unintended bid and those who relied to their detriment on it, much depends on what each of those parties could and should have known.[29] Insofar as the others could and should have known the 'bidder' was a newcomer innocent in the ways of this particular auction room, it would have been unreasonable for them to base

[24] Hobbes 1651, ch. 14. [25] Miller and Wertheimer 2010; Renzo 2022.

[26] Miller and Wertheimer (2010, p. 85) say that in cases like this (but explicitly not, for some unexplained reason, in the auction case) that 'a consent transaction in which it is reasonable for *A* to believe that *B* has tokened consent can be morally transformative even without valid consent'. On my analysis, it would not be 'morally transformative' in the sense of genuinely occasioning a shift between fundamental normative categories; but it would nonetheless provide a *pro tanto* moral reason for treating *B* 'as if he consented' and requiring *B* to bear the burden of his mistake accordingly (see Section 1.4.2 and Chapter 4).

[27] See Sections 1.4.2 and 5.1.1 above. [28] See further Sections 1.4.2, 2.4 and Chapter 4 above.

[29] See Sections 4.4.1 and 4.5 above. Section 1.4.3.3 would just hold him liable to compensate others fully for the costs that they have incurred in reliance upon his false consent; but as suggested in Section 1.4.3.5, there are special features surrounding auctions such that that is impossible and requiring him to go through with the purchase is the second-best option.

any expectations on the fact that he scratched his head at a crucial moment.[30] Insofar as the innocent could and should have known that he was in a convention-governed setting where financial obligations could be incurred, and he failed to ascertain what those conventions were, we might reasonably reckon him liable for the purchase of the vase.

This is not quite a case of *literally* consenting without knowing that you have consented. Virtually no one thinks that the unwitting head-scratcher at the auction genuinely consented to the purchase of the vase.[31] He had not performed the mental 'act of consent' which is a necessary condition of genuine consent. But if he could and should have known that scratching his head at the auction would be taken as a sign of consent, we might think that he should be bound to purchase the vase for the price indicated, nonetheless. Furthermore, the reason we think he should be so bound is grounded in some facts *about* consent—not, in this case, the fact that *he did* consent but, instead, the fact that *others reasonably took him to be* consenting. He is bound *as if* he consented, because he sent signals that he could and should have known reasonably led others to believe he was giving consent.

Such a person's liability is, as I have said, grounded in his negligence—his culpable ignorance of the conventions governing the auction—rather than on his genuine consent to the purchase.[32] For someone's ignorance to be culpable, it must (by definition) be the case that he 'could and should have known' that of which he is ignorant. That may seem to raise a second-order question of 'how could and should he have known that he could and should have known?'

One way of answering that question might be to say that for that to be true, it must be the case that there was something he *actually did* know, in however a rudimentary or sketchy way, that should have made him investigate further. On that analysis, if someone has absolutely no reason for thinking that he 'could and should know' something, then it cannot be the case that he could and should have been expected to find it out. And then it would not be the case that someone should be 'bound-as-if-consenting' without knowing, in some rudimentary way, at least that he could and should have known that what he was doing would be taken as a sign of consent.

That was the conclusion suggested in Section 4.6.3.2, at least. Some may resist that resolution of the issue on the grounds that it ties 'what you should have

[30] We might still think that the costs should be shared in the case of a bid socially signalled in innocent error, however, as proposed in Section 1.4.3.4.

[31] Communicationists are of course an exception. I have for example previously quoted Saunders (2012b, p. 71) as saying 'that consenting is an action, rather than a mental attitude. It is not simply that the action is necessary and the mental attitude insufficient. It is also that the action is sufficient and [the] mental attitude unnecessary. Someone who has performed the relevant consent action—whether that be signing an explicit declaration or some action understood as tacit consent—cannot escape their obligation simply by saying that they did not mean to give their consent. Their intentions are irrelevant to what they in fact did.' See similarly Bolinger (2019); cf. Wispelaere (2012).

[32] See Sections 1.4 and 4.4.1.

known' unnecessarily tightly to 'what (in some sense) you actually knew'. We need to preserve more critical distance between those two concepts, they may say. They may go so far as to argue that there must be some wholly independent standard of what you should have known, not at all connected to what you actually knew. Otherwise, gross dereliction of your epistemic duties—deliberately turning a completely blind eye to what others might reasonably expect of you, epistemically—would excuse you from such epistemic duties altogether. Surely that cannot be correct.[33] There is certainly something to be said, if only purely pragmatically, in favour of that line of reasoning.

Whichever way we come down on that latter issue, the larger conclusion remains the same. The conclusion is just this. While you cannot genuinely consent without knowing that you are consenting, you can unknowingly send social signals that lead others to reasonably believe that you are consenting. And that can justify us in treating you 'as if you consent'. You can in that way incur the burdens of consenting (or, more precisely, the same burdens as if you consented) without knowing that you are doing so.

5.1.2 Consent as a Social Practice

Another way in which consenting without knowing might be possible is if 'consenting' is equated with 'engaging in a social practice'.

Certain elements of this view are utterly standard. Clearly, consenting is pre-eminently a social act: we give consent to one another. Equally clearly, consenting is a practice governed by social conventions concerning what constitutes giving consent. There is nothing novel in any of that.

There are however two novel elements of the account here in view. The first lies in treating the 'rules governing the practice' as *themselves* things to which one consents when engaging in the practice. The second lies in treating 'engaging in the practice' as *itself* constituting consent to it.

Consent understood in this way is thus importantly different from the sort of consent in on-going practices that was discussed in Section 3.3.3. What was there under discussion was consent to a *particular instantiation* of the practice; and consent to that particular instantiation was presumed on the basis of *previous actual* consent (explicit or tacit) to the practice. The view here under discussion claims that: (1) it is the rules constituting the practice *themselves* to which one consents by engaging in the practice; and (2) engaging in the practice *constitutes* consenting to the practice (whether one knows or intends that). The latter feature

[33] Holmes (1881/1963, p. 41) raises a similar objection to accepting pleas of 'ignorance of the law' as an excuse for violating them: admitting that excuse would incentivize people to avoid finding out what the law requires.

of this view is what gives rise to the possibility that someone might end up consenting (on this account, *genuinely* consenting) without knowing that he was doing so.

In my previous discussions I have distinguished between 'bound-as-if-consenting' and 'bound-because-consenting'. The example of scratching one's head at an auction illustrated the difference. If the person did that knowing that that was a conventional signal of a bid in that auction house and intended thereby to make a bid, then he consented to purchase the vase at the price the auctioneer had just stated. But if the person simply scratched his head to alleviate an itch, with no intention of thereby making a bid and not knowing that others would take him to be so doing by that gesture, then he has not genuinely consented to purchase the vase at that price. If however that person was culpably negligent in not finding out the rules of the auction house—if he could and should have known that head-scratching constituted bidding under the conventions of that auction house—then he should be liable 'as if he consented' to purchase the vase at the nominated price. He did not 'genuinely consent' because the mental element required for that is missing, but he is bound all the same.

On the novel account of consenting here in view, in contrast, a person who engages (even unknowingly) in a practice—bidding at an auction by scratching his head, for example—would be bound *as* (not 'as if') consenting. Engaging in the practice, on this view, just does constitute consent to the rules of that practice. Arthur Applbaum motivates that view by way of an example from American gridiron football:

> What are we to make of the football halfback who, before the game, pins to his jersey a note that reads, in large letters, 'I do not consent to be tackled', and then proceeds to take his place on the field, accepts a handoff, and runs with the football toward the goal line? One is tempted to say that he no longer plays football.[34] .... But an equally plausible understanding is that... he cannot coherently deny consent so long as he takes the football in hand. Carrying a football under those circumstances means that one has consented to be tackled, no matter what he may signal or even intend to the contrary.[35]

Consent divorced from intention in this way might not do all of the moral work that we ordinarily expect of that notion, perhaps.[36] But as Applbaum's example persuasively suggests, it is at least a coherent and perhaps even tempting view that by participating in a practice we thereby consent to its rules.

[34] As an aside, Applbaum (1999, p. 119) interjects at this point: 'If so, then he has indeed withdrawn his consent, he may not be tackled—and the referee should eject him from the game.' I shall say more along those lines in Section 10.2.1.

[35] Applbaum 1999, p. 119.

[36] As Applbaum (1999, p. 120) goes on to say.

Some might resist this novel view in the following manner. First, they would observe that 'engaged *in*' is an action. Second, they would observe that actions, by definition, must be intentional. From those two propositions they would conclude that it is conceptually impossible for anyone to engage in a practice unintentionally or, hence, to consent to the rules of that practice by doing so.

Very well. Rephrase the point, and it retains the same force. The inadvertent bidder at the auction has '*engaged* the practice', in the sense of 'triggering it', even if he has not (knowingly, intentionally) 'engaged *in*' it. He activated the social machinery that constitutes the practice of consenting—and on the social practice account here in view, that just is what it is to consent. Whether he did so unintentionally or unknowingly is immaterial. The social machinery has been activated, and that (on this novel view) is all that matters for consent to have been given.

Following Rawls, notice that social practices ('promising' for him, 'consenting' for me) are essentially rule-governed. Among other things, each contains stipulations as to 'what defenses the practice . . . allows'.[37] In the 'promising' case that is of particular interest to Rawls, simply saying 'it was best on the whole not to keep my promise on this occasion' is not, within the social practice of promising, allowable as a defence for breaking one's promise. So too, it might be argued, within the practice of consenting in force in any particular place, simply saying 'I did not know that others would take what I did as a sign of consent' not be allowable as a defence for failing to permit that to which you socially consented.[38]

What follows from 'not having a defence'? In Rawls's case, what follows is that there is no doubt that you made a promise, and the only question concerns whether you were excused or justified in not keeping it—which, in the absence of a defence, you are not. In the case of unwittingly consenting, we might similarly suppose that the question likewise merely concerns whether you were excused or justified in not permitting that to which you consented. That is to say, the fact that you gave consent is not in doubt, merely the consequences you must bear for failing to honour the consent that you have (knowingly or unknowingly) signalled within the terms of the social practice.[39]

[37] Rawls 1955, p. 17.

[38] On the analysis of consenting as a social practice, whether or not that is true just depends on the conventions that have grown up around the practice of consenting in any particular place. It is not a necessary and universal truth about consenting in general. Still, although contingent, it may well be a common fact about the conventions surrounding the practice of consenting in most places. In some, perhaps many, places those conventions might contain the further rider 'if he could and should have known his signals would be thus understood'. In my earlier discussions (Section 1.4 and Chapter 4) that phrase was associated with 'as if consent', but there is no reason that the conventions constituting the practice of consenting could not include just such a rider. But neither of course is there any reason that they must. It all just depends upon what conventions have grown up in any particular place.

[39] Alternatively, and more weakly, when saying that your claim that 'I didn't know' is 'no defence' we might be saying merely that it does not relieve you of the burdens that would have befallen you if you had known (as you could and should have done) that others would interpret your signals as

The social practice account of consent is akin to the Communicationist account, insofar as the social practice of consent is defined purely in terms of external performances rather than internal mental intentions. In those terms, the unwitting consent-giver has engaged the practice of giving consent, whether or not he intended to do so. In triggering the conventional social machinery for 'giving consent' within the social practice of consent, he actually 'consented'. That is just what it is to consent, where consenting is understood as a social practice in this way.[40] Hence, on this revisionary 'engaging a social practice' view of giving consent, you might truly consent without knowing that you are doing so.

This is a novel, intriguing account of consent. But my aim in this book is to explicate more ordinary understandings of what is involved in consenting. Hence, I will pursue this approach no further, and nothing in the rest of the book will turn on it.

5.2 Consenting Without Knowing to What You Are Consenting

Can you consent without knowing what it is you are consenting to? Conventional wisdom would once again say that you cannot. But again, that is not quite right. I shall make four connected arguments in support of that claim.

The first pair of arguments points toward a conclusion that you can indeed consent without knowing (exactly) what it is to which you are consenting. I shall begin by arguing that valid consent can be given even if what is being consented to is specified only very loosely. I shall then proceed to argue what is being consented to can never be specified completely tightly.

The second pair of arguments points toward the conclusion that you can at the very least be treated 'as if you consented' to the default rules that are socially in place for filling in any gaps in your incompletely-specified consent. Given you had a chance to opt out of them but you didn't, perhaps you can be said to have consented to those default rules. In any case, I shall argue that you can properly be treated 'as if you consented' to those default rules even if you did not know their content, just so long as you could and should have known they exist and you could have discovered their content. Hence you can consent—or anyway, you can properly be treated 'as if you consent'—without being altogether certain to what, exactly, you are consenting.

consent. But that simply says, once again, you should be treated 'as if you had consented', even if really you did not, as has already been discussed; here I want to see if anything more than that can be extracted from the analysis of the social practice of consent.

[40] I hasten to add that that is not the only way to understand consenting as a social practice. We might alternatively understand the practice of consenting as 'a social process of conventions which are not "agreed to" but shared' (Patterson 1990, p. 942). Something more like that is what underlies my discussion in Section 3.3.3 for example.

5.2.1 *Carte Blanche* Consent

Consent, it is standardly said, must be specific.[41] In the paradigm case, a particular person, *X*, gives consent to another particular person, *Y*, to perform some particular action, φ, that would been impermissible for *Y* to perform without *X*'s consent.

The consent-receiver *Y* need not be identified by name and need not be a single, specific individual. An Australian grazier may consent to Aboriginal people in general crossing his land to access their sacred site. The owner of a beachfront mansion may consent for anyone who wants to cross her land to access the sea to do so. A keeper of a public house may consent for any member of the public to enter it.[42] It is ordinarily supposed, however, that even if the consent-receiver is specified as being any member of a set, even the universal set, the consent-giver must be precise about that in specifying to whom he is giving consent.[43]

But just how tightly does the consent-giver need to specify φ, that which he is giving consent for *Y* to do? On the face of things, it would seem that that can be specified really rather loosely and it would still count as morally binding consent.

Some would insist consent cannot be specified *too* loosely. Consider Leslie Green's analogous remark about promising: if I say, 'I promise to do something for you,... the act-type is so open as to defeat any point in promising, for it is inherently unclear what would count as keeping the promise.'[44] But that 'pointlessness' critique speaks purely to pragmatics, not to conceptual necessities. It may be conceptually impossible to promise something that is impossible for you to do.[45] But it is certainly not conceptually impossible for you to make a pointless promise. Furthermore, the promise in question is not *completely* pointless. In effect, it imposes an imperfect duty on the promise-giver to 'do something sometime or another' for the promise-receiver. Although the promise-giver is under no duty to do anything in particular for the promise-receiver, he is morally remiss if he does not ever do anything for her. Being the beneficiary of an imperfect duty is not nearly as useful as being the beneficiary of a perfect duty, to be sure. But it is not completely pointless.

[41] Or 'determinate', as Kleinig (1982, pp. 104–5; 2010, p. 18) puts it. The *Restatement of the Law (Second), Torts* says that: 'To be effective, consent must be... to the particular conduct'; but then, in acknowledgment of the points I am about to make, it immediately goes on to add, 'or to substantially the same conduct' (ALI 1979, § § 892A(2)(b)).

[42] Blackstone 1765, bk. 3, ch. 12.

[43] That may seem redundant in the case of the universal set. But consider someone saying, 'I hereby consent to people walking on my lawn': you cannot just *assume* that that means 'all people'; it may mean merely 'some people' or 'certain people'. If the consent-giver means 'all people' he needs to say so, and the consent-giver must have said that in order for the consent-receiver to be legitimate in inferring that.

[44] Green 1988, pp. 176.

[45] Grotius 1625, bk. 1, ch. 11, sec. 8. Hobbes 1651, ch. 14. Pufendorf 1672/1710, bk. 3, ch. 7, sec. 1.

The 'consenting' analogue to Green's example of pointless promising would be: 'I consent for you to do something'. Not knowing what, exactly (or even roughly), you have my consent to do, that consent would be pretty useless to you. But, again, at least I have your consent to something, however unspecified that may be; and you would be morally remiss if, on literally every occasion, you said, 'No, I did not consent to *that.*' Furthermore, it is not conceptually incoherent to give consent in this radically unspecified way; it is just not very useful, from the consent-receiver's point of view.[46] Suppose I had said instead, 'I consent for you doing anything you want'. What I have given consent to is equally radically unspecified (and in that case, extremely usefully so, from the consent-receiver's point of view).

Let us now turn to some more specific examples of open-ended consent. Suppose a surgeon is explaining to a patient the complicated procedure that he is proposing to perform on her. And suppose the patient says in reply, 'Just do whatever you think best, doc'. The surgeon should probably ask a few follow-up questions, just to make sure the patient really means it. But having done due diligence in that regard, it would certainly seem that the surgeon does indeed have the patient's consent to perform the procedure on her.

Some may say that in a case like that the surgeon has failed to secure properly informed consent from the patient.[47] But does that constitute a failure to consent or a failure to inform? That is to say, does the fault lie in the *carte blanche* nature of the consent—in the fact that the consent is not to a sufficiently specific action to qualify as genuine consent? Or does the failure of properly informed consent lie instead in the fact that the patient's reply suggests that she did not really understand the details of the complicated procedure that the surgeon was describing? The latter seems to me the more plausible interpretation.

Consider another case of relatively open-ended consent. My neighbour asks, 'Can I borrow your car tonight?', and I reply, 'Sure'. What is he going to do with the car? I don't know. He didn't say; I didn't ask. He might be going to the cinema, or he might be hauling lumber, or he might just be going for a joyride. Have I consented to his doing any of those things? It would seem to be so. After all I consented to him using the car tonight, without imposing any more specific limitations on how he might use the car. Note well, however: that is to say that I consented without knowing (exactly, anyway) what I was consenting to.

5.2.2 Implicit Limitations

When I said 'sure' without specifying any limits on the use to which my neighbour puts my car, did he really thereby acquire my consent to make literally *any* use of it

[46] Unless, of course, it is left up to the consent-receiver to determine to what the consent applied.
[47] Faden and Beauchamp 1986, p. 277. Cf. Katz (1994/1999, p. 246) and Brock (1987, pp. 106–7).

he pleases, however? Maybe he is going to use it to rob a bank. Have I consented to *that* when I said, 'Sure, you can use my car tonight'?

Maybe not, on the grounds that morally you cannot transfer more powers than you yourself possess. You may not use your car to rob a bank yourself. And since it is not morally permissible for you to do that, your consent cannot morally empower your neighbour to do so either.

So weaken the case to involve using the car in a way you would be morally permitted to use it yourself, but you (and indeed most people) clearly would not—driving it through waves crashing over the breakwater during a Category 4 hurricane, for example. Do I really have to add a rider specifically excluding his using my car in that way in order to prevent my 'Sure, you can use my car tonight' from extending to *that* use of it?

What that and analogous examples seem to point to are conventional understandings of what is generally within the scope of uses envisaged when people are being asked consent to use their car.[48] As in Section 3.3.5, when someone is asking to borrow your car for some use that falls outside the customary referents of what is involved in 'borrowing a car', the onus is on them to state specifically the intended use and seek your explicit consent for that variation to those conventional understandings.[49]

Notice, however, that that leaves a wide range of conventional uses to which your neighbour might put the car he borrowed from you. Although he would be required to set out explicitly what he intended to do with the car if he intended something outside that range, he need not specify what he is proposing to do with the car if it is within that range of conventional uses. So, unless he is intending to make some highly unusual use of your car, you can once again consent to his using it without knowing (exactly) which of those conventional uses of it he has in mind.

5.2.3 Consent Can Never Be Specified Completely Tightly

Suppose I am less trusting of my neighbour and I therefore attach a rider to my consent, specifying things that I do *not* consent to him doing with my car. 'Sure, you can borrow my car tonight', I might say, but adding, 'just don't haul dirty boxes in it!'

Still, any use of the car that is not expressly prohibited by such a rider (or implicit limitations of the sort discussed in Section 5.2.2 above) would seem still to be permitted by my blanket, 'Sure'. That again leaves me consenting to a plethora

[48] See Ssection 1.3.2.2. [49] Kleinig 2010, pp. 17–18.

of non-prohibited uses—once again, consenting without knowing (exactly) what I was consenting to.

I might try to narrow your consent down to just one very precise use of my car. I might say to my neighbour, 'Sure, you can use my car to collect your wife from Canberra airport—but *only* that, not to do anything else with my car.' But that still leaves much open: which of two equally direct routes he takes to the airport; whether he parks in the north or south parking lot; how fast he drives; what lane he uses; and so on.[50] When consenting to my neighbour's using my car to collect his wife from the airport, and that alone, I would seem to have consented to his using my car in any of those ways without my knowing (exactly) what I was consenting to in those respects.[51]

In short, however tightly I specify what it is that I consent to my neighbour doing with my car, it seems inevitable that the neighbour will be left with some discretion of that sort in how he does what my consent permits him to do with the car. I do not know in advance in which of those ways the neighbour will exercise that discretion. I might not even be able to imagine all of the ways in which he might do so—or indeed what all dimensions of discretion might be left to him even on the 'tightest' imaginable specification of what I consent to.[52] Nevertheless, when the neighbour uses my car in the way I specified, he does so with my consent. Hence, I have consented without knowing (exactly) to what I was consenting.[53]

[50] Pallikkathayil (2020, p. 115) observes that, 'when borrowing a car, one need not specify each and every turn one intends to make while driving'. I would add, more strongly, that when consenting to someone's borrowing your car, you *cannot* specify in advance each and every turn the borrower is to take while driving.

[51] The inevitable incompleteness of the specification of duties is a familiar point in connection with promissory duties, and perfect duties more generally. To adapt one of the standard examples from those discussions, suppose that I consent to loan you $20 on condition you repay it by noon next Monday, and you promise to do so. Now, a promissory obligation is standardly said to be a 'perfect duty', and the standard analysis of the difference between perfect and imperfect duties is that the latter leave the duty bearer with considerable discretion whereas the former do not. But it is not true that perfect duties leave duty bearers with no discretion whatsoever. Your duty to repay me $20 by noon next Monday is as perfect as they come. But it still leaves you with discretion as to how to repay the money (with one $20 note, two $10 notes, four $5 notes, a cheque, direct bank transfer, etc.) and when (11am the next Monday, 9pm the day before, etc.). Chisholm 1963, p. 4, fn. 6; see similarly Hill 1971, p. 155.

[52] As Manson (2018, p. 68) says, 'All consent is "broad" consent, and all consent involves ignorance of countless facts about the actions that are permitted by consent. If *A* consents to *B*'s use of her camera, she may have no idea what pictures *A* will take. If *A* consents to *B*'s use of her car, she may not know that at this junction she will turn left, at that, turn right.... [T]his kind of "open-but-bounded" feature of consent... is a general feature of communication.' Hart (1961, pp. 124–32) speaks similarly about the inevitability of 'open texture' in laws.

[53] Even if I could in principle list all the possible acts he might perform on the basis of my consent (which may or may not be true), if I have not worked through that long list at the time of giving my consent then I have consented without knowing all of what is on it. Furthermore, and perhaps more tellingly, I have consented to his request to 'borrow my car' without knowing what *exactly* he meant by that, not knowing what he intended to or would end up doing under the description of 'borrowing my car'.

5.2.4 Gap-filling

There thus seem inevitably to be gaps both in any specification of what we consent to and of how that consent is limited. Typically, we make use of some institutional or conventional rules for filling in those gaps. The consent-giver can make explicit provision otherwise; but if he does not those rules fill in any gaps he left in conferring the consent.

5.2.4.1 A Contract Law Analogy

According to a famous slogan of contract law, 'Chancelry mends no man's bargain'.[54] But courts *do* regularly 'complete' people's bargains.[55] Contract lawyers have long known that contracts are invariably incomplete and full of gaps.[56] A large body of law has grown up concerning what can be imputed to contracting parties to fill in those gaps.[57] When concluding a contract that will be 'completed' by the courts in these ways, many of the details of which those consenting to the contract might be unaware (although they certainly could and arguably should have been aware of them), people can once again be said to be consenting without (fully) knowing what they will be taken to be consenting to.

Let us take this as our recurring example here the following.[58] You promise to provide me with a horse tomorrow; you didn't specify 'on condition that the person who borrowed it today has returned it by then', but that is implicit. How are we to understand 'implicit' here?[59] One way would be this: 'we both had that condition in mind, but just did not bother articulating it'.[60] Another way would be 'it is a condition that did not occur to either of us, but it is a stipulation we both

[54] Lord Nottingham, *Maynard v. Mosley* (1676) 3 Swanst. 651, 655. Many dispute whether that is in fact true (Waddams 1976; Atiyah 1979); but for present purposes, no matter.

[55] As the *Restatement of the Law (Second), Contracts* puts it, 'When the parties to a bargain sufficiently defined to be a contract have not agreed with respect to a term which is essential to a determination of their rights and duties, a term which is reasonable in the circumstances is supplied by the court' (ALI 1981, § 204).

[56] Early on, Pufendorf (1672/1710, bk. 3, ch. 6, sec. 2, para. 1) noticed that 'most covenants leave some slight exceptions and conditions to be understood'. He went on to warn, 'But we must have a care of stretching these indulgences any farther than is well consistent with the carrying on of trade and business in the world; least they should prove of ill consequence to the validity of the contracts, by rendering them too slippery and uncertain.'

[57] See, e.g.: Barnett 1992; Kalevitch 1993.

[58] This is a variation on an example from Pufendorf (1672/1710, bk. 3, ch. 7, sec. 2, para. 2).

[59] See the related discussion in Section 3.4.

[60] Take for example the case of *Taylor v. Caldwell* (1863) 3 B. & S. 826, 122 E.R. 309 (Q.B.). 'In that case, the music hall burned down, through no fault of the owner. The disappointed impresario sued the owner for failure to supply the hall. The court rejected his claim, invoking what is now called "implied term theory". The court presumed that its task was to get to the real, though sometimes unarticulated intentions of the parties. As a result, it held that, despite never expressly mentioning it, the parties intended ("they must have contemplated") that the continued existence of the music hall was a precondition to the performance. No hall, no breach. Thus, the court found for the music hall owner' (Langille and Ripstein 1996, p. 66).

would have agreed to if we had thought of it'.[61] The former would be a case of mental but uncommunicated consent, which is socially a very anaemic form of consent.[62] The latter would be a case of hypothetical consent, which as I have argued in Section 2.2.2 is no kind of consent at all.[63]

A third way of understanding 'implicit' might be Pufendorf's 'nature of the business', as discussed in Section 3.2.2 above. It is in the nature of the business of hiring out horses that I actually have horses to hire out. From that obvious fact, both of us could and should have inferred that built into my consent for you to use my horse tomorrow must be the implicit condition that the horse I hired out today has been returned in time for you to use it tomorrow.[64] That is not to say that either of the contracting parties actually had that in mind when agreeing to the arrangement. But it is to say that both of them could and should have known, given the nature of the business, that that was an implicit condition in the contract. And that they could and should have known is enough to hold them bound to that implicit term of the contract 'as if they consented' to it.[65]

5.2.4.2 Defeasible Presumptions and Consent by Silence

When engaging in the filling in of gaps in people's contracts, courts often appeal to what reasonable people would or should have agreed to. But in doing that they are self-consciously imposing their own judgments on contracting parties, rather than adducing what the particular contracting parties themselves actually consented to in even the most attenuated sense. Hence judicial gap-filling is often regarded as going 'beyond consent', and instead 'imposing upon' people rules not of their choosing.[66] And that is all the more true when legislatures stipulate rules for gap-filling, without even the pretence of considering what those particular contracting parties implicitly did or hypothetically would have consented to.[67]

[61] Langille and Ripstein (1996, pp. 66–7) characterize this as 'the dominant contemporary view'.

[62] See Section 1.2.2 above.

[63] Unless Epstein (1989, p. 106) is right that we can take 'what rational parties would have agreed to' as 'strong evidence of what these parties did, in fact, agree to where there is silence or ambiguity'. Surely there are some things that are so 'obvious' to all parties that none of them bothers stating them. But equally surely, among boundedly-rational agents (Simon 1982) there are many things that escape everyone's notice. And there is no reason to think that those things that 'rational parties would have agreed to' are more likely to be noticed but not enunciated—if anything, it seems more likely that if noticed they would be enunciated. So Epstein's 'strong evidence' claim itself seems to be way too strong.

[64] Equally, what is implied in my consent might be that I had horses to lend. Which of these ways the gap left in the explicit consent is to be filled is, as I say, socially conventional and may well vary from one community to the next.

[65] See the discussion in Sections 1.4.2 and 4.4.1.

[66] As Barnett (1992, pp. 822–3) writes in describing the received wisdom from which he dissents: 'Gap-filling terms—sometimes referred to as "implied-in-law"—are said to be imposed by the legal system for reasons of principle or policy rather than consented to by the parties.'

[67] See generally Barnett (1992).

But note this important feature of a vast majority of those judicially or legislatively imposed rules for filling in gaps in contracts. They are rules to be used 'unless contracting parties specify otherwise in the contract'.[68] The parties are thereby put on notice that (a) this will be how their contract will interpreted and (b) they can overwrite that interpretation by specifying a different arrangement in the terms of their contract itself. In this sense the judicially or legislatively imposed rules for gap-filling are not imposed at all. They are merely default rules, from which parties can deviate through their explicit acts of will.

In this sense, the judicial gap-filling rules are akin to opting-out rules governing organ donation or the chairman of a meeting announcing he will take the motion to be agreed unless he hears any objections.[69] In those cases inaction is taken to signal consent. By analogy in the gap-filling cases, failure to specify any alternative clause in the contract can be construed as consent to judges filling in the gaps in their contract.[70]

Of course, the rules judges use in filling in those gaps are complicated and address situations that occur only rarely. Hence there is no reason to think that parties to common-garden contracts necessarily know the particulars of every rule that judges will use in that gap-filling process should they fail to specify some alternative arrangement.[71] Still, they could and should have known that such gap-filling rules exist; and they could and should have known that they could avoid having those rules applied to their contract by specifying some alternative provision explicitly in it. They have consented without knowing exactly what they were consenting to—'consented', that is, to judges filling in the gap, but 'without knowing what they were consenting to', in not knowing the exact content of the rules that the judges would use in so doing.

In the case of a well-publicized opt-out rule governing organ donation, I argued that by not opting out a person was genuinely (albeit tacitly) consenting to donate his organs, because the statute put him on notice that that would be interpreted in that way.[72] In the case of gap-ridden consent, it may be much harder for consenting parties to anticipate what gaps might emerge and what rules will be used to fill them. So we may not want to say, in the case of gap-ridden consent, that people

[68] As Barnett (1992, p. 825) points out, 'many of the provisions of Article 2 of the Uniform Commercial Code . . . are default rules, because they apply "unless otherwise agreed". Eighteen of the twenty-eight provisions of Part 2 of Article 2, which specify the "General Obligation and Construction of Contract", contain this or comparable language.'

[69] Discussed in Sections 3.3.4 and 3.2 respectively.

[70] 'Given the opportunity to deviate from the default rules, it is unrealistic to depict implied-in-law default rules as being "imposed upon" the parties in the tort-like sense that this phrase has acquired over the years' (Barnett 1992, p. 865). See similarly Langille and Ripstein (1996, p. 80).

[71] As Macneil (1978, p. 884) says, 'The classical American contract is founded not upon actual consent but upon . . . . whole masses of contract content one, or even both, parties did not know . . . . For example, ordinary run-of-the-mill purchasers of insurance are, in classic law, deemed to have consented not only to all the terms in the policy, which they did not read and could not have understood if they had, but also to all the interpretations the law would make of those terms.'

[72] See Section 3.3.4.

genuinely (albeit tacitly) consent to those rules being applied by failing to stipulate some other rule to govern those contingencies when giving their consent. Nevertheless, the fact that they could and should have known they could do so might well be grounds enough for treating them 'as if they consented' to that, once again. As in the case of culpably negligent false consenters, so too with the people here in view: there is something that they could and should have known; and there was something they could have done to avoid that from happening, if they so desired.

On this weaker reading of the case, we justify people being held to default rules and defeasible presumptions precisely because they could have overwritten them but they did not. Even if in the circumstances it would not be right to say that they genuinely consented to being bound by those rules and presumptions, the fact they could have overwritten them and did not is more than enough to justify holding them to those rules and presumptions 'as if' they consented to them. And that, once again, is very close (if not quite identical) to treating them 'as if they consented' without knowing (exactly) to what they were consenting.

5.2.4.3 Limits to Gap-filling?

The institutionalized nature of those rules governing gap-filling may make those cases very special ones, incapable of being generalized more broadly. It is precisely because there is an institutionally-specified default that people could and should have known that their failure to make alternative arrangements can be taken as 'consent-on-notice' to have that default applied in filling in gaps in consent that they have given.

How, if at all, might that logic apply in the absence of such institutionalized default rules? In more private affairs where such institutionalized default rules are lacking, is there anything that people could and should know about how others will fill in gaps in their consent? And if there is not, must that not mean that others are not entitled to fill in gaps in the consent that they have been given by other people at all?

Some people seem to embrace that latter conclusion, at least for high-stakes cases involving consent. Pallikkathayil gives this example:

> Suppose Andrew and Beth agree to have sex. During their interaction, Beth faints. Is Andrew permitted to continue while Beth is unconscious? No, because what Beth consented to was conscious sex not unconscious sex. Without prior discussion of this specific circumstance, consent to sex while unconscious cannot be assumed.[73]

[73] Pallikkathayil 2020, p. 122.

That seems to be the correct conclusion in that case. But insofar as it does, is that because consent gap-filling in non-institutionalized personal relations ought to be prohibited in general, or is it something special about sexual consent (or high-stakes consent more generally)?

I would argue that it is the latter. For a start, notice that Pallikkathayil's conclusion is continuous with the more general advice that official organizations like the London Metropolitan Police offer concerning 'rape and sexual assault': you should get consent from your sexual partner anew 'each time you start a new type of sexual activity'.[74] They offer no principles for individuating 'types' of sexual activity, but it hardly seems a stretch to say that 'sex while conscious' is one type and 'sex while unconscious' is another. So the conclusion in Pallikkathayil's example is continuous with our ordinary ways of thinking about consent to sexual relations.

Now, the reason we think that way about sexual consent might not be *altogether sui generis*. That way of thinking might not apply to sexual consent alone but instead stretch to consent in high-stakes settings more generally, of which sexual relations are only one dramatic instance. That leaves open the possibility, however, that the prohibition on non-institutionalized consent gap-filling might not extend to low-stakes instances of consent.

So consider next a trivial example of consent gap-filling. You consented to loan me your car at 2pm today, but I was running late and didn't get there until 2:01pm. Did I really act without consent when driving off with your car one minute later than agreed? I didn't ask you about borrowing your car at 2:01pm, you didn't explicitly consent to that. Yet is it not a perfectly reasonable extrapolation from what you did consent to (my borrowing your car at 2pm) that my borrowing it at 2:01pm was within the scope of that consent?[75] Or suppose you consented to loan me your car today to drive to the coast. I took it as agreed, but the road was closed and as far as I got with your car was Braidwood rather than Bateman's Bay. Did I really act without your consent?[76] I didn't ask about borrowing your car to drive to Braidwood. But isn't it a reasonable extrapolation from what you did agree to (borrowing your car to drive to Bateman's Bay) that

[74] Metropolitan Police (2019), linking to the website of Consent Is Everything (2019).

[75] Where to draw the temporal line is of course uncertain at the margins: 2:01pm seems definitely in-scope; 3pm is less clear; sometime tomorrow is definitely out-of-scope. Dougherty (2021a, p. 144) offers an even more trivial example, consent to borrowing my pen. Dougherty writes: 'Borrowing the pen at 10am [to which you had consented] would be a different action from borrowing the pen at 11am.' They would be different actions, to be sure—but that they are different actions is not at all the issue. The issue, instead, is whether your consent to my borrowing the pen at 10am extends to the separate act of my borrowing it at 11am. Dougherty analyzes that in terms of whether 'the consent-giver *intends to cover*' (my emphasis) the latter in the consent he gave to the former. If so, that would decisively settle the matter and no further enquiries would be required. But then it would not be a case of 'gap-filling' at all—he consented to borrowing the pen at 11am, end of story. The problem of gap-filling arises only when the consent-giver's intentions are unclear or indeed absent.

[76] This is an Australian variation on an example from Tadros (2022, pp. 457–8).

your consent extended to my borrowing it to drive to Braidwood—particularly since passing through Braidwood is the only way to get from Canberra (where we were) to Bateman's Bay? Examples such as those lead me to conclude that there can be no principled objection to consent gap-filling even in non-institutionalized settings, at least in relatively low-stakes cases.

The reason I think we can justifiably engage in gap-filling even where there are no formal (e.g., legal) institutional rules to guide us in that is that there are socially conventional ones that play the same role. Dougherty gives this example:

> In general, when a host tells their guest to make themselves at home, there are social conventions concerning what the guest is allowed to do. For example, our society's conventions prohibit a guest from trying on their host's clothes but permit a guest to leaf through the books on their host's shelves.[77]

One way of reading that is as suggesting that 'that is what the host actually intended by what he said'. Read that way, it would not be a case of 'gap-filling' at all—it would merely be a standard case of consent.[78] But suppose the circumstances were such as to make it clear that the host could not have had any such thing in mind when inviting the guest to 'make themselves at home'—it was supposed to be a brief pause before the two of them left for a drive, but the host then had to take an urgent and protracted telephone call leaving the guest at loose ends in a way that the host could never have envisaged when uttering those words. The host could not have had in mind his guest's leafing through his books when he said, 'Make yourself at home'. Yet if that is within the scope of what that phrase conventionally means in their society, then the guest would be perfectly entitled to fill in the gaps in the host's consent in that way. The host could and should have known that that is how his words would be interpreted (and he should therefore have said, explicitly 'but do not touch my books!' if he wanted to block that interpretation). The host in that case could be said to have consented (or anyway could justifiably be treated 'as if he consented') to his guest reading his books so, without knowing (or anyway, certainly without it being remotely near the front of his mind) that that was what he was consenting to his guest doing when saying 'make yourself at home'.

77 Dougherty 2021a, p. 159.

78 Tadros (2022, pp. 459) offers a related analysis suggesting, in effect, that gaps in consent can be filled by actions that are sufficiently 'closely related' to the things to which the consent-giver actually consented, where 'closeness' is defined in terms of the consent-giver's subjective perception of 'differences in kind or degree of value'. Perhaps in intimate settings, where the consent-receiver knows or could and should have known those subjective perceptions of the consent-giver, those should be controlling. But outside those more intimate settings, I would argue, social conventions can properly be allowed to rule—as they do in interpreting signs of consent, as I argued Sections 1.3.1 and 2.3.2 above.

This conventionalist approach to gap-filling provides us with yet another response to Pallikkathayil's example of Beth, who consents to have sex with Andrew but who then faints. Nothing was said about unconscious sex, one way or the other, before Beth fainted. There was no on-going relationship between them from which might give Andrew good reason to presume from past instances that Beth consents to unconscious sex with him.[79] Neither—and here is the novel contribution of the conventionalist approach—do the social conventions of our society dictate that part and parcel of what it is to consent to sexual relations is to consent to sex acts being performed on the consent-giver while unconscious.[80] So the thing that makes it all right for the guest to leaf through his host's books does not make it all right for Andrew to perform sex acts on Beth while unconscious.

[79] As was the case in Section 3.3.3 above.

[80] Of course social conventions could have been otherwise. One could imagine such a society (although I am not sure how many of us would care to live in it). I take it to be a brute empirical fact that our society's conventions are not like that, however.

6
Evoking and Invoking Consent

This chapter is concerned with how consent is evoked in the first instance and invoked in the second. To evoke consent is 'to call it forth'.[1] To evoke consent is bring it into being; it is to procure and to secure it, in the first place. Invoking consent is something you can do only once you already have it. When invoking consent, you appeal to the fact that you have it in justifying your actions.[2]

6.1 Evoking Consent

Sometimes you volunteer your consent to someone without its being specifically sought. In *Great Expectations* Estella offers her cheek to Pip saying, 'You may kiss me if you like'.[3] Other times you offer such consent to the world at large. The apple tree in your garden has produced a surfeit of fruit; so you set a basket full of apples at the end of your driveway with a sign reading, 'Free'. You thereby consent for anyone and everyone who may be passing to take what they want of those apples. Likewise, as Blackstone has it,

> a man may justify entering into an inn or public house, without the leave of the owner first specially asked; because, when a man professes the keeping of such inn or public house, he thereby gives a general license to any person to enter his doors.[4]

Very often, however, one seeks another person's consent by explicitly asking for it ('may I...?').[5] When the old Natural Lawyers discussed cases of this sort, they did so mostly by way of explicating how elaborately the consent-giver needed to communicate his consent in order for it to be valid. When a consent-seeker's request has set the context, a mere nod on the part of the consent-giver would

[1] *Oxford English Dictionary*, qv. 'evoke (v.)', def. 1; this definition is said to connote 'the use of magical charms', which may be at least metaphorically appropriate given Hurd's (1996) famous article, 'The Moral Magic of Consent'. Less metaphorically, the *OED*'s clunkier definition 2b might be more apt—'to call (a feeling, faculty, manifestation, etc.) into being or activity'.

[2] The *Oxford English Dictionary*, qv. 'invoke (v.)', def. 1b, defines 'to invoke', in the relevant sense, as 'to appeal to, in confirmation of something'.

[3] Dickens 1861, ch. 11.

[4] Blackstone 1765, bk. 3, ch. 12.

[5] Indeed, many such as Cowart (2004, p. 520) build such a request into the 'core principle of consent', which she characterizes as: 'The giving of permission *in response to a request* by *H* to do *X* that *H* does not have a right to perform without permission, but if granted will be performed by *H*.'

Consent Matters. Robert E. Goodin, Oxford University Press. © Robert E. Goodin 2024.
DOI: 10.1093/oso/9780192889027.003.0006

suffice, in Pufendorf's example.[6] But I think there is much more morally at stake in asking for consent than just backgrounding a nod.

6.1.1 Asking for Consent Can Itself Be Morally Problematic

At least sometimes the sheer act of asking for consent can itself be morally problematic. You are seated next to a stranger on a bus. You turn to her and ask, 'May I put my hand on your breast?'[7] Of course it would be wrong to touch her breast without asking. But it is also almost as wrong even to ask.[8] Simply asking, in that case, would itself be a morally offensive form of harassment.

There are other things that are so trivial that, even though you should ask for consent, you cannot possibly give offence by asking for it. You are standing behind someone in the Heathrow Immigration queue, and you ask to borrow her pen to complete your landing card. Now, pens are private property, and consent theorists insist that you must get the owner's consent to use them;[9] the lady would be perfectly within her rights to refuse. But outside of special circumstances (like an outbreak of a highly contagious disease which can be transmitted on pens), it is hard to see that there could be anything morally problematic in your asking.

6.1.2 Can Asking for Consent Be Coercive?

At the other extreme, there are some 'asks' that are so big that they can come across as menacing. Suppose that a stranger comes up to you and asks, 'May I borrow your car (or your daughter)?' You might laugh off the request ('Don't be ridiculous!'); or you might ask, 'What for?' But if the stranger is physically intimidating or brandishing a weapon, you will reasonably infer that he is demanding rather than requesting, and he will take what he wants anyway if you refuse.[10] You will read that request for consent as 'a request you cannot refuse'.[11]

[6] '[A] bare nod will serve, if the thing...have been before requested' (Pufendorf 1672/1710, bk 3, ch. 6, sec 15, para 1).

[7] The example is not original with me, but due attribution would presumably be an unkindness.

[8] Certainly, anyway, in the absence of any good reason to think that the request would be welcome (see further Section 6.1.3 below). Your thinking 'I am so attractive she would be flattered to be asked' obviously does *not* constitute such a reason.

[9] Gerver 2020, p. 27; Dougherty 2021a, p. 144; Chadha 2021, pp. 343–4.

[10] Wertheimer (1996, p. 102) contemplates a parallel case: 'We do not say that a panhandler threatens *B* if he says, 'Do you have any money to spare?' But does a large and tough-looking *A* threaten *B* when he says 'I would appreciate it if you would give me your wallet', but issues no threat as to what he will do if *B* refuses? We are inclined to think that some nonverbal behaviors are reasonably understood as proposing to make *B* worse off if *B* refuses, and that it is also reasonable to expect *A* to understand this.'

[11] Parallel to a 'coercive offer' (Held 1972; Zimmerman 1981; cf. Wertheimer 1987, ch. 13; 1996, pp. 102–5).

Even something so trivial as asking the lady in the Heathrow queue to borrow her pen might be vaguely coercive, in another way. In the absence of special circumstances, it is such a trivial thing that, having been asked, she can hardly refuse. Of course she would be within her rights to do so; but it would be so socially inappropriate of her to refuse that that is not really a viable option for her.[12] 'Coercive' may be too strong a term here; but simply asking puts social pressure on her, at least; and at least sometimes social pressure can be such as to make us doubt whether she really means what she says when consenting or refusing consent.[13] We would generally think that it would have been far better (and at least in part for that reason) for her to have noticed your need of a pen and offered it without being asked.

For a final example of how simply asking for consent can be coercive, take this standard case from discussions of sexual consent. Not only does 'no mean no', but once you have been told 'no' you must not keep asking. Of course you may not engage in sexual conduct without asking for consent. But repeatedly asking for consent that you have already been denied is itself morally offensive.[14] At the very least it is 'badgering'. Some say it is literally 'coercive'.[15] In any case, someone who agrees only after having been badgered in that way does not consent wholly 'voluntarily'. She consents under duress, of a sort.[16] We might rightly doubt, in that case, whether even 'yes' really 'means yes'.[17]

[12] Manson (2018) gives the example of being asked by a stranger if they can take the empty seat next to you on a train. Brownlee (2020, p. 110) goes so far as to say, in the case of a stranger saying 'hello' to you on the street, that it would be morally impermissible for you not to respond; 'social niceties, etiquette and morality' are of a cloth, she says, in that all 'convey our willingness to recognize and respect each other's humanity'.

[13] Cases like that might include Chapter 9's hunger strikers and the case there also discussed of someone whose refusal to consent to a transfusion was ruled invalid due to the 'undue influence' of her mother, a Jehovah's Witness (Section 9.5). See more generally Mill (1859, ch. 4).

[14] Wertheimer (2003, p. 161) offers the following as a case of morally impermissible Persistence: '*A* makes advances which *B* rejects. *A* repeats his advances five times. On the fifth occasion, *B* says, "You don't take no for an answer, do you? If it'll make you happy, go ahead."' Husak (2006, p. 268) rightly observes however that 'further details that must be specified before we can decide whether persistence is commendable, objectionable, or merely annoying. Were *A*'s advances repeated over several weeks or over several minutes? How did *B* behave in the interim? How unqualified were her rejections? Tone of voice, inflection, and other mannerisms make an enormous difference to how *A*'s behavior should be evaluated.'

[15] Santos-Longhurst (2019), for example, claims: 'Repeatedly asking someone to engage in a sexual act until they eventually say yes is not consent, it's coercion.'

[16] I.e., under 'verbal coercion' (Conly 2004; Leahy 2014). On Wertheimer's (1987) classic account, a proposal cannot be coercive if making it and carrying it out would be within your rights. But that is precisely what is at issue in the case at hand: you may be within your rights to ask once or twice, but are you within your rights to keep pestering a person once they have firmly said 'no'?

[17] Alongside doubts we may have on that score arising from more standard considerations of 'coercion, misrepresentation, and competence' (Wertheimer 1996, p. 89).

6.1.3 Do You Need Consent to Ask for Consent?

An important feature driving the earlier example of asking the stranger on the bus 'May I touch your breast?' is that she is indeed a stranger. Why that matters is not the sheer fact you were unacquainted with one another—it would be equally morally obnoxious to ask that of an acquaintance or even the vast majority of your good friends. What makes it morally obnoxious, when it is, is that you have no remotely good reason for thinking that the request would be a welcome one (and almost necessarily so, in the case of a complete stranger).[18]

To force this point into the form of a paradox, one might say only slightly hyperbolically that 'you need consent to ask for consent'.[19] That is a bit hyperbolic, because of course the standard of evidence required is presumably much lower in the one case than in the other. And the paradox is slightly forced, because of course the other person is consenting to different things in the two cases. It is perfectly possible that someone might 'consent' to being asked, even if she would not consent to that which is asked. To switch examples: my neighbour may appreciate me asking 'can I help you carry those groceries upstairs?', even if she invariably replies, 'No thanks, I can manage.' Still, the trope of 'needing consent to ask for consent' captures something of the dynamic at work here.

Perhaps not all requests for consent rise to the same level of moral obnoxiousness as asking the stranger on the bus, 'May I touch your breast?' Sometimes such requests might simply be 'oddly inappropriate', more a breach of etiquette than morality. Often they will fall somewhere in between, violations of social norms and mores towards which we take a critical reflective attitude but of a qualitatively different sort.[20]

It may be oddly inappropriate, but perhaps nothing more, to ask the stranger seated next to me in a cold airplane, 'May I borrow that sweater if you are not going to use it?' But it would not seem nearly so inappropriate to ask my host at an informal dinner party, 'May I borrow a sweater? I'm feeling a bit chilled . . .'

What is the salient difference between those cases? Perhaps it is that dinner party hosts have an obligation to make their guests comfortable, in a way that strangers seated next to one another on airplanes do not. That obligation does not license me going into the host's bedroom and rummaging around for a sweater. But it does license me at least to ask, because (knowing my host to be attentive and

[18] Contrast this with the case of a woman presenting for a medical examination which she knew would involve the doctor examining her breasts for suspicious lumps that may be cancerous.

[19] To avoid infinite redress, we must add 'you need *unsought* consent to ask for consent'—although adding that makes it less paradoxical, of course. Another less paradoxical formulation would be that 'you need to be invited to make the request'—although that retains a whiff of paradox (it is not logically impossible for you to invite a request that you then proceed to refuse, perhaps, but doing so is nevertheless a morally obnoxious form of jerking someone around).

[20] Brennan et al. 2013, ch. 4.

conscientious) I reasonably expect my request would be if not exactly welcomed (after all, it's an implicit criticism of their standard of home heating) anyway regarded as a perfectly appropriate one.

On-going relationships and continuing (or recurring) practices among repeat-players (of the sort discussed in Section 3.3.3) can ground reasonable expectations that my requesting your consent for something to which you have consented in the past would not be deemed inappropriate. Of course you may refuse consent to the new request, perhaps because you think 'I've done my bit' or because 'it didn't turn out so well last time'. That explains why, if it is a remotely 'big' request, I should probably ask once again instead of simply presuming your consent. But if you have agreed on previous occasions, that fact certainly provides grounds at least for me thinking that 'there is no harm in asking'.

If you refuse that request, what it means for our on-going practice depends very heavily on the terms of the refusal. If you say, 'I don't want to do that anymore', then obviously that puts to an end the practice and any grounds for presuming either consent or even permission to ask for further consent; and it would be coercive 'badgering' once again to keep asking. But if you just offer some episodic excuse ('I need the car today myself'), then it would be perfectly proper for me to take that at face value and presume that there would be nothing inappropriate about asking to borrow the car on some subsequent occasions. If however you keep offering such seemingly episodic excuses, that would seem to indicate that those are just 'polite excuses' and you really want to put the previous practice to an end, and once again it would constitute coercive 'badgering' for me to keep asking beyond some point.

6.2 Invoking Consent

Invoking consent is something you can only do when you actually already have consent, and you invoke that fact in justification of the moral permissibility of your actions when that is challenged. Such challenges might sometimes come from the very same person who has given you the consent. More often they will come from third parties. I shall proceed to discuss each case in turn.

6.2.1 Vis-à-Vis the Principal

Here is an example of the first sort of case. I say to my son, 'What were you doing taking the car last night?' He replies, 'Don't you remember? You consented for me to use it last night.'

How effective that reply will be, morally, depends upon whether or not the consented-to act has been fully completed at the time the reply is given. If I really had given valid consent to his using the car last night, and I had not subsequently revoked that consent, then I have no moral grounds for complaint the next morning. I might wish I had not consented, but I cannot at that point undo the fact that I had indeed consented and my son had acted with my permission at the time he borrowed the car.[21]

The matter is less clear-cut if I lodge my challenge before the consented-to act has been undertaken (or completed). Seeing my son get into the car, I ask, 'What are you doing?' My son says, 'Don't you remember you consented for me to use your car today?' That would be an argument-stopper if it was said as he was returning the car, of course. But if instead it was said ahead of his driving away, that is not necessarily the case. At that point I can still say, 'Well, I've changed my mind; you can't use my car today.' Chapter 7 will discuss considerations involved in deciding whether or consent may legitimately be revoked.

Even if the consent can be revoked, the former-consent-receiver may still use the other's previous consent as an argument in entreating him to stick with his prior commitment. My son could say, for example, 'What has changed? If all the reasons for and against letting me use the car remain now just as they were when you initially consented to me using it, it is just plain unreasonable for you not to honour that consent now.' That is to say that, if on the balance of reasons it was right to have consented previously, it would be wrong for me to revoke the consent now on the balance of the same set of unchanged reasons. But that is not to say that my son actually still has the consent that I now have (however wrongly) revoked. Just as 'ought-to consent' does not confer consent (Section 3.5), so too 'ought-not-to-revoke consent' does not necessarily mean that the consent has not been revoked. Nor is it to say that it would be appropriate for him to harp on about it, once having been told (however unreasonably) a firm and final 'no': doing so would once again be a morally unacceptable form of 'badgering'.[22]

6.2.2 Vis-à-Vis a Third Party

More often, you find yourself invoking consent as a defence against third-party challenges to the legitimacy of your actions. You insert the key and get into Jim's car, turn on the ignition and start to drive it away. John, the parking lot attendant

[21] As I argue at greater length in Section 7.2.1 below.

[22] If he needed the car that I promised to loan him to go to an important job interview, it may not be morally inappropriate for him to press me on my refusal. But once he has received a genuinely 'firm and final "no"', however unjustified it may have been, it would be morally inappropriate for him to press further.

on duty,[23] shouts, 'What are you doing? That's Jim's car!' You reply, 'It's okay, he agreed to let me use it this afternoon.'[24]

Of course your claiming to have Jim's consent does not make that claim true. John may well want to demand proof of that claim, as any conscientious parking lot attendant should. And he may not be fully satisfied when you hold out Jim's distinctive key ring, saying, 'Look, Jim gave me his keys!' (After all you might have stolen the key ring.) John may well want to have Jim himself confirm that he consented to the loan; and being in a position of responsibility with respect to Jim's car, he would be fully within his rights to do insist on that.[25] Or for a more troubling example, slaves in the Antebellum South, when encountered by a third party upon a public roadway, could be (and regularly were) required to produce documents from their masters consenting to their leaving the plantation on some errand.[26]

6.2.3 Authorization versus Consent

In discussions of consent, these cases are sometimes described as ones involving 'authorization'.[27] But there is a world of difference between saying 'I am doing it with his permission' and 'I am doing it on his authority'. Doing it on his authority is doing it in his place and on his behalf. You are claiming to be his agent, and

[23] I set up the example in this way deliberately to skirt the issue of whether any old third party is morally entitled to challenge someone for violating another's rights. I am inclined to think that they are: violations of rights are morally important; they are an affront to the moral community at large; any member of that moral community is thus entitled to challenge those appearing to violate them. But arguing for that conclusion would take me far from the concerns of this chapter, which are equally well served by stipulating that the challenger (here, the parking lot attendant on duty) has a special responsibility to protect the rights in question (of the owners of the cars entrusted to his care not to have their cars taken without their consent).

[24] Valentine (2018, p. 515) provides another example: 'I take $5 from your wallet, and a bystander asks "why?" Answer 1 is that you consented.'

[25] Hobbes (1651, ch. 16) says similarly that a 'covenant made with [someone's agent] is not valid without his counterassurance' that that agent has authority to act for that person in that particular respect.

[26] Among the generally accepted rules there was that: 'A slave was not to leave the estate without a pass which gave his destination and the time he was to return' (Stampp 1963, p.149).

[27] This was central to Plamenatz's (1938/1968, ch. 1 and pp. 167, 171) attempt to tease out a sense of 'consent' that would make good the claim that 'representative democracy is government by consent'. The two are similarly equated in: Hart 1955, p. 184; Simmons 1976, pp. 275–6; Faden and Beauchamp 1986, pp. 277–80; Beauchamp and Childress 2009, pp. 118–20; and Miller and Wertheimer 2010, p. 81. Feinberg is of two minds on the matter. In his later work he offers a broadly sceptical analysis very much along the lines I give immediately below (Feinberg 1986a, pp. 176–7). But earlier he had written that 'to give one's consent to an action is to be, in some sense, a party to it' (Feinberg 1984, p. 115). Maybe that is sometimes the case (as when '*X* consents to join the gang', for example). But it is not true as a matter of conceptual necessity. When *X* consents to *Y*'s φ-ing, *X* merely removes a moral obstacle to *Y*'s φ-ing. Removing that obstacle may be a necessary condition, morally speaking, for *Y*'s φ-ing; but at most that would make *X* *complicit* in *Y*'s φ-ing, an accessory to it rather than a principal in it, which is what 'being a party to it' would ordinarily mean (Lepora and Goodin 2013, p. 33).

making choices on his behalf that he has authorized you to make.[28] In Hobbes' terms, the person who has authorized the agent is morally the 'author' of what the agent does in his name.[29] Locke, at one point, claimed that something like that was involved in consenting to political rule;[30] so too, on one reading, did Rousseau.[31] But nothing remotely like that is going on in most cases of consent.

Depending on the content of the proposition being consented to, consenting may sometimes be 'authorizing' (as when 'I consent for you to act on my behalf in this matter'—although 'I commission you to' or 'I authorize you to' would be more natural expressions in that context). Likewise, depending on the content of the proposition being consented to, consenting may sometimes be 'marrying' (as when 'I consent to take this woman as my lawfully married wife') or 'renting a house' (as when 'I consent for you to use my house in exchange for the stipulated monthly sum in rent'). But in each case, that is a function of the particular thing being consented to. It is not something that is true about the nature of consent in general.

When *X* consents to *Y*'s φ-ing, *X* merely waives his rights against *Y*'s φ-ing or (what I take to be an equivalent expression) gives *Y* permission to do something, φ, that would be wrong for *Y* to do without *X*'s permission.[32] *X* does not positively endorse *Y*'s φ-ing necessarily (although sometimes of course *X* might). Still less does *X* authorize *Y* to φ on *X*'s behalf. (When *X* consents to a boxing match with *Y*, *X* gives his permission for *Y* to hit him if he can—but *Y* is hardly acting as *X*'s *agent* when raining blows on *X*'s body.[33]) When *X* consents to *Y*'s φ-ing, *X* merely removes what would otherwise have been one moral barrier to *Y*'s φ-ing.

When you authorize someone to act on your behalf, you create a principal–agent relationship. In such a relationship, the agent is supposed to do what is in the principal's interests or to follow the principal's instructions. When you consent to someone doing something, no such expectation is ordinarily created. On the contrary, you would ordinarily expect the consent-receiver to do what is in his interests, not your own—certainly not necessarily, anyway.

[28] As in Pufendorf's (1672/1710, bk. 3, ch. 11) discussion of agents contracting on behalf of others.

[29] Hobbes 1651, ch. 16.

[30] '[I]f the supreme authority and power of making laws be conferred on the magistrate by the consent of the people..., then it is evident that they have resigned up the liberty of their actions into his disposure, and so all his commands are but their own votes, and his edicts their own injunctions made by proxy which in mutual contract they are bound to obey...' (Locke 1660, pp. 1–2; Locke 1660/1967, p. 126).

[31] Gewirth (1962, p. 129) writes: 'If a man has consented to government, then the government's acts become his own acts, and hence he in effect governs himself and is politically free. Consent thus furnishes the answer to what Rousseau [1762, bk. 1, ch. 6] called the problem of *droit politique*, the problem of how "to find a form of association... in which each person, while uniting himself with all, may still obey himself alone and remain as free as before."'

[32] In the above examples, *X* waives his rights against *Y*'s acting as *X*'s agent or occupying *X*'s marital bed or house without *X*'s consent.

[33] To adapt an example from Feinberg (1986a, p. 177).

Of course it may sometimes be the case that what is in his interests is also in your own.[34] And sometimes you might independently be in a fiduciary relationship with someone to whom you give consent to do some more specific thing that is in your interest. You consent to your surgeon removing your inflamed appendix or to your attorney cutting a plea bargain with the prosecutor. But in those latter cases what makes you expect the consent-receiving fiduciary to do what is in your interests is not the fact of a consenting relationship but instead the fact of a (wholly independent) fiduciary relationship.[35]

Sometimes mutual consent is akin to the mutual exchange of promises such as constitutes a contract.[36] Each party consents on condition that the other does likewise, and with the expectation that her interests will be served by entering into the mutually consenting relationship. But in such arrangements, what *X* consents to benefits *Y*, and what *Y* consents to benefits *X*. In cases of authorization, the principal benefits directly from what the agent does on his authority. In cases of mutual consent, in contrast, the consent-giver benefits only indirectly—not from the consented-to act itself being performed, but instead from the other's performance of the action upon which she made her own consent conditional.

6.3 Invoking Consent When You Should Not

When you have valid consent from someone, you have their permission to do what they have consented for you to do. They have waived their rights in that respect, and they cannot complain if you do what they consented to your doing. Still and all, it might be wrong for you to do it. You may not be committing a wrong *against them*—after all they have waived their right against you doing it. But it might be wrong in some larger sense.

Go back to the case of the lady in the Heathrow immigration queue whose pen you ask to borrow. Imagine it was the favourite pen of her recently deceased father, to whom she was deeply attached. She is irrationally reluctant to give her father's pen to a stranger, even if there is every reason to expect he will return it. But she has enough self-awareness to realize that her reluctance is irrational and she realizes that refusing your innocuous request would be socially inappropriate. So she reluctantly consents to loan you the pen. You sense her reluctance; nevertheless, you now have her consent. What should you do? I submit that you

[34] For example, consensual sex is mutually pleasurable—at least that is the hope and expectation going into it.

[35] This has already been mentioned in Section 4.6.3.1 and it will reappear in Section 8.4. Sometimes that fiduciary relationship might itself be based on consent (as it typically is with your lawyer or your surgeon)—but sometimes it is not (as in the case of your guardian).

[36] ALI 1981, §§ 1–2.

should just wave off the offer, saying 'Thanks anyway', and turn to the neighbour on the other side of the queue to ask for his pen.

For perhaps the most dramatic example of this sort of norm at work, consider the practice of duelling. In days of old, when you impugned someone's honour, they would challenge you to a duel at dawn, with pistols drawn at twenty paces. When you accepted the challenge you consented to the duel and all that it involved, including the chance of being shot and killed; in challenging you to a duel, your opponent did likewise. The honourable thing to do, having accepted the challenge to a duel, was to turn up at the appointed hour, take one of the pistols out of the box, walk the paces and turn to fire. But the decent thing to do was to fire into the air. Honour was thus satisfied, and no one got hurt.[37]

When Vice President Aaron Burr instead shot directly at Alexander Hamilton, he marked himself as an irredeemable cad. Hamilton had consented to the duel, to be sure. Burr had Hamilton's permission to kill him if he could, no doubt. But it was consent that clearly should not have been acted upon, even according to the norms prevailing at the time.

[37] Ellsberg 1956; Elster 1990; Brennan et al. 2013, pp. 123–4.

7
Revoking Consent

There are many things you may do to, or with, others only if they have given their consent to your doing so. But what if they no longer consent? On the face of it, the answer would seem obvious. If their consent is morally required for the action to be permissible, then once they no longer consent that action would no longer be permissible.[1]

That may be too quick, however. Just as there are some things to which we morally may not consent (selling oneself into slavery is the classic example[2]), so too might there be some circumstances in which consent, once given, may not be revoked.[3] That view has a long history. Some of the examples once offered now seem quite antiquated.[4] Others still seem compelling. A 'security agreement'

[1] Dougherty (2014, p. 38) for example argues that 'present dissent trumps past consent'; 'typically, when someone gives their consent, they can withdraw this consent later' (Dougherty 2021a, p. 56). He does not elaborate the exceptions to which his 'typically' might be alluding. But Wertheimer (2003, p. 154, n. 32) explains that he says 'ordinarily' in the same context in order 'to leave open the possibility that [the consent-giver's] subsequent refusal in a Ulysses case [of self-binding] does not trump her earlier consent token'. The criminal law similarly tends 'to privilege contemporaneous expressions of consent or nonconsent over prior conflicting preferences' (Husak 2010, p. 116).

[2] Locke (1690, § 24) declares flatly 'no man can by agreement pass over to another that which he has not in himself—a power over his own life'. See similarly: Rousseau 1762, bk. 1, ch. 4; Mill 1859, ch. 5, pp. 299–300. This view is of long standing: while selling oneself into slavery was permitted in ancient Rome, it was outlawed in the ninth century by order of Emperor Leo VI (888/1932, constituto 59, vol. 17, pp. 257–8). Hobbes (1651, ch. 14) and Tadros (2016, ch. 14) offer other examples of rights that you cannot consent to alienate. These issues are often discussed these days in connection with consent to medical treatment (Director 2019, p. 1070) and participation in medical experiments (Chwang 2008).

[3] Even though the agent meets the ordinary requirements of competence for consenting or refusing consent. Director (2019, p. 1070), for example, argues that one reason people cannot revoke consent to surgery is that the medical issues are so complex that the patient is incompetent to judge them (although that invites questions about the patient's competence to consent to surgery ahead of time either). We are looking, here, for cases of consent that morally *may not* be revoked—not merely for cases of a person being not competent to give or revoke it.

[4] Grotius (1625, bk. 1, ch. 3, sec. 8, subsec. 1) offers two examples of 'a Power which, tho' at first one was at Liberty to confer it or not, cannot afterwards be revoked by him that has once conferred it'. His first example concerns the transfer of political authority: 'Valentinian told his Soldiers, who had made him Emperor, when they desired something which he did not like, "It was indeed in your Power to chuse me your Emperor, O ye Soldiers! But after you have chosen me, what you request depends on me, and not on you. It is your Duty, as Subjects, to obey, and mine to consider what is proper to be done."' Grotius' second example is 'when a Woman chuses herself a Husband, whom she must from that Time always obey'. In English law under Henry VIII (1540), too, marriage was an 'indissoluble' private contract (Blackstone 1765, vol. 1, ch. 15, sec. 1, p. 423). In an infamous passage elaborating on that thought, Sir Matthew Hale (1736, vol. 1, p. 629) writes, 'the husband cannot be guilty of rape committed by himself upon his lawful wife, for by their mutual matrimonial consent and contract the wife hath given herself up in this kind unto her husband which she cannot retract'. As Lord Keith of

Consent Matters. Robert E. Goodin, Oxford University Press. © Robert E. Goodin 2024.
DOI: 10.1093/oso/9780192889027.003.0007

whereby you consent for your house to serve as collateral in case you default on a loan is a prime example of consent that cannot be revoked: of course you can, by mutual agreement, substitute something else as collateral, but you cannot unilaterally withdraw the house as collateral once the loan has been made based on it.[5] The aim of this chapter is to provide a normative account of under what conditions consent, once given, may or may not be revoked.[6]

Of course the consent-giver might have specifically stipulated, in originally granting consent, that it lapses after a certain period. When I say, 'I consent for you to borrow the car tonight', that consent automatically lapses at midnight; and when I say, 'I consent for you to hit me in the 10 rounds of our boxing match', that consent automatically lapses when the bell has rung for the last time. Such cases do not involve revocation of consent—consent was never given beyond the stipulated conditions, in the first place. In a variation on that scenario, the consent-giver might have specifically stipulated, in the original granting of consent, that it can be revoked at any time.[7] Labour contracts and international treaties, for example, almost invariably contain some such 'withdrawal' or 'termination' provisions.[8] Those cases are less problematic because in the original grant of consent the consent-giver has reserved the right to revoke it, and the consent-receiver in thereby put 'on notice' that that might happen. Some of the same issues I describe below may still arise even in those cases. But to simplify the exposition I shall here focus upon cases where consent is being revoked without appeal to any such provisions internal to the original granting of it. Likewise, I shall here bracket cases where consent cannot be revoked purely because, in giving it, the consent-giver stipulated that it could not be revoked.[9] In this chapter, I shall be looking for features intrinsic to consent and the

Kinkel said, however, in handing down judgment in *Regina v R* [1991] UKHL 12, 'In modern times any reasonable person must regard that conception as quite unacceptable'; and that rationale is now repudiated by all courts (Witmer-Rich 2011, pp. 387–8).

[5] ALI 2010, Art. 9. See further: Gilmore 1965; Witmer-Rich 2011, pp. 386–7.

[6] Note that there may also be cases, not to be further discussed here, in which people are not allowed to sign away their own right to revoke consent. One example might be matrimonial: marriage is a consensual relation, and you can enter into a prenuptial agreement governing what rights each party has over property in the event of dissolution of the marriage; but you cannot as part of that agreement legally extinguish your right to seek dissolution of that marriage (ULC 2012). Likewise, you can consent to your house serving as security for a loan, but you cannot legally sign away your 'right to redeem' your title to your house by paying off the loan (Curzon 1967, p. 91). Those may not be perfect examples, perhaps, because it may be questioned whether dissolving a marriage or redeeming title to your house really constitutes 'revoking' your previous consent. But they give the flavour of the thing, anyway.

[7] Director (2019, p. 1070) envisages a case where such a proviso is explicitly contained in someone's consent to sexual interaction.

[8] Those typically stipulate a period before which withdrawal is not permitted or a 'period of notice' that must be given before it can take effect (Koremenos 2016, pp. 140–57).

[9] When consenting to Thetis' request, for example, Zeus said: 'I'll nod my head. Among gods that's the strongest pledge I make. Once I nod my assent, nothing I say can be revoked, denied or unfulfilled' (Homer 800a BCE, bk. 1, lines 524–7). Ulysses consented to his men binding him to the mast and instructed them to ignore his pleas to be released (Homer 800b BCE, bk. 12); and such irrevocable 'Ulysses contracts' are common in social and political life (Elster 1979, ch. 2; 2000, ch. 1) and the practice of psychiatric medicine (Walker 2012).

circumstances surrounding it, rather than to stipulations that the consent-giver made when giving it, that might make it revocable or irrevocable.

7.1 What Revoking Consent Involves

Revoking consent would involve the following scenario:

(1) it was initially impermissible for *Y* to do φ to *X*;
(2) *X* then consented to *Y*'s doing φ to *X*, making it thereafter permissible for *Y* to do φ to *X*;
(3) *X* has now revoked that consent, making it once again impermissible for *Y* to do φ to *X*.[10]

To say that someone may revoke his previously-given consent would be to say (in Hohfeld's terminology) that he has a 'power' to regain the rights that he waived in originally giving that consent.[11]

As with the giving of consent, so too with its revocation: all the standard validity conditions apply.[12] The revocation must be intentional, there must be no force or fraud, it must be done by someone who is competent to do so.[13] Furthermore, the revocation of consent must be communicated clearly to the party to whom consent had previously been given, in order socially for that consent to count as having been revoked.[14]

[10] Dougherty (2021a, p. 120) phrases his version of (3) slightly differently: '*X* deliberately engages in behaviour *B* that indicates that *X* is re-imposing on *Y* the duty from which *Y* had been released by this consent'. I agree the effect of *X*'s revocation is that *Y* is now back under the same duty as before the consent was given, but I disagree about the process. *X* is not (re)imposing a duty on *Y*. Individuals not in authority cannot impose, or hence reimpose, duties on other people (not in that way, anyway). What is going on when *X* revokes his consent to *Y* is instead that *X* is withdrawing the waiver through which his previous consent had shielded *Y* from that duty.

[11] Hohfeld 1923. Feinberg (1984, p. 115) quotes approvingly Salmon's (1957, p. 261) claim, 'He cannot waive his right and then complain of its infringement.' But there is nothing paradoxical about someone simultaneously having both a Hohfeldian 'no-right' (as does the consent-giver, having waived his rights) and also a Hohfeldian 'power' to regain the rights that he has waived. He just needs first to exercise his 'power' to regain the rights and, only then, exercise his regained 'rights' to block the other's actions. Some may query the *value* to *Y* of *X*'s waiving *X*'s right against *Y*'s φ-ing if *X* can reclaim his right against *Y*'s φ-ing whenever *X* wants (Locke 1690, § 194)—but that overlooks the fact that, in between the time *X* waived and reclaimed his right against *Y*'s φ-ing, *Y* had *X*'s permission to φ and that in itself may be valuable to *Y*.

[12] But note that in Sections 8.5 and 11.3 I shall offer arguments for sometimes 'respecting a person's wishes' even if they do not meet the competence requirements for literally giving or withholding consent.

[13] Westen (2004, pp. 248–54) offers various examples of consent that cannot be revoked. But most of them involve people who are arguably incapable or incompetent (unconscious, drunk, psychologically 'frozen' by fright, absent, asleep or suffering a personality disorder); his other examples vaguely concern contracts, on which see Section 7.3.2.1 below.

[14] As the FCC (2015, ¶ 63) ruled in relation to consumers revoking their consent to receive robocalls on their mobile phones, 'consumers may revoke consent in any manner that clearly expresses a desire not to receive further messages'; it explicitly ruled 'that callers may not infringe on that ability by

Some suppose that it is a matter of conceptual necessity that any consent that can be given with moral effect can be revoked with moral effect.[15] By way of a rationale for that position, perhaps what is standardly said of the British Parliament could be said of morally autonomous agents more generally: no sovereign can bind its equally sovereign successors.[16] As Grotius put it, the right to revoke what a person previously willed follows straightforwardly from a person's 'liberty... to change his mind'.[17]

Others suppose the opposite, that consent by its nature can never be revoked. That might be thought to be so on the grounds that, as Hobbes puts it, a person has a 'duty not to make void that voluntary act of his own'.[18] In the context of consent to transfer property, Locke similarly asks 'can there be anything more ridiculous than to say: "I give you and yours this for ever",... and yet it is to be understood that I have a right, if I please, to take it away from you again tomorrow?'[19] You cannot consent to give me a perpetual easement allowing me to cross your property and then simply say, 'I changed my mind'.[20]

The same schizophrenia is found in contemporary legal discussions of revoking consent. In tort law, consent is basically always revocable.[21] In contract law, consent is never unilaterally revocable.[22]

This chapter will chart a path in between those more extreme positions. To foreshadow, I will argue that:

designating an exclusive means to revoke'. But the courts have ruled that a person's saying, 'We're ready to go now', is not sufficient to count as withdrawal of that person's previously-given consent for the police to search his car (US Court of Appeals 2004, p. 1029; see further Holcomb 2005).

[15] By 'with moral effect' in both instances I mean the giving or revoking of the consent changes (back) the moral status of the (de)consented-to act.

[16] Dicey 1939, p. 64.

[17] Grotius 1625, bk. 1, ch. 3, sec. 8, n. 4. True, in the case of an individual consent-giver, the 'successors' are not different agents but rather merely different stages of the same agent (Feinberg 1986a, pp. 84–6). Insofar as we see each person-stage as 'sovereign', the analogy still stands. But if 'personal sovereignty' attaches instead to the single ongoing entity, then it can be argued that the any person-stage should be empowered to make irrevocable commitments so the entity as a whole to pursue enduring projects and life-plans (Feinberg 1986a, p. 83; see also Parfit 1973).

[18] Hobbes 1651, ch. 14.

[19] Locke 1690, § 194. Although we colloquially use the term 'consent' in this connection, it is arguably really more a case of promising—and promises, unlike consent, can never be unilaterally revoked. See Sections 2.2.4 and 7.3.2.1.

[20] The reason may be that you have given the other a right—and rights give morally protected choices to the rights-holder, not the rights-bestower. Contemplating such a case, the *Restatement (Second) of Torts* says: 'the consent has become irrevocable... because the license given is coupled with an interest conferred upon the actor, which is itself a property right of which he cannot be deprived' (ALI 1979, § 892A, comment i). Seen that way, this is (in terms of Section 2.2.4's distinction) more like a case of a rights-conferring promise than of permission-granting consent. To foreshadow: in many of the examples given of consent that is irrevocable, that will often prove to be the case.

[21] According to the *Restatement (Second) of Torts*, 'upon termination of consent its effectiveness is terminated'; and 'consent is terminated when the actor knows or has reason to know that the other is no longer willing for him to continue the particular conduct' (ALI 1979, § 892A (5) and cmt. i).

[22] Consent can 'become irrevocable by contract' (ALI 1979, § 892A (5), cmt. i). See similarly ALI 1981, § 287, cmt. and *Reyes v Lincoln Automotive Financial Services*, 861 F3d (2d Cir. 2017). As I argue in Section 7.3.2.1 below, however, that is due to particular promissory features of contracts rather than anything to do with consent in general.

1) There are certain cases in which consent is irrevocable. Those are cases where it is logically impossible to revoke consent, because the consented-to act has already occurred (although there are various ways of construing that).[23]
2) In all other cases, consent is conditionally revocable. The condition in question is that the person revoking consent must (ordinarily) reimburse those from whom consent is being revoked for costs they have reasonably incurred in consequence of the consent having previously been given.[24]
3) Where that condition cannot be met, it is morally impermissible to revoke consent. That is the case where those costs do not, by their nature, admit of compensation. While the consent-giver is morally powerless to revoke consent in such a situation, it may also be the case that the consent-receiver morally ought not hold the consent-giver to that consent. That is the case where the consent-giver has substantially greater stakes in his consent not being acted upon than the consent-receiver has in acting upon it.[25]

Questions arise as to how we should construe the 'condition' set out in 2. Should it be seen as an *external* condition that morally ought also be satisfied when exercising a power to revoke consent, without the existence of said power being itself in any way dependent upon that condition being met? Or should it be seen as a condition that is morally *internal* to—part and parcel of—the power to revoke consent, such that you are morally powerless to revoke consent unless that condition is met?

In one way, it might not matter. A morally scrupulous and morally infallible agent will make sure to satisfy the conditions (insofar as he possibly can), whichever way we construe them. On the other hand, not everyone is morally scrupulous and no one is morally infallible. Hence it is important to work out the correct way to construe those conditions. If the condition that compensation be paid is internal to the power to revoke, the consent-giver would ordinarily be morally powerless to revoke consent without compensating the consent-receiver, whereas if it is external compensating would merely be some additional thing that morally he ought to do (but in practice he may or may not).

With the *giving* of consent, we are more inclined toward the external approach. There may be conditions under which consent should be given, but those are external standards. It is perfectly possible to give consent to something to which it

[23] See Ssection 7.2.

[24] See Section 7.3 below. The exceptions to which 'ordinarily' refers are set out at the beginning of that section.

[25] This is a possibility foreshadowed in Section 1.5 above and further discussed in Section 7.3.2.5 below.

should not be given. It is perfectly possible to fail to give consent to something to which it should be given.[26]

With the *revoking* of consent, I suggest we ought to be more inclined toward the internal approach. That is to say, you are ordinarily morally powerless to revoke your consent unless, at the same time (with some exceptions as discussed in Sections 7.3 below), you restore the person from whom consent is now being revoked to the same condition he would have been in had consent never been given.[27] The rationale for that is simply this: if you are going to undo your consenting, you must undo it *completely*.[28]

7.2 When Is Consent Irrevocable?

The permissibility of revoking consent turns on timing. Specifically, it may be permissible to revoke consent at some times, but not others, in relation to the timing of the performance of the consented-to act.[29]

7.2.1 After the Consented-to Act is Over

There are three distinct arguments against revoking consent to something that has already been done with your consent. Firstly and most fundamentally, doing so is conceptually impossible. That is to say, logically it cannot be done. But it is also true (in ways that bear on my subsequent discussions[30]) that doing so would, in any case, be pragmatically pointless and morally objectionable. For those second two reasons, it ought not be done even if it could be.

As regards the conceptual objection, recall my earlier argument for thinking it is logically impossible to give consent retrospectively, after the consented-to act

[26] See Section 3.5.

[27] By 'ordinarily' I mean of course to refer to the fact that this is to say no more than that there are strong *pro tanto* reasons to think that that is the case, but there might be other *pro tanto* reasons that are sometimes even stronger to think that it is not. High-stakes cases involving bodily integrity—sex and surgery for example—might often be cases of the latter sort (see Sections 1.1, 3.2.2, 5.2.4.3 above and 8.4 and 11.1 below).

[28] See further Section 7.3.2.4 below.

[29] This section will focus upon one temporal endpoint—the point *after* which consent can never be revoked. Section 7.3 discusses the role of others' having relied to their detriment on your previously-given consent in limiting your power to revoke it. That consideration fixes the other endpoint—the point *before* which consent can always be revoked. You are at liberty to revoke it at any point before others have come to rely on it. Likewise, both promises (Grotius 1625, bk. 2, ch. 11, sec. 16) and contractual offers (ALI 1981, § 36 (1)(c)) can be revoked if that is done before they have been accepted by the other party.

[30] In Section 7.3.1.

has already occurred.[31] You cannot change the past.[32] If the act would have been morally permissible only with your consent, which the actor did not have at the time of acting, then the actor committed a wrong in so acting at the time of acting. Nothing you now do can change that fact.[33]

Something similar can be said about the conceptual impossibility of retrospectively revoking your previously-given consent after the consented-to act is over. You cannot change the past. If the act was morally permissible with your consent, which the actor *did* have at the time of acting, then the actor committed no wrong in so acting at the time of acting. Nothing you now do can change that fact.

That is my reason for thinking that consent must logically be irrevocable after the consented-to act is over. But notice as well that, even if that were conceptually possible, there would be both pragmatic and moral reasons against doing it.

Pragmatically, it would be pointless to revoke your consent once someone already has done that to which you no longer consent. It would be pragmatically pointless in the sense that he has already done it, and he cannot now undo it in response to your revoking your consent. Giving or withholding or revoking consent is supposed to guide the actions of others, and actions that have already occurred cannot be so guided.[34] Just as there can be no backward causation, so too can there be no backward action-guidance.[35]

Morally, retrospectively revoking consent would constitute a violation of natural justice. Retroactive laws that criminalize conduct that has already occurred fail to give people fair warning and a fair opportunity to obey the law-not-yet-on-the-books at the time they act.[36] So too with retrospectively revoking consent to actions that have already been performed. What you have done would become

[31] See Section 2.2.1.

[32] You can of course provide recompense for wrongs done in the past—that is what compensation in tort law is all about, after all. But payment of compensation does not render past wrongs retrospectively right, or even 'all right'. Morally, the wrongs remain wrongs, even after full compensation has been paid.

[33] 'The fact that it was wrong to do at the time you did it', anyway. You can forgive, pardon or excuse the wrong, subsequently, of course, and in that way expunge blame for having done the wrong (as acknowledged in Section 2.2.1). But while that expunges blame for the wrong it does not change the fact that the wrong had been done. Indeed, 'expunging blame' presupposes the (continuing) existence of a wrong in the past, for which blame is being expunged.

[34] As I acknowledged in Section 2.2.1, your present actions can of course be guided by your present expectations about the other person's future actions. But that would be a case of your action being guided, not by *their* 'giving, withholding or revoking of consent', but rather by *your* anticipation of that. It is a case of *you* exercising control over your actions, not of *their* exercising control over their 'protected sphere' in the ways consent is supposed to facilitate (as I said at the very beginning of Chapter 1).

[35] I use the familiar term 'action-guiding' here, although strictly speaking consent does not positively direct action; it merely redefines the scope of what action is morally permissible. Still, that is action-guidance of a sort, defining moral boundaries that others' action may or must not cross.

[36] Bentham 1843, pt. 1, ch. 17, sec. 1; Woozley 1969; Fuller 1969, pp. 51–62. Some might say the Nuremburg Trials were an exception to this principle—rightly convicting perpetrators of a crime that was not a crime at international law at the time it was committed. But the judgments handed down make it clear that the justices regarded the crimes committed as crimes at international law at the time they were committed (IMT 1946).

impermissible only after you had already done it, at which point you could not alter your behaviour in light of the 'changed' normative status of your action.[37] That would be a denial of natural justice in the same way that retrospective laws are.

Here are some examples of cases in which it is commonly agreed that consent cannot be revoked because the consented-to act has already occurred:

- Recall this homely example from Section 6.2.1: If you have consented to your son's borrowing your car for the night, you can revoke your consent at any time up to the appointed hour on the night in question. But come the next morning, you cannot revoke your consent to his having borrowed the car last night.
- Here is a more consequential example from publishing ethics: Before a medical journal publishes a case report involving an identifiable individual, the patient (or their proxy in case of a child patient) must consent to publication. They 'may revoke consent at any time before publication, but once the information has been published, revocation of the consent is no longer possible'.[38]
- Here is an example from medical ethics: Parental consent is required before their children receive vaccinations. Parents 'can revoke or withdraw their consent at any time prior to a vaccination taking place'—but not afterwards.[39]
- And here is a final example from the law governing adoptions: When parents consent to the adoption of their child, many jurisdictions allow them to revoke that consent up until a certain point.[40] The exact point varies—but in no jurisdiction can birth parents revoke their consent to adoption after the court has issued the final decree.[41]

[37] 'Changed' in scare-quotes, because of course I am arguing that so such change can or should be allowed to occur.

[38] COPE 2016. That formulation is ambiguous as between 'morally possible' and 'practically possible' (i.e., once that issue of the journal has been published it is not practically possible to recall all copies of it that are in circulation). That it might be the practical rather than moral sense of 'possible' to which that quotation refers is suggested by another COPE (2015) ruling 'that consent can be revoked and that a journal should respect the wishes of a patient if they wish to revoke consent [even after the case report concerning them has been published]. The journal should then remove the paper from their website but leave a place marker, with a note saying that the paper has been removed and stating the reasons why. The journal should inform the patient that although the paper has been removed, there is little that can be done regarding copies already in circulation.'

[39] NSW Health 2019.

[40] In many jurisdictions, revocation is permitted only at the discretion of the court, with due regard to the best interests of the child.

[41] Anon. 1961. The point at which consent becomes irrevocable, or revocable only at the discretion of the court, varies by jurisdiction. It is never after the final court decree, but is sometimes well before that (when the child has been placed in the prospective adoptive home, for example, or once the court has issued the intermediate interlocutory order). Those earlier points presumably reflect, at least in part, the fact that by then others (the prospective adoptive parents) have come to rely on the consent of the parents giving up their child for adoption; I will say more about such considerations below.

7.2.2 When the Consented-to Act Has Commenced? Is Completed? In Between?

As that last example suggests, however, it is sometimes not so straightforward to determine the point at which the consented-to act has occurred and therefore consent can no longer be revoked. That uncertainty sometimes arises because the consented-to act takes place over a period of time rather than at an instant in time. In such cases, which should be considered the 'point of no return' for revoking consent: when the act first commenced, or when the act is finally completed, or somewhere in between?

In some cases we are inclined to think that consent may be revoked at any point while the consented-to act is still on-going.[42] In the US, the consent of criminal suspects is required for police to question them without their lawyer being present. They must also be told, 'If you decide to answer questions now without a lawyer present, you have the right to stop answering at any time.'[43] Similarly, a doctor may conduct an ordinary (non-emergency) medical procedure on a patient only with the informed consent of that patient or that patient's proxy[44]; and the patient or proxy can revoke that consent at any time during the procedure, even after it has commenced, in which case the physician must cease the procedure at the earliest safe opportunity.[45] Likewise, a scientific experiment can be conducted only with the consent of the participant in that experiment, who may revoke that consent and withdraw from the experiment at any point.[46]

[42] That is Guerrero's (2021, p. 373) position, for example: '[C]onsent can be withdrawn or altered at any moment up until the consented-to state of affairs is concluded. If the state of affairs I have consented to has not yet begun or is still ongoing, I can withdraw my consent.'

[43] This version of the warning is reported in, e.g., US Court of Appeals 2011, p. 121. As the US Supreme Court (1966, p. 444–5) said in the original *Miranda* ruling, 'If... [the suspect] indicates in any manner and at any stage of the process that he wishes to consult with an attorney before speaking, there can be no questioning.... The mere fact that he may have answered some questions or volunteered some statements on his own does not deprive him of the right to refrain from answering any further inquiries until he has consulted with an attorney and thereafter consents to be questioned.'

[44] See Section 11.2 below.

[45] According to the relevant Australian standard, 'good medical practice involves... accepting that patients have the right to refuse medical treatment or to request the withdrawal of treatment already started' (AMC 2016, 3.12.5). Kleinig (2010, p. 9) says similarly, 'A person who consents to a medical procedure or therapeutic regime may, after a time (though perhaps not any time), withdraw his or her consent'.

[46] Under the 'Common Rule' in the *US Code of Federal Regulations* (US DHHS 1991, Title 45, § 46.116.a.8), those seeking informed consent for participation in medical research must provide to potential subjects 'a statement that participation is voluntary,... and the subject may discontinue participation at any time without penalty or loss of benefits to which the subject is otherwise entitled' (reproduced in Emanuel et al. 2003, p. 46). This encodes into US law the principle of the World Medical Association's Helsinki Declaration that, 'In medical research involving human subjects capable of giving informed consent,... the potential subject must be informed of the right to refuse to participate in the study or to withdraw consent to participate at any time without reprisal' (WMA 1964, principle 26).

In other cases, however, we may be inclined to say the 'point of no return' for revoking consent is when the act first commenced. That was the old common law approach to sexual intercourse, for example. Having sex without the other's consent constitutes the assault of rape. Consent makes intercourse permissible. But under the traditional (now defunct) rule of common law, an initially consenting party could not revoke that consent once penetration had occurred, despite the sex act continuing after that.[47]

In yet other cases, the 'point of no return' for revoking consent comes somewhere in between commencement and completion of the consented-to act. Here is an example in the neighbourhood of that. If the police have neither a warrant nor reasonable grounds to suspect you have committed a crime, they may search you or your property only with your consent. If you have given your consent, you may revoke it at any time during the search—up until the point that some evidence of illegality is discovered.[48] Thereafter, the police may continue the search whatever you say. Having now found reasonable grounds for the search, they no longer require your consent to continue it; after that point, you have no right for the police not search your property; there is no longer any right to be waived by your consenting or to be reclaimed by your revoking it. The consented-to act, the search, remains ongoing but you cannot (with moral effect, anyway) revoke your consent to it any longer.

Finally, there may be some actions that are on-going and are never finally completed. In legislative proceedings, for example, members who vote in favour of a bill can be said to consent to its passage into law.[49] Depending on the rules of the

[47] Lyon 2004, p. 291; Parker 2013, pp. 1070–3. The old rule is well summarized by a California Court of Appeals as follows: 'the presence or absence of consent at the moment of initial penetration appears to be the crucial point in the crime of rape.... [I]f consent is given at the moment of penetration, that act of intercourse will be shielded from being a rape even if consent is later withdrawn during the act' (Best 1985, p. 242, emphasis added). Why should that have ever been thought to be so? Perhaps because it was thought that a 'categorical change' had occurred at the moment of penetration (she had then become a 'fallen woman', or ceased to be a 'virgin', or whatever). In Blackstone's (1765, ch. 4, sec. 3) day the civil law held that a 'prostitute or common harlot' was 'incapable of any injuries' by rape for this reason. If that is the explanation, then this becomes just another example of 'no retrospective revoking of consent' rather than a distinctive one as I treat it in the text. It can certainly be agreed that penetration is a very special *prima facie* wrong (Dempsey and Herring 2007, see similarly Best 1985, p. 243), without thinking as the old common law rule would have it that nothing after that matters so far as consent is concerned.

[48] '[C]learly a person may limit or withdraw his consent to a search and the police must honor such limitations. But, where a suspect does not withdraw his valid consent to a search for illegal substances before they are discovered, the consent remains valid and the substances are admissible as evidence' (US Court of Appeals 1986, p. 817). The exceptions subsequently adumbrated (airport passenger screening, prison visitation) serve to prove the rule (Holcomb 2005).

[49] The standard enacting clause in English legislation has, since the fifteenth century, been couched in terms of 'the advice and consent of the Lords Spiritual and Temporal, and Commons, in this present Parliament assembled' (May 2019, pt. 4, ch. 26, para. 9). This might seem like a sense of 'consent' different from 'permissive consent' which I earlier said would be the focus of this book (Chapters 1 and 2). But in a democracy, where legislators are acting as representatives of those who will be subjected to the laws, it might make sense to say that they are waiving rights on behalf of their constituents in consenting to have laws imposed on them. I am grateful to Garrett Cullity for this formulation.

assembly, they may be able to withdraw their consent by changing their votes up until the moment the votes have been tallied and the outcome officially declared.[50] On the face of it, that looks like the point at which the consented-to act (the enactment of the legislation) has occurred, and hence the point beyond which consent cannot be revoked. Notice, however, that parliamentary procedure standardly permits any member who voted in favour of a motion to 'move to reconsider' that motion.[51] That is not quite to say that, in legislative proceedings, there is literally no 'point of no return' for revoking one's consent.[52] But the example does suggest a certain 'fuzziness' as to when exactly it is a 'done deal', at least in legislative settings.

7.2.3 Consent to On-going Activities

Acts that occur over a period of time—and on-going activities and practices, more generally—thus pose distinctive issues for revoking consent.[53] Once something has been done it cannot be undone, which is what makes it impossible to revoke consent retrospectively.[54] But with activities that continue over a period of time, there is the possibility of stopping them mid-course. That in turn creates the possibility for people who initially consented to those activities to revoke consent mid-course.

Certainly we think nowadays that that is the right way to think about consent to sexual intercourse. While the old common-law rule used to be that a party could not withdraw consent to sexual intercourse after penetration, literally every US state now employs the opposite rule.[55] The firm legal rule now is that consent can be withdrawn at any time during sexual intercourse, and it constitutes rape if one party persists with intercourse after the other party has withdrawn consent.[56] That

[50] In larger-scale electoral settings, 'once one's vote has been made, one cannot (usually) retract whatever it is that one has consented to. Even if voting is still in progress, one's pulling the lever or depositing a slip in the ballot box places one at a point of no return' (Kleinig 2010, pp. 8–9).

[51] Robert 1876/1951, § 36.

[52] The right to 'move to reconsider' is circumscribed in various ways, as discussed in Section 7.3.1 below.

[53] Just as they did for giving consent, in Sections 3.3.3 and 5.1.2 above.

[54] Just as Section 2.2.1 argued it is impossible to give consent retrospectively—retrospective consent cannot undo the wrongness of the act that was done before consent had been granted. Some might think 'posthumous harm' some backward-reaching causation, although an alternative interpretation is not literally to the now-dead person but rather to his on-going memory or projects that survive beyond him.

[55] In 2019 North Carolina became the last US to embrace that rule (Padilla 2019; North Carolina General Assembly 2019, sec. 5(a)). There, that was done through a legislative enactment; in other states it has been done through court decisions. This position is widely endorsed by both philosophers (Brogaard 2018) and lawyers (Parker 2013; Ehrlich 2016).

[56] The new rule is well encapsulated in the trial judge's instruction to the jury in the first case in modern times to consider the question: 'During deliberations at trial, the jury asked the judge "whether consent can be withdrawn" and the judge responded affirmatively. The court's instruction stated:

contemporary consensus has now been written into the American Law Institute's revised *Model Penal Code*.[57]

Maybe that is also the right way to view legislative proceedings, as a series of repeated deliberations each of which constitutes an opportunity for consenters to renew or revoke their consent. Rousseau seemed to be thinking of politics in this way when he suggested that each session of the legislative assembly be opened with an obligatory vote on whether or not to renew consent to the existing laws, constitution and administration. In defence of that rule, he wrote that 'there is in the state no fundamental law which cannot be revoked, not even the social compact'.[58]

I have argued in Section 3.3.3 above, previous consent to an on-going practice can ground a legitimate presumption of continuing consent to that practice.[59] That presumption is a *defeasible* one, however. The strongest defeater of that presumption would of course be for the consent-giver to communicate clearly and explicitly to the consent-receiver that she no longer consents. But a range of much less clear and explicit signals may well suffice—if not literally to 'revoke consent', anyway to cancel the presumption of continuing consent. With the presumption of continuing consent thus cancelled, the consent-seeker must simply seek to reconfirm consent. This is simply to say that, when you are doing things that require someone else's consent, you must practice 'due diligence' in ensuring that you have it.[60]

A presumption-based approach offers one promising solution to the puzzle posed by the case of someone who does something that is conventionally taken to signal consent without actually intending to consent.[61] The receiver of that message is (at least weakly) entitled to presume that the other has consented;[62]

"consent initially given could be withdrawn and if the intercourse continued through use of force or threat of force and that the act at that point was no longer consensual this would constitute the crime of rape"' (Lyon 2004, p. 293, referring to *State v. Way*, 254 S.E.2d 760 at 761 (N.C. 1979)).

[57] Section 213.0(3)(e) of the *Model Penal Code*, as approved by the American Law Institute in October 2016, says on this point: 'Consent may be revoked or withdrawn any time before or during the act of sexual penetration or sexual contact. A clear verbal refusal—such as "No," "Stop," or "Don't"—establishes the lack of consent or the revocation or withdrawal of previous consent' (American Law Institute 2016). On the history of this revision see Morinigo (2016).

[58] Assemblies 'ought always be opened with two propositions, which no one should be able to suppress, and which should pass separately by vote. The first: "Whether it pleases the sovereign [assembly] to maintain the present form of government." The second: "Whether it pleases the people to leave the administration to those at present entrusted with it"' (Rousseau 1762, bk. 3, ch. 18). More recently, Calabresi (1982) has proposed that after a certain period of time statutes should expire unless they are renewed.

[59] The fact that the thing to which consent is being presumed is (or is part of) an on-going practice to which that person had previously consented forms an important part of what Dougherty (2018, p. 105) calls the 'background context' that you can and should take into account when assessing whether someone else consents.

[60] Dougherty 2018, p. 105; 2021a, ch. 11.

[61] Wertheimer 2003, ch. 7; Bolinger 2019.

[62] Assuming the sender of the signal knew (or could and should have known) what the receiver would understand it to mean, and there is no reason to think that the consent-receiver knew (or could and should have known) that the sender meant something different by it (ALI 1981, § 20).

and the onus is on the sender of the signal to clearly communicate, 'No, that is not what I meant.'[63] Saying that does not so much 'revoke consent' as clarify the fact that consent was never given—however justified the receiver of the previous message was in believing it had been, prior to that follow-up message being received. Once the follow-up has been received, of course, it would no longer be permissible for the recipient of the faux consent to do things to or with the sender for which her consent is required. But on this analysis he would have been justified in presuming he could do so, up until that follow-up clarification had been received.

7.3 Reliance Interests and Revoking Consent

The previous section discussed cases in which consent is irrevocable—you lack the power to revoke consent—because doing so is logically impossible. Now let us turn to cases in which it is logically possible to revoke consent and ask, 'Under what conditions ought doing so be morally permissible?'

As previously indicated, one strong reason that you should do as you have promised and permit what you have consented to is that other people have reasonably relied to their detriment on your promise or your consent.[64] Just as others' reliance is a *pro tanto* reason for you to do as you promised or consented, so too there is a *pro tanto* reason for you not to revoke consent you have previously given when, and because, others have already acted in reasonable reliance upon that consent.

If you do revoke consent you should ordinarily compensate them for the harm to those reliance interests that that causes.[65] Indeed, the moral permissibility of your revoking consent should ordinarily be *conditional* on your compensating them in that way, your power to do the one morally depending on your also doing the other.

There may be some exceptions to compensation requirements. One exception might come when the damage to the other's reliance interests is slight, and a

[63] Similarly with 'customary consent' as in Sections 3.3.4 and 3.3.6.

[64] See Sections 1.3.3 and 2.4 above. The clearest case of reliance interests being taken to ground claims is found in contract law (Fuller and Perdue 1936). 'Promissory estoppel', already briefly discussed (in Sections 1.4.2 and 5.1.1), arises in the following situation: you make a promise to someone, upon which you should reasonably expect her to rely; and she has indeed relied to her detriment on your promise. Then, even if your promise was unilateral, it is nonetheless legally binding upon you 'if injustice can be avoided only by enforcement of the promise' (ALI 1981, § 90). On the face of it, the correct remedy would be for the aggrieved party to be reimbursed the costs of his reliance; but, in part because those are hard to calculate, courts sometimes instead order one of the other remedies discussed below (Metzger and Phillips 1983, pp. 544–5; Becker 1987).

[65] A similar remedy for culpably negligent false consent has been proposed in Section 1.4.3.3.

simple apology would be more appropriate than compensatory damages.[66] (That would be the case where someone withdraws consent to sexual intercourse when the only cost that you have already incurred is that you have already unwrapped your condom, for example.) A second exception might be that, due to some special circumstances surrounding the case, the consent-receiver should be construed as having 'voluntarily assumed the risk' that the consent-giver would revoke his consent. (Those conducting medical experiments involving human subjects should expect some attrition in the pool of subjects; hence it would be inappropriate to require participants withdrawing from experiments to compensate the researchers for the costs incurred in experimenting on them before they withdrew.) In most cases, however, your power to revoke your consent should indeed be conditional upon your compensating those who have relied to their detriment on the consent you had given them that is now being revoked.

These are the same sorts of reliance interests as discussed in previous chapters.[67] Here, as before, one person incurred costs in reasonably relying upon what she took to be the other person's consent. In the 'mistake' cases earlier, that was a reason for treating someone 'as if he consented' when really he did not.[68] In the present case, however, the other person *really had* consented. There was no mistake about it; the other really had mentally consented at the time he socially signalled the consent that he now wishes to revoke.

The present case therefore does not, as did the previous ones, involve treating someone 'as if he consented'. Here he actually consented. Of course, now he no longer does; now he wants to revoke the consent that he had previously given. The question in these cases is whether he should be allowed to do so, and on what conditions, in light of others already having reasonably relied to their detriment on his earlier consent.

The 'revocation' cases differ from 'mistake' cases in a second way, as well. Previously, when saying someone 'reasonably relied' upon the other's consent, 'reasonably' was first and foremost a reference to the reasonableness of his having taken the other's signals as indicating that she mentally consented. In the 'mistake' cases she did not mentally consent, of course; but it is proper to treat her 'as if she consented', because it was reasonable for him to have understood her signals to indicate that she did.

In revocation cases, 'reasonably' refers in part to the extent of the costs that the consent-receiver incurred in relying upon the consent he had truly been given. What are 'reasonable' costs, and what are 'exorbitant' ones, is obviously going to

[66] As Corbin (1952, §200) says of the corresponding rule in contract law, 'the action or forbearance [in reliance] must amount to a substantial change of position. The abandonment of a peppercorn or the turning over of the hand will not be enough. A generous promise of a gift of $100 will not be made enforceable by the fact that the promisee walks a few blocks to the bank in the reasonable belief that the promise will there be performed.'

[67] See Sections 1.3.3 and 2.4.

[68] As was the case in Sections 1.4.2 and Chapter 4.

be highly context specific. But here is an example that will give a sense of it. Suppose I consent to your using my boat, which is moored at a distant port, to go deep-sea fishing; and suppose I then revoked my consent, after you had made your travel plans but before you have used the boat. I owe you compensation for costs 'reasonably incurred' in reliance on my now-revoked consent. So, for example, I owe you compensation for the unreimbursable costs of the flight that you booked to the distant city where the boat is moored. But it would be unreasonable for me to be expected to pay the full cost of the First Class ticket you actually purchased, rather than that of an Economy Class ticket that you could equally well have purchased to get there at the same time on the same day.

'Reasonably rely' might also refer to the reasonableness of expecting that the other's consent will persist and not be revoked. If someone is notoriously fickle and well-known for revoking consent, the consent-receiver could and should have known there is a significant risk of it being revoked; and it would be unreasonable for the consent-receiver to incur any substantial costs in reliance on his consent.[69] This consideration should not serve as a barrier to compensation altogether (unless the consent-giver could and should have been known to be completely fickle). But it should serve to reduce the compensation proportionally to the risk that the consent-receiver could and should have known there to be of the consent-giver revoking consent.

7.3.1 Reliance Interests

Notice that reliance is also at work in many of Section 7.2's examples of cases in which consent cannot be revoked. Acting in reliance on your consent, you son has already borrowed the car, the medical journal has already published the article, your child has already been vaccinated or adopted.

Of course, those are all also cases of revoking consent after the consented-to act has occurred, which makes it conceptually impossible for that consent now to be

[69] By 'unreasonable' I here mean 'pragmatically imprudent'. Remember, the aim here is to determine how much the receiver of the revoked consent deserves to be compensated, not how much the fickle person revoking it deserves to be punished for any bad behaviour. Remember, too, that the consent-receiver has no right (or any other sort of morally-grounded expectation) that the consent will continue. Contrast that with the case of a promise, in which you do have a right that the promise-giver not unilaterally revoke: if you know the promise-giver is likely to welch on his promise, it may still be imprudent for you to incur any great costs in the expectation that he will keep it; but you have a moral right that he keep his promise, and so you would be morally entitled to full (rather than risk-discounted) compensation for all of your (non-exorbitant) reliance expenses if he defaults on his promise. Or consider your moral right to walk unmolested, even in a dangerous neighbourhood: you have a moral right not to be molested, even if getting molested there is what you should statistically expect walking alone in that neighbourhood; and in a tort action for injuries received when you are indeed molested there, the compensation due to you should not be discounted by what you could and should have known about the probability of being molested there.

revoked. But as I pointed out in Section 7.2.1, revoking consent would also be a violation of 'natural justice'. That is certainly a powerful moral consideration against retrospectively revoking consent. That does not render the 'reliance' aspect otiose, however. Quite the contrary: the *reason* that retrospectively revoking consent would be an offence against natural justice is that others have already acted in reliance on your previous consent that you now want to revoke. That is precisely what would be unjust about it.

Others having already performed the consented-to act is the limiting case of others having acted in reliance on your consent. But they might have done all sorts of other things, short of the consented-to act itself, because they had your consent to that action. In so doing they might have incurred costs, whether out-of-pocket expenses or the costs of foregoing other opportunities.[70] Your having given your consent knowing that others were likely to rely upon it in this way, and their having done so, it would be unfair for you now to pull the carpet out from under them by revoking your consent and rendering those costs gratuitous.[71]

Parliamentary procedure similarly points to 'reliance' as grounds for not allowing legislators to revoke their consent to a proposition. As I have said, legislators signal their consent to legislation by voting for it; and they revoke that consent either by changing their votes before the assembly has finalized its decision or by 'moving to reconsider' a bill after it has been passed.[72] But parliamentary procedure dictates that '[t]he motion to reconsider cannot be applied . . . when the vote has been partially executed . . . or something has been done as a result of the vote that the assembly cannot undo, or to an affirmative vote in the nature of a contract, when the other party to the contract has been notified of the vote . . .'[73] There, revoking consent (via a 'motion to reconsider' anyway[74]) is prohibited precisely when, and because, others have come to rely on it.

[70] The emphasis here is on '*other* opportunities' forgone. When consent is revoked, you also suffer an 'opportunity cost' in no longer being able to do the previously consented-to thing: but in the terminology set out below, that is your 'expectation interest', not your 'reliance interest'.

[71] This is Hobbes' (1651, ch. 14) thought in explicating the 'duty not to make void that voluntary act of his own': Hobbes goes on to say that 'to undo that from which the beginning he had voluntarily done' is to do an 'injustice and injury' to the person in favour of whom he had relinquished his right. Kleinig (2010, p. 9) similarly comments, 'Consent creates reliance and those who have obtained our consent may be seriously disadvantaged if consent is subsequently withdrawn. A late withdrawal of consent to giving a lecture may sometimes reasonably result in liability for the costs associated with setting it up.'

[72] As discussed in Section 7.2.2. Of course the legislature could also repeal the previous enactment, in which case the restriction discussed in the text would not apply.

[73] Robert 1876/1951, § 36.

[74] The legislature can repeal laws it has previously enacted, 'revoking' the law (*Oxford English Dictionary*, q.v. 'repeal (v.)', definition 1b). But notice: that does not literally 'erase' the old law, in the sense of causing it never to have been law. When the 21st Amendment to the US Constitution repealed the 18th, the 18th did not disappear from the list and all intervening Amendments all move up one place. It was the law of the land between the time it was enacted and it was repealed; prosecutions under it were not quashed; sentences were not automatically commuted.

7.3.2 Irrevocable, or Revocable with Compensation?

Morally, what is the appropriate response to other people's having reasonably acted in (costly) reliance upon your previous consent? Does that warrant an absolute prohibition on revoking consent—denying altogether the consent-giver any moral power to revoke it—as in the parliamentary procedure example just discussed? Or ought we instead simply require consent-revokers to compensate others for the costs they have reasonably incurred when relying on their consent?

The fullest treatment of 'reliance interests' is found in contract law, so let us look to that for ideas in addressing those questions.[75] Contracts combine consent and promises, which differ from one another in certain respects. But as Section 2.4 has shown, they are alike in that both invite reliance. Hence, seeing how reliance interests are taken into account in breach-of-contract settings can usefully inform us as to how to approach the reliance interests that are damaged by revocation of consent as well.

To foreshadow, my conclusion will be that others' reliance to their detriment on your consent is not ordinarily a sufficient reason for prohibiting you from revoking that consent. But their reliance does constitute a strong reason for making your power to revoke consent conditional in form. The power to revoke consent ordinarily is, and ought to be, morally conditional upon the consent-giver compensating consent-receivers for the costs they reasonably incurred in relying upon the consent that is now being revoked.[76]

7.3.2.1 The Wrongfulness of Revoking Consent to Contracts

Because contracts cannot be cancelled unilaterally, contracts have long been thought to be the clearest case of a kind of consent that, once given, cannot be revoked.[77] Whether that fact about contracts really reflects on the revocability of consent in general, however, requires further analysis.

In one way, contracts not being unilaterally cancellable might just be a special case of the irrevocability of consent once the consented-to act has occurred. Here is how that argument would go. Each party can revoke his offer—which we might

[75] For the seminal discussion see Fuller and Perdue (1936).

[76] And where those costs are by their nature such that no compensation is possible, or the consent-giver cannot afford to pay it, the consent-giver is therefore ordinarily powerless to revoke his consent. ('Ordinarily' here is meant in the same way as previously stated, in footnote 27 in Section 7.1.) It may sometimes be the case, however, that the consent-receiver would be morally wrong to hold him to it, as discussed in Sections 1.5 and 7.3.2.5.

[77] Dougherty 2014, p. 29. One party to a contract 'may not alter a bilateral contract... without the consent of a counterparty'; *Reyes v Lincoln Automotive Financial Services*, 861 F.3d 51 (2017); cf. Daly 2018.

think of as his 'consent to a contract being concluded on these terms'[78]—at any time before the other party has accepted that offer.[79] At law, a contract is concluded at the point at which both parties have accepted one another's offers. Once that has happened, the consented-to act—'a contract being concluded on these terms'—has occurred. After that point, neither can unilaterally revoke their consent for precisely that reason. As argued in Section 7.2.1, it is a general truth about consent, nowise peculiar to the case of contracts, that consent cannot be revoked after the consented-to act has already occurred.[80]

Another even more natural reason for thinking that contracts are not unilaterally revocable is that contracts encode enforceable promises[81]—and as I have already said, promises cannot be revoked.[82] Just as going back on a promise without the promise-receiver's agreement is a moral wrong, breaching a contract without the other party's agreement is a legal wrong.[83] But while you cannot release yourself from a promise, the person to whom it was made *can* release you. That explains why contracts can be cancelled bilaterally, with each party releasing the other from her contractual obligations. Note well, however: it is a case of each releasing the *other* from his promissory obligations, not a case of anyone revoking his *own* consent to the contract.

How does any of this bear on revoking consent more generally, however? Consent to a contract may be one kind of consent. But it is a very special kind of consent—one that bundles up consent together with a promise. Not all consent is like that. It is perfectly coherent to give your consent to something while at the same time saying, 'But be warned, I might change my mind and revoke my consent—no promises!' As I said at the outset of this chapter, contracts and international treaties take that form all the time. So even if consent is not unilaterally revocable where it involves a promise, that tells us nothing whatsoever about whether it is unilaterally revocable in other cases.

[78] We speak colloquially in this way. But as argued in footnote 23 to Section 4.4.1, 'offers' in contractual negotiations involve (in terms of Section 2.2.2 above) 'conditional promises' rather than (or anyway, in addition to) 'consent'. The remaining paragraphs in this section explore the 'promise' rather than 'consent' interpretation.

[79] ALI 1981, § 42.

[80] 'Security agreements'—offering your house as collateral for the loan—can be seen as a special case of this rather than as the sort of exceptional case that Witmer-Rich (2011, pp. 386–7) takes them to be.

[81] ALI 1981, § 1. That conventional wisdom within the law that contractual 'agreement is an exchange of promises' is tricky to explicate philosophically, however (Gilbert 1993).

[82] See Section 2.2.4 above. But as noted there, and again immediately above, promises (like contractual offers) *can* be revoked before they have been accepted by the other party.

[83] Dougherty 2014, pp. 30, 39. It may also be a legal wrong, even outside narrowly contractual settings, if the promisee reasonably relies on the promise to her detriment and the promisor could reasonably have expected her to do so—that is the case of 'promissory estoppel', already discussed (ALI 1981, § 90; see also Sections 1.4.2 and 5.1.1 above). At international law, 'the termination of a treaty or withdrawal of a party may take place' only 'by consent of all the parties' unless the treaty in question makes explicit provision otherwise (UN 1969, art. 54).

7.3.2.2 Legal Remedies for Breach of Contract

While it is always wrong to break a promise or breach a contract, the remedy ordered by courts when a contract has been breached is only rarely 'specific performance', requiring that the promise-giver (as nearly as possible) do precisely what was promised.[84] It is far more common for courts to order the breaching party to pay damages in lieu of doing what was promised.[85]

Contract law offers multiple ways of calibrating the appropriate amount of damages to be paid. The two most relevant for present purposes are those already mentioned: (1) damages can be calibrated according to the promise-receiver's 'expectation interest', i.e., how well off the promise-receiver would have been had the promise been carried out; (2) alternatively, damages can be calibrated according to the promise-receiver's 'reliance interest', i.e., how well off the promise-receiver would have been had the promise never been made.[86] The former relates to the promise-receiver's expected gains from the promise being kept, whereas the latter relates to the actual losses the promise-receiver has incurred as a result of the promise having been made (and relied upon).

7.3.2.3 Strict Performance and Prohibiting Revocation of Consent

Contracts paradigmatically give rise to 'expectation interests'. A contract is a 'bargained' agreement.[87] Each party to it has consented to it expecting to benefit in some way from the contract being carried out. Indeed, in contracting, each has given the other a right in that respect. That is why, when one party fails to deliver as promised, it might be thought that the other party should be compensated for those disappointed expectations of gain.[88]

Outside of contractual settings, however, the giving of consent is not typically preceded by negotiations where parties are each obviously bargaining for expected

[84] ALI 1981, §§ 307, 358(1). This is 'specific delivery or restoration of the subject-matter', in Blackstone's (1765, bk. 3, ch. 8) terms.

[85] This is 'pecuniary satisfaction in damages', in Blackstone's (1765, bk. 3, ch. 8) terms.

[86] See Sections 1.4.3 and 2.2.5 above. 'Judicial remedies... serve to protect one or more of the following interests of the promisee: (a) his "expectation interest," which is his interest in having the benefit of his bargain by being put in as good a position as he would have been in had the contract been performed; (b) his "reliance interest," which is his interest in being reimbursed for loss caused by his reliance on the contract by being put in as good a position as he would have been in had the contract not been made' (ALI 1981, § 344).

[87] '[T]he formation of a contract requires a bargain in which there is a manifestation of mutual assent to the exchange and a consideration.... To constitute consideration, a performance or a return promise must be bargained for. A performance or return promise is bargained for if it is sought by the promisor in exchange for his promise and is given by the promisee in exchange for that promise' (ALI 1981, §§ 17, 71). Kenessey (2020) argues, more contentiously, that promises in general are 'proposals in joint practical deliberation'.

[88] As the doctrine of 'promissory estoppel' has expanded from unilateral 'donative' cases to more 'commercial' ones, this has become increasingly true there as well (Becker 1987).

gains.[89] The interests at stake there are, as I have said, primarily 'reliance interests', costs incurred in consequence of the now-revoked consent having been given in the first place.[90] Focusing on reliance interests of that sort, our aim would to make the one person as well off as she would have been if the other person's revoked consent had never been given.[91]

Would prohibiting a person from revoking consent be a good way of doing that? Insisting that '*X* permit *Y* to do what *X* consented to permit *Y* to do' would, in effect, be to require specific performance on *X*'s part. It is to require *X* to do exactly as he said he would, rather than compensate *Y* in some other way. At law, however, 'specific performance' is ordinarily ordered only to protect 'expectation interests', *not* 'reliance interests'.[92] And there is good reason for that. A promise-receiver's expectation interests pertain to how well off the promise-receiver would be had the promise-giver done as promised. Making the promise-giver do as promised is a way of guaranteeing that. A promise-receiver's reliance interests pertain to how well off the promise-receiver would have been had the promise never been made. Making the promise-giver do as promised is hardly a way of 'undoing' the promise.

Reliance interests are defined in terms of how well off the other would have been had the promise/consent never been given. The right way to restore him to that position is to reimburse him for the costs he has incurred in relying upon that promise/consent. Putting him in the same position he would have been in had the promise/consent been honoured, by requiring 'specific performance' of the contract or prohibiting revocation of the consent, is ironically to put him in a *different* position than he would have been had the promise/consent never been given. That is the very opposite of what we are supposed to be doing in protecting someone's reliance interests.

7.3.2.4 Making Revocability Conditional on Due Compensation

What we are morally worried about when someone revokes consent, I submit, are the costs the other person has incurred by acting in reasonable reliance upon that

[89] Maybe 'expectation interests' might be an appropriate measure of compensation for revoking consent in very special cases that are similar to contract in relevant respects—e.g., where the consent was similarly mutual, with the consent of each being conditional upon the consent of the other, with each having some substantial 'stake' (i.e., expectation interest) in what the others has consented to, and with the exchange being concluded with sufficient solemnity to signal to all parties its seriousness.

[90] See Sections 1.5, 2.2.5 and 2.4 above.

[91] This is another way in which contract differs from promise, over and above those surveyed in Shiffrin (2007). Note that when courts award damages for breach of 'preliminary agreements' those are typically for reliance interests (Schwartz and Scott 2007).

[92] And then only when damages would not be adequate to protect the expectation interests in view (ALI 1981, § 359).

consent. Refusing to allow revocation of consent altogether is not the right way to address those concerns, as I have just shown. Instead, we ordinarily ought to permit the consent-giver to revoke consent, conditional upon his compensating those to whom consent had been given for the costs that those consent-receivers had reasonably incurred in relying upon it.[93]

The compensation requirement grows out of a concern for parity of treatment as regards the consent-giver and the consent-receiver. Revoking consent would restore the *status quo ante* for the consent-giver: it restores to him the rights that he waived when giving the consent that he is now revoking. But if the *status quo ante* is to be restored to one party to the consent transaction, it must be restored to all parties. That means that the consent-receiver must also be restored to the same situation he would have been in had the consent never been given. That is why compensation should ordinarily be paid to him, sufficient to reimburse him for all the costs that he has reasonably incurred in relying upon the consent that is now being revoked.[94]

Notice that that is precisely what is done when, for example, planning authorities revoke consent they have given to someone to use land in a certain way. Take the UK, for example. There, planning authorities are permitted to revoke or modify such consent as has been previously given. In doing so, however, they must 'serve notice on the owner' that that consent is being revoked; and they must pay compensation to 'any person interested in the land [who] has incurred expenditure in carrying out work which is rendered abortive by the revocation or modification, or has otherwise sustained loss or damage which is directly attributable to the revocation or modification'.[95]

The implications of the consent-revocation rule here being proposed would be as follows:

- Firstly, it obviously sets the presumption against any general prohibition on revoking consent to actions unless they have already occurred. Compensation for costs people have incurred when acting in reasonable reliance on the other's now-revoked consent is the most that should ordinarily be required.

[93] As I have said in explicating 'ordinarily' in this context (in footnote 27 in Section 7.1), this principle might not apply to high-stakes cases, such as surgery and sex.

[94] It must restore him to exactly the same position as before, which requires what I have elsewhere dubbed strong 'means-replacing' rather than weak 'ends-displacing' compensation (Goodin 1989).

[95] UK *Town & Country Planning Act*, §§ 22.2, 22.4. However, 'no compensation shall be payable... in respect of loss or damage consisting of the depreciation in value of any interest in the land by virtue of the revocation or modification' (§ 22.4). In the terms from contract law discussed above, that is to say compensation will be paid for damage done to the owner's reliance but not expectation interests. Similarly in Australia, the New South Wales Environmental Planning and Assessment Act 1979 stipulates that 'any... person entitled to rely on the [revoked] consent... is entitled to recover... compensation for expenditure incurred pursuant to the consent... which expenditure is rendered abortive by the revocation or modification of that consent' (§§ 96A.5, 96A.7).

- Second, payment of such compensation should morally ordinarily be required as a condition of permitting him to revoke that consent.[96] Morally, consent-givers should ordinarily be powerless to revoke their consent unless they pay due compensation for the costs that consent-receivers have reasonably incurred in relying on the consent that is now being revoked.
- Third, the measure of compensation that is required should be no more than is needed to recompense the costs of consent-receivers' reasonable reliance on the now-revoked consent. The measure is not how well off they would have been had the previously-consented to act been performed (their 'expectation interests'). It is merely how much they are out-of-pocket for the previously given consent having now been revoked.

7.3.2.5 Uncompensatable Losses

What about cases where substantial *un*compensatable harm would be done to the other party, were you to revoke your previously-given consent?[97]

Above I have argued that, morally, the power to revoke consent is ordinarily predicated upon payment of compensation to those who have incurred costs in reasonably relying upon that consent.[98] Where it is, if the costs are such that, by their nature, they are incapable of being compensated that condition cannot be satisfied and, hence, the consent-giver morally would ordinarily lack the power to revoke his previous consent.[99] That follows straightforwardly from the conditional nature of the moral power to revoke consent.[100]

Someone who would suffer uncompensatable losses if the other person were to revoke his consent therefore ordinarily continues to have the other's consent, even

[96] As I said in footnote 93 to this section, 'ordinarily' here serves (among other things) to exempt consent to high-stakes activities, such as for example sexual intercourse or surgery. In such cases, perhaps consent-givers should be permitted to revoke their previous consent even if they cannot afford to compensate consent-receivers for expenses that they have already reasonably incurred in relying on that consent.

[97] Bentham (1843, pt. 1, ch. 16) similarly identifies a set of commodities that are 'susceptible of a value in affection' that should be exempt from 'forced exchanges'.

[98] I should add '*full* compensation'. In tort suits for the wrongful death of a relative, plaintiffs are paid *some* compensation (e.g., for lost earnings of the deceased) even though no payment can compensate them fully for the loss of their loved one.

[99] Similarly, at contract law specific performance—which, as I have said, is akin to prohibiting revocation of consent—is ordered when, and because, the other's losses from breach would be impossible to compensate or to calculate (ALI 1981, §§ 359(1), 360. See also: Fuller and Perdue 1936, pp. 64–5; Metzger and Phillips 1983, pp. 544–5; Becker 1987). The underlying reasoning is that, if compensation would be required to right the wrong and compensation is impossible, then we must simply prevent the wrong from occurring in the first place.

[100] Here I focus on costs that are 'by their nature' incapable of being compensated. But obviously it is equally true that if the costs are by their nature capable of being compensated, and the consent-giver simply cannot afford to pay them, then the condition morally imposed on revoking consent cannot be met and consent cannot ordinarily be revoked.

if the other would now like to revoke it. But there are circumstances in which people ought not invoke the other's consent and act on the permission that it gives them.[101] Morally, they would be within their rights to do so; but all things considered, it might be morally wrong for them to do so.

It is important to remember in this connection that, just because you deem something to be irreplaceable and nothing would compensate you for its loss, that does not necessarily mean that you deem that thing to be of particularly great value. A classically economistic way to think about irreplaceable goods is through the distinction between the 'protection value' and the 'insurance value' a person places on them.[102] If something (some family heirloom, for example) is irreplaceable for you, you will spend money to protect it but none to insure it (insurance compensation would be pointless, as nothing can replace it). The difference between the 'protection' and 'insurance' values that you assign to something is a good measure of just how irreplaceable it is for you. But notice: even things that are deemed by those standards to be highly irreplaceable are rarely infinitely valuable to you. You would not spend *any* amount of money to protect them from harm.[103]

Hence it is possible that, even though consent-receiver *Y* would suffer losses that are uncompensatable in form were *X*'s consent to *Y*'s φ-ing revoked, those losses might not be of any great magnitude. And on the other side, consent-giver *X* might suffer substantially greater losses (maybe even of something *X* regards as irreplaceable) if *Y* were to act upon *X*'s consent and proceed to φ.

In such cases, because *Y*'s losses would be uncompensatable if *X* were to revoke his consent, *X* is ordinarily morally powerless to revoke it. Once *Y* has been given *X*'s consent to *Y*'s φ-ing, *Y* always has it; and nothing *X* subsequently does can change that fact, where uncompensatable losses are at stake for *Y*. Nevertheless, because *X* would suffer so much greater losses from *Y*'s φ-ing than *Y* would suffer from *Y*'s not-φ-ing, *Y* morally ought to refrain from acting on *X*'s permission for him to φ. That is the case, even though *Y* would be perfectly within his rights to go ahead and φ.

7.4 Conclusion

In short, there are three broad approaches we might take toward revoking consent. We might say, with Hobbes, that it should always be prohibited. We might say, with Grotius, that it should always be permitted. Or we might say that it should be permitted, but only in certain circumstances or on certain conditions. In this

[101] As discussed in Sections 1.5 and 6.3.

[102] Cook and Graham 1977.

[103] Goodin 1983.

Chapter, I eschewed the first two more extreme alternatives and offered instead a proposal along the latter lines.

The first plank of that proposal is that there are certain circumstances under which consent can never be revoked. Those are basically ones in which the consented-to act has already been performed. Not only would it be pragmatically pointless and a violation of natural justice to do so (although that is true too). More importantly, it is conceptually impossible to revoke consent in such circumstances—being powerless to change the past, you are simply incapable of either consenting or revoking consent to things that have already happened. There are of course complications about when exactly that cutoff occurs, about when 'the consented-to act has already been performed', as we have seen in Section 7.2. But at least in broad outline, the principle is straightforward.

The second plank of my proposal is that, those circumstances apart, revoking consent is morally permissible—but ordinarily only on condition that the person revoking it compensates the person from whom it is revoked for costs he had reasonably incurred in reliance on the now-revoked consent. There may be exceptions to that rule, where the costs are small or where the consent-receiver voluntarily assumed the risk that the consent-giver would revoke the consent. But where reliance interests are substantial and there is no credible case for voluntary assumption of the risk, compensation must be paid to the party whose reliance interests are damaged in order for the revocation of consent to be morally permissible.[104]

If follows from the second plank of my proposal that, where reliance interests are such that they cannot be compensated and neither of those exceptions apply, the consent-giver is morally powerless to revoke his consent. A necessary condition for doing that is lacking. But it is worth bearing in mind that, just because you have someone's consent to do something, that does not necessarily mean that you should do it. Morally, you might have someone's permission to do something that, all things considered, morally you ought not to do.[105]

[104] The compensation that is due can, however, be discounted proportionately to the risk that the consent-receiver could and should have known there to be that the consent-giver would revoke consent.

[105] There are all sorts of reasons that you morally ought not to do something other than that you lack the requisite consent to do it. And, remember, being given consent does not provide a positive reason to do something; it merely negates one reason not to do it.

PART III
SPECIAL CASES

8

Consent of the Unconscious and the Incompetent

Kinky Sex

Sexually forcing yourself upon someone else without their consent is assault, pure and simple.[1] As such, it is both immoral and illegal. The other's granting of consent can transform that otherwise impermissible intrusion into an act that is morally permissible. But in the absence of the other person's clear consent, it must be presumed that they do not consent to sexual relations. The consent must actually be communicated, not necessarily verbally but nonetheless in a way that clearly attests to the will of the consenting party.[2] The consenting party must be competent to consent and must be acting voluntarily and free of force or fraud.[3] For purposes of the present discussion, I will simply take all that as read.

Although once controversial, it is nowadays also a platitude both morally and legally that consent to sexual relations is revocable at any time during intercourse.[4] Someone who initially consented to sexual relations is morally entitled to revoke that consent at any time during the sex act. Once consent has been revoked, it becomes immediately impermissible for the other party to persist in sexual acts on the party who no longer consents to them.[5] The sheer fact that someone initially consented to sex does not commit that person to continuing to consent, nor does

[1] Owing to the gender sensitivities surrounding these topics, I shall here use 'they' and 'their' as gender-neutral singular terms, grammatically grotesque though that is.

[2] That is to say, consent requires both the appropriate mental element and a 'performative' (Wertheimer 2003, ch. 8; Kleinig 2010, pp. 9–12; Miller and Wertheimer 2010, pp. 84–6). The latest version of the American Law Institute's *Model Penal Code* says, 'Consent may be express or it may be inferred from behavior—both action and inaction—in the context of all the circumstances' (ALI 2016, sec. 213.0(3)(b)).

[3] Failure of the last condition is central to 'rape by deception' cases, which the law in places sometimes fails to criminalize (Rubenfeld 2013; Pundik 2015) but which philosophically surely count as invalid consent beyond some threshold (Dougherty 2013; cf. Manson 2017).

[4] The American Law Institute's *Model Penal Code* says, 'Consent may be revoked or withdrawn any time before or during the act of sexual penetration or sexual contact' (ALI 2016, sec. 213.0(3)(e)). (I take those two terms, 'revoke' and 'withdraw', to be synonymous in this context; and I will systematically use 'revoke' for consistency with Chapter 7 above.) As has been discussed in in Sections 7.2.2 and 7.3 above, common law traditionally held that a woman could only withdraw consent to sexual intercourse before penetration but not thereafter, but that traditional rule has now been supplanted in all US states (Lyon 2004).

[5] That is to say, I presume that the circumstances set out in Section 7.3.2.5 above will almost (perhaps literally) never be met where a person wants to revoke their consent to sexual relations. In

Consent Matters. Robert E. Goodin, Oxford University Press. © Robert E. Goodin 2024.
DOI: 10.1093/oso/9780192889027.003.0008

it permit the other to presume continuing consent in the face of conflicting evidence.

But what if someone is incapable, for one reason or another, of communicating the fact that they have changed their mind about giving or withholding consent to the sexual encounter? That poses problems because consent, at least in its interpersonal form, is more than merely something within one's own head. To serve its social function, consent must be communicated to the person to whom it is being given or from whom it is being withdrawn.[6] And that is precisely what is, *ex hypothesi*, impossible in the sorts of cases that will be under discussion in the bulk of this chapter.[7] At the end of the chapter I turn to consider the case of someone who is capable of communicating but who is incompetent to give or revoke consent in some other respect.[8]

Were we focusing exclusively on cases of 'giving consent', that problem would seem to admit of an easy solution. The obvious rule should be 'do not do anything that would require someone else's consent, unless their consent has been clearly communicated to you'.

Revoking consent poses harder problems. There, the other person has previously communicated clear consent to you, but they now have changed their minds. They no longer consent. Given that they are unable to communicate that to you, however, you have no way of knowing that fact. Had they been capable of communicating any change of mind to you, you might (or might not) have been entitled in the absence of any such communication to presume that their initial consent persists. But given that they are unable to communicate a change of mind, and given you know that that is the case, you are much less clearly entitled (indeed, arguably are not entitled at all) to any such presumption.[9] Those are the issues that lie at the heart of this chapter.

8.1 Non-verbal Revocation of Consent

At law, all sorts of things other than explicit verbal instruction can constitute sufficient evidence of consent to sex or of revocation of previous consent to sex.[10] Some philosophers may want to deny that (or severely circumscribe the extent to which) non-verbal forms of communication can constitute the *giving* of consent to

terms of the rule set out in that earlier section, the stakes of the person wanting to revoke consent (bodily integrity) will almost always (perhaps literally always) outweigh the stakes of the person wanting to persist in sexual relations.

[6] As argued in Sections 1.2.2 and 2.3.1.

[7] In Sections 8.1 through 8.4.

[8] In Section 8.5.

[9] Even of consent to the same sexual act on the same occasion, much less the same act on some later occasion—except perhaps in the case of 'on-going consent' among long-term sexual partners as discussed in Section 3.3.3 above.

[10] ALI 2016, secs. 213.0(3)(b), (c) and (e).

sex.[11] But even they would presumably accept that non-verbal forms of communication can clearly constitute the *refusal* or *revocation* of consent to sex.

Suppose someone originally consented to engage in bondage sex and was bound and gagged accordingly. If gagged, they may not be able to verbally articulate their subsequent revocation of consent. Being bound, they may not be able to push away their attacker. But they can nonetheless communicate in other ways—through grunts, squirming, scowls, and so on—that they no longer welcome the other's sexual intrusions.

True, they can only communicate 'after a fashion', and their communications may be open to multiple interpretations. But just as sex is assault in the absence of clear communication of consent, so too ought it count as assault in the presence of any indication, however ambiguous (within broad limits), of revocation of consent. That too can, I think, nowadays be taken to be a platitude.[12]

8.2 Consent of the Uncommunicative

Let me now push the hypothetical scenarios into more uncharted territory. Suppose that, instead of a case of bondage sex, we are dealing with a case of 'conscious simulated necrophilia'.

Imagine one person, with the other's fully informed consent, injects them with a strong sedative rendering them incapable of any motion whatsoever, in order to perform sexual acts on their motionless body.[13] That person, once so sedated, is incapable of communicating in any way whatsoever, either verbally or physically. Yet while incapable of motion, imagine that the sedated person nonetheless remains conscious throughout the sexual encounter.

Now imagine that the sedated person, who is still conscious albeit motionless, changes their mind in the middle of the sexual encounter and ceases to consent to it.[14] The sedated person is incapable of giving any indication whatsoever that they now no longer consents. And being incapable of communicating in any way, the

[11] Cf.: Dougherty 2015; Pallikkathayil 2020.

[12] Which is not of course to say that there is no philosopher who dissents from it. Hurd (1996, p. 137) notoriously offers the case of someone having sex with a mute quadriplegic, saying that 'he does not, as a moral matter, rape her if she in fact possesses the subjective mental state required' for consent, even if she can do nothing to communicate consent. Although Hurd does not address withdrawal of consent in connection with that example, presumably she would say the same about that.

[13] Call that the 'Romeo and Juliet scenario' (Shakespeare 1591, act 4, scene 3, pp. 270–1). Of course such a drug could not be safely used without a respirator.

[14] This is a variation on Wertheimer's (2003, pp. 48ff.) 'Quadriplegic' case. The present case is importantly different from his, however: in the case here under discussion, the sedated person *did* give consent before falling into that state, in a way that Wertheimer's Quadriplegic did not.

sedated person is incapable of 'revoking' their consent, insofar as 'revoke' is an active verb and the sedated person is *ex hypothesi* incapable of any action.[15]

Yet the other party has no way of knowing that the sedated person no longer consents. All that they know is that the sedated person previously consented. And, for all they can possibly know, the sedated person continues to do so. Still, from an objective perspective it is morally impermissible to persist in performing sexual acts on the no-longer-consenting party. It is always objectively wrong to do that. But, here, that would be blameless wrongdoing, because the perpetrator had initiated the sexual adventure with the consent of the victim and had no way of knowing—or, indeed, reason for supposing—that that consent ceased to be present. The wrong may therefore be excused, on grounds of unavoidable ignorance.[16] Excused or not, however, the wrong remains wrong.[17]

One way of resisting that conclusion might be to analogize this case to that of Ulysses, who in effect consented to waive any right to revoke his consent to his crew's binding him to the mast until after they had safely passed the Sirens.[18] Perhaps it can be said that the participant in simulated necrophilia, in consenting to being sedated, consented to waive any right to revoke their consent during the period they were under sedation.[19] They certainly rendered the right moot, insofar as it would be (and they knew, or could and should have known, it would be) impossible to effect revocation by communicating it to the other participant. But rendering a right moot is not the same as waiving it. In consenting to be sedated, that participant has also rendered moot (incapable of being claimed by them during the period of their sedation) all other rights they may have against everyone and anyone. But it would be crazy to say that in consenting to be sedated that person has waived their right against your taking their car without their permission or selling their house out from under them. Why should we think of their right to revoke their consent to sex acts while sedated any differently?[20]

[15] Notice that it does no good, in this case, to say that the sedated party should have built a clause into their consent agreement to cover this case (as in Director [2019, p. 1070]), because being incapable of communication at the time of changing their mind the sedated person would have no way of activating that clause.

[16] Of course, while the ignorance itself may have been unavoidable, acting in ignorance was utterly avoidable—just do not have sex in those circumstances (on which see Section 8.3 below).

[17] This is to follow Alexander (2014).

[18] Homer 800b BCE, bk. 12.

[19] Of course, Ulysses—and likewise mental health patients who sign 'Ulysses contracts' giving their doctors permission to ignore requests they make when in the midst of a psychotic episode (Walker 2012)—have good reasons for disavowing the preferences and beliefs that they can anticipate changing in unfortunate ways during the period over which they waive any right to revoke their consent (Elster 1979, ch. 2; 2000, ch. 1; Van Frassen 1995). The participant in simulated necrophilia has, at least in the story as told, no reason to expect either (i) that their preferences will change while sedated or (ii) that if their preferences do change, those new preferences will be in any way inferior to their preferences before being sedated.

[20] Here is a counterexample: when enlisting in the military, you do so for a fixed period of time without any power to terminate your service before the end of that period (although you can of course connive to get yourself dishonorably discharged). But I am inclined to regard that as a 'fixed-term slavery contract', morally suspect for that reason. Cf. Simon 1951.

8.3 At Whose Risk?

Now step back from that case, to reflect upon this further question. Does the very fact that consent cannot be revoked by a completely sedated party mean that such sexual practices should be deemed morally impermissible altogether?[21]

There are strong grounds for supposing that that ought to be so. Recall the parallel argument against allowing one to sell oneself into slavery. As John Stuart Mill says, there are no grounds in autonomy for respecting someone's choice to abnegate their autonomy.[22] By the same token, we may suppose that people ought not be allowed to consent to arrangements that physiologically preclude them from communicating the fact that they have revoked their consent when mentally they have done so. Following this line of reasoning, we ought not regard their consent to such arrangements as being morally valid.

If we take that line, then the one party's consent to being sedated (for these purposes anyway[23]) was morally inoperative. The other party would have been acting without the valid consent of the person to be sedated, both before and after they were sedated. Even if the victim purportedly consented, that consent was morally invalid—and those acts were nonetheless morally impermissible all along.

That would be an awfully strong conclusion.[24] A weaker (but still pretty strong) conclusion might be that, knowing that it could not be known whether the other party changed their mind once sedated, the perpetrator would have been acting morally completely at their own risk in that sexual encounter. True, if the sedated party had changed their mind, the perpetrator would have had no way of knowing that fact. But on this account, that would not excuse the perpetrator. Instead the perpetrator would be liable for any moral wrong committed, however faultless he may have been in committing it.[25]

[21] The same issue would presumably arise with 'bondage sex', wherein much of the erotic appeal lies in having sex with someone who pretends not to consent—it would, anyway, unless the participants had previously negotiated 'safe words' or other signals that could be used to indicate that they genuinely wanted to stop and they were not just pretending to do so for the sake of the sex game (Kukla 2018, pp. 79–90).

[22] Mill 1859, ch. 5, pp. 299–300.

[23] This case differs from consenting to the administration of anesthesia for surgery, for reasons to be discussed in in the next section.

[24] In generalized form, it would for example rule out all sorts of 'Ulysses contracts' whereby one binds oneself against temptations and weakness of will (Homer 800b BCE, bk. 12; Elster 1979, ch. 2; 2000, ch. 1).

[25] Having voluntarily assumed the risk, per Section 4.4.2 above; perhaps it might even be deemed to be an 'ultra-hazardous activity' meriting strict liability, per Section 4.6.3. The latter would be akin to the strict liability that was imposed on purveyors of intoxicating liquor during Prohibition in the US. Note however that, post-Prohibition, 'dram shop laws' made liability depend on negligence (i.e., serving alcohol to someone whom the server knew or should have known was intoxicated), which is absent in the case discussed in the text (Krentzman 1996, pp. 1258–9).

8.4 Consent of the Unconscious

Next let us imagine a case of 'unconscious simulated necrophilia'. In that case, the person who consented to simulated necrophilia sex is not merely sedated but is rendered literally unconsciousness.[26] Would that change anything?

In several ways, it may seem that it should not. In this case, just as in that other, the person consented in advance to the sexual encounter. In this case, as in that, once sedated they are incapable of communicating any change of mind during its course. The only difference is that, by rendering the person unconscious, the sedative has rendered them incapable even of changing their mind.

Of course, it makes no *practical* difference whether they are capable of changing their mind, given that they are incapable of communicating that fact—which they are on both this scenario and the last. Still, rendering the person incapable of changing their mind (performing the mental act of revoking consent) seems worse somehow. Why? Perhaps because preventing someone from forming and revising judgments abnegates the victim's moral autonomy, whereas leaving them conscious and incapable merely of action abnegates only their physical autonomy. Both are important, but perhaps judgment is morally far more central to autonomy than is action.

Some might see the problem as residing in the fact that when a person has been rendered unconscious their moral autonomy has been 'put on hold'. This analysis fully acknowledges that the person consented to the proposed arrangements before they were rendered unconscious and that their giving of that consent was a genuinely autonomous act.[27] But, the analysis would go on to say, once unconscious their consent is 'on autopilot'—and even if the agent had autonomously switched on the autopilot, the actions of the autopilot are not fully the agent's own. I have rejected this line of analysis in Section 1.2.1.1, however. There I argued that mental consent should be seen as a mental 'act of commitment' that remains in force until and unless it is undone by another mental act of a similar sort—and it does so even if the person who had performed that act has mentally moved on to think about other matters or, indeed, if they have lost consciousness altogether (falling asleep in the earlier case, being sedated in this one).

Some might persist with broadly the same line of argument by invoking the Attitudinalist claim that a 'consenting state of mind' is ontologically required for

[26] This is a much harder case than one of mere fainting, which Pallikkathayil (2020, p. 122) breezily dismisses saying that 'without prior discussion of this specific circumstance, consent to sex while unconscious cannot be assumed.' In the case here in view, the person *had* consented to unconscious sex.

[27] In Dworkin's (1986) phrase, they have exercised 'precedent autonomy' in giving you an advance directive.

consent to exist.[28] It is not just (as I have been saying) that you cannot be *sure* you have their consent at the time you perform those acts. Rather, these theorists would insist, someone who is unconscious at the time you perform the acts is mentally incapable of consenting or refusing consent to them at all.[29] If Attitudinalists are correct that consent ontologically requires a person to be of a 'consenting state of mind' at the time the consented-to act occurs, and a person is not of that (or indeed any other) state of mind at the time you perform the consented-to sexual acts on them, then it is morally impermissible for you to perform those acts—whatever the other person may have said ahead of time.[30]

Perhaps there may be something *special* about sex that requires a 'consenting state of mind' at the time the sex act occurs. (I shall say a little more on that topic in the next section.) But as I have already shown in Section 1.2.1.1, consent *in general* does not require a 'consenting state of mind' at the time the consented-to act occurs. Recall the case offered there of my son borrowing the car to go to midnight mass. I am soundly asleep at the point at which my son drives off, so he does not have my occurrent consent at the time he performs the consented-to act. But it would be absurd to say that he has taken my car without my consent. In that case, at least, it seems that I do not need to be awake when he performs the consented-to act in order for him to genuinely have done it with my consent.

Even allowing for that counterexample, many people are likely to say, 'But consent to sexual relations is different!' The most general way of characterizing that difference is presumably in terms of the size of the stakes.[31] Something more should be required, in terms of consent, for high-stakes activities such as sexual relations, compared to low-stakes activities such as the trivial borrowing of a car. But consider what we require by way of consent to another equally high-stakes activity: invasive surgery.

Requiring that the consent-giver actually be of a 'consenting state of mind' at the time the consented-to act was performed would rule out advance directives of all sorts even where we think they should be honoured. I will discuss advance directives more fully shortly.[32] But for now let us focus on the case of an advance

[28] Discussed and discounted in Section 1.2.1.

[29] Except perhaps in a 'dispositional' sense (Feinberg 1986a, pp. 173–4). Take 'the case in which someone who objects to a treatment is asleep or unconscious when he needs it; in that case we can say (using a dispositional sense of objecting) that he continues to object then' (Dworkin 1986, p. 12). But 'dispositional consent' is, as Westen (2004, p. 271) points out, 'hypothetical consent'—about which Dworkin (1975, pp. 18–9) was elsewhere rightly scathing. See further Sections 1.2.1.1, 2.2.2 above and 11.2 below.

[30] That was the holding of the Supreme Court of Canada in *R. v J.A.*, 2S.C.R. 440, para. 66: 'The definition of consent for sexual assault requires the complainant to provide actual active consent throughout every phase of the sexual activity. It is not possible for an unconscious person to satisfy this requirement, even if she expresses her consent in advance.' An exception might be people in a long-term on-going sexual relationship, who (as argued in Section 3.3.3 above) might have given one another 'on-going consent'.

[31] Critically discussed in Section 5.2.4.3 above.

[32] In the next section and again in Section 11.2 below.

directive that almost everyone would surely agree ought to be honoured: consent to a surgical procedure that must be conducted under general anaesthesia.[33]

Of course the patient must give consent to the surgery in the first place. And had the patient remained conscious during the surgery they would of course be entitled to revoke that consent at any point, and the surgeon would then have to stop as soon as it is medically safe to do so. But suppose the surgery is performed under general anaesthesia rendering the patient unconscious. It will then be impossible for the patient to give continuing consent throughout the operation. Still, we think the surgeon should be morally permitted to conduct the surgery.

One way of reading that case is as showing, once again, that consent is an 'act of commitment' that remains in force even while the patient is unconscious. That would be the most obvious, and the most defensible way, to preserve surgery on unconscious patients as involving genuine consent. Furthermore, that is the way that they are generally regarded—that is what it said atop the 'Consent to Surgery Form' that the surgeon had the patient to sign prior to surgery, after all.[34]

Applying these lessons to the case of simulated necrophilia sex, the upshot is this. Sex acts performed on the unconscious party might be consensual if they had consented to that—if they had performed an 'act of commitment' to that effect that remains binding even while they are unconscious—in advance of being rendered unconscious.[35]

[33] Discussing a case to which I will return in Section 8.5, den Hartogh (2022, ch. 15) argues that 'advance euthanasia directives in case of dementia' cannot be valid because someone with severe dementia cannot at that point participate in such shared decision-making. But then again, neither can a surgical patient once anesthetized. If shared decision-making at some earlier point is good enough in the latter case, it is unclear why it should not be in the former.

[34] As argued in Section 4.6.3.1 and elaborated in Sections 11.2 and 11.3, the surgeon is in a fiduciary relationship with the patient (Joffe and Truog 2010; Miller and Wertheimer 2010, p. 92; and Snyder 2012, p. 75)—and that may render surgery on the unconscious permissible even in the absence of consent. Even if surgeons have a pecuniary interest in the fee they will be paid for the surgery, they are nonetheless under strong injunctions of professional medical ethics to put the interests of their patients first. The modern version of the Hippocratic Oath, as codified in the Physician's Pledge contained in the Declaration of Geneva, has the physician pledging, 'The health and well-being of my patient will be my first consideration' (WMA 1948, clause 2). As the American College of Physicians' Ethics Manual further elaborates: 'Although the physician should be fairly compensated for services rendered, a sense of duty to the patient should take precedence over concern about compensation' (Snyder 2012, p. 75, see also pp. 88–9) .

It is also the case that the patient had authorized the surgeon to conduct surgery on them while unconscious. But 'authorizing' is not the same as 'consenting' (Section 6.2.3). Furthermore, what authorization does is create a 'principal–agent relationship', whereby the surgeon becomes the agent of the principal for the purposes specified. At common law, however, an agent's authority to act was traditionally terminated once the principal became legally incompetent (ALI 1958, §§ 122(1), 133). By 1984, however, all US states had enacted statutes providing for 'durable power of attorney' that remained valid even after the principal became legally incapacitated (Boxx 2001, p. 12).

[35] The other two arguments canvassed in the footnote immediately above do not transfer from the case of the surgeon to the case of simulated necrophilia. Except perhaps among long-term partners, it seems unlikely that any fiduciary relationship generally exists among parties to simulated necrophilia sex. Show me any equivalent of the Hippocratic Oath for perpetrators of kinky sex! The person who

8.5 Consent of the Incompetent

Now compare the situation of the consent of people who are uncommunicative (perhaps even unconscious) with that of people who are conscious and communicative but incompetent. The interesting cases, for my purposes, will be those involving someone who was competent to consent at one point in time but has ceased being so.

My running example will be that of someone who becomes really very seriously inebriated. For purposes of this discussion, let us stipulate (although some of might disagree[36]) that anyone who is *that* seriously inebriated cannot validly consent to sexual intercourse.[37] But imagine this scenario. Suppose someone said, 'Please get me blind drunk and then make love to me!'[38]

That case falls interestingly in between the cases offered in Sections 8.2 and 8.4. In the former case, the person consented to simulated necrophilia sex and then was rendered mute but conscious. The person who consented when sober to having sex once drunk similarly (let us assume) remains conscious despite being blind drunk. But like the person in Section 8.4 who consented to simulated necrophilia sex and was then rendered unconscious, the person who consented when sober to 'having sex when drunk' is, once drunk, unable (because, we are here assuming, seriously drunk and hence incompetent) to make moral transformations through any voluntary act of will.

Now, many of the same cautions offered in Section 8.3 clearly apply in the case of the person who consented when sober to having sex when drunk. Maybe we ought to regard the proposal, 'Please get me drunk them make love to me!', as akin to a slavery contract and dismiss its moral authority on the same grounds—people ought not, and ought not be allowed to, consent to arrangements that preclude them from revoking consent.

The more interesting wrinkle, to my mind, is this. What if the person who consented when sober to 'having sex when seriously drunk' says, once drunk, that

sedates the other for those purposes is hardly acting purely for the best interests of the person sedated: those perpetrating simulated necrophilia sex have interests of their own in play as well, and those interests will commonly predominate over any concern that they have for the interests of the unconscious object of their sexual attentions. Furthermore, in the case of kinky sex the sedater is not the 'authorized agent' of the sedated in respect of anything other than, perhaps, the administration of the sedative (Wertheimer 1996, p. 109).

36 Particularly if the person had become intoxicated voluntarily (Hurd 1996, p. 141; Wertheimer 2001; 2003; 2010; Buchhandler-Raphael 2017).

37 It is a fuzzy line, of course (Dixon 2001a; Director 2022)—but again, let us just stipulate that the intoxicated person is clearly over the line.

38 Such a scenario is contemplated in passing, but not further discussed, by Wertheimer (1996, p. 106, n. 32; 2003, p. 156ff.; 2010, p. 213). Boni-Saenz (2016) and Director (2019) advocate for 'sexual advance directives' being respected in the case of 'people with persistent acquired incapacity living in long-term care institutions' (p. 4); but Boni-Saenz (2016, p. 14, fn. 74), at least, is 'skeptical [about]... the utility of sexual advance directives for temporary incapacity'.

they no longer consent?[39] *Ex hypothesi*, a person, once that drunk, is incompetent to consent to sex. But is a person who is incompetent to consent, because so seriously drunk, also incompetent to revoke the previously given consent to sex?

On the face of it, incompetence seems to disqualify a person from making any moral transformations at all through voluntary acts of will. And that should, on the face of it, work the same in both directions—for giving consent and for revoking consent likewise.[40]

Many of us, however, would intuitively want to say that the drunk's expressed desire not to have sex should be respected, even if the converse (a drunk's consenting to have sex) should not be.[41] How can we make normative sense of that intuition?

One way would be to say that, just as you should not have sex with someone who is unconscious whatever they said beforehand granting you consent to do so, so too you should not have sex with someone who is seriously drunk whatever they said beforehand. But as Section 8.4 has shown, it is far from clear that that is the right way to handle the advance consent of someone who is now unconscious, which puts a question mark over its extension to the case of the drunk as well. In any case, on that account the drunk's saying 'No!' would also be morally irrelevant, in a way that it seems (to me, anyway) not to be.

A second way of making sense of the intuition would be by saying that you need *occurrent* consent at the time you perform the consented-to act, which *ex hypothesi* you do not have in the case of sex with someone who is unconscious

[39] In defending advance sexual directives, Boni-Saenz (2016, pp. 26–30) focuses a very different sort of case where the person consents to sexual relations both before and after becoming incompetent. The same is true of Director's (2019, p. 1070) baseline case, although he goes on to consider a case like the one under discussion here; but there he explains away why 'saying "no" when drunk' has moral force by stipulating that the consent-when-sober contains the (explicit or implicit) proviso 'unless I say "no" at the time'. In a way that just re-poses the same problem: how does anything that is said by someone too-drunk-to-be-competent suffice to activate that proviso? But to avoid that evasive manoeuvre, let us simply suppose that no such proviso was attached to their consent. Indeed, for the starkest version of the case here under discussion, imagine that they said when sober, 'And ignore anything I say to the contrary at the time'. Director (2019, p. 1070) says 'it is highly unlikely that anyone would agree to such a directive', which is probably ordinarily true—but remember, here we are considering 'kinky sex' and there it often is not (Kukla 2018).

[40] Maybe a different, lower standard of 'competence' should be required for revoking consent than for giving it in the first place. This view comports well with the 2009 German statute that allows a medical advance directive to 'be informally revoked at any time, even [by persons] with limited decision-making capacity' (Wiesing et al. 2010, p. 779). But this solution fails in the case at hand for the same reason given in response to the 'different evidentiary standards' proposal below.

[41] There is a certain amount of case law on the topic. Consider for example the Kansas case of *State v Chaney*. There, the Court of Appeals had argued that: 'Consent is a two-edged sword; on the one side is consent and on the other is refusal to consent. If the victim can do one, he or she can do either.' But the Kansas Supreme Court overruled them on that point, saying, 'It is not outside the realm of reason to think that a victim can be too drunk to provide valid consent to sex yet remain capable, on some level, of rejecting unwanted aggression' (*State v Chaney*, 5 P.3d 492, 496 Kan. 2000). Director (2019, p. 1070) is tempted by that conclusion but struggles to justify it.

or drunk.[42] In both of those cases, your sexual partner would be incapable of consenting at the time you perform the sexual act—in the one case because unconscious, in the other because seriously drunk. I argued above that occurrent consent is not morally required as a general rule. But maybe there is something special about sex that makes that rule true there, even if it is not elsewhere. Perhaps that is because there is something special about consenting to sex. Or perhaps that is because of something about the nature of sexual relations and their value: for example, some perfectionists may build 'mutuality' into that, thereby making it impossible to have meritorious sexual relations with someone who is unconscious.

A third way to make sense of the intuitive asymmetry might be to say that different standards of proof should apply in the case of giving and revoking consent. That seems correct. Whenever consent is morally required, surely there is a presumption against concluding that you have it—and where something serious is at stake, that is a strong presumption.[43] 'More likely than not' cannot be the right standard of proof; something more like 'beyond a reasonable doubt' should surely be required.[44] If so, a somewhat questionable piece of evidence that you do not have consent would be morally conclusive in that direction, in a way that a similar piece of evidence that you do have consent would not be equally morally conclusive in that direction.

Does that really help with the case of the no-longer-consenting person who is seriously drunk, however? It might, in borderline cases where you are simply not certain whether the other is sufficiently inebriated as to count as incompetent for consent purposes.[45] But where the other is clearly so inebriated as to be completely incompetent, the differing standards of proof for giving and revoking consent cannot help. What someone who is *clearly* incompetent says cannot count as evidence in either direction.[46]

A fourth approach might be to say that we should respect the wishes—or anyway *certain sorts* of wishes, to be elaborated below—of someone even if when expressing those wishes they are not in a fit state to validly give or withhold or revoke consent. In the case under discussion, this could have the seemingly-odd consequence of allowing incompetent (drunken) wishes to override competent (sober) consent. But that would not merely be an ad hoc response to the case at

[42] Some say something like that is true of seeking informed consent to medical procedures (Hertogh 2009), assuming that that process is conceived of as 'shared decision-making' (President's Commission 1982, vol. 1, ch. 1; Katz 1984, pp. 86–7; cf. Faden and Beauchamp 1986, pp. 278–9; Katz 1994).

[43] As argued in Section 1.1 above.

[44] ALI 1979, § 892D, comment a. Dougherty 2015, pp. 252–3.

[45] Director (2022), for example, explores this 'grey area'.

[46] Likewise, even if (as discussed in footnote 40 to this section) a lower standard of competence is required for revoking consent than for granting it in the first place, someone who is *completely* incompetent does not clear that bar no matter how low it is set.

hand. There are other cases where that would yield what seems to me the intuitively correct conclusion.

Consider some medical examples.[47] Someone, when completely competent, signs an advance directive specifying what treatments they want their physicians to administer to them in particular circumstances should they become incompetent to make those decisions. Suppose that in that advance directive they instruct their physicians to undertake some invasive, painful, long-shot treatment should a certain condition befall them. Suppose that condition does befall them, and they are now drugged up to their eyeballs with strong pain killers that render them incompetent to give or withhold consent. Still, they are conscious, and they beg their physicians not to act on their prior instructions and instead let nature take its course. I, for one, would be very reluctant to hold them to their prior word, even accepting that they are not now of a completely sound state of mind.

Or, again, take the case of a patient who is now suffering severe dementia. Suppose that patient had signed an advance directive clearly requesting euthanasia in such circumstances. But suppose the patient now clearly wishes to continue living. I think we should respect those wishes even though the patient is no longer competent and even though respecting those wishes goes against the patient's competent-self's prior consent.[48]

With these examples in hand, we are now in a position to characterize which sorts of wishes are to be respected in that way. In the two examples just offered, the incompetent persons are expressing a wish for the 'moral default' treatment that would be required if they do not consent to something else.[49] No one can be subjected to invasive medical procedures, much less euthanasia, without their consent.

Now take the case, possibly more contentious, of a Jehovah's Witness who has signed an advance medical directive not to be given blood transfusions. Suppose he has suffered an accident that leaves him in desperate need of a blood

[47] Director (2019, p. 1068) resists the extension to cases of medical advance directives. His resistance seems based mostly simply on the fact that it is counterintuitive. The only arguments he offers in support of those intuitions ultimately hinge on the 'proviso in the original consent' manoeuvre grounding his intuitions in the drunken-sex case, which seems to me a jerry-rigged response that is much inferior to the alternative analysis I here offer. See the discussion in footnote 39 to Section 8.5.

[48] Many cases of this sort have arisen in The Netherlands since the legalization of euthanasia there in 2002: physicians are very reluctant to act upon patients' advance directives to euthanize them if they become severely demented (de Boer et al. 2011; Karasz 2019). I can find only one reported case of anything remotely like holding a demented patient to their advance directive for euthanasia against their current wishes (Karasz 2019)—yet even then it was not clear whether the patient was 'resisting a lethal injection' as opposed to merely 'getting up and wandering off' (as dementia patients are wont to do) as it was being administered (Asscher and van den Vathorst 2020, p. 72).

[49] The same rule is found in human research ethics concerning experimentation on minors. Being minors they are incompetent to give consent; consent ('permission') must be obtained from surrogate decision-makers (usually their parents). But if the Institutional Review Board deems the minor sufficiently competent to give meaningful 'assent' (if not 'consent'), the minor's assent is also required. That is mandated by the 'Common Rule' in the *US Code of Federal Regulations* (US DHHS 1983, Title 45, §46.408.a; for discussion see Leikin 1993).

transfusion, and suppose that he is now (in his current seriously deranged state) begging the attending physicians to give him one. Were he fully competent when he asked for the transfusion, that case would be an easy one: his current competent consent would then clearly override his previous equally competent refusal of consent. But *ex hypothesi* he is not now fully competent. Some would say, in consequence, that 'his former decision remains in force because no new decision by a person capable of autonomy has annulled it'.[50]

But had the attending physician not known of the patient's advance directive or religious convictions and a transfusion was urgently required, the physician would have given the injured person a transfusion on the grounds it is in the patient's best medical interests. Confronted with a deranged patient who refuses urgently needed medical treatment to which he had consented when he was competent to do so, the doctor would have no hesitation in ignoring his deranged wishes. The case here in view is the opposite: the deranged patient is demanding urgently needed medical treatment against the directions of his previous, competent self. But the fact that the patient is asking for what is in his best medical interests as they are conventionally understood should surely carry *some* weight with the doctor who is trying to decide whether to honour the patient's current (albeit deranged) wishes or the patient's previous (fully competent) advance directive. That is not because there is any uncertainty about the patient's current competence—*ex hypothesi*, the patient here is totally incompetent. It is merely because the patient, however impaired his judgment, is actually asking for the moral default, here, what is medically in his best interests.

Return now to the case of drunken sex. The person, when fully competent, had consented to having sex when blind drunk but, once drunk, clearly said 'No!' Even though drunks are not morally competent to give, withhold or revoke consent, the fact that the person is asking for the moral default—no unwanted sexual relations—surely makes that incompetent person's request worthy of respect.[51]

This is I think best seen as analogous to the case discussed in Section 6.3 in which, although clearly you have someone's permission to do something, morally you ought not to act upon that consent. Strictly speaking you still have the person's consent; being seriously drunk, the person is incompetent to revoke it. But the fact that what the drunk is asking for, when asking you not to act on their prior consent, is the moral default points to independent moral reasons for your not acting on that consent even if you still have it.

[50] Dworkin 1995, pp. 227–8. See also Dworkin's (1986, pp. 11–12) earlier discussion of this case.

[51] In a way that it clearly would not be if the person when competent had insisted on the moral default and only when drunk agreed to sexual relations.

9

Consent of the Mute

Medical Interventions in Hunger Strikes

It is a central principle of medical ethics that patients must give informed consent to any medical intervention, and patients who initially consented may revoke their consent at any time during the medical intervention.[1] The same is also true of decisions to withhold consent. People who previously declined to consent to a medical procedure must be able to change their minds with moral effect, as long as that procedure remains medically appropriate.[2]

But what if, as in the previous chapter, people find themselves in one way or another unable to communicate the fact that they have indeed changed their minds? The last chapter's cases involved people who initially consented to something (there, sexual intercourse) but subsequently changed their minds; they wanted to revoke their consent, but they found it pragmatically impossible to communicate that fact. This chapter will focus on consent to medical interventions during hunger strikes.[3] The change-of-mind that will be involved in these cases goes in the opposite direction, from initially refusing to now wanting to consent, but once again finding it pragmatically impossible to communicate that desire. The two sets of cases are importantly different in many ways.[4] But the pragmatic impossibility of communicating the fact that one has changed one's mind about consent poses real problems in both sets of cases.

[1] According to the relevant Australian standard already quoted, 'good medical practice involves... accepting that patients have the right to refuse medical treatment or to request the withdrawal of treatment already started' (MBA 2009, 3.12.5; see similarly Australian Medical Association 2004, sec. 2.1.6).

[2] Note well, however: 'revoking your past refusal of consent to φ' is not, in and of itself, 'giving your consent to φ' (see Sections 3.5 and 9.3.2).

[3] The bulk of this chapter assumes that conscious hunger strikers are mentally competent to give or withhold consent, arguably unlike anorexics (Tan et al. 2003). Section 9.5 takes up the case of comatose hunger strikers.

[4] One important point of difference is that the last chapter's cases involve a personal act and whereas this chapter's cases typically involve hunger-striking as a political act (Aitchison 2022). Another point of difference is the power imbalances involved. Some sets of sexual partners are more unequal than others, to be sure, but few are as unequal as prisoners and their warders; and 'the reason food refusal is often chosen as the act of assertion of autonomy is that often all other areas of autonomy have been removed as options' (Reyes et al. 2013c, p. 100). Remember, however, the relations here in view are between prisoners who are on hunger strike and their physicians, who are bound by medical ethics to 'remain independent from their employer [i.e., the prison's management] in regard to medical decisions' (WMA 1991/2017, ¶ 6; see similarly Reyes et al. 2013b, pp. 65–6).

Consent Matters. Robert E. Goodin, Oxford University Press. © Robert E. Goodin 2024.
DOI: 10.1093/oso/9780192889027.003.0009

Often the reason hunger strikers find it pragmatically impossible to communicate their change-of-mind about consenting to medical interventions is that they have socially painted themselves into a corner.[5] The British Medical Association explains their predicament in a Background Paper for the World Medical Association on its guidance to physicians treating hunger strikers: 'Physicians need to be aware that at the start of hunger strikes there can be pressure for hunger strikers to prove that their intentions are serious', which 'may push them into making an ill-considered advance refusal of [artificial feeding] or resuscitation'—commitments that they subsequently feel unable to alter, for fear of losing face and undermining the efforts of their peers.[6]

Sometimes those conundrums can be resolved through confidential conversations between the hunger striker and the physician, in which the patient consents to medical interventions that the physician promises to keep secret.[7] But sometimes those arrangements cannot be kept completely secret. That is particularly so in prison settings, which will be the focus of this chapter. There, the physician often has to reveal to prison authorities that the hunger striker has consented to being fed artificially, in order to prevent them from 'force-feeding' him.[8] Physicians must be 'frank with hunger strikers about the limitations of what they can and cannot do, including situations in which the physician may not be able to maintain confidentiality'.[9] Fears that confidentiality might be breached in such ways often prevents hunger strikers from explicitly consenting, even confidentially, to treatment.

That gives rise to the issue at the heart of this chapter. Sometimes a hunger striker may be willing to be fed, but he is not willing to ask or explicitly agree to be fed.[10] The hunger striker would be glad to be fed, but he needs to be able credibly to say to his significant others (family, peers, etc.), 'I did not ask for that, it was something that the doctor did without my consent.'[11] Coming from a hunger striker who is in prison, that claim can be far more credible than when coming

[5] They 'paint themselves into a corner' and do not 'know how to back off' (Reyes et al. 2013b, p. 64).

[6] BMA 2006, p. 41.

[7] Several of the cases discussed by the BMA (2006) background paper are of this sort. Lo (2019, ch. 10) similarly recommends that when discussing blood transfusions with Jehovah's Witnesses, physicians conduct those discussions with patients in private so they are protected from undue influence by family and friends who are also Jehovah's Witnesses.

[8] BMA 2006, p. 39. Note that there is an important distinction between 'artificial feeding' and 'force-feeding', as discussed below.

[9] WMA 1991/2017, ¶ 9.

[10] There may be an analogy here to Jehovah's Witnesses who regard it as a sin to consent to a blood transfusion but not to receive one if it is done by a court order without their consent (Banja 2009; BBC 2009; Lo 2019, ch. 10; Pavlikova and van Dijk 2022, p. 391).

[11] The physician is then left with the 'diplomatic task' of simultaneously 'inserting an intravenous line, while "allowing" the hunger striker to declare vociferously that the "hunger strike continues..."' (Reyes et al. 2013a, p. 34). 'The prison doctor must be ready to shoulder this blame, having the interest of the patient as a priority.' There are various reports from Latin America and the Middle East of precisely that happening (Reyes et al. 2013b, p. 64).

from someone on hunger strike in the community and being cared for by his personal physician.

What is the physician to do, confronted with a patient who mentally consents but who refuses to explicitly affirm that fact? Ordinarily, the answer would be clear: a physician is prohibited from administering treatment to a conscious, competent patient without a clear sign of his consent. But, as I shall argue, the special circumstances surrounding incarcerated hunger strikers can render sufficient tacit consent of a much more passive sort.[12]

9.1 The Nature of Hunger Strikes

A hunger strike occurs when someone refuses food (and in extreme cases water) for a sufficiently long period to put their health at risk, with the aim of getting some specific demands satisfied.[13] Hunger strikes can of course take place anywhere; several of Gandhi's took place in his own home, for example. But here I shall concentrate upon ones occurring inside prisons.

Often hunger strikers have been imprisoned for politically motivated crimes and go on hunger strike to demand recognition of that fact in prison. Such was the demand of British suffragettes at the beginning of the twentieth century and of Bobby Sands and the other Provisional IRA hunger strikers in the Maze prison three-quarters of a century later. A quarter century after that, detainees went on hunger strikes to protest the length and terms of their confinement at Guantánamo Bay. Other prisoners have gone on hunger strikes to demand that their trial date be brought forward, or that they be released on bail pending trial, or that they be provided with a religious diet in prison.[14]

[12] Delmas (2023) argues that incarcerated people have a *special* 'right to hunger strike'—'a right to petition for redress, in light of incarcerated people's structural vulnerability to abuse and given inadequate grievance mechanisms'. She derives that special right 'from the right to resist oppression and stresses the normative permissibility of the use of coercive tactics to defend one's liberty interests in the face of carceral oppression'. But no special right is required. Everyone has a right not to be forcibly fed against their will, whether imprisoned or not and whether the terms and conditions of their imprisonment are just or not.

[13] Different hunger strikers differ in what they are prepared to eat or drink. To some extent this is culturally specific. 'Most so-called "total fasts" involve protesters accepting water but abstaining from all foodstuffs. Different cultures, however, have different notions of how fasting should be defined. Salt (either NaCl alone or together with a combination of minerals) is often added to the water, as is sometimes sugar or other sweet substances such as honey. Some cultures define fasting in terms of abstaining from solid food (substances that need to be chewed) or from food that is cooked or heated' (BMA 2006, p. 38). In terms of what they are demanding, 'the hunger striker will often be prepared to accept a fallback position, accepting much less than initially asked for' (Reyes et al. 2013c, p. 98).

[14] Silver 2005, pp. 633–6. Whether going on hunger strike is an efficacious way of securing those other goals varies. In some famous cases it was, in others not. In Guantánamo, for example, hunger strikers were less likely to get a 'release recommendation' (Deutschmann 2016, p. 570).

Hunger strikers are rarely suicidal.[15] They risk their lives for some cause, to be sure, and they often say they are 'prepared to die' for that cause.[16] But they aim at some such further goal, such as those just mentioned, rather than intending their own death.[17] As the British Medical Association's background paper for the World Medical Association pointedly remarks, 'A hunger strike is not equivalent to suicide. Individuals who embark on hunger strikes aim to achieve goals important to them but generally hope and intend to survive.'[18]

9.2 Medical Responses to Hunger Strikes

The most notorious 'medical' response to life-threatening hunger strikes in custody is literal forced-feeding, as was originally inflicted on imprisoned British suffragettes. They were strapped down and, resisting all the while, had feeding tubes forcibly inserted into their nostrils, with deleterious consequences for their digestive, circulatory and nervous systems.[19]

British authorities relented and found more-or-less satisfactory work-arounds in the case of the suffragettes.[20] In other places, literal forced-feeding continued to be practised, even when apparently contrary to higher court rulings.[21] The US military famously force-fed Guantánamo Bay prisoners during hunger strikes there.[22] Any given state's publicly-declared policy on hunger strikes can vacillate strategically between threatening forced-feeding and wantonly allowing hunger strikers to die—although in practice prison authorities, not wanting to create martyrs, typically do their best behind the scenes to avoid the latter.

Within medical ethics, opposition to forced-feeding and non-consensual assisted (or artificial) feeding is clear and univocal. There is a widespread

[15] Using both terms in a colloquial manner; in technical terms, a person can be medically defined as a 'hunger striker' only if any suicidal intent is ruled out.

[16] 'Hunger strikers rarely wish to die but some may be prepared to do so to achieve their aims' (WMA 1991/2017, ¶ 1). In practice, however, 'most hunger strikers desperately want to find a way out of the confrontation and often stop fasting if they obtain some minor form of concession from the authorities' (BMA 2006, p. 42).

[17] O'Keeffe 1984.

[18] BMA 2006, p. 42. Even when they are (typically falsely) accused of intending their own death, it is typically for some larger socio-political purpose. The UK Secretary of State for Northern Ireland, for example, tendentiously speculated that Bobby Sands may have 'committed suicide... under the instructions of those who felt it useful to their cause that he should die' in order to be a martyr for the Republican cause (Aitkins 1981).

[19] Williams 2008.

[20] Under the 'Prisoners (Temporary Discharge for Ill Health) Act of 1913', hunger striking suffragettes were released when their health began to suffer, only to be reinterred when their health had recovered, at which point they went on hunger strike again. Hence its nickname: the 'Cat and Mouse Act'.

[21] Silver (2005) provides a shocking list of US state court decisions permitting forced-feeding, apparently in flat contravention to Supreme Court rulings.

[22] US DoD 2006, ¶ 4.7.1, p. 947. Reyes et al. 2013b.

consensus, underpinned by the Declaration of Malta of the World Medical Association, that:

> Artificial feeding, when used in the patient's clinical interest, can be ethically appropriate if competent hunger strikers agree to it. However, in accordance with the WMA Declaration of Tokyo, where a prisoner refuses nourishment and is considered by the physician as capable of forming an unimpaired and rational judgment concerning the consequences of such a decision, he or she shall not be fed artificially...
>
> ...
>
> All kinds of interventions for enteral or parenteral feeding against the will of the mentally competent hunger striker are to be considered as 'forced feeding'. Forced feeding is never ethically acceptable. Even if intended to benefit, feeding accompanied by threats, coercion, force or use of physical restraints is a form of inhuman and degrading treatment.[23]

The basic rule is thus absolutely clear: patients may be artificially fed if, and only if, they consent. Two things complicate application of that firm rule, however. In order for a patient's consent or refusal of consent to carry any moral weight (a) the patient must be mentally competent to consent and (b) the consent or refusal of consent must have been made voluntarily.[24]

9.3 Is Refusal of Consent Really Voluntary?

It is axiomatic that 'consent and refusal are invalid if the result of coercion'.[25] Medical ethicists sometimes query whether prisoners can ever give valid consent at all, given that they are under the coercive regime of the prison.[26] Over and above any coercion brought to bear by prison authorities, however, hunger strikers are often also subject to the coercive influence of peer pressure. Hunger strikes are often group activities, and participants are under pressure from their peers and their supporters both to join and to continue the hunger strike. So when hunger strikers refuse artificial feeding, they sometimes do so under duress—from their peers, rather than from prison authorities (who typically want them to eat, not to refuse food). I shall first survey some testimony of that happening (Section 9.3.1) and then discuss what morally follows (Section 9.3.2).

[23] WMA (1991/2017, ¶¶ 21, 23), elaborating on WMA (1975/2016, ¶ 8).
[24] WMA 1991/2017, ¶¶ 10, 16. BMA 2006, pp. 36–8.
[25] BMA 2006, p. 41.
[26] Cf. Cohen 1978; US DHSS 1978; CIOMS/WHO 2002, guideline 11.

9.3.1 Peer Pressure to Continue Hunger Striking

The World Medical Association's Declaration of Malta emphasizes at various places that:

> Physicians should respect individuals' autonomy. This can involve difficult assessments, as hunger strikers' true wishes may not be as clear as they appear. Any decisions lack moral force if made by use of threats, peer pressure or coercion.
>
> ...
>
> Physicians need to ascertain the individual's true intention, especially in collective strikes or situations where peer pressure may be a factor.
>
> ...
>
> Physicians need to satisfy themselves that food or treatment refusal is the individual's voluntary choice. Hunger strikers should be protected from coercion. Physicians... should be aware that coercion may come from the authorities, the peer group, or others, such as family members.[27]

In a background paper for World Medical Association deliberations on updating the Declaration of Malta, the British Medical Association elaborates:

> The informed and voluntary nature of individuals' food refusal are key aspects that physicians need to ascertain once mental competence has been established.
>
> ...
>
> Detainees may... suffer coercion from peer groups in subtle as well as obvious ways. These often complex situations can lead to the point where it becomes virtually impossible for a protester to cease fasting voluntarily.... Physicians must do their utmost to speak to each patient privately, out of earshot of all other people.... Those orchestrating collective hunger strikes are often reluctant to allow such talks, as this undermines their authority. This is possibly the most complex situation to deal with in determining whether hunger strikers are indeed genuine volunteers.
>
> ...
>
> Where protesters appear to be fasting under duress, a solution may be to separate those individuals in hospital on a medical pretext, thereby extracting them from the influence of others and allowing them, if they agree, to resume nourishment on medical grounds. Pressure may still come from relatives or the media.

[27] WMA 1991/2017, ¶¶ 4, 2, 16.

> Families often alert the media, hoping this will heighten the pressure on the authorities to make concessions but it can also increase pressure on the protester not to give way.[28]

The BMA background paper recounts the case of a physician attending participants in a collective, politically-motivated hunger strike. Upon closer questioning, one hunger striker 'agreed that she did not want to die'. She 'agreed to accept nourishment which was given on a medical pretext to avoid pressure being brought to bear upon her by her peer group'. But obviously it was essential that 'the conversation between them was kept confidential'.[29]

They report another case of another collective hunger strike in which

> the degree of commitment to the fast varied considerably.... [S]ome prisoners were absolutely determined to fast until they died.... Other prisoners in the same strike however, told the doctor privately that they were willing to accept an intravenous line or naso-gastric tube as long as they could maintain the pretence publicly that these interventions were done against their will.

The two groups were separated from one another 'without in any way indicating that some were willingly accepting nutrition', and the willing prisoners received artificial feeding.[30]

9.3.2 What Morally Does and Does Not Follow?

Exactly how much help can we get, in those circumstances, from the axiom that 'consent and refusal are invalid if the result of coercion'?[31] In addressing that question, I shall start with two brush-clearing exercises. The two most dramatic things that might intuitively seem to follow simply do not. But a third conclusion—less dramatic perhaps, but pragmatically hugely important—most definitely does follow.

First, remember that the case in view involves a *refusal* of consent (here, to being artificially fed while on a hunger strike). If coercion invalidates, that is what it would here be invalidating. But note well, invalidating a refusal to consent is not the same as positively securing consent.[32] Invalidating the refusal would, morally,

[28] BMA 2006, p. 37. As Reyes et al. (2013a, p. 33) report, 'It is not uncommon for prisoners to be "volunteered" to go on a hunger strike, by their peers or by an unofficial prisoner hierarchy. In extreme cases, such hierarchy may even "force" a prisoner to keep fasting way beyond whatever moment he or she would have stopped. The physician has a duty to detect such a case, so as to help him or her break loose from such coercion' (see similarly Reyes et al. 2013b, pp. 65, 66). On the ways in which social pressure can compromise consent, see Pallikkathayil (2020).

[29] BMA 2006, pp. 37–8. [30] BMA 2006, pp. 42–3. [31] BMA 2006, p. 41.

[32] As already argued in Section 3.5 above.

merely bring us back to the situation in which the person neither gives nor refuses consent. If what we are talking about is something that may be done to a person only with that person's consent, then that is simply not enough to justify doing it. And artificial feeding, at least of a patient who is still conscious and competent to consent, is surely something that does require a patient's consent. Hence, even if the coercion in view were to invalidate the hunger striker's refusal to consent to artificial feeding, that would not suffice to justify subjecting the patient to artificial feeding without that patient's further positive consent.

Second, notice that *who* is doing the coercing might matter morally, when it comes to coercion invalidating consent and refusal to consent. Philosophers are divided on whether, when and why third-party duress invalidates consent.[33] But in contract law, at least, force and fraud famously invalidate consent only if the force or fraud is perpetrated by the other party to the contract (or someone in league with them). If perpetrated by someone who is not party to the contract (and not in league with anyone who is), then it does not invalidate the contract.[34] So, for example, if I contract with you to sell you my house in order to raise a ransom to free my kidnapped daughter, I consent to that contract under duress—but the duress comes from the kidnapper, not you (the other party to the contract for the sale of my house), and for that reason the duress does not invalidate our contract for the sale of my house to you. In the case under discussion in this chapter, likewise, the coercion inducing the hunger striker to refuse treatment comes not from anyone who would be directly involved in treating him (the physician or prison officials) but instead from someone else (his family, friends or fellow hunger strikers).[35] So even if there is coercion somewhere in the background, and even if coercion generally invalidates consent or refusal to consent, the coercion in question comes from the wrong people for it to have that effect morally.

Let us set aside those two possible confusions about what third-party coercion might do, then. Let us turn instead to discuss what that third-party coercion *can* do. Coercive pressure from their peers can (and often does) compromise the capacity of the hunger striker to *signal* clearly to the physician, in conventionally explicit ways, that he does indeed consent to artificial feeding. That fact, in turn, licenses the attending physician to seek, and to act upon, consent of a tacit and

[33] Cf., e.g.: Millum 2014; Dougherty 2021b; Gerver 2021; Tadros 2021, pp. 214–17.

[34] Here is the example given in the *Restatement of the Law of Contracts*: '*A*, who is not *C*'s agent, induced *B* by duress to contract with *C* to sell land to *C*. *C*, in good faith, promises *B* to pay the agreed price. The contract is not voidable by *B*' (ALI 1981, § 175(2), comment c, illustration 10).

[35] In the case set out in the immediately prior footnote, if *C* had known that *B* was acting under duress from *A* and knowingly took advantage of that fact when contracting with *B*, the contract would be voidable by *B*. In the hunger strike case, the attending physician will typically know that the hunger striker was refusing consent to artificial feeding under duress, as a result of peer group pressure. But the physician could only be said to be 'taking advantage' of the duress the hunger striker is under if the physician were looking for an excuse not to provide him with needed medical treatment—which is the very opposite of what a conscientious physician would be seeking, of course.

more oblique form (to be elaborated in the next section) than might ordinarily be required for an invasive medical procedure. Note well, however: the patient's positive consent is still required. The only thing that has changed in consequence of peer pressure on an imprisoned hunger striker is *what counts as adequate evidence* that positive consent has indeed been given.

9.4 Uncommunicative Patients

The cases discussed in Section 9.3.1 are 'easy' cases, precisely because there the patients in the end gave their explicit consent (albeit privately) to artificial feeding. Once the attending physician has the patient's explicit consent to treatment, that renders moot any questions concerning the validity of any previous refusal of consent.[36]

Let us now consider a case where that element of explicit consent is missing. Take the case of a hunger striker whom the physician has strong reason to believe: (a) refuses consent to artificial feeding as a result of duress from family, friends or other hunger strikers; (b) actually wants to be artificially fed; but (c) is unwilling to consent explicitly, even in private, for fear of 'losing face with their peer group'.[37]

As in case of bondage sex discussed in the previous chapter, the hunger strikers here in view are incapable—here socially, rather than physically—of verbalizing their consent or non-consent. Still, like Section 8.1's bound-and-gagged parties to bondage sex, mute hunger strikers are nonetheless capable of communicating their consenting or non-consenting intentions in all sorts of *non-verbal* ways.[38]

Imagine this scenario. The physician enters the hunger striker's room with all the paraphernalia required for intravenous feeding. She carefully explains to the patient what is involved in setting up the intravenous line. She tells the patient that she will not proceed with that procedure if he objects, and that she will stop at any

[36] Why should physicians respect even the patient's initial refusal to consent? Perhaps the answer is simply this: the physician should purely out of courtesy nonetheless respect that person's announced wishes (even if they are not completely his own), so long as there is no grave medical reason not to do so. I have argued for respecting people's wishes, even when they cannot validly give or withhold consent, in Section 8.5 and will return to that topic in Section 11.3.

[37] 'For example, if doctors ask hunger strikers to give advance instructions at the start of a fast saying whether or not they would refuse resuscitation at a later stage, it may be difficult for the hunger strikers to do anything other than refuse artificial feeding, without losing face with their peer group' (BMA 2006, p. 36). Similar issues might arise in other situations than hunger strikes—for example with Jehovah's Witnesses who need and want a life-saving blood transfusion but who refuse to say so explicitly fearing ostracism by their fellow Jehovah Witnesses.

[38] To be clear: I am here still requiring *some* indication of consent. I will therefore not be able to capture the sort of case that Reyes et al. (2013b, p. 64) report, in which the doctor resuscitated a 'vociferous political hunger striker' contrary to the prisoner's written instructions. Reyes et al. conclude that '[t]his prison doctor did well', on the grounds that, 'As the hunger striker confessed to the author [Reyes], he was actually delighted to find himself alive and well—but he did not want either the authorities or the prison doctor to know this!'

point in the procedure at which the patient objects. She then proceeds, very slowly, to perform those procedures, telling the patient what she is doing at each step and reminding him that she will stop any time he asks her to. Now, suppose the patient—although fully conscious and mentally competent—allows her to proceed without saying a word. Can that count as his giving her 'tacit consent' to artificial feeding?[39]

Clearly, there are *some* cases in which we are prepared to treat silence as signalling consent.[40] Recall the case of the chairperson of a meeting asking 'Any objections?' and no one objecting: the chairperson is entitled to take their silence as consent to the proposition on the table.[41] Similarly, we sometimes take people's non-verbal gestures as consent to lower-level medical interventions. Ben Saunders gives this example:

> [I]f the doctor says to a patient 'you need an injection—hold still' then the patient, by not withdrawing their arm or objecting, can be said to have implied their consent.... [I]mplicit consent is still actual consent and the doctor does no wrong in taking it as a licence to proceed.[42]

Courts have held likewise. When a passenger joined a queue to receive the smallpox inoculation that was a precondition for disembarking at that port and stood silently as the doctor administered it, the court ruled that she had consented to the inoculation and could not subsequently sue for medical battery.[43]

Ex hypothesi, in the hunger-strike scenario under discussion the patient heard and understood the physician's invitation to say he did not consent. *Ex hypothesi*, he heard and understood that the physician would proceed with the artificial feeding procedure if he did not object. So this would seem to constitute a clear case of tacitly consenting via 'silence-on-notice', as discussed in Section 3.3.4 above.

Still, an invasive medical procedure—particularly one nullifying something very important to the hunger-striking patient, like the political gesture being

[39] Prison authorities claim—disingenuously—that 'most hunger-striking patients' at Guantánamo Bay 'do not struggle and fight against insertion of the naso-gastric tube'. Reyes et al. (2013b, p. 62) show that those claims are demonstrably false but go on to say, counterfactually, 'If this were to be the case, i.e. voluntary acceptance of the feeding, it would *not* constitute *force*-feeding, but artificial feeding. The latter... is not a transgression of ethics as by definition it implies voluntary acceptance of medical intervention from the hunger striker.'

[40] See Sections 3.2 and 3.3.4 through 3.3.5 above.

[41] Kleinig 2010, p. 11; cf. Dougherty 2015, p. 230; Pallikkathayil 2020.

[42] Saunders 2012b, p. 70. The National Health Service guidance on 'How consent is given' states similarly: 'Someone could also give non-verbal consent, as long as they understand the treatment or examination about to take place—for example, holding out an arm for a blood test' (NHS 2019).

[43] Knowlton 1891. That is a US case. But English courts hold similarly: 'an adult patient who is mentally and physically capable of exercising a choice must consent if medical treatment of him is to be lawful, although the consent need not be in writing and may sometimes be inferred from the patient's conduct in the context of the surrounding circumstances'; Lord Donaldson, *In re T*, 4 All ER 649 [1992] at 653.

made by the hunger strike—is a much more serious matter than adoption of a routine proposal by an assembly or getting a routine injection.[44] We may therefore reasonably want to insist on higher standards for assessing consent in such settings.[45]

The case of inferring the hunger striker's tacit consent from 'silence on notice' can be usefully contrasted with another hypothetical scenario, proposed by Stephen Schulhofer. This scenario involves an athlete with knee problems, for which his surgeon recommends an operation. The athlete vacillates; the surgeon grows impatient.

> So the surgeon signals an anesthesiologist to ready the drugs that will flow through an intravenous tube already in place. One last time the surgeon... reminds the athlete, 'You don't have to go ahead with this. If you really want me to stop, just say so.' But the athlete, his brain still clouded with doubts, fears, hopes, and uncertainties, says nothing. So the surgeon starts the anesthesia and just *does* it.[46]

'Consent?' Schulhofer asks. 'Of course not', he scoffs. 'But why not?' Schulhofer asks. 'The athlete was not compelled to submit. Nobody forced him.... Surely his silence proves that he was not unwilling. If he really objected, all he had to do was say so.' Nonetheless, Schulhofer thinks that the athlete's 'physical autonomy was unquestionably violated because no choice was ever made.... Non-consent is simply anything that is not positive consent...'[47]

Schulhofer may be overly confident in that conclusion. On the face of it, his case would seem analogous to the chairperson of the meeting asking 'Any objections?' and, hearing none, taking that as a signal of consent to the motion. Furthermore, the hesitant athlete would not be required to make any heroic sacrifice (like the earlier case of 'chopping his arm off at the elbow'[48]) to signal that he did not consent to the surgeon's proposed plan of action. Still, even if there were no objectively costly barriers to his speaking up, we can imagine from Schulhofer's description that the athlete suffered a debilitating mental condition (his brain was 'clouded') that prevented him from speaking up. And that may be enough to get Schulhofer the conclusion he wants in the circumstances that he stipulates.

Even if that is the correct conclusion in Schulhofer's hypothetical, however, there are two important points of difference between his case and the hunger strike case here under discussion. The first point of difference is that there is no

[44] Even as regards adoption of a proposal by an assembly, when the proposal is very serious—a declaration of war, for example—we would surely demand a more positive expression of assent (a roll-call vote, for example) than mere 'assent by silence'.

[45] See Section 1.1 above. That is presumably why Saunders (2012b, p. 70) goes on to say of his injection example, 'I am not recommending this as general medical practice.'

[46] Schulhofer 1992, p. 74.

[47] Schulhofer 1992, pp. 74–5.

[48] See Section 3.2 above.

medical urgency in performing knee surgery on the athlete, whereas there is in the case of nourishing the medically precarious hunger striker.[49] In the former case, the impatient surgeon is merely at risk of missing his tee-off time at the golf club. In the latter case, the physician's hunger striking patient is at risk of dying.

The second point of difference is that the hunger striker has (and the physician knows he has) compelling reasons not to say he consents to the medical intervention, even if he genuinely does so. And knowing that the hunger striker's refusal to give explicit consent is not fully voluntary, and may therefore not be genuine, makes it more justifiable for the physician to try to discover whether or not the hunger striker consents in some other non-verbal way.[50] Schulhofer's surgeon, in contrast, has no reason for thinking that the athlete has any compelling reason not to say that he consents to knee surgery if he genuinely does so.[51] Hence there is no justification for the surgeon not to take the athlete's failure to give verbal consent at face value as constituting 'not consenting'.

9.5 Comatose Patients

Finally, consider the case of hunger strikers who have lost consciousness. Much ink has been spilt on the question of whether hunger strikers may properly be resuscitated. That is a highly marginal case medically, however, given how poor the prognosis generally is for someone whose body has been that badly compromised by a protracted hunger strike.[52]

In the previous chapter we were dealing with someone who consented to something (there, sexual relations) in advance but who is now incapable of confirming or denying whether they still consent (because they are comatose or paralysed and incapable of communication).[53] In the hunger strike case, we are dealing with a patient who instead refused consent to resuscitation before losing consciousness, and the question is now whether a physician must necessarily honour that request once the hunger-striking patient has lost consciousness.

[49] In explaining why to respect the patient's initial refusal to consent, footnote 36 in Section 9.4 above suggested that the physician should purely out of courtesy respect the patient's announced wishes (even if they are not completely his own) so long as there is no grave medical reason not to do so. When the hunger striker's medical condition worsens, however, such courtesies should give way to medical necessity.

[50] While the non-verbal signal here in view is less conventional than a firm nod of the head, for example, it can be equally clear in communicating the intent of the hunger striker. Perhaps it is not quite as clear as was the consent of a woman to a smallpox inoculation who 'held up her arm to be vaccinated' and 'did not tell [the physician] she did not want to be vaccinated', only to go on to (unsuccessfully) sue for medical assault (Knowlton 1891). But that is a pretty outrageous case.

[51] His 'attitude may be deeply ambivalent' (ALI 1980, pt. 2, p. 302). But, as Schulhofer (1992, p. 74) concedes, 'surgical patients are almost always like that'.

[52] de Grooth et al. 2017. Majewski, Ball and Finn 2019.

[53] See Sections 8.4 and 8.2 respectively.

Legal codes differ on this matter. 'In some countries, patients' known wishes dictate what the physician does after consciousness is lost. In others, this is not an option and physicians may be prosecuted if they fail to intervene to save the hunger striker's life.'[54] Codes of medical ethics differ on that matter as well. The World Medical Association's Declaration of Malta dictates that, 'Advance refusals of treatment must be followed if they reflect the voluntary wish of the individual when competent.'[55] But that Declaration acknowledges that physicians will feel conflicted in such cases.[56] And the Islamic Code of Medical Ethics requires life-saving interventions in such circumstances.[57] Policies and codes differ because there are two components of the patient's best interests in play: '"benefit" includes respecting individuals' wishes as well as promoting their welfare';[58] and different commentators and communities strike the balance between them differently.[59] The upshot is that there is no universal 'moral default' to guide us here, as there was in last chapter's cases.[60]

I will not here attempt to resolve the issue of whether, when and why to respect advance directives in general.[61] Instead, for the purposes of this chapter I shall focus upon the issue that most commonly arises with advance directives 'not to be artificially fed' or 'not to be resuscitated' specifically in connection with hunger strikes.

The upshot of the previous discussion is that '[s]ome advance instructions truly reflect the individual's wishes but others do not', and '[p]hysicians need to assess the evidence' on that score in each particular case.[62] Having said that 'Advance refusals of treatment must be followed if they reflect the voluntary wish of the individual when competent', the World Medical Association's Declaration of Malta goes on to say that:

[54] BMA 2006, p. 40. And within any given jurisdiction, such as England, advance directives are binding on physicians only until challenged in courts, which do not then regard them as particularly binding (Michalowski 2005).

[55] WMA 1991/2017, ¶ 18.

[56] 'An emotional challenge arises when hunger strikers who have apparently issued clear instructions not to be resuscitated reach a stage of cognitive impairment. The principle of beneficence urges physicians to resuscitate them but respect for individual autonomy restrains physicians from intervening when a valid and informed refusal has been made' (WMA 1991/2017, ¶ 2).

[57] 'In situations where urgent and immediate surgical or other interference is necessary to save life, the Doctor should go ahead according to the Islamic rule "necessities override prohibitions". His position shall be safe and secure whatever the result achieved, on condition that he has followed established medical methodology in a correct way. The "bad" inherent in not saving the patient outweighs the presumptive "good" in leaving him to his self-destructive decision. The Islamic rule proclaims that "warding off" the "bad" takes priority over bringing about the "good"' (Declaration of Kuwait 1981, 'Responsibility and Liability').

[58] WMA 1991/2017, ¶ 5. Note well the phrasing in terms of 'wishes' rather than 'consent'—I have made much of the difference before (in Section 8.5) and will again later (in Section 11.3).

[59] In the case of sex with a comatose person, we could conclude decisively that 'having sex when it is unwanted' is uncontroversially worse than 'not having sex when it is wanted'. No such uncontroversial ranking is possible as between the two considerations in play in the hunger strike case.

[60] In Section 8.5 above.

[61] I return to say a little more about that in Section 11.2 below, however.

[62] BMA 2006, p. 41.

> In custodial settings, the possibility of advance instructions having been made under pressure needs to be considered. Where physicians have serious doubts about the individual's intention, any instructions must be treated with great caution.
>
> ...
>
> Physicians may rarely and exceptionally consider it justifiable to go against advance instructions refusing treatment because, for example, the refusal is thought to have been made under duress.[63]

If a hunger striker's advance instructions of 'no artificial feeding' or 'no resuscitation' were subject to coercive pressure, even just from peers and not from prison authorities, there is a real risk that they might not reflect the genuine will of the patient. Insofar as the physician has good reason to believe that that is so, they may not necessarily be morally binding on the physician—anyway, certainly not *as* morally binding as if they would be if there were no such question of coercion hanging over them.

When physicians decide to act against a comatose patient's advance directive—just as in Section 8.3's case of a person having sex with someone who is currently incapable of communicating that she no longer consents—physicians are 'acting as their own risk'.[64] The Declaration of Malta dictates that 'Physicians acting against an advanced refusal of treatment must be prepared to justify that action to relevant authorities including professional regulators.' And '[i]f, after resuscitation and having regained their mental faculties, hunger strikers continue to reiterate their intention to fast, that decision should be respected'.[65] Be those caveats as they may, the larger point is that it should be morally permissible for physicians to act at their own risk in this way, overriding a hunger striker's advance directive when they have good grounds for believing that those may not have reflected the genuine will of the patient.

For a parallel case of advance treatment instructions being ignored on grounds of 'undue pressure', consider the decision of English courts in *Re T*. The case involved pregnant Miss T who had to have a Caesarean section after a traffic accident. Doctors advised her that blood transfusions were often required after the sort of operation that she was about to undergo and asked for her consent to that. After spending considerable time discussing it with her mother, who was a Jehovah's Witness (Miss T herself was not), Miss T refused consent. When Miss T's condition deteriorated and she fell unconscious, the hospital petitioned the court to allow them to give Miss T blood despite her refusal of consent. The court agreed, questioning the genuineness of Miss T's refusal of consent and citing 'undue influence' of her mother on her decision.

[63] WMA 1991/2017, ¶¶ 18 and 20.

[64] Reyes et al. 2013b, p. 64.

[65] WMA 1991/2017, ¶ 20.

When hearing the case on appeal the Master of the Rolls, Lord Donaldson, first emphasized the strong presumption in favour of respecting the instructions of the patient. 'The law', he said, 'requires that an adult patient who is mentally and physically capable of exercising a choice *must* consent if medical treatment of him is to be lawful'.[66] But Lord Donaldson then went on to discuss at length the 'vitiating effect of outside influence' on that rule:

> A special problem may arise if at the time the decision is made the patient has been subjected to the influence of some third party. This is by no means to say that the patient is not entitled to receive and indeed invite advice and assistance from others in reaching a decision, particularly from members of the family. But the doctors have to consider whether the decision is really that of the patient.... The real question ... is: does the patient really mean what he says or is he merely saying it ... to satisfy someone else or because the advice and persuasion to which he has been subjected is such that he can no longer think and decide for himself? ...
>
> When considering the effect of outside influences, ... the relationship of the 'persuader' to the patient may be of crucial importance. The influence of parents on their children or of one spouse on the other can be ... much stronger than would be the case in other relationships. Persuasion based upon religious belief can also be much more compelling and the fact that arguments based upon religious beliefs are being deployed by someone in a very close relationship with the patient will give them added force and should alert the doctors to the possibility—no more—that the patient's capacity or will to decide has been overborne. In other words the patient may not mean what he says.[67]

Based on that reasoning, the court agreed that doctors should be allowed to ignore Miss T's refusal of consent and proceed to give her a blood transfusion.

I suggest that the same reasoning should be applied in the case of hunger strikers. Should they become unconscious, their advance instructions refusing artificial assisted feeding or resuscitation may properly be overridden if there are strong grounds for believing that their will in giving those instructions had been 'overborne' by interventions of others (family, friends, fellow hunger strikers, etc.).[68]

[66] *Re T*, 4 All ER 649 [1992], at 653. [67] Lord Donaldson, *Re T*, 4 All ER 649 [1992], at 662.

[68] To anyone worried that 'this gives the physician an incentive to let the patient become unconscious', I would reply that physicians are (supposed to be, and much most typically are) striving to act in the best medical interests of their patients; and the medical prognosis for hunger-strikers once comatose is much worse.

9.6 Conclusion

Let me conclude with two brief reflections on the more practical implications of my analysis.

First, I should emphasize what should in any case be obvious. It is no part of my brief to argue that *all* refusal of assisted feeding on the part of all hunger strikers is necessarily invalid; neither, even more emphatically, do I think that *every* hunger striker should be artificially fed or resuscitated. My argument has merely been that peer-group pressure may sometimes prevent a hunger-striking prisoner from explicitly communicating his genuine consent to artificial feeding. Under such peer-group pressure hunger strikers sometimes 'paint themselves into a corner' and do not 'know how to back off'.[69] My argument is just that it is the duty of the doctor (or anyone working in the hunger striker's interest) to give the hunger striker multiple ways out of that corner, including various creative modes of consenting (clearly, if only tacitly) to artificial feeding if he genuinely desires it.

Second, even where the attending physician has good reason to doubt the genuineness of a hunger striker's refusal of assisted feeding at the outset, she ordinarily ought at least initially respect that refusal. That is merely to say that she should respect a patient's announced wishes (even if they are not completely his own) so long as there is no grave medical reason not to do so.[70] There was no such reason at the outset of the hunger strike, but there comes to be one over the course of a hunger strike. Even if the hunger striker initially genuinely refused consent to artificial feeding (i.e. he would have said he refused even in the absence of peer pressure), he might later in the hunger strike have changed his mind—but, by reason of peer pressure he might not be able to come right out and say so. Again, that argues for the physician offering the hunger striker alternative non-verbal modalities of signalling his consent to assisted feeding (if he does indeed now consent) without 'betraying the cause' by actually saying so in as many words.

[69] Reyes et al. 2013b, p. 64.

[70] See similarly Sections 8.5 and 11.3.

10

Consent by Extension

Voting and Political Authority

There is a long tradition of attempting to use consent to ground legitimate political authority and content-independent duties to obey the laws enacted by such authorities. The vast majority of those attempts have failed abysmally.

Explicit consent is a non-starter. Only a miniscule proportion of the population nowadays have explicitly consented to the authority of those who rule over them politically. Maybe it used to be more common in olden times, when people explicitly swore fealty to their liege-lord—insofar as his word was law, that might have amounted to a promise to obey the law.[1] Maybe, at a stretch, we could regard swearing allegiance to the American flag as consenting to political authority there.[2] But even in the 1950s that was done only in primary schools, mostly by children too young to give valid consent.[3] Naturalized citizens and people taking oaths of public office are about the only adults who today explicitly consent to political authority, and even they typically swear oaths that stop short of having them literally promise to obey the laws.[4] In any case, they are only a tiny proportion of most countries' populations.[5] If we are looking for a way to say that

[1] But note well, both here and below: 'a promise' rather than 'consent', which Chapter 2 has shown to be different.

[2] In support of that proposition, I offer this anecdote. When renouncing my US citizenship in the wake of Donald Trump's election, consular officials required me to do so before the American flag. Unswearing allegiance to its flag was intimately intertwined, in that way, with formally repudiating the political authority of that state.

[3] As Simmons (1993, p. 219) also observes.

[4] The US Naturalization Oath of Allegiance merely has new citizens swear, 'I will support and defend the Constitution and laws of the United States of America'—but 'supporting and defending the laws' is not quite the same as actually 'obeying' them. The US president's oath of office has him swearing to 'preserve, protect and defend the Constitution'—but, again, not to 'obey' it (except insofar as that is implied by 'I will faithfully execute the Office of President'). US senators pledge, 'I will bear true faith and allegiance' to the Constitution—but that is more a promise not to commit treason than to obey the laws. Members of the US Army swear an Oath of Enlistment promising, 'I will obey the orders of the President of the United States and the orders of the officers appointed over me'—but nothing is said about obeying the laws beyond following those orders.

[5] More people—although still far short of a majority of citizens—apply for passports. But applicants for a US passport, for example, merely swear an oath that they have not renounced US citizenship or sworn allegiance to or fought in the army of any foreign state (US Department of State 2021). Thus, Simmons (1976, p. 289) is right to dismiss applying for a passport as a consent-based way of grounding a duty to obey the laws. Perhaps there is some country whose national anthem contains a promise to obey the laws, so every time people sing it at an athletic event they are consenting to obey the law—but I know of no such national anthem.

Consent Matters. Robert E. Goodin, Oxford University Press. © Robert E. Goodin 2024.
DOI: 10.1093/oso/9780192889027.003.0010

(virtually) everyone in a political community is under a political obligation to obey laws duly enacted, we must look elsewhere.

Recognizing that that was true even in his own day, Locke turned instead to tacit consent, such as walking on the king's highways and enjoying the protection of his laws.[6] But the problems with that move are too obvious.[7] For a start, that is not the common understanding of what follows from walking on the king's highways, so it cannot reasonably be construed as unspoken-but-nonetheless-intentional consent to the king's rule, much less a commitment to obey his laws. (Roadside signs sometime identify the government responsible for building or maintaining the road, but have you ever seen a sign advising those travelling on a road that doing so will be taken as consent to the political authority of that government?) Furthermore, as Hume tartly pointed out, consent cannot reasonably be inferred from something you cannot realistically avoid doing.[8]

In the wake of those obvious failures, appeal is made to the notion of hypothetical consent.[9] That, however, is merely to say that those arrangements are ones you would consent to if asked, or perhaps ones you 'ought-to' consent to. But 'would' or 'ought to' is not 'did'.[10] For consent to be morally transformative, it has to be something that you actually did, either explicitly or tacitly or presumptively. Consent that has not (yet) been given cannot be morally transformative (yet).[11]

Talking about what you would consent to might be an evocative way of drawing attention to the good reasons for consenting, and those may be good reasons for doing what you would have consented to do even without your having consented. But it is those wholly independent 'good reasons', rather than anything to do with consent, that would be doing the moral work there.[12]

Those are familiar dead ends. I do not intend to explore them further here. Instead I shall focus on two other arguments for deriving political obligation from consent in ways suggested by Chapter 3 above. First I shall examine whether we can somehow infer from 'the nature of the business of democratic politics' that people participating in it actually do thereby tacitly consent to political authority. Next I shall examine whether political obligation can be somehow derived from

[6] Locke 1690, sec. 119.

[7] Which is not to say that some people do not persist in it. Steinberger (2004, pp. 219–20) for example lists the following among the forms of 'active participation in the institutions of the state' that could be taken as tacit consent to its political authority: calling the police or fire department, sending your children to public schools or using the public library.

[8] Hume 1760.

[9] Contemporary theorists of hypothetical consent follow Kant (1793/1991, p. 79) in saying that 'we need by no means assume that this contract... actually exists as a *fact*.... It is... merely an *idea* of reason... This is the test of the rightfulness of every public law.... [I]f it is at least possible that a people could agree to it, it is our duty to consider the law as just, even if the people is at present in such a position or attitude of mind that it would probably refuse its consent if it were consulted.'

[10] As argued in Sections 2.2.2 and 3.5.

[11] Struggle as he might make the best general case he can for hypothetical consent, Enoch (2017, p. 35) concedes that applying it to politics 'just seems entirely ludicrous.'

[12] As argued in Section 2.2.2 above.

'implicit consent', whereby your expressly consenting to one thing commits you (logically or pragmatically) to consenting to something else that is implicit in what you actually consented to. To foreshadow: while both of those approaches get further than previous consent-based approaches, neither is ultimately successful in generating any very general obligations to obey the law either.

10.1 The Nature of the Business of Democratic Politics

It is often treated as something of a platitude that 'liberal democratic consent theory expresses itself in the practice of voting' or 'through devices like elections, referendums and so on, one might say that actual processes of consent go on in a democracy'.[13] But those platitudes are purely gestural, leaving undone the hard work of explaining exactly how voting is connected to consent.[14] After all, voting is expressing a preference; consent is making a commitment. How is a commitment to be extracted from an expression of a preference?

Here is one way. When in a restaurant I tell the waiter, 'I would like the duck laksa', I am expressing a preference. But I am also 'placing an order'. And in the context of a commercial restaurant, placing an order entails a commitment to pay for the food I have ordered. The context and associated conventions there provide just the sort of connection that we are here seeking between an expression of a preference and a consent-based commitment.

Borrowing a phrase form Pufendorf, I discussed (in Section 3.2.2 above) cases in which you can infer that people actually (albeit only tacitly) consent to certain things that are inherent in or anyway conventionally associated with the 'nature of the business' in which they are voluntarily engaged. His prime example was a variation on the one just given: when you order a meal in a pub it is in 'the nature of the business' that you consent to pay for it. The aim of this section is to see if something like that can be made to work politically, such that it is in 'the nature of business of democratic politics' that those who participate in that process thereby consent to being governed by the laws made through it.

[13] The first quotation is from Kleinig (1982, p. 91, cf. pp. 107–9). The second is from Weale (1999, p. 80), who proceeds to dissent from that view. Pateman (1979, p. 83) similarly dissents from the view according to which 'most consent theorists assume that . . . consent, when present, in liberal democracies is given through liberal democratic voting . . .'. Cf. Green 1988, pp. 168–9; Simmons 1993, pp. 218–24.

[14] There is a further question that I shall not address as to whether, even if voting can in principle confer consent, the consent thus given counts as 'valid consent'. Standard validity conditions apply to political as well as other forms of consent, and one can well imagine that force or fraud might sometimes invalidate electoral consent (Tanasoca 2022). It is harder to imagine that any substantial number of voters failing the 'mental competence' condition—and note well, the 'mental competence' has nothing to do with being well informed. Cf Brennan (2019, pp. 209–10) who would disenfranchise voters on the latter basis alone.

10.1.1 Binding Politicians

Take first the case of politicians themselves. Another familiar example of being bound by 'the nature of the business' is this: when you voluntarily enter a contest with publicly known rules, you are thereby consenting to abide by those rules.[15] Let us apply that thought to the case of a politician standing for re-election to public office.

It is in the nature of elections (democratic or otherwise) that those who are elected assume the office to which they have been elected. Of course, no one expects a politician standing for re-election to explicitly *say* that he consents to vacating that office if he is not re-elected, any more that we expect a politician to say that he will return to his medical practice if he fails to win this election. Saying that would send the wrong signal to voters, suggesting to them that the politician half-expects to lose, thereby increasing the chances of precisely that happening. Still, we have every reason to suppose that the politician understands and accepts that it is in the nature of the business of elections that losers lose office. And we therefore have every reason to suppose that a politician who stands for re-election actually does consent (however tacitly) to vacating office if he loses the election.

That is not some esoteric, arcane rule of electoral law or procedure. Instead it is a familiar fact with which anyone remotely acquainted with the practice can reasonably be expected to know. It is in the well-known 'nature of the business' of elections that winners win office and losers lose it.[16] That is what elections are *about*, after all—who will occupy office. The fact that it is general knowledge that that is 'in the nature of the business' of elections warrants us in assuming that any politician standing in such an election actually does tacitly consent to that arrangement.

We may of course be wrong in making that assumption in the case of any particular politician. He may have absolutely no intention of vacating office, even if he loses the election. But then he would be acting in bad faith in standing in that election at all.[17] He would be acting under false pretences, pretending to participate in an election when he does not actually consent to one of the constitutive features of an election, which is that the winner of the election assumes the office that he won in the election.

So even if we were mistaken about the politician's consenting to leave office if he loses, the fault for that mistake lies with him, not us. And that gives us independent grounds, quite apart from whether he actually consented to vacating

[15] Saunders 2010, p. 84. Singer 1973, pp. 47–59.

[16] Przeworski (2015) shows that empirically the practice is far from universal, but it is a habit quickly acquired once introduced into a country. Let us just say that when talking about 'democracies' here we are thinking about 'consolidated democracies' where the habit has been acquired.

[17] Lau 2014.

office if he lost the election, for forcibly evicting him from office if he loses and refuses to go.

On the precepts laid down in Chapter 4, if a person is at fault in causing a mistake, that person should be the one to bear the burdens of that mistake. The politician could and should have known the rest of us will regard it as 'in the nature of standing for re-election' that one is thereby committing oneself to vacating office if one loses. In those circumstances, it was the politician's responsibility to tell us if that is not actually something he was consenting to (however tacitly) through the act of standing for re-election.[18] If the politician knowingly lured us into mistaken beliefs about that, it is he who morally should bear the burdens of our mistaken beliefs about his consent. Those are sufficient grounds all on their own to justify us in evicting him from office if he loses, 'as if he consented' to leaving if he lost even if he did not really consent to doing so.[19]

10.1.2 Binding Voters

So much for politicians and what they tacitly consent to in the nature of the business of standing for office. Let us turn our attention now to voters and what they tacitly consent to in the nature of the business of voting in a democratic election. To keep things as simple as possible, let us assume a direct democracy, where citizens are voting on a referendum proposal that will automatically become law if it wins enough votes.

The natural extension of the 'politician standing for office' case is to say that, by voluntarily participating in a collective decision-making process, voters are consenting for that process to be determinative of the collective decision.[20] It is a pure tautology that it is in the nature of the business of a collective decision-making process that it makes collective decisions. Furthermore, that is not some arcane or obscure fact that can be known only among the *cognoscenti*. It is plain on its face that the point of a collective decision-making process is to make collective decisions. When invoking the process, that simply must be what you are doing collectively.

Something similar might perhaps be said about the individuals who make up that collectivity. It is in the nature of the business of a democratic referendum that, in voting, voters make laws. Each is casting a vote in a process in which the votes, taken together, constitute the collective decision. Each is—and ought to know that

[18] See Section 3.3.6. [19] See Section 1.4.3.2 and Chapter 4.

[20] I pass lightly over the irony that, in systems where voting is compulsory, citizens can therefore not be said to be voluntarily giving valid consent to political authority or hence be under any moral obligation to obey laws made by them. That conclusion might be avoided if the penalty for non-voting is sufficiently low as not really to be coercive; in Australia for example it is only A$20, roughly US$14 or £11 (AEC 2019, para. 30).

he is—doing something that is partially constitutive of making the collective decision. In making the law in that way, each voter is consenting to the law being made in that way. That is just in the nature of the business of his making the law in that way.

In any given democratic political community there are also typically formal or informal norms and conventions of 'fair play' and 'good sportsmanship' further specifying what is 'in the nature of the business of voting in a referendum'. Those supplementary norms and conventions further reinforce the general understanding that, by voting in it, each individual participant consents to winning propositions becoming law.[21] Insofar as that is well-established in the norms and conventions of the community, we have every reason to believe that voters understand those facts when casting their votes in a referendum. Even if a few of them do not, they could and should have done so, and on those grounds we would be justified in treating them 'as if' they consented.

An analogous point has sometimes been made with respect to the more complex case of voting for representatives. Here is how Plamenatz puts it:

> Where there is an established process of election to an office, then . . . anyone who takes part in the process consents to the authority of whoever is elected to the office. . . . The citizen who votes at an election is presumed to understand the significance of what he is doing, and if the election is free, he has voluntarily taken part in a process which confers authority on someone who otherwise would not have it. He may bitterly regret the election of the successful candidate . . . , but if the election was free and he freely took part in it, he consented to the authority of the man elected.[22]

It is in the nature of the business of voting for representatives that one consents to the winning candidate being elected as our representative, and once again we have every right to assume that voters actually do consent to that (even if only tacitly) when voting for representatives.

Again, we may be mistaken in assuming that any given voter actually consents (albeit tacitly) to the outcome of a referendum becoming law or the outcome of an

[21] At the very least each is consenting to the outcome of the process 'being the collective decision' and to its 'becoming law' (assuming those two are analytically identical in the sort of referendum here in view). Weale (1999, p. 81) similarly writes: 'If we are to maintain the idea that participation in the democratic process is a form of consent, it is . . . going to be necessary to distinguish that part of the meaning of a person's act that derives from his or her intention and that part which derives from the meaning that is attached by the institutional context in which they act.' The institutional context gives participation that meaning, even if the private intention of the participant is otherwise. My argument here is that we can legitimately presume that voters tacitly intend what is 'in the nature of the business' of a referendum (or anyway that they can be legitimately treated 'as if they consent' because they could and should understand that that is how their actions will be understood, unless they explicitly and publicly disavow that understanding of them).

[22] Plamenatz 1938/1968, pp. 170–1.

election installing the winning candidate in office. But, in the absence of explicit contra-indications, we had every right to assume that he did given that doing so is 'in the nature of the business' of voting in a representative democracy. If we are mistaken in that assumption, once again the responsibility for the mistake lies with the voter who deviates, without giving due notice, from such obvious community understandings;[23] and he should be the one who bears the costs of the mistake, here, by being treated 'as if he consented' even when (secretly) he did not. Especially if others have incurred costs in acting in reliance upon his false signals, he has contracted a quasi-contractual duty to accept the outcome as the outcome, even if it is one to which (secretly) he has not 'really' consented.[24] On this 'who bears the burden of mistakes' analysis, it is a matter of 'fairness' rather than literal 'consent', to be sure.[25] But the duty to accept the outcome as the outcome, even though differently grounded in this case, is none the less strong. Furthermore, its grounding is not all *that* different: it is still consent-related, in the sense that the referendum voter gave conventional signals of consent from which others reasonably inferred that he actually did consent to the outcome of the referendum becoming law or the winning candidate in the election taking the office to which she was elected.[26]

10.1.3 Bound to What?

Just how far do moves of this sort get us toward legitimating political authority and establishing a general obligation to obey the law *qua* law? Not all that far, for various reasons.

First and most obviously, not everyone votes in every referendum (and not everyone is even entitled to do so). This argument offers us no leverage on why non-voters have an obligation to obey the law enacted as a result of a referendum.[27]

Second, and only a little less obviously, all that that argument gives us is the conclusion that those who voted in the referendum consent to a proposition that is passed in the referendum becoming law. Fine, now it is law. But that leaves open the question of 'why obey the law'.[28] And you had better not just say: 'Because it is the law; that is just analytic, what it means for something to be law.' That is

[23] As argued in Section 3.3.6 above.

[24] Siegler 1968, p. 260; Singer 1973, pp. 47–59; cf. Kleinig 1982, p. 109; Simmons 1976, pp. 287–8; Postow 1980; cf. Simmons 1981. See further Sections 1.4.2 and 5.11.

[25] Weale 1999, p. 200. Rawls (1971, p. 347) similarly argues with respect to promising that 'we are under an obligation to do as we promised by the principle of fairness'.

[26] See Section 1.4.2 above. [27] Simmons 1993, p. 221. Weale 1999, p. 81.

[28] It is not analytically true, just because a law was made by some legitimate authority, there is necessarily the case that you have a duty to obey that law (Applbaum 2010).

precisely the question we were trying to answer, 'Why obey the law just because it is the law?'[29]

Third, and most interestingly, that argument leaves open the question of how to derive anyone's consent to the political system in general. What a theory of political obligation is seeking is some story about why people have at least a *prima facie* duty to obey *any and all* laws duly enacted within this political system. But all that the 'you voted in the referendum on this particular proposition' argument gives us is a conclusion that, by the nature of the business, you thereby consented to the outcome of the referendum being ensconced as the collective decision *on that particular proposition.*[30]

Can we infer from the fact that, by voting in that referendum you consented to that *one* collective decision being made in that way, you consent to *all* collective decisions being made in that way? Or to all decisions made under the constitution that provides for all sorts of other ways of making legally binding decisions in addition to the referendum? Just how far can we go in presuming consent to the (very) general from consent to the (very) particular?[31]

The 'nature of the business' move, recall, is supposed to be a way of grounding tacit consent. The thought is that, even though you may not have said so in as many words, surely you knew to what you were consenting when casting your ballot, just as surely as you knew to what you were consenting when ordering a meal in the pub. It is in the nature of voting in referenda that you consent for a collective decision thereby to be made through that process, just as it is in the nature of ordering food in a pub that you consent to pay for it. Everyone knows (or could be expected to know) that, and consent to that, when engaging in those practices. For anyone who does not, the responsibility for the mistaken understanding lies squarely with them; and they should be the ones to bear any burdens arising from the mistake.

That however is essentially an empirical claim about what people know or can reasonably be expected to know about the meaning that will be attached to their actions.[32] It would be utterly disingenuous to pretend ignorance of the fact that referenda make collective decisions, and that therefore when participating in a

[29] You might say 'it is in the nature of the business of law that it commands obedience', and hence that those who voluntarily engaged in processes of law-making consented by the nature of the business of making law to its 'commanding obedience'. But I can consent to the law *making* those commands without consenting to *obey* its commands.

[30] Of course, things would have been different if the referendum had been on the constitution itself, as sometimes happens.

[31] Simmons (1993, pp. 220–1) argues similarly *a propos* representative democracy that 'it will not be immediately evident what consent is being given *to*.... [O]ne would have to assume that since what is typically voted *for* is a candidate for a political office of limited term, consent is given only to the authority of that candidate for that term. This seems far short of the overarching power to the authority of government that was supposed to be given in the act of voting.'

[32] As Weale (1999, p. 200) says, 'If there is a general understanding that turning out to vote is a way of signaling to others that one is prepared to abide by the result, then the act of voting is equivalent to

referendum you are consenting to a collective decision being made by that referendum.[33] But there is no reason to think that there is any widespread conventional understanding of the meaning of 'voting in a referendum on some particular proposition' that you necessarily thereby consent to some different matter being decided by another referendum, much less that you consent to the system of government as a whole (not just rules governing referenda but all other aspects of the constitutional structure).[34]

10.2 Implicit Consent: To What Are Voters Logically Committed?

Plamenatz wants to argue:

> When you vote for a person or a party that wins an election, you directly consent to his or her authority, and you also consent indirectly to the system of government. Even when your vote is cast for persons who intend to change the system, you consent to it until it is changed. For you make use of the system in order to change it.... It does not matter what your motive for voting is, any more than it matters what your motive is in making a promise.[35]

Leave aside those who voted for people or parties that lost the election. Even so, as we have just seen, we cannot even get as much as Plamenatz here wants out of any tacit-consent story about the 'nature of the business' of democratic politics.

an act of express consent to the result of the election.' Whether that 'if' clause is satisfied is fundamentally an empirically matter. Kleinig (1982, p. 109) is right to say that 'whether such a belief is induced is to be decided, not a priori, but by seeing what serious expectations are in fact engendered'. Kleinig goes on to say: 'I doubt whether, in the contemporary climate [i.e. even back in 1982], participation creates any strong general expectation of conformity.' For my part I doubt whether, even in today's climate, there are many who genuinely doubt that the collective decision-making process in which they have participated has resulted in a genuine collective decision—although it may be more doubtful whether we can nowadays expect everyone to abide by those decisions and act in conformity with them.

[33] Thus, I think Simmons (1976, p. 289) overreaches badly when writing: 'One may, and probably the average man does, register and vote with only minimal awareness that one is participating at all, and with no intention whatsoever of consenting to anything.' Say what you will about voter ignorance, it beggars belief that someone voting in a referendum can be 'only minimally aware' that he is engaged in a lawmaking process; nor can anyone credibly pretend not to realize that others will reasonably expect participants in the lawmaking process to accept the laws made thereby. When it comes to the broader implications of voting in a referendum for consent to the political system as a whole, however, such scepticism seems much more warranted.

[34] As Weale (1999, p. 82) says, 'in the political case there is simply not this rich institutional background [as would be required] to provide an authoritative interpretation to the acts of individuals'. In reply to the claim that 'voting in a democratic election is necessarily a way of consenting because there are clear conventions [to that effect] governing such elections', Simmons (1993, p. 224) likewise replies that 'the conventions governing such elections are hardly crystal-clear'.

[35] Plamenatz 1963, vol. 1, pp. 239–40.

Might we fare better by trying an 'implicit-consent' story akin to those developed in Section 3.4 above? The upshot of the discussion of this section will be discouraging in that regard.

10.2.1 It's Analytic! Or Is It?

Recall one of the examples from that earlier discussion. When you consent to my frying fish you also consent to my cooking fish because, by definition, 'frying' just is a form of 'cooking'. Can a similar definitional gambit succeed in getting consent to obey the law out of voluntarily participating in a process to make the law?

Some say 'yea'. They say that, whenever one consents to participate in some rule-governed activity,

> one also consents to abide by the rules that constitute and regulate the activity or association in question. Consent follows logically from participation here because adherence to the rules of the activity determine what it means to participate in the activity; and correspondingly, participation is not possible except by adherence to the rules.[36]

So, for example, when you join in a game of baseball, you consent to the umpire's decisions being binding, because the umpire's decisions being binding is one of the constitutive rules of the game of baseball. If you didn't accept the umpire's decisions as binding, you would simply not be playing 'baseball'. You may be playing some other ball-and-bat game that is identical in every other respect. But absent that one key constitutive rule, it just would not be 'baseball'.[37]

The example of the politician running for re-election might arguably fit into the same pattern. It is simply analytic—it is built into the very notion of 'election to office'—that the person who wins election to office is entitled to assume the office. That is just what it means to win election to office.

On that account, unless the politician standing for re-election to office at least implicitly consented to vacating office if he lost, he was not really running for re-election at all. It certainly *looked* like that was what he was doing, to be sure. If he had won, he would have *claimed* that that is what he had done: won re-election.

[36] Carr 1990, p. 338. In the Section 10.1.1 application, the thought was that it is in the nature of the business that when engaging in a rule-governed activity the politician tacitly consents to abide by those rules. The thought in this section is that a politician is logically committed to abiding by the rules that constitute the business.

[37] Rawls 1955, p. 25; cf. Simmons 1976, p. 287. Recall Applbaum's (1999, p. 119) example along the same lines of the American gridiron football player who pins to his jersey a sign saying 'I do not consent to be tackled' and then takes the field, accepts the handoff and runs with the ball toward the goal: ' One is tempted to say that he no longer plays football... and the referee should eject him from the game.' See Kukla's (2018, p. 91) similar remarks about participating (consensually) in a boxing match.

But, the advocate of this approach would say, those claims are purely fraudulent on his part. However much the politician insists that he is standing for re-election, he is doing no such thing if he does not at least implicitly consent to the rules constituting the practice and intend to abide by the outcome of that election.

Perhaps those appearances are not really all that deceptive, however. Here is another way of looking at that situation. We could say that the politician truly is standing for re-election, on the grounds that if he had won re-election he would have claimed political authority based on having won re-election. That is to say, he consents to the proposition that 'winning an election confers political authority'. What he does not consent to is the proposition that 'winning an election is the *only* thing that can confer political authority'. There are other things that confer political authority (such as the proven capacity to lead the country in times of crisis), he might suppose; and if he loses the election he intends to claim political authority on one of those other bases. Having implicitly consented to the proposition that winning an election confers (some) political authority, he would of course have to concede that the other person who won the election has some claim to office under that heading. But even admitting as much, it is still open to him to claim that he has still greater political authority deriving from that other source.

Something similar might be said of the voter in a referendum. It may be analytic that the operation of a collective decision procedure makes a binding collective decision, in the same way that it is analytic that an election to office decides who is to occupy office. But it is not really analytic that a voter must, purely by definition of what it is 'to vote', accept (even implicitly) that she is under an obligation to obey the laws thereby enacted.[38]

Suppose there is an institutional requirement that, before receiving their ballot paper, voters must swear an oath that they consent to accepting the outcome of the referendum. But now imagine a voter who insincerely swears just such an oath. She does not really consent to accepting the result of the referendum as law, if the vote goes against her. Such a voter would have obtained her ballot paper under false pretences. She would have committed a fraud. Nevertheless, when she drops the ballot paper into the ballot box, there can be no doubt she has indeed 'cast a vote'.[39] The intentions and backstory behind her vote, and what constitutes 'a vote', are wholly separate matters.[40] Dropping her market ballot paper into the ballot box is conceptually all that is involved in 'casting a vote'.

[38] Contrary to Singer's (1973, p. 50) claim that 'there is a conceptual connection between consenting and voting'.

[39] See further Section 2.3.1.

[40] Green (1988, p. 171), for example, says: 'it seems groundless to insist that there is a conceptual connection between voting and consenting if this is merely the claim that it would be wrong to call it voting if it did not express consent. There is nothing linguistically improper about describing an anarchist's action in marking her ballot for the least bad candidate as "voting." . . . [T]he conceptual connection argument offers an answer to the wrong question. We are not to ask, "Why would anyone set up a practice of voting knowing that participating in it will not express consent" but rather, "Is it

What are we to say of a voter who would accept the outcome of an election as authoritatively binding only if her side won? Well, she was voting in bad faith if she did not intend to accept the outcome. She was being a 'bad sport' in refusing to accept the outcome. She is behaving unfairly in refusing to accept the results of the election if and only if they go against her.[41] She is misbehaving in all sorts of ways. The winners have every right to rule (over her, among all others) notwithstanding her protestations, and they have every right to bring the full force of law to bear upon her if she resists. We can say all of those things. All that we cannot say, I think, is that 'she did not really cast a vote after all, because voting analytically entails consenting to whoever wins having political authority'.

Hence I do not think that either of those two appeals to analiticity go through. Even if they did, note that we would still not have arrived at an obligation to obey the law. Even if it were somehow analytic that those standing for election to office must by definition consent to the winner of that election holding office, the most that would show is that they have consented to the political authority of those holding offices to make laws. Whether unsuccessful office-seekers have any obligation to obey the laws, just because they are laws, is another matter that is yet to be resolved. Similarly with a voter in a referendum: even if it were somehow analytic that those voting in a referendum must by definition consent to the proposition on which they are voting becoming law if it wins enough votes in the referendum, the question remains why they are under any obligation to obey the law just because it is law.

Some might say that that, too, is simply analytic. It is built into the notion of 'law' that it imposes obligations that it be obeyed.[42] To be sure, laws impose legal obligations—that is indeed analytic. But do legal obligations give rise to *moral* obligations? They purport to, perhaps. But what the law purports to do is one thing; what it actually does, morally, is quite another. We are looking for a reason to think that we really do have an obligation, morally, to obey the law just because it is the law. The fact that the law purports to impose a moral obligation is no reason to think that it actually does so, any more than the fact that the pretender Louis Alphonse de Bourbon, Duke of Anjou, purports to be the king of France makes him king of that country.

None of this is to deny that there are good reasons to obey the law, of course. There clearly are good reasons of all sorts, often couched in terms of 'fairness' and 'reciprocity' and others in terms of 'reliance'. It is merely to say that you cannot argue that the obligation to obey the law, just because it is law, 'is analytic'. You

possible to make sense of the individual decision to vote even if that individual does not regard herself as thereby expressing her consent?" The answer to the latter question is decisively in the affirmative: she may vote to minimize her losses.'

[41] See the discussion of 'fairness' in Section 3.5 above and sources cited there.

[42] The *Oxford English Dictionary* (qv. 'law (n.)', def. 3d) defines 'law' as: 'Rules or injunctions that must be obeyed'.

cannot get those obligations out of the definition of 'law' and that alone. You need further arguments. And, as is the larger claim of this chapter, you cannot get those obligations out of the 'consent' of those subject to those laws, either.

10.2.2 Consent to Lower-order Rules Logically Implies Consent to Higher-order Ones

Suppose the argument in Section 10.1.2 goes through, and by participating in a collective decision-making process you are thereby consenting to the collective decision being made through that process. I argued in Section 10.1.3 that even if that is the case, the question remains why your consenting to one particular decision being made through the particular collective decision-making process in which you participated should be taken as your consenting to the general political system in which that process is embedded.

Here is one implied-consent sort of answer that might be given to that challenge. That particular collective decision-making process gives rise to particular laws that are binding in your community only by virtue of some higher-order general rule (call it a 'constitution') that makes that the case. Given that fact, consenting to the former logically commits you to consenting to the latter because the latter is what gives the former its authority. Or so the argument might go.

The argument might go through if put the other way around. If you consent to the higher-order rule, then perhaps from your consent to that rule we can derive the conclusion that it is logically implicit that you consent to any lower-order rule made under the higher-order one. The argument there would be that the lower-order rule is not really a different rule at all, to which separate consent must be given. Rather, it is merely an application of the higher-order rule to which you have already consented—it is, as it were, merely that higher-order rule in a different guise.

Consenting to the lower-order rule does not commit you to consenting (still less does it 'constitute' consenting) to the higher-order rule, however. I can sign a legally binding contract in a theocratic state without consenting to the deity from whom that state claims highest authority. Residents of occupied territories can consent to marry one another under the laws of the occupiers, without consenting to the authority of the occupying forces. Tourists can consent to obey the traffic laws of the country they are visiting without consenting to the rule of the monarch who made them. All sorts of people can consent to lower-order rules without consenting to the higher-order rules from which they purport to derive their authority.

Note that the existence of lower-order rules does not logically depend upon the existence of higher-order ones, necessarily. You can—primitive societies do—have what Hart calls a system of 'primary norms' (norms that just say, 'Do this, do that') without having any 'secondary norms' that specify how those norms come into being, are changed, and so on.[43] Voting rules are themselves secondary norms, of course; they govern how primary norms are to be made. But you can have that level of secondary norms without having any higher-order secondary norms atop them. A primitive band can conduct a vote to decide who will lead the hunt without there being any other secondary norms among them governing anything else.

10.2.3 Pragmatically Implied?

A more promising approach might be one that trades in pragmatics rather than sheer logic.[44] Perhaps when consenting to something becoming law you are (or at least it is pragmatically implied that you are) consenting to all of the social and institutional infrastructure that is required to make law be law-on-the-ground and not just law-on-the-statute-books. Actually, statute books themselves—or anyway some system for promulgating the law—might be part of that institutional infrastructure that is required to make law law-on-the-ground. So too might be systems for interpretation and application and perhaps for enforcement of the law.

Could the tourist who is consenting to a country's traffic laws for the duration of his passage through it really be said to be consenting to all that institutional infrastructure as well? I do not think that would be too far a stretch. He is certainly subjecting himself to the judicial system of that country, before which he may be made to appear if he breaches one of its traffic laws on his journey. Likewise the newlyweds in the occupied territory: they are counting on the occupiers' law to recognize their new status, tax them at the 'married' rather than 'single' rate, register the birth of their children, etc. Likewise with my contract signed under the laws of some theocratic state: I am counting on the courts of that state to enforce the contract if the other party defaults, even if I am not counting on their god to strike him dead.

Suppose, *arguendo*, that consenting to a law being law pragmatically implies consenting to the state apparatus required to give effect to that law. That still does not necessarily extend to all of the state apparatus—or even to all uses that might

[43] Hart 1961, ch. 5.

[44] Notice that there is another familiar pragmatic argument that will not do the work here required. It may well be true, as Singer (1973, p. 55) says, that unless enough people are prepared to accept the outcome of an election 'there would cease to be any point in voting . . . , since the majority verdict would not be accepted, and hence would decide nothing'. As Siegler (1968, p. 261) puts it, 'if nobody who voted consented to the authority of the winner or to the system there could be no genuine notion of a free election. It might be that a free political system depends on popular consent in that without it there could be no such thing. And therefore there is a logical connection between voting and consenting'. But as Siegler (1968, p. 261) goes on to say, 'the connection is *not* one of entailment in individual cases'; the system-level presupposition is simply that enough voters accept the outcome, not that each and every one of them do so.

be made of those parts of the state apparatus to which I thereby consent. When I sign a contract in England, perhaps it indeed is pragmatically implied that I consent to the operation of the courts and officers of the court in England that are required to enforce that particular contract. But it is not necessarily pragmatically implied that I consent to the operation of English courts and officers of the court to enforce all the other contracts I have signed (in other jurisdictions, for example). And in consenting to the operation of the English courts and officers of the court required to enforce my contract, I do not consent to those being used to do something else altogether (brutalize peaceful political protestors, for example).

Hence, even this most promising approach for finding consent to the political system as a whole has strict limits. We might be able to say that consent to certain elements of the state apparatus is pragmatically implied in our consenting that some law be law. But there seems to be no way of arguing that consent to the entire state apparatus is pragmatically implied.

10.3 Conclusion

We have long been familiar with abject failures of all of the standard ways of trying to use consent to ground political authority and the obligation to obey the law. The aim of this chapter has been to see if either of the two more novel ways suggested in Chapter 3 can be made to work for these purposes.

Those approaches do manage to get further than do the familiar discredited approaches. Their success is nevertheless only very partial. Considerations of what is 'in the nature of voting' might get us the result that those who take part in a law-making process tacitly consent or may legitimately be treated 'as if they consent' to *that* law being made by that process. But those considerations do not get us to the conclusion that those voters thereby consent to *other laws* being made by that process, or to *other processes* of making law under the same constitution; nor do they necessarily thereby *consent to obey* even the very law that they take part in making, as opposed to consenting merely that it become law. Or again, it may be pragmatically implicit in our consenting to a law being law that we consent to the institutional infrastructure required to give effect to *that* law. But that does not mean that we consent to all the rest of the state apparatus *beyond* that.

In short, 'consent by extension' seems subject to some pretty strict limits. Certainly that is so, at least in the political case. And perhaps—indeed, perhaps 'presumably'—that is true more generally as well.

11
Epilogue
Consent in Its Place

Consent is intimately connected to rights. Consent is morally transformative, in that it gives permission to the consent-receiver to do something that would otherwise constitute a violation of the consent-giver's rights. Consent is morally important just because, and (but only) insofar as, those rights are morally important. But just how important is that? That is the question around which this final chapter revolves, returning to the larger moral controversies foreshadowed at the beginning of the book.

Deontologists elevate rights to the highest normative alter. They put them on a moral pedestal above all else. 'Rights are trumps', proclaims Dworkin hyperbolically.[1] My retort would be that moral life is more than a card game, and some of the other moral considerations in play can sometimes be of far more importance than many of the 'rights' in Dworkin's deck.[2]

Let's not rehearse here the tiresome disputes between consequentialists and deontologists over whether it can ever be morally permissible to intentionally sacrifice one person to save a great many. We all know the famous intuition-pumps that work in in both directions.[3] The battle lines there are too well drawn. Everyone knows what they 'have to say', given their larger moral allegiances; and no one can think remotely outside their confining moral box in relation to those terribly familiar cases. It really is a dialogue of the deaf—an ethical analogue of trench warfare.

11.1 The Varying Importance of Consent

Let us focus instead on this simple, novel example.[4] A convicted criminal has been sentenced to death, and his imminent execution can now only be averted by the governor's signing an order commuting his death sentence.

[1] Dworkin 1977, p. xi; 1984.

[2] When not sloganeering, Dworkin (1977, pp. 90–4) himself acknowledges as much.

[3] On the one hand there is Williams' (1973, pp. 98–100) example of Jim and Pedro: Pedro will kill 20 Indians unless Jim kills one of them, in which case Pedro will spare the rest; Williams and many others think it would be wrong of Jim to do so. On the other hand, many think it was right (in obviously unfortunate circumstances) for the British government to use its double-agents to redirect the German buzz bombs away from London and toward less populated areas, so that fewer (albeit different) people died (Burri 2020).

[4] I promised in the Preface to abjure 'crazy' cases. What follows is, alas, far from unrealistic in today's US where public executions are burgeoning and politics is increasingly plutocratic; the only thing remotely unrealistic about the example is the suggestion that many US governors would dare to pardon anyone on Death Row these days.

Consent Matters. Robert E. Goodin, Oxford University Press. © Robert E. Goodin 2024.
DOI: 10.1093/oso/9780192889027.003.0011

Suppose the governor is staying at a rich backer's mansion on the night of the scheduled execution, and suppose he did not bring with him a pen of his own. The only way he can sign an order commuting the sentence would be to use one of his host's pens. Unfortunately, his host drank way too much and has passed out; he will not be *compos mentis* until well after the execution is scheduled to take place; and the governor did not think to ask his host's consent to use one of his pens for that purpose before he got stuck into the booze.

The governor would be violating his host's property right by using his host's pen without his consent.[5] To make things worse, from a consent point of view, suppose further that the governor knows that his host actually thinks the condemned man should be executed—so the governor has every reason to suppose that his host would have refused permission to use the pen for that purpose, had the governor asked.[6]

Now, there are all sorts of weighty moral issues swirling around in this example. Is the death penalty morally permissible, and under what circumstances?[7] Is it morally proper for an elected official to overrule the results of a judicial process, and under what circumstances?[8] And are those circumstances present in the case at hand?

Those are all weighty moral considerations that must be carefully balanced in the governor's decision of whether or not to pardon the condemned man. But no one except a philosopher riding a hobbyhorse could conceivably imagine that the consideration of whether to use the host's pen without his consent should figure remotely largely in those moral deliberations.[9] Perhaps a deontologist, grasping at straws, might say, 'Well, at least at the margin it should be a tie-breaker...'[10] But the margin at which such an utterly trivial moral consideration could break a tie is surely measured in microns.[11]

[5] I am not making this up: consent theorists really do talk about consent being required to use someone else's pen (Tadros 2016, p. 210; Gerver 2020, p. 27; Dougherty 2021a, p. 144; Chadha 2021, pp. 343–4).

[6] Garrett Cullity (private communication) suggests 'that using someone's pen falls within the scope of what you've been permitted to do in being invited to their house', and 'you wouldn't be violating any right if you just pick it up and use it (any more than you would be if you use the towel in the bathroom without asking for permission first)'. While that may ordinarily be so, the governor's knowing that the owner would object to his pen being used for that purpose seems to change things in that regard. Anyone still worried by such thoughts can just change the example from 'using a pen' to something else ('making an expensive long-distance telephone call' or 'borrowing his car to get to the prison in time') that clearly would not fall within the scope of what would ordinarily be permitted by being invited into someone's home.

[7] Cf. van den Haag and Conrad (1983) and Bedau (1997).

[8] Love 2010.

[9] Enoch (2017, p. 15) makes much of the fact that 'normatively mattering can be a matter of degree' when he is trying to make the case that 'hypothetical consent' morally matters, even if not as much as 'actual consent'. That is an unacknowledged echo of Waldron's (1993, p. 49) 'wrongness is a matter of degree' talk, in the same connection.

[10] Enoch (2017, p. 14, n. 20) for example grasps at this straw.

[11] The other weightier considerations might sometimes be deontological ones. The condemned man might be said, by a deontologist, to have a right against being killed for his crime; or a deontologist

In that example, consent seems to be of vanishingly small moral importance in the larger scheme of things. But clearly there are other cases in which consent is hugely important. Consent to sexual relations is a currently prominent example of that. Sex without valid consent constitutes a serious assault, a violation of the assaulted person's rights both legally and morally. Forced marriage—marriage without the free consent of one or both parties—constitutes a violation of human rights on an even more on-going basis.[12] Cutting into, or experimenting on, a person's body without their consent is another gross moral offence, except in a medical emergency where doing so is required to save that person's life or otherwise avert grievous harm to that person.[13]

In between are cases of commandeering one's property in emergency situations—taking your car, when it is the only transport available and you are not around to ask, in order to transport someone who is badly injured to hospital, for example.[14] When doing that, I owe you an explanation and an apology, to be sure (and perhaps payment for cleaning the bloodstains from your car). But morally you would surely be in the wrong not to accept that explanation and apology. Legally, no doubt, you could sue me. Morally, however, you have no legitimate grounds for complaint in those circumstances.

The long and short of it is just this. Rights are not trumps. They are merely *pro tanto* moral considerations, of greater or lesser weight. (Doubtless they are special kinds of moral considerations, but what makes them special need not here detain us: all that matters, for present purposes, is that they are considerations that *weigh* rather than *trump*.) The moral importance of securing someone's consent to something just depends on how morally important are the rights that would thereby be waived.[15] They can be, perhaps often are, very important indeed. But they can be, and certainly at least sometimes are, less weighty than countervailing

might say it is wrong to kill people whatever they have done. But it is also possible—indeed, common—to conduct a moral debate over the permissibility of the death penalty in purely consequentialist terms (Bedau 1997; Donohue and Wolfers 2005; Sunstein and Vermeule 2005).

[12] According to the Universal Declaration of Human Rights, 'Marriage shall be entered into only with the free and full consent of the intending spouses' (UN 1948, art. 16.2). That was reiterated in the International Covenant on Economic, Social and Cultural Rights (UN 1966, art. 10.1) and the Convention on Consent to Marriage, Minimum Age for Marriage and Registration of Marriages (UN 1964).

[13] Declaration of Geneva (WMA 1948, clause 3); Nuremburg Code (1947, principle 1); Declaration of Helsinki (WMA 1964, art. 26).

[14] Feinberg (1978, p. 102; 1980, p. 230) famously offered the case of a backpacker caught in a snowstorm breaking into someone else's unoccupied cabin for shelter, which although a clear violation of the other's property rights Feinberg deems justified in the circumstances. Some, following Pufendorf (1672/1710, bk. 2, ch. 6, sec. 5), would characterize that as a 'right of necessity'—setting it up as a 'rights versus rights' confrontation (see further Mancilla 2016 and others cited therein). In my version of the example, the person taking the car without permission can have no such right *himself*, however much the injured third party needs to get to hospital (although see ALI [1979, § 891] on the 'delegability of privileges').

[15] And the moral permissibility of proceeding without their consent depends on the moral importance of those rights compared to that of the countervailing considerations at stake. I here leave open the question of how to calibrate 'the moral importance' of the rights in question or the 'gravity' of violating them—Archard (2007) and Tadros (2016, pp. 252–63) survey some alternatives. All that my argument here requires is that their moral importance is indeed graded.

moral considerations.[16] In those cases, it would certainly be nice to get consent if we conveniently can, if only as a courtesy—but doing so is in no way a moral *sine qua non* for proceeding.[17]

11.2 Asking Consent to Do More Work than It Can

Non-American physicians are often amazed at US medical ethicists' utter fixation on 'informed consent' as an absolute, inviolable standard.[18] Even in the US in earlier periods (not that long ago) doctors took a more paternalistic attitude toward patient care.[19] While they usually tried to explain to their patients what they were going to do to them and why, back then they were gratified rather than galled when their patients responded with an uncritical, 'Whatever you say, doc!' In other parts of the world, even today, 'informed consent' is not always considered such an essential part of 'good medical practice'.[20] Even where it is formally required, physicians often do not go to nearly such great lengths to secure it.

This is nowhere more evident than in the treatment of comatose or incompetent patients.[21] US physicians are supposed to seek out and slavishly follow patients' 'advance directives'. Absent those, they seek out 'surrogate decision-makers' (typically

[16] In Thomson's (1986, pp. 40–2, 51–5) and Feinberg's (1978, pp. 101–3; 1980, pp. 229–31) terminology, the right is merely 'infringed' and not 'violated' when the infringement was morally justified and hence no moral wrong was committed in infringing it. Still, for them (as for me), it remains the case that a right was infringed and compensation is owed for any damage done in consequence (see similarly Pufendorf 1672/1710, bk. 2, ch. 6. sec 6).

[17] Pufendorf (1672/1710, bk. 2, ch. 6, sec. 5, para. 1) thinks that someone can sometimes claim something as a 'right of necessity', but he is at pains to emphasize that that person ought in the first instance 'to apply himself to the owner, desiring to receive it from his disposal' rather than simply seizing it immediately. See similarly Grotius (1625, bk. 2, ch. 2, sec. 7). Oberdiek (2004, p. 329, n. 11) says 'I see no moral grounds on which *B* must ask *A* for such permission because even if *A* withheld permission *B* would still be justified' in doing what infringes (but in the Thomson/Feinberg terminology does not 'violate') *A*'s rights. That strikes me as socially, and maybe even morally, obtuse. Even if I have loaned you something on condition I may reclaim it whenever I need it, surely it is only polite for me to ask for it back rather than simply to grab it. Insofar as such small courtesies can be seen as ways of manifesting 'respect for a person', they may even be morally enjoined.

[18] For an example, see the influential textbook by Beauchamp and Childress (2009, pp. 117–35).

[19] 'The idea that, prior to any medical intervention, physicians must seek their patients' informed consent was introduced into American law in a brief paragraph in a 1957 state court decision, and then elaborated on in a lengthier opinion in 1960' (Katz 1994, p. 72, referring respectively to *Salgo v Leland Stanford Jr. University Board of Trustees*, 317 P.2d 170, 181 (Cal. Dist. Ct. App. 1957) and *Natanson v Kline*, 350 P.2d 1093 (Kan. 1960); see also Brock 1987). There may have been intimations of the view in much earlier texts and practice, but this represents the first full flowering of anything like a developed doctrine (Faden and Beauchamp 1986, ch. 3).

[20] It is in, e.g., the UK (NHS 2019; RCSE 2021) and Australia (AMC 2016, sec. 4.5), although only in a footnote to the Australian Medical Association's *Code of Ethics* (Australian Medical Association 2004, sec. 2.1.4 fn. 4). But there is no mention of 'informed consent' in the World Medical Association's *International Code of Medical Ethics* (WMA 1949), which refers only to 'a competent patient's right to accept or refuse treatment'.

[21] As also discussed in Sections 2.2.2, 8.5 and 9.5 above.

family members) to consent on behalf of the comatose patient. Absent both of those, US physicians throw up their hands and just 'do what is in the best interests of the patient'.[22] But even then they insistently characterize those treatment choices in terms of 'presumed consent'[23]—which is to say, what they presume their patients do or hypothetically would or retrospectively will consent to.[24]

There can be large question marks over how 'consent' is supposed to work in each of those cases, however. Advance directives are the most persuasive. They represent 'acts of consent' (or, of course, 'non-consent'), performed by that patient in the past, which the patient has not afterwards revoked. And acts of consent like that are valid until and unless revoked.[25]

Even so, advance directives can be dicey. How can we be sure the patient had not changed her mind—by which I mean, in terms of Section 1.2.1.1, performed the mental act of withdrawing consent—but just not gotten around to rewriting her advance directive?[26] The advance directive suffices to get the physician off the hook legally: it is the fault of the patient for not updating the advance directive, not the fault of the doctor for following it. But that merely resolves the issue of liability, not consent. The fact that the patient is at fault for not updating her advance directive does not alter the fact that she no longer mentally consents to the procedure that she had previously specified in it.

Advance directives as a way of literally 'giving consent' can also be paradoxical, depending upon how exactly they are framed. Advance directives by their nature purport to give 'conditional consent'. Now, there is nothing problematic about conditional consent in general.[27] When taking out a loan and offering my house as collateral, I give my conditional consent to the lender foreclosing on my house if I default on the loan. We do that sort of thing all the time. The potential paradox with advance directives is this: they can sometimes seem to be purporting to give consent to something precisely on condition you are incompetent to give it.[28]

[22] AMA 2019, sec. 2.1.2.

[23] Recall the American College of Physicians' *Ethics Manual*, quoted earlier as saying: 'In medical emergencies, consent to treatment necessary to maintain life or restore health is usually presumed unless it is known that the patient would refuse the intervention' (Snyder 2012, p. 77).

[24] Eyal 2019.

[25] As I have argued in Section 1.2.1.1 and Chapter 7.

[26] This point is sometimes made in terms of 'personal identity', and of course if the patient has changed so fundamentally as to be in effect a different person since signing the advance directive that makes it all the more inappropriate guidance (Buchanan 1988, p. 281; Wrigley 2007; Kuflik 2010, p. 148–9). But merely changing her mind, a much more common or garden phenomenon, is more than enough to generate the problem here in view.

[27] Pufendorf 1672/1710, bk. 3, ch. 8, sec. 3. I am speaking here of what Chadha (2021, pp. 344–52) calls 'conditionally tokening consent'.

[28] In contemplating whether causing someone's death harms the person, Feinberg (1984, p. 80) similarly recalls the old adage from Epicurus: 'Where she was, death was not, and where death was, she was not' (*Letter to Menoeceus*, para. 3). Adapting the slogan to the present case: 'Where competence is consent is not, and where consent is competence is not.'

True, you were competent when conditionally consenting. But we need to enquire as to how precisely the 'condition' stands in relation to that to which you were conditionally consenting. As discussed in Section 2.2.2, the condition can be 'internal' to the proposition being consented to ('I consent [to φ if γ]'); alternatively, the condition can be 'external' to the proposition being consented to ('If γ [I consent to φ]').[29] On the internalist reading, you actually give your consent before becoming incompetent. That is fine.[30] But on the externalist reading, you do not give your consent until the condition—your becoming incompetent—arises. That is clearly paradoxical. Incompetents are incompetent to consent. Thus, at the very least, we need to clean up the way advance directives are phrased, so as to avoid paradoxical locutions of the (all too common) form, 'If I fall into an irreversible coma I consent to being ventilated.'

Even greater problems arise in making sense of 'consent' given by surrogate decision-makers. They are asked to consent 'on behalf' of the comatose patient. But unless they have literally been given 'durable power of attorney' by the patient before she fell into the coma—and have been formally authorized in that very particular way[31]—they have no authority (certainly not legally, and probably not morally either) literally to *act on behalf* of the comatose patient. Instead it is a case of 'substituted judgment', with the surrogate making the decision *instead* of the patient.[32] Codes of ethics insist that: 'Physicians should emphasize to surrogates that decisions should be based on what the patient would want, not what surrogates would choose for themselves.'[33] But surmising what the patient 'would want' is not always straightforward, even for family and close friends.[34] And in any case, following the patient's wishes is different from obeying her orders, and what she '*would* want' is importantly different from what she '*does* want' which is what is crucial for purposes of assessing consent.[35]

Presuming the consent of a comatose patient is even more problematic. Being comatose, a patient does not currently consent to anything. What she would hypothetically consent to, or will later retrospectively consent to, is importantly different from her actually consenting to it now. Unless there was some prior 'act of consent' before the patient became comatose—through an advance directive for example—there is no consent that can be presumed. Consent might come later, or it might come if certain counterfactuals came to be realized, but it does not exist at

[29] Gilbert 1993; Chadha 2021, pp. 346–7.

[30] That is just like the case, discussed in Section 1.2.1.1, of my giving my son my consent to his using the family car tonight after I am asleep. On the analysis there given, I performed the act of consent while still awake; and that act of consent is an act of commitment that binds me (even while asleep), until and unless I perform some other act revoking it.

[31] Note well: 'authorization' is distinct from 'consent', as I argued in Section 6.2.3.

[32] Dworkin 1988, pp. 85–99. Kuflik 2010, p. 131.

[33] Snyder 2012, p. 78.

[34] 'Much depends on the transparency of the patient's attitudes, values and commitments, as well as on the designated agent's character and intelligence' (Kuflik 2010, p. 149).

[35] A point that figures, in a slightly different way, in my critique of hypothetical consent in Section 2.2.2 above.

the time the doctor administered the treatment, which was when it was needed to make the doctor's actions morally permissible.[36]

Contrast these US consent-fixated ways of dealing with comatose patients with how it is done by doctors in different parts of the world. Codes of medical ethics elsewhere—ranging from the UK Royal College of Surgeons' to the Islamic Code of Medical Ethics—sensibly omit any pretence of consent and simply say, straightforwardly, that physicians should simply do what is in the comatose patient's best interests.[37] The latter is of course a strictly consequentialistic approach, devoid of any consent-based charades, as regards comatose patients anyway.

I am not here proposing to go quite that far, necessarily. I would regard advance directives whose continuing validity is beyond doubt as acts of consent (or non-consent) that should be respected in the same way that the explicit consent or non-consent of conscious and competent patients should be.[38] And as I shall go on to argue in the next section, I also think that there is something to be said (less strongly, perhaps) for simply respecting the expressed wishes of patients even if they are not fully competent to give or withhold consent. But in the remaining cases—of unconscious patients without any formal advance directives or even any firmly expressed previous—I think physicians should simply do what is in the patient's best interests unencumbered by concerns about fictitious consent.

11.3 Simply Respecting People's Wishes

It is very plausible to suppose that we ought to abide by the expressed wishes of a person concerning what should happen to him, his body or his property once he is no longer capable of making those decisions for himself. But I suggest that we should do that out of respect for the person now past, pure and simple—without necessarily trying to force some fiction about current consent upon a person who is now manifestly incapable of consenting.[39]

Respecting a person's rights to autonomy and self-determination are clearly part—a very large part—of what it is to respect the person. Those considerations are why a person's actual consent matters, morally. Still, those considerations far from exhaust what it is to respect the person. Simply respecting a person's wishes

[36] As I have argued in Sections 2.2.1 and 2.2.2 above.

[37] Declaration of Kuwait 1981, 'Responsibility and Liability'; NHS 2019; RCSE 2021. In the UK advance directives limiting life-preserving treatments are formally permitted but infrequently followed; indeed, there is an explicit presumption written into the Mental Capacity Act 2005 in favour of preserving life in any cases of any uncertainty about the validity of the advance directive (Michalowski 2005, p. 959).

[38] Per my analysis in Section 1.2.1 above.

[39] I am assuming here that the deceased had expressed her wishes in a way that stopped well short of anything that could be regarded as an 'act of consent' (or 'non-consent').

is another important way of respecting the person.[40] And that is so, even if those wishes are not (or, anyway, not now) connected to any autonomy or self-determination rights, powers or interests the person may have or have had.[41]

This will come as an odd thought only to a consent theorist with tunnel vision. But others—democratic theorists, for example—are quite accustomed to consulting the wishes and preferences of people who will be affected by a decision, even if they do not strictly speaking have rights (certainly not any right of veto) in the matter.

For reasons outlined in the previous section, it might be better to think of advance directives as a way of communicating people's wishes, rather than as a form of conditional consent. It is also a good way of explaining why knowing that someone had previously refused consent in similar circumstances might be morally relevant, even when (as in emergency medical care of comatose patients without advance directives or surrogate decision-makers) consent is not strictly required. Other things being equal, the wishes of the person ought to be respected for their own sake, even when they cannot be taken as tokens of consent.

That is also much the more natural way of treating people's preferences concerning the disposition of their bodies and properties after their death.[42] Bequests could, of course, be forced into the framework of conditional consent ('I consent that [my property be transferred to you, if I die]'). But the concept of consenting cadavers—or even cadavers being morally bound by the consent of their live predecessors—is very peculiar indeed. And so too, in much the same way, is that of cadavers consenting to the transfer of their (former) property. We can sensibly talk about 'advance directives' and 'acts of commitment' that people have previously made enduring and having continuing force even if they are no longer conscious; but it makes far less sense to talk of a person's commitments having continuing force once that person no longer exists. Far better in both cases, I suggest, to talk in terms of 'respecting the wishes' that those people

[40] The past or present wishes of the person, in the case of someone who is now incapable of consenting; the wishes of the past person, in the case of someone now deceased.

[41] Kuflik (2010, p. 140) talks of 'hypothetical consent' as being a 'reasonable way of' extending respect for someone's right to decide what will happen in and to his or her own body, even in circumstances in which that person's capacity for decision making cannot be concurrently exercised'. Respecting the *actual* wishes of presently incapacitated people seems a far better way of doing that, however, than does respecting purely *hypothetical* choices that we impute to them in some counterfactual circumstances.

[42] Among the 'contexts in which consent (or some suitably related idea) is typically hypothesized', Kuflik (2010, pp. 131–2) discusses the case of 'respect for those who have died', saying: 'Friends and relatives are trying to honor a recently deceased person by handling some of that person's posthumous affairs in a way that they believe that person *would have* wanted them to do and indeed *would have authorized* them to do, if only (or so they believe) the deceased had managed to anticipate and more explicitly address such matters with greater specificity.' But I cannot see how the second italicized passage ('would have authorized') adds anything to the first ('would have wanted').

who are now dead had while they were still alive.[43] It is a way of honouring their memory, which is something we should do, at least for a while.[44]

Trying to force bequests into the framework of conditional consent runs into the same logical difficulties identified in the previous section with advance directives for medical care. On the externalist account of conditional consent, the testator would be saying, 'If I die [I consent to my title to my property being transferred to you]'. But that is absurd. Once you are dead, you cannot consent to anything.[45]

The internalist reading of conditional consent, as I have said, avoids that absurdity. There, the testator is merely saying, 'I consent to [my title to my property being transferred to you if I die].'[46] That does not run into the same problem. The person was alive at the time the consent was given. But problems of a different sort may well then arise.

To see why, recall a distinction common across Grotius, Hobbes and Pufendorf between: (a) 'I promise to give you this tomorrow' (in which case it has not yet been given to you); and (b) 'I give you this and I will deliver it tomorrow' (in which case it has been given today, and delivery is all that is pending).[47] Construing bequests as internalist-style conditional contracts—which is the only way to avoid the previous absurdity—makes them promises of form (b). But that is then to say that the transfer of property would have been effected by the signing of the will, and all that is pending is delivery of the goods. Yet in that case you would have lost your power to change your will—which is an absurdity of another sort.[48]

One way of avoiding that absurdity might be by construing a bequest as conditional consent such as 'I consent to [my title to my property being transferred to you if I die]'—as I earlier phrased it—rather than as a conditional promise for it to do so. But, strictly speaking, if title to property is to be transferred from one person to another, something more than mere consent (more than the mere waiving of rights) must be involved. Something like a promise, vesting

[43] Feinberg 1984, pp. 79–95. It is a matter of 'keeping faith with the dead', in Feinberg's (1980, p. 174) phrase.

[44] But not in perpetuity—I wholly agree with Lam (2019) on that.

[45] Pufendorf 1672/1710, bk. 4, ch. 10, sec. 2. As Feinberg (1980, p. 174) similarly observes in advocating the opposing internalist reading of bequests: 'the duties of courts and trustees to honor testamentary directions, and the duties of life insurance companies to pay benefits to survivors, are, in a sense, only conditional duties before a man dies. They come into existence as categorical demands for immediate action only upon the [man's] death. So the view that death renders them null and void has the truth exactly upside down.'

[46] Pufendorf 1672/1710, bk. 4, ch. 10, sec. 5. Sometimes further conditions are added, such as 'if the building purchased by this donation bears my name in perpetuity'—which creates problems of the sort Lam (2019) rightly laments.

[47] Grotius 1625, bk. 2, ch. 11, secs. 2--. Hobbes 1651, ch. 14. Pufendorf 1672/1710, bk. 3, ch. 5, sec. 8.

[48] Pufendorf 1672/1710, bk. 4, ch. 10, sec. 2. The reason this absurdity arises with bequests is that they involve the transfer of title to property; and once title has been transferred it cannot be taken back by the original owner. With advance directives for medical treatment no analogous problem arises, so long as that consent is revocable; and none of the reasons discussed in Chapter 7 would seem to suggest it should not be.

claim-rights (rather than just liberties) in the other, must be involved. And while consent is sometimes revocable, promises are not.[49] Hence the absurdity noted above.

Far better, I suggest, not to of think of last wills and testaments in terms of consent at all. They are not an exercise of autonomy, as so many want to treat them.[50] They are instead merely an expression of the previous wishes of a person who has since passed away. That does not make them any the less worthy of respect. Neither does following them as mere 'past wishes' betoken any less respect for the person now deceased.[51] If anything, honouring his wishes (something over which we have discretion) is more respectful of the person than following his orders (something over which we have no discretion, assuming he was in a position of authority to give such orders).

[49] See Section 2.2.4 above.

[50] Just note the familiar phrase, 'last *will* and testament'. Testaments are, Grotius (1625/1910, bk. 2, ch. 9, secs. 1–2) insists, a 'declaration of his will'.

[51] If you think there is something odd about 'respecting something (here, a person) that does not exist (any longer)', rephrase it as 'respecting his memory'.

References

Aitchison, Guy. 2022. Fragility as strength: the ethics and purpose of hunger strikes. *Journal of Political Philosophy*, 30: 535–58.

Aitkins, Humphrey. 1981. Humphrey Aitkins comments on the death of Bobby Sands. BBC Nine O'Clock News, 7 May 1981. Available at <https://www.bbc.co.uk/programmes/p00hfzhb>.

Akerlof, George A. 1970. The market for 'lemons': qualitative uncertainty and the market mechanism. *Quarterly Journal of Economics*, 84: 488–500.

Alderson, Priscilla. 2012. Children's consent and 'assent' to healthcare research. Pp. 174–89 in *Law and Childhood Studies*, ed. Michael Freeman. Oxford: Oxford University Press.

Alexander, Larry. 2014. The ontology of consent. *Analytic Philosophy*, 55: 102–13.

Alexander, Larry; Heidi Hurd; and Peter Westen. 2016. Consent does not require communication: a reply to Dougherty. *Law & Philosophy*, 35: 655–60.

Altham, J.E.J. 1985. Wicked promises. Pp. 1–21 in *Exercises in Analysis*, ed. Ian Hacking. Cambridge: Cambridge University Press.

American Law Institute (ALI). 1934. *Restatement of the Law (First), Torts*. St. Paul, MN: ALI.

American Law Institute (ALI). 1958. *Restatement of the Law (Second), Agency*. St. Paul, MN: ALI.

American Law Institute (ALI). 1979. *Restatement of the Law (Second), Torts*. St. Paul, MN: ALI.

American Law Institute (ALI). 1980. *Model Penal Code and Commentaries*. Philadelphia: ALI.

American Law Institute (ALI). 1981. *Restatement of the Law (Second), Contracts*. St. Paul, MN: ALI.

American Law Institute (ALI). 2010. *Uniform Commercial Code*. St. Paul, MN: ALI.

American Law Institute (ALI). 2016. Updated 'consent' definition. *In the News: Member News*, 21 December. Available at <https://perma.cc/825F-MD64>.

American Law Institute (ALI). 2019. *Restatement of the Law Third, Torts: Intentional Torts to Persons, Tentative Draft No. 4*. St. Paul, MN: ALI.

American Medical Association. 2019. *Code of Medical Ethics*, originally adopted 1847. Available at <https://www.ama-assn.org/delivering-care/ethics/code-medical-ethics-overview>.

Andonova, Elena and Holly A. Taylor. 2012. Nodding in dis/agreement: a tale of two cultures. *Cognitive Processing*, 13 (supplement 1): S79–82.

Anon. 1946. Labor law: implied-in-fact contract after expiration of collective wage agreement. *Columbia Law Review*, 46: 856–60.

Anon. 1961. Revocation of parental consent to adoption: legal doctrine and social policy. *University of Chicago Law Review*, 28: 564–73.

Anscombe, G.E.M. 1958. On brute facts. *Analysis*, 18: 69–72.

Anscombe, G.E.M. 1963. Two kinds of error in action. *Journal of Philosophy*, 60: 393–401.

Applbaum, Arthur Isak. 1999. *Ethics for Adversaries*. Princeton, NJ: Princeton University Press.

Applbaum, Arthur Isak. 2010. Legitimacy without the duty to obey. *Philosophy & Public Affairs*, 38: 215–39.

Archard, David. 2007. The wrong of rape. *Phlosophical Quarterly*, 57: 374–93.

Arrow, Kenneth J. 1963. Uncertainty and the welfare economics of medical care. *American Economic Review* 53: 941–73.

Asscher, Eva Constance Alida and Suzanne van de Vathorst. 2020. First prosecution of a Dutch doctor since the Euthanasia Act of 2002: what does the verdict mean? *Journal of Medical Ethics*, 46: 71–5.

Atiyah, P.S. 1979. *The Rise and Fall of Freedom of Contract*. Oxford: Clarendon Press.

Austin, J.L. 1962. *How to Do Things with Words*. Oxford: Clarendon Press.

Austin, J.L. 1971. Performative-constative. Pp. 13–22 in in *The Philosophy of Language*, ed. J.R. Searle. Oxford: Oxford University Press.

Austin, J.L. 1979. Performative utterances. Pp. 233–52 in *Philosophical Papers*, 3rd edn, ed. J.O. Urmson and G.J. Warnock. Oxford: Clarendon Press.

Australian Electoral Commission (AEC). 2019. *Electoral Backgrounder: Compulsory Voting*. Available at <https://www.aec.gov.au/About_AEC/Publications/backgrounders/compulsory-voting.htm>

Australian Medical Association. 2004. *Code of Ethics*. Revised 2016. Available at <https://ama.com.au/articles/code-ethics-2004-editorially-revised-2006-revised-2016>.

Australian Medical Council (AMC). 2016. *Good Medical Practice: A Code of Conduct for Doctors in Australia*. Available at <https://www.amc.org.au>images>Final_Code>.

Banja, John D. 2009. Overriding the Jehovah's Witness patient's refusal of blood. *Pain Medicine*, 10: 878–82.

Barnett, Randy E. 1992. The sound of silence: default rules and contractual consent. *Virginia Law Review*, 78: 821–911.

BBC. 2000. Australian PM denies touching Queen. Asia-Pacific Front Page, 27 March; available at <http://news.bbc.co.uk/2/hi/asia-pacific/692302.stm>.

BBC. 2009. Jehovah's Witness ethics. Medical ethics: blood transfusions. Available at <https://www.bbc.co.uk/religion/religions/witnesses/witnessethics/ethics_1.shtml>.

Beauchamp, Tom L. and James F. Childress. 2009. *Principles of Biomedical Ethics*, 6th edn. New York: Oxford University Press.

Becker, Mary C. 1987. Promissory estoppel damages. *Hofstra Law Review*, 16: 131–63.

Bedau, Hugo Adam, ed. 1997. *The Death Penalty in America: Current Controversies*, New York: Oxford University Press.

Bennett, Christopher. 2018. The alteration thesis: forgiveness as a normative power. *Philosophy & Public Affairs*, 46: 207–33.

Bentham, Jeremy. 1776/1977. *A Comment on the Commentaries and a Fragment on Government*, ed. J.H. Burns and H.L.A. Hart. London: Athlone Press; originally published 1776.

Bentham, Jeremy. 1843. *Principles of the Civil Code*. Vol. 1 in *Works*, ed. John Bowring. ed. John Bowring. Edinburgh: William Tait. Available at <https://oll.libertyfund.org/title/bowring-the-works-of-jeremy-bentham-vol-1#lf0872-01_head_161>.

Berkeley, George. 1732. *Alciphron*. Dublin: G. Risk, G. Ewing and W. Smith. Available at <https://www.google.com.au/books/edition/Alciphron_or_the_Minute_Philosopher_in_s/S-WljxmSMh4C?hl=en&gbpv=1&dq=george+berkeley+Alciphron&printsec=frontcover>

Best, Justice. 1985. *People v. Vela*, 172 Ca. App. 3d 238 (Fifth District). Available at <https://law.justia.com/cases/california/court-of-appeal/3d/172/237.html>.

Blackstone, William. 1765. *Commentaries on the Laws of England.* Oxford: Clarendon Press.

Bolinger, Renée Jorgensen. 2019. Moral risk and communicating consent. *Philosophy & Public Affairs*, 47: 179–207.

Bolinger, Renée Jorgensen. 2021. The moral grounds of reasonably mistaken self-defense. *Philosophy and Phenomenological Research*, 103: 140–56.

Boni-Saenz, Alexander A. 2016. Sexual advance directives. *Alabama Law Review*, 68: 1–47.

Boxx, Karen E. 2001. The durable power of attorney's place in the family of fiduciary relationships. *Georgia Law Review*, 36: 1–62.

Boyd, William L., III. 1991. Implied-in-fact contract: contractual recovery against the government without an express agreement. *Public Contract Law Journal*, 21: 84–128.

Bratman, Michael. 1984. Two faces of intention. *Philosophical Review*, 93: 375–405.

Brennan, Geoffrey; Lina Eriksson, Robert E. Goodin and Nicholas Southwood. 2013. *Explaining Norms.* Oxford: Oxford University Press.

Brennan, Jason. 2019. Democracy as uninformed non-consent. *Journal of Applied Philosophy*, 36: 205–11.

Brett, Nathan. 1998. Sexual offenses and consent. *Canadian Journal of Law and Jurisprudence*, 11: 69–88.

British Medical Association (BMA). 2006. WMA Declaration of Malta: a background paper on the ethical management of hunger strikes. *World Medical Journal*, 52 (#2): 36–43. Available at <https://pjp-eu.coe.int/documents/41781569/42171356/World+medical+association+on+the+ethical+management+of+hunger+strikes.pdf/781b5720-d6f0-41de-83e3-430ebd02c0df>.

Brock, Dan W. 1987. Informed consent. Pp. 98–126 in *Health Care Ethics*, ed. Donald Van Den Veer and Tom Regan. Philadelphia: Temple University Press.

Brogaard, Berit. 2018. Why agreement is not consent: thinking about morality and sex. *Psychology Today*, 31 March; available at <https://www.psychologytoday.com/au/blog/the-mysteries-love/201803/why-agreement-sex-is-not-consent>.

Brownlee, Kimberley. 2020. *Being Sure of Each Other.* Oxford: Oxford University Press.

Brudney, Daniel. 1991. Hypothetical consent and moral force. *Law and Philosophy*, 10: 235–70.

Buchanan, Allen. 1988. Advance directives and the personal identity problem. *Philosophy & Public Affairs*, 17: 277–302.

Buchhandler-Raphael, Michal. 2017. The conundrum of voluntary intoxication and sex. *Brooklyn Law Review*, 82: 1031–108.

Burri, Susanne. 2020. Why moral theorising needs real cases: the redirection of V-weapons during the Second World War. *Journal of Political Philosophy*, 28: 247–69.

Calabresi, Guido. 1970. *The Costs of Accidents.* New Haven, CT: Yale University Press.

Calabresi, Guido. 1982. *A Common Law for the Age of Statutes.* Cambridge, MA: Harvard University Press.

Cantor, Norman L. 1996. Discarding substituted judgment and best interests: toward a constructive preference standard for dying, previously competent patients without advance instructions. *Rutgers Law Review*, 48: 1193–272.

Carr, Craig L. 1990. Tacit consent. *Public Affairs Quarterly*, 4: 335–45.

Carter, Rosemary. 1977. Justifying paternalism. *Canadian Journal of Philosophy*, 7: 133–45.

Chadha, Karamvir. 2021. Conditional consent. *Law & Philosophy*, 40: 335–59.

Chisholm, R.M. 1963. Supererogation and offence: a conceptual scheme for ethics. *Ratio*, 5: 1–14.

Chwang, Eric. 2008. Against the inalienable right to withdraw from research. *Bioethics*, 22: 370–8.

Chwang, Eric. 2009. A defense of subsequent consent. *Journal of Social Philosophy*, 40: 117–31.

Cicero, Marcus Tullius. 44. *De Officiis*, trans. Walter Miller. London: Heinemann, 1928; originally published 44.

Cohen, Carl. 1978. Medical experimentation on prisoners. *Perspectives in Biology and Medicine*, 21: 357–72. Reprinted in part in Emanuel et al. 2003, pp. 262–6.

Committee on Publication Ethics (COPE). 2015. Revoked parental consent. Case no. 15–09. Available at <https://publicationethics.org/case/revoked-parental-consent>.

Committee on Publication Ethics (COPE). 2016. *Journals' Best Practices for Ensuring Consent for Publishing Medical Case Reports*. Available at <https://publicationethics.org/files/Best_Practices_for_Ensuring_Consent_for_Publishing_Medical_Case_Reports_guidance_from_COPE.pdf>.

Conly, Sarah. 2004. Seduction, rape and coercion. *Ethics*, 115: 96–121.

Consent Is Everything. 2019. Consent—how to get it. Available at <http://www.consentiseverything.com/>.

Cook, Philip J. and Daniel A. Graham. 1977. The demand for insurance and protection: the case of irreplaceable commodities. *Quarterly Journal of Economics*, 91: 143–56.

Cooperrider, Kensey. 2019. Universals and diversity in gesture: research past, present and future. *Gesture*, 18: 209–38.

Corbin, A.L. 1952. *Corbin on Contracts*. One volume edition. St Paul, MN: West.

Council for International Organizations of Medical Sciences (CIOMS) and World Health Organisation (WHO). 2002. *International Ethical Guidelines for Biomedical Research Involving Human Subjects*. Geneva: CIOMS/WHO. Reprinted in Emanuel et al. 2003, pp. 56–80.

Cowart, Monica R. 2004. Understanding acts of consent: using speech act theory to help resolve moral dilemmas and legal disputes. *Law & Philosophy*, 23: 495–525.

Curzon, L.B. 1967. *Equity*. London: Macdonald and Evans.

Daly, Michael P. 2018. Trial courts split on whether consumers can unilaterally revoke contractual consent. *National Law Review*, 14 Sept. Available at <https://www.natlawreview.com/article/trial-courts-split-whether-consumers-can-unilaterally-revoke-contractual-consent>.

Daniels, Norman. 1996. *Justice and Justification: Reflective Equilibrium in Theory and Practice*. New York: Cambridge University Press.

Daniels, Norman. 2016. Reflective equilibrium. *Stanford Encyclopedia of Philosophy*, ed. Edward Zalta. <https://plato.stanford.edu/entries/reflective-equilibrium/>.

Davidson, Donald. 1980. *Essays on Actions and Events*. Oxford: Clarendon Press.

de Boer, Marike E.; Rose-Marie Dröes; Cees Jonker; Jan A. Eefsting; and Cees M.P. M. Hertogh. 2011. Advance directives for euthanasia in dementia: how do they affect resident care in Dutch nursing homes? Experiences of physicians and relatives. *Journal of the American Geriatrics Society*, 59: 989–96.

de Grooth, Harm-Jan; Irma L. Geenen; Armand R. Girbes; Jean-Louis Vincent; Jean-Jacques Parienti; and Heleen M. Oudemans-van Straaten. 2017. SOFA and mortality endpoints in randomized controlled trials: a systematic review and meta-regression analysis. *Critical Care*, 21 (1): article 38. Available at <https://doi.org/10.1186/s13054-017-1609-1>.

Declaration of Kuwait. 1981. Islamic Code of Medical Ethics. First International Conference on Islamic Medicine, Kuwait, 1981. Reprinted in *World Medical Journal*,

29 (5) (1982): 78–80. Available at <https://www.encyclopedia.com/science/encyclopedias-almanacs-transcripts-and-maps/islamic-code-medical-ethics-kuwait-document>.

Delmas, Candice. 2023. The right to hunger strike. *American Political Science Review*, forthcoming <doi:10.1017/S0003055423000400>.

Dempsey, Michelle Madden and Jonathan Herring. 2007. Why sexual penetration requires justification. *Oxford Journal of Legal Studies*, 27: 467–91.

Den Hartogh, Govert. 1989. Made by contrivance and the consent of man: abstract principle and historical fact in Locke's political philosophy. *Interpretation*, 17: 193–222.

den Hartogh, Govert. 2011. Can consent be presumed? *Journal of Applied Philosophy*, 28: 295–307.

den Hartogh, Govert. 2022. *What Kind of Death: The Ethics of Determining One's Own Death*. New York: Routledge.

Deutschmann, Emanuel. 2016. Between collaboration and disobedience: the behavior of the Guantánamo detainees and its consequences. *Journal of Conflict Resolution*, 60: 555–82.

Dicey, A.V. 1939. *The Law of the Constitution*. 9th ed. London: Macmillan.

Dickens, Charles. 1861. *Great Expectations*. London: Chapman & Hall.

Director, Sam. 2019. Consent's dominion: dementia and prior consent to sexual relations. *Bioethics*, 33: 1065–71.

Director, Samuel. 2022. Sober thoughts on drunken sex: intoxication and consent to sexual relations. *Social Theory and Practice*, 48: 235–61.

Dixon, Nicholas. 2001a. Alcohol and rape. *Public Affairs Quarterly*, 15: 341–54.

Dixon, Nicholas. 2001b. Boxing, paternalism and legal moralism. *Social Theory & Practice*, 27: 323–44.

Donohue, John J. III and Justin Wolfers. 2005. Uses and abuses of empirical evidence in the death penalty debate. *Stanford Law Review*, 58: 791–846.

Dougherty, Tom. 2013. Sex, lies and consent. *Ethics*, 123: 717–44.

Dougherty, Tom. 2014. Fickle consent. *Philosophical Studies*, 167: 25–40.

Dougherty, Tom. 2015. Yes means yes: consent as communication. *Philosophy & Public Affairs*, 43: 224–53.

Dougherty, Tom. 2018. Affirmative consent and due diligence. *Philosophy & Public Affairs*, 46: 90–112.

Dougherty, Tom. 2021a. *The Scope of Consent*. Oxford: Oxford University Press.

Dougherty, Tom. 2021b. Why does duress undermine consent? *Nous*, 55: 317–33.

Dworkin, Gerald. 1972. Paternalism. *Monist*, 56: 107–26.

Dworkin, Gerald. 1988. *The Theory and Practice of Autonomy*. Cambridge: Cambridge University Press.

Dworkin, Ronald. 1975. The original position. Pp. 16–53 in *Reading Rawls*, ed. Norman Daniels. New York: Basic Books.

Dworkin, Ronald. 1977. *Taking Rights Seriously*. London: Duckworth.

Dworkin, Ronald. 1984. Rights as trumps. Pp. 153–67 in *Theories of Rights*, ed. Jeremy Waldron. Oxford: Oxford University Press.

Dworkin, Ronald. 1986. Autonomy and the demented self. *Milbank Quarterly*, 64 (supplement 2): 4–16.

Dworkin, Ronald. 1995. *Life's Dominion*. London: HarperCollins.

Ehrlich, Susan. 2016. Post-penetration rape: coercion or freely given consent? Pp. 47–70 in *Discursive Constructions of Consent in the Legal Process*, ed. Susan Lynn Ehrlich, Diana Eades and Janet Ainsworth. Oxford: Oxford University Press.

Ellsberg, Daniel. 1956. Theory of the reluctant duellist. *American Economic Review*, 46: 909–23.

Elster, Jon. 1979. *Ulysses and the Sirens*. Cambridge: Cambridge University Press.
Elster, Jon. 1990. Norms of revenge. *Ethics*, 100: 862–85.
Elster, Jon. 2000. *Ulysses Unbound*. Cambridge: Cambridge University Press.
Emanuel, Ezekiel J.; Robert A. Crouch; John D. Arras; Jonathan D. Moreno; and Christine Grady, eds. 2003. *Ethical and Regulatory Aspects of Clinical Research: Readings and Commentary*. Baltimore, MD: Johns Hopkins University Press.
Enoch, David. 2017. Hypothetical consent and the value(s) of autonomy. *Ethics*, 128: 6–36.
Enoch, David. 2022. Autonomy as non-alienation, autonomy as sovereignty, and politics. *Journal of Political Philosophy*, 30: 143–65.
Epstein, Richard A. 1989. Beyond foreseeability: consequential damages in the law of contract. *Journal of Legal Studies*, 18: 105–38.
Estlund, David. 2005. Political authority and the tyranny of non-consent. *Philosophical Issues*, 15: 352–67.
Estlund, David. 2008. *Democratic Authority: A Philosophical Framework*. Princeton, NJ: Princeton University Press.
Estrich, Susan. 1992. Palm Beach stories. *Law & Philosophy*, 11: 5–33.
Eyal, Nir. 2019. Informed consent. *Stanford Encyclopedia of Philosophy*; Available at <https://Plato.Stanford.Edu/Entries/Informed-Consent/#Idecon>.
Faden, Ruth R. and Tom L. Beauchamp. 1986. *A History and Theory of Informed Consent*. New York: Oxford University Press.
Federal Communications Commission (FCC) 2015. *TCPA Omnibus Declaratory Ruling and Order*. FCC 15-72. Available at <https://www.fcc.gov/document/tcpa-omnibus-declaratory-ruling-and-order>.
Feinberg, Joel. 1978. Voluntary euthanasia and the inalienable right to life. *Philosophy & Public Affairs*, 7: 93–123. Reprinted in Feinberg 1980: pp. 221–51.
Feinberg, Joel. 1980. *Rights, Justice and the Bounds of Liberty*. Princeton, NJ: Princeton University Press.
Feinberg, Joel. 1984. *Harm to Others*. Vol. 1 of *The Moral Limits of the Criminal Law*. New York: Oxford University Press.
Feinberg, Joel. 1986a. *Harm to Self*. Vol. 3 of *The Moral Limits of the Criminal Law*. New York: Oxford University Press.
Feinberg, Joel. 1986b. Victims' excuses: the case of fraudulently procured consent. *Ethics*, 96: 330–4.
Ferzan, Kimberly Kessler. 2016. Consent, culpability, and the law of rape. *Ohio State Journal of Criminal Law*, 13: 397–439.
Ferzan, Kimberly Kessler and Peter Westen. 2017. How to think (like a lawyer) about rape. *Criminal Law & Philosophy*, 11: 759–800.
Frankel, Tamar. 1983. Fiduciary law. *California Law Review*, 71: 795–836.
French, Peter A. 2002. Honor, shame and identity. *Public Affairs Quarterly*, 16: 1–15.
Fuller, Lon. 1969. *The Morality of Law*. 3rd edn. New Haven, CT: Yale University Press.
Fuller, Lon L. and William R. Perdue. 1936. The reliance interest in contract damages. *Yale Law Journal*, 46: 52–96, 373–420.
Gaius. 170/1988. *The Institutes of Gaius*, trans. W.M. Gordon and O.F. Richardson. Ithaca, NY: Cornell University Press, 1988; originally published 170.
Gambetta, Diego. 1993. *The Sicilian Mafia: The Business of Private Protection*. Cambridge, MA: Harvard University Press.
Gerver, Mollie. 2020. Inferring consent without communication. *Social Theory and Practice*, 46: 27–53.
Gerver, Mollie. 2021. Consent and third-party coercion. *Ethics*, 131: 246–69.

Gewirth, Alan. 1962. Political justice. Pp. 119–69 in *Social Justice*, ed. Richard B. Brandt. Englewood Cliffs, NJ: Prentice-Hall.

Gilbert, Margaret. 1993. Is an agreement an exchange of promises? *Journal of Philosophy*, 90: 626–49.

Gilmore, Grant. 1965. *Security Interests in Personal Property*. Boston: Little, Brown.

Goldman, Alan H. 1977. Plain sex. *Philosophy & Public Affairs*, 6: 267–87.

Goodin, Robert E. 1976. *The Politics of Rational Man*. London: Wiley.

Goodin, Robert E. 1982. *Political Theory & Public Policy*. Chicago: University of Chicago Press.

Goodin, Robert E. 1983. The ethics of destroying irreplaceable assets. *International Journal of Environmental Studies*, 21: 55–66.

Goodin, Robert E. 1985a. Erring on the side of kindness in social welfare policy. *Policy Sciences*, 18: 141–56.

Goodin, Robert E. 1985b. *Protecting the Vulnerable: A Re-Analysis of Our Social Responsibilities*. Chicago: University of Chicago Press.

Goodin, Robert E. 1988. *Reasons for Welfare: The Political Theory of the Welfare State*. Princeton, NJ: Princeton University Press.

Goodin, Robert E. 1989. Theories of compensation. *Oxford Journal of Legal Studies*, 9: 56–75.

Goodin, Robert E. 1995. *Utilitarianism as a Public Philosophy*. New York: Cambridge University Press.

Goodin, Robert E. 2005. Toward an international rule of law: distinguishing international law-breakers from would-be law-makers. *Journal of Ethics*, 9: 225–46.

Goodin, Robert E. 2023. Consent as an act of commitment. *European Journal of Philosophy*, DOI: 10.1111/ejop.12852.

Green, James A. 2016. *The Persistent Objector Rule in International Law*. Oxford: Oxford University Press.

Green, Leslie. 1988. *The Authority of the State*. Oxford: Clarendon Press.

Grice, H.P. 1957. Meaning. *Philosophical Review*, 66: 377–88.

Grice, H.P. 1975. Logic and conversation. Pp. 64–75 in *The Logic of Grammar*, ed. Donald Davidson and Gilbert Harman. Encino, CA: Dickenson Publishing Co.

Grotius, Hugo. 1625/1901. *The Right of War and Peace*, trans. A.C. Campbell. New York: M. Walter Dunne, 1901; originally published 1625. Available at <https://oll.libertyfund.org/title/grotius-the-rights-of-war-and-peace-1901-ed#preview>.

Guerrero, Alexander. 2021. The epistemology of consent. Pp. 348–88 in *Applied Epistemology*, ed. Jennifer Lackey. Oxford: Oxford University Press.

Hale, Matthew. 1736. *History of the Pleas of the Crown*. London: E. and R. Nutt and R. Gosling.

Hare, R.M. 1964. The promising game. *Revue Internationale de Philosophie*, 70: 398–412. Reprinted pp. 115–27 in *Theories of Ethics*, ed. Philippa Foot. Oxford: Oxford University Press, 1967.

Hart, H.L.A. 1955. Are there any natural rights? *Philosophical Review*, 64: 175–91.

Hart, H.L.A. 1961. *The Concept of Law*. Oxford: Clarendon Press.

Healey, Kieran. 2006. Do presumed-consent laws raise organ procurement rates? *DePaul Law Review*, 55: 1017–43.

Healey, Richard. 2015. The ontology of consent: a reply to Alexander. *Analytic Philosophy*, 56: 354–63.

Held, Virginia. 1972. Coercion and coercive offers. Pp. 49–62 in *Nomos XIV: Coercion*, ed. J. Roland Pennock and John W. Chapman. New York: Aldine-Atherton.

Henry VIII. 1540. An act concerning pre-contracts of marriage, and touching degrees of consanguinity. 32 Henry VIII, c. 38.

Hertogh, C.M.P.M. 2009. The role of advance euthanasia directives as an aid to communication and shared decision-making in dementia. *Journal of Medical Ethics*, 35: 100–3.

Hill, Thomas E. Jr. 1971. Kant on imperfect duty and supererogation. *Kant-Studien*, 61: 55–77.

Hobbes, Thomas. 1651. *Leviathan*. London: Andrew Crooke.

Hohfeld, Wesley N. 1923. *Fundamental Legal Conceptions as Applied in Judicial Reasoning*. New Haven, CT: Yale University Press.

Holcomb, Jayme W. 2005. Revoking consent to search. *FBI Law Enforcement Bulletin*, 74 (2): 25–32. Available at <https://www.thefreelibrary.com/Revoking consent to search.-a0131193469>.

Holmes, Oliver Wendell Jr. 1963. *The Common Law*, ed. Mark DeWofle Howe. Boston: Little Brown; originally published 1881.

Homan, Kees. 2006. NATO, common funding and peace support operations: a comparative perspective. Netherlands Institute of International Relations 'Clingendael'. Available at <https://www.clingendael.org/sites/default/files/pdfs/20061000_cscp_art_homan.pdf>.

Homer. 800a BCE. *The Iliad*, trans. Ian Johnston. Nanaimo, BC: Vancouver Island University, 2019. Available at <http://johnstoniatexts.x10host.com/homer/iliadallpdf.pdf>.

Homer. 800b BCE. *The Odyssey*, trans. Samuel Butler. London: A.C. Fifield, 1900. Available at <https://www.gutenberg.org/ebooks/1727>.

Hume, David. 1760. Of the original contract. Pt. 2, ch. 12 of *Essays, Literary, Moral and Political*. London: A. Millar.

Hurd, Heidi M. 1996. The moral magic of consent. *Legal Theory*, 2: 121–46.

Husak, Douglas N. 2006. The complete guide to consent to sex: Alan Wertheimer's 'Consent to Sexual Relations'. *Law & Philosophy*, 25: 267–87.

Husak, Douglas N. 2010. Paternalism and consent. Pp. 107–30 in *The Ethics of Consent: Theory and Practice*, ed. Franklin Miller and Alan Wertheimer. New York: Oxford University Press.

International Military Tribunal (IMT). 1946. Judgment of 1 October 1946. *The Trial of German Major War Criminals. Proceedings of the International Military Tribunal sitting at Nuremberg, Germany*, Part 22 (22nd August, 1946 to 1st October, 1946). Available at <https://crimeofaggression.info/documents/6/1946_Nuremberg_Judgement.pdf>.

Joffe, Steven and Robert D. Truog. 2010. Consent to medical care: the importance of fiduciary context. Pp. 347–74 in *The Ethics of Consent: Theory and Practice*, ed. Franklin Miller and Alan Wertheimer. New York: Oxford University Press.

Justinian. 535. *Justinian's Institutes*, trans. Peter Birks and Grant McLeod. Ithaca, NY: Cornell University Press, 1987.

Kalevitch, Lawrence. 1993. Gaps in contracts: a critique of consent theory. *Montana Law Review*, 54: 170–224.

Kant, Immanuel. 1785. *The Metaphysics of Morals*, trans. Mary Gregor. Cambridge: Cambridge University Press, 1991.

Kant, Immanuel. 1793. On the common saying: this may be true in theory but it does not apply in practice. Pp. 61–92 in *Kant's Political Writings*, 2nd edn., ed. Hans Reiss, trans. H.B. Nisbet. Cambridge: Cambridge University Press, 1991.

Kantor, Brian. 1979. Rational expectations and economic thought. *Journal of Economic Literature*, 17: 1422–41.

Karasz, Plako. 2019. Doctor acquitted in euthanasia of patient who may have changed her mind. *New York Times*, 12 September, sec. A, p. 12. Available at <https://www.nytimes.com/2019/09/11/world/europe/netherlands-euthanasia-doctor.html>.

Katz, Jay. 1984. *The Silent World of Doctor and Patient*. New York: Free Press.

Katz, Jay. 1994. Informed consent—must it remain a fairy tale? *Journal of Contemporary Health Law and Policy*, 10: 69–91. Reprinted pp. 241–9 in *A Health Law Reader*, ed. John H. Robinson, Roberta M. Berry and Kevin McDonnell. Durham, NC: Carolina University Press, 1999.

Keedy, Edwin R. 1908. Ignorance and mistake in the criminal law. *Harvard Law Review*, 22: 75–96.

Kennedy, I.; R.A. Sells; A.S. Daar; R.D. Buttmann; R. Hoffenberg; M. Lock; J. Radcliffe-Richards; and N. Tilney. 1998. The case for 'presumed consent' in organ donation. *Lancet*, 341 (9116): 1650–2.

Kenessey, Brendan De. 2020. Promises as proposals in joint practical deliberation. *Nous*, 54: 204–32.

Kleinig, John. 1982. The ethics of consent. *Canadian Journal of Philosophy*, Supplementary Volume 8, 91–118; reprinted as *New Essays in Ethics and Public Policy*, ed. Kai Nielsen and Steven C. Patten.

Kleinig, John. 2010. The nature of consent. Pp. 3–22 in *The Ethics of Consent: Theory and Practice*, ed. Franklin Miller and Alan Wertheimer. New York: Oxford University Press.

Knowlton, Marcus Perrin. 1891. *O'Brien v Cunard Steamship Company*, 154 Mass. 272, 28 N.E. 266.

Kolodny, Niko and R. Jay Wallace. 2003. Promises and practices revisited. *Philosophy & Public Affairs*, 31: 119–54.

Koremenos, Barbara. 2016. *The Continent of International Law: Explaining Agreement Design*. Cambridge: Cambridge University Press.

Krentzman, Jessica L. 1996. Dram shop law—gambling while intoxicated. *Villanova Law Review*, 41: 1255–86.

Kuflik, Arthur. 2010. Hypothetical consent. Pp. 131–62 in *The Ethics of Consent: Theory and Practice*, ed. Franklin Miller and Alan Wertheimer. New York: Oxford University Press.

Kukla, Rebecca. 2018. That's what she said: the language of sexual negotiation. *Ethics*, 129: 70–97.

Lackey, Jennifer. 2018. Silence and objecting. Pp. 82–96 in *Voicing Dissent: The Ethics and Epistemology of Making Disagreement Public*, ed. Casey Johnson. London: Routledge.

Lackey, Jennifer. 2021. Sexual consent and epistemic agency. Pp. 321–47 in *Applied Epistemology*, ed. Jennifer Lackey. Oxford: Oxford University Press.

Lam, Barry. 2019. The invisible hand from the grave. *Journal of Ethics and Social Philosophy*, 15: 197–221.

Langille, Brian and Arthur Ripstein. 1996. 'Strictly speaking—it went without saying'. *Legal Theory*, 2: 63–81.

Lau, Joanne C. 2014. Voting in bad faith. *Res Publica*, 20: 281–94.

Leahy, Susan. 2014. 'No means no', but where's the force? Addressing the challenges of formally recognising non-violent sexual coercion as a serious criminal offence. *Journal of Criminal Law*, 78: 309–25.

Leikin, Sanford. 1993. Minors' assent, consent or dissent. *IRB: A Review of Human Subjects Research*, 15 (2): 1–7. Reprinted in Emanuel et al. 2003, pp. 252–8.

Leo VI (Roman Emperor). 888/1932. *New Constitutions*. Vol. 17, pp. 204–97 in *The Civil Law*, trans. & ed. S.P. Scott. Cincinnati, OH: Central Trust Co., 1932; originally published 888.

Lepora, Chiara. 2021. Humanitarian ethics: on complicity. Chapter 18 in *Doctors in Prisons*, ed. International Committee of the Red Cross and the World Medical Association; on-line course. Available at <https://course.wcea.education/app/course-worldmedicalassociation/elearning/medical-professional/doctors-in-prisons/196456#/>.

Lepora, Chiara and Robert E. Goodin. 2013. *On Complicity and Compromise.* Oxford: Oxford University Press.

Lewis, David. 1969. *Convention.* Oxford: Blackwell.

Liberto, Hallie. 2017. The problem with sexual promises. *Ethics*, 127: 383–414.

Liberto, Hallie. 2018. Promises and the backward reach of uptake. *American Philosophical Quarterly*, 55: 15–26.

Lo, Bernard. 2019. *Resolving Ethical Dilemmas: A Guide for Clinicians.* 6th ed. Philadelphia: Wolters Kluwer Health.

Locke, John. 1660. *First Tract on Government.* Pp. 115–82 in Locke, *Two Tracts on Government*, ed. Philip Abrams. Cambridge: Cambridge University Press, 1967.

Locke, John. 1660. *Two Tracts on Government*, ed. Philip Abrams. Cambridge: Cambridge University Press, 1967; originally cmposed 1660.

Locke, John. 1690/1960. *Second Treatise of Government*, ed. Peter Laslett. Cambridge: Cambridge University Press, 1960; originally published 1690.

Love, Margaret Colgate. 2010. The twilight of the pardon power. *Journal of Criminal Law and Criminology*, 100: 1169–212.

Lyon, Matthew R. 2004. No means no: withdrawal of consent during sexual intercourse and the continuing evolution of the definition of rape. *Journal of Criminal Law and Criminology*, 95: 277–314.

McConnell, Michael W. 2008. Opinion of the court. *US v Verdin-Garcia*, 516 F.3d 884 (10th Cir.).

MacCoun, Robert. 1993. Is there a 'deep-pocket' bias in the tort system? Issue Paper, Institute for Civil Justice. New York: RAND Corporation.

McDonald, Lucy. 2021. Your word against mine: the power of uptake. *Synthese*, 199: 3505–26.

Macneil, Ian R. 1978. Contracts: adjustment of long-term economic relations under classical, neoclassical and relational contract law. *Northwestern University Law Review*, 72: 854–905.

Majewski, David; Stephen Ball; and Judith Finn. 2019. Systematic review of the relationship between comorbidity and out-of-hospital cardiac arrest outcomes. *BMJ Open*, 9(11): e031655. Available at <https://doi.org/10.1136/bmjopen-2019-031655>.

Malm, H.M. 1996. The ontological status of consent and its implications for the law of rape. *Legal Theory*, 2: 147–64.

Mancilla, Alejandra. 2016. *The Right of Necessity.* London: Rowman & Littlefield.

Manson, Neil C. 2013. Normative consent is not consent. *Cambridge Quarterly of Healthcare Ethics*, 22: 33–44.

Manson, Neil C. 2016. Permissive consent: a robust reason-changing account. *Philosophical Studies*, 173: 3317–34.

Manson, Neil C. 2017. How not to think about the ethics of deceiving into sex. *Ethics*, 127: 415–29.

Manson, Neil C. 2018. The scope of consent. Pp. 65–74 in *The Routledge Handbook of the Ethics of Consent*, ed. Andreas Müller and Peter Schaber. London: Routledge.

May, Erskine. 2019. *Treatise on the Law, Privileges, Proceedings and Usage of Parliament*, 25th edn. Available at <https://erskinemay.parliament.uk/>.

McConnell, Michael W. 2008. Opinion of the court. *US v Verdin-Garcia*, 516 F.3d 884 (10th Cir.).

McDonald, Lucy. 2021. Your word against mine: the power of uptake. *Synthese*, 199: 3505–26.

Medical Board of Australia (MBA). 2009. *Good Medical Practice: A Code of Conduct for Doctors in Australia.* Canberra: Australian Health Practitioner Regulation Agency.

Merton, Robert K. 1949. On sociological theories of the middle range. Pp. 39–53 in Merton, *Social Theory and Social Structure.* New York: Simon & Schuster.

Metropolitan Police, London. 2019. What is rape and sexual assault? https://www.met.police.uk/advice/advice-and-information/rsa/rape-and-sexual-assault/what-is-rape-and-sexual-assault/

Metzger, Michael B. and Michael J. Phillips. 1983. The emergence of promissory estoppel as an independent theory of recovery. *Rutgers Law Review*, 35: 472–557.

Michalowski, Sabine. 2005. The refusals of life-saving medical treatment: the relativity of an absolute right. *Modern Law Review*, 68: 958–82.

Midgley, Mary. 1974. The game game. *Philosophy*, 49: 231–53.

Mill, John Stuart. 1859. *On Liberty*. Vol. 18, pp. 212–310 in John Stuart Mill, *The Collected Works of John Stuart Mill*, ed. John M. Robson. Toronto: University of Toronto Press, 1977. <http://oll.libertyfund.org/titles/mill-the-collected-works-of-john-stuart-mill-volume-xviii-essays-on-politics-and-society-part-i>

Miller, Franklin and Alan Wertheimer. 2010. Preface to a theory of consent transactions: beyond valid consent. Pp. 79–105 in *The Ethics of Consent: Theory and Practice*, ed. Miller and Wertheimer. New York: Oxford University Press.

Millum, Joseph. 2014. Consent under pressure: the puzzle of third party coercion. *Ethical Theory and Moral Practice*, 17: 112–27.

Mirrlees, James A. 1971. An exploration in the theory of optimal income taxation. *Review of Economic Studies*, 38: 175–208.

Morinigo, Jennifer. 2016. The evolution of the Model Penal Code 'consent' definition. *The ALI Adviser*, 6 September. Available at <http://thealiadviser.org/sexual-assault/evolution-of-model-penal-code-consent-definition/>.

Murphy, Jeffrie G. and Jean Hampton. 1988. *Forgiveness and Mercy*. Cambridge: Cambridge University Press.

National Health Service (NHS). 2019. Overview: consent to treatment. Available at <https://www.nhs.uk/conditions/consent-to-treatment/>.

New Zealand Ministry of Justice. 2020. Going to court: costs and disbursements. Available at <https://www.justice.govt.nz/courts/going-to-court/without-a-lawyer/representing-yourself-civil-high-court/costs-and-disbursements/>.

North Carolina General Assembly. 2019. An act to protect children from sexual abuse and to strengthen and modernize sexual assault laws. Session Law 2019–245. Available at <https://www.ncleg.gov/EnactedLegislation/SessionLaws/PDF/2019-2020/SL2019-245.pdf>.

NSW Health. 2019. NSW School Vaccination Program: Procedure for Withdrawal of Consent (Information for Parents). Available at: <https://www.health.nsw.gov.au/immunisation/Pages/withdraw_consent.aspx>.

Nuremberg Code. 1947. Permissible medical experiments. *U.S. v Karl Brandt et al.* In Emanuel et al. 2003, p. 29.

Oberdiek, John. 2004. Lost in moral space: on the infringing/violating distinction and its place in the theory of rights. *Law & Philosophy*, 23: 325–46.

O'Keeffe, Terence. 1984. Suicide and self-starvation. *Philosophy*, 59: 349–63.

O'Neil, Collin. 2012. Lying, trust and gratitude. *Philosophy & Public Affairs*, 40: 301–33.

Owens, David. 2008. Promising without intending. *Journal of Philosophy*, 105: 737–55.

Owens, David. 2011. The possibility of consent. *Ratio*, 24: 402–21.

Owens, David. 2012. *Shaping the Normative Landscape*. Oxford: Oxford University Press.

Padilla, Mariel. 2019. North Carolina lawmakers pass bill to close sexual assault loopholes. *New York Times*, 1 November. Available at <https://www.nytimes.com/2019/11/01/us/north-carolina-sexual-assault-loophole.html>.

Pallikkathayil, Japa. 2020. Consent to sexual interactions. *Politics, Philosophy & Economics*, 19: 107–27.

Parfit, Derek. 1973. Later selves and moral principles. Pp. 137–69 in *Philosophy and Personal Relations*, ed. Alan Montefiore. London: Routledge & Kegan Paul.

Parker, Sarah O. 2013. No means no . . . sometimes: developments in post-penetration rape law and the need for legislative action. *Brooklyn Law Review*, 78: 1067–95.

Partridge, P.H. 1971. *Consent and Consensus*. London: Pall Mall Press.

Pateman, Carole. 1979. *The Problem of Political Obligation*. Chichester: Wiley.

Patterson, Dennis M. 1990. Law's pragmatism: law as practice and narrative. *Virginia Law Review*, 76: 937–96.

Pavlikova, Barbara and Jitse P. van Dijk. 2022. Jehovah'sWitnesses and their compliance with regulations on smoking and blood treatment. *International Journal of Environmental Research and Public Health*, 19: 387–93.

Plamenatz, John. 1963. *Man and Society*. London: Longman.

Plamenatz, J.P. 1968. *Consent, Freedom and Political Obligation*. 2nd edn. Oxford: Oxford University Press; originally published 1938.

Plato. 399 BCE/1961. *Crito*, trans. Hugh Tredennick. Pp. 27–39 in *Plato: The Collected Dialogues*, ed. Edith Hamilton and Huntington Cairns. Princeton, NJ: Princeton University Press, 1961; originally published 399 BCE.

Postow, B.C. 1980. A possible ground of political obligation. *Southern Journal of Philosophy*, 18: 63–9.

Potts, Michael; Joseph L. Verheijde; Mohamed Y. Rady; and David W. Evans. 2010. Normative consent and presumed consent for organ donation: a critique. *Journal of Medical Ethics*, 36: 498–9.

President's Commission for the Study of Ethical Problems in Medicine and Biomedical and Behavioral Research. 1982. *Making Health Care Decisions: The Ethical and Legal Implications of Informed Consent in the Patient–Practitioner Relationship*. Washington, DC: Government Printing Office.

Prichard, H.A. 1940. The obligation to keep a promise. Pp. 169–79 in *Moral Obligation and Duty & Interest*. Oxford: Oxford University Press, 1968.

Przeworski, Adam. 2015. Acquiring the habit of changing governments through elections. *Comparative Political Studies*, 48: 101–29.

Pufendorf, Samuel. 1672/1710. *Of the Law of Nature and Nations*, trans. Basil Kennett. Oxford: Lichfield; originally published 1672.

Pundik, Amit. 2015. Coercion and deception in sexual relations. *Canadian Journal of Law & Jurisprudence*, 28: 97–127.

Rawls, John. 1955. Two concepts of rules. *Philosophical Review*, 64: 3–32.

Rawls, John. 1967. Civil disobedience and the duty of fair play. Pp. 3–18 in *Law and Philosophy*, ed. Sidney Hook. New York: New York University Press.

Rawls, John. 1971. *A Theory of Justice*. Cambridge, MA: Harvard University Press.

Rawls, John. 1999. *A Theory of Justice*, rev. ed. Cambridge, MA: Harvard University Press.

Raz, Joseph. 1981. Authority and consent. *Virginia Law Review*, 67: 101–31. Reprinted in Raz 1986, pp. 70–105.

Raz, Joseph. 1986. *The Morality of Freedom*. Oxford: Clarendon Press.

Reiman, Jeffrey. 2013. A moral equivalent of consent. *Ratio Juris*, 26: 358–77.

Renzo, Massimo. 2017. Rights forfeiture and liability to harm. *Journal of Political Philosophy*, 25: 324–42.

Renzo, Massimo. 2022. Defective normative powers: the case of consent. *Journal of Practical Ethics*, 10 (1): 49–77. doi: https://doi.org.10.3998/jpe.2382.

Reyes, Hernán; Scott A. Allen; and George J. Annas. 2013a. Physicians and hunger strikes in prison: confrontation, manipulation, medicalization and medical ethics (part 1). *World Medical Journal*, 59 (1): 27–36.

Reyes, Hernán; Scott A. Allen; and George J. Annas. 2013b. Physicians and hunger strikes in prison: confrontation, manipulation, medicalization and medical ethics (part 2). *World Medical Journal*, 59 (2): 60–7.

Reyes, Hernán; Scott A. Allen; and George J. Annas. 2013c. Physicians and hunger strikes in prison: confrontation, manipulation, medicalization and medical ethics (part 3). *World Medical Journal*, 59 (3): 97–101.

Rid, Annette and David Wendler. 2014. Use of a Patient Preference Predictor to help make medical decisions for incapacitated patients. *Journal of Medicine and Philosophy*, 39: 104–29.

Robert, Henry M. 1876/1951. *Robert's Rules of Order*. Revised edn. Chicago: Scott, Foresman.

Rousseau, Jean-Jacques. 1762. *The Social Contract*. Pp. 164–278 in *The Social Contract and Discourses*, trans. G.D.H. Cole. New edn. London: Everyman/Dent, 1973.

Royal College of Surgeons of England (RCSE). 2021. Consent. In RCSE, *Good Surgical Practice*. Available at <https://www.rcseng.ac.uk/standards-and-research/gsp/domain-3/3-5-1-consent/>.

Ruben, David-Hillel. 1972. Tacit promising. *Ethics*, 83: 71–9.

Rubenfeld, Jed. 2013. The riddle of rape-by-deception and the myth of sexual autonomy. *Yale Law Journal*, 122: 1372–443.

Salmon, John. 1957. *Salmon on Jurisprudence*, ed. Glanville Williams, 7th edn. London: Sweet & Maxwell.

Santos-Longhurst, Adrienne. 2019. Your guide to sexual consent. *Healthline*, 12 February. Available at <https://www.healthline.com/health/guide-to-consent>.

Saunders, Ben. 2010. Normative consent and opt-out organ donation. *Journal of Medical Ethics*, 36: 84–7.

Saunders, Ben. 2012a. Opt-out organ donation and tacit consent: a reply to Wilkinson and De Wispelaere. *Journal of Medical Ethics*, 38: 75–6.

Saunders, Ben. 2012b. Opt-out organ donation without presumptions. *Journal of Medical Ethics*, 38: 69–72.

Scanlon, T.M. 1990. Promises and practices. *Philosophy & Public Affairs*, 19: 199–226.

Scanlon, T.M. 1998. *What We Owe to Each Other*. Cambridge, MA: Harvard University Press.

Schulhofer, Stephen J. 1992. Taking sexual autonomy seriously: rape law and beyond. *Law & Philosophy*, 11: 35–94.

Schulhofer, Stephen J. 1998. *Unwanted Sex: The Culture of Intimidation and the Failure of Law*. Cambridge, MA: Harvard University Press.

Schwartz, Alan and Robert E. Scott. 2007. Precontractual liability and preliminary agreements. *Harvard Law Review*, 120: 661–707.

Searle, John R. 1964. How to derive ought from is. *Philosophical Review*, 73: 43–58.

Searle, John R. 1965. What is a speech act. Pp. 221–39 in *Philosophy in America*, ed. Max Black. London: Allen & Unwin. Reprinted in Searle 1971, pp. 39–53.

Searle, John R. 1969. *Speech Acts*. Cambridge: Cambridge University Press.

Searle, John R., ed. 1971. *The Philosophy of Language*. Oxford: Oxford University Press.
Searle, John R. 1995. *The Construction of Social Reality*. Harmondsworth: Penguin.
Selden, John. 1689. *Table Talk*. London: E. Smith. Reprinted in *Table Talk from Ben Johnson to Leigh Hunt*, ed. James Thornton. London: Dent, 1934.
Sender, Courtney. 2018. He asked permission to touch, but not to ghost. *New York Times*, 7. September. Available at <https://www.nytimes.com/2018/09/07/style/modern-love-he-asked-permission-to-touch-but-not-to-ghost.html>.
Shakespeare, William. 1591. *Romeo and Juliet*. Vol. 1, pp. 247–77 in *The Complete Works of William Shakespeare*, ed W.G. Clark and W. Aldis Wright. Garden City, NY: Doubleday, n.d.
Shakespeare, William. 1596. *The Merchant of Venice*. Vol. 1, pp. 331–55 in *The Complete Works of William Shakespeare*, ed W.G. Clark and W. Aldis Wright. Garden City, NY: Doubleday, n.d.
Shavell, Steven. 2019. The mistaken restrictions of strict liability to uncommon activities. *Journal of Legal Analysis*, 10.
Shiffrin, Seana Valentine. 2007. The divergence of contract and promise. *Harvard Law Review*, 120: 708–53.
Shiffrin, Seana Valentine. 2008. Promising, intimate relationships and conventionalism. *Philosophical Review*, 117: 481–524.
Sidgwick, Henry. 1907. *The Methods of Ethics*. 7th edn. London: Macmillan; originally published 1874.
Siegler, Frederick. 1968. Plamenatz on consent and obligation. *Philosophical Quarterly*, 18: 256–61.
Silver, Mara. 2005. Testing Cruzan: prisoners and the constitutional question of self-starvation. *Stanford Law Review*, 58: 631–62.
Simmons, A. John. 1976. Tacit consent and political obligation. *Philosophy & Public Affairs*, 5: 274–91. Reprinted, with revisions, in Simmons 1979, pp. 75–100.
Simmons, A. John. 1979. *Moral Principles and Political Obligations*. Princeton, NJ: Princeton University Press.
Simmons, A. John. 1981. Reasonable expectations and obligations: a reply to Postow. *Southern Journal of Philosophy*, 19: 123–7.
Simmons, A. John. 1993. *On the Edge of Anarchy: Locke, Consent and the Limits of Society*. Princeton, NJ: Princeton University Press.
Simon, Herbert A. 1951. A formal theory of the employment relationship. *Econometrica*, 19: 293–305.
Simon, Herbert A. 1982. *Models of Bounded Rationality*. Cambridge, MA: MIT Press.
Simons, Kenneth W. 2006a. The conceptual structure of consent in criminal law. *Buffalo Criminal Law Review*, 9: 577–653.
Simons, Kenneth W. 2006b. A Restatement (Third) of intentional torts? *Arizona Law Review*, 48: 1061–102.
Simons, Kenneth W. 2019. Actual, apparent, hypothetical and implied-in-law consent in tort law. Paper presented to Moral, Social & Political Theory Seminar, Australian National University, 25 March. Available at: <https://www.dropbox.com/s/39n8jffv1pp0q9u/Actual%20hypo%20consent%20in%20tort%20law%202.15.19%20ANU.docx?dl=0>.
Singer, Peter. 1973. *Democracy & Disobedience*. Oxford: Oxford University Press.
Singer, Peter. 1974. Sidgwick and reflective equilibrium. *The Monist*, 58: 490–517.
Smith, Holly. 1983. Culpable ignorance. *Philosophical Review*, 92: 543–71.
Snyder, Lois for the American College of Physicians Ethics, Professionalism and Human Rights Committee. 2012. American College of Physicians ethics manual, 6th edn. *Annals of Internal Medicine*, Supplement. 156 (1, pt. 2): 73–104.

Southwood, Nicholas and Daniel Friedrich. 2009. Promises beyond assurance. *Philosophical Studies*, 144: 261–80.

Sreenivasan, Gopal. 2009. 'Oh, but you should have': Estlund on normative consent. *Iyyun*, 58: 62–72.

Stampp, Kenneth M. 1963. *The Peculiar Institution: Slavery in the Ante-bellum South*. New York: Knopf.

Stark, Cynthia A. 2000. Hypothetical consent and justification. *Journal of Philosophy*, 79: 313–34.

Steinberger, Peter. 2004. *The Idea of the State*. Cambridge: Cambridge University Press.

Strawson, P. F. 1964. Intention and convention in speech acts. *Philosophical Review*, 73: 439–60. Reprinted in Searle 1971, pp. 23–38.

Stroud, Seward R. 1939. Right of a physician to recover an implied-in-fact contract. *Michigan Law Review*, 37: 768–73.

Suetonius. 121/1957. *The Twelve Caesars*, trans. Robert Graves. Harmondsworth: Penguin; originally published 121.

Sunstein, Cass R. and Adrian Vermeule. 2005. Is capital punishment morally required? Acts, omissions and life-life tradeoffs. *Stanford Law Review*, 58: 703–50.

Tadros, Victor. 2016. *Wrongs and Crimes*. Oxford: Oxford University Press.

Tadros, Victor. 2021. Consent to sex in an unjust world. *Ethics*, 131: 293–318.

Tadros, Victor. 2022. Beyond the scope of consent. *Philosophy & Public Affairs*, 50: 430–66.

Tan, Jacinta; Tony Hope; and Anne Stewart. 2003. Competence to refuse treatment in anorexia nervosa. *International Journal of Law and Psychiatry*, 26: 697–707.

Tanasoca, Ana. 2022. Political consent under false pretences. Mimeo., Macquarie University.

Tännsjö, Torbjörn. 1990. *Conservatism for Our Time*. London: Routledge.

Tersman, Folke. 2018. Recent work on reflective equilibrium and method in ethics. *Philosophy Compass*, 13: e12493.

Thomson, Judith Jarvis. 1986. *Rights, Restitution and Risk*, ed. William Parent. Cambridge, MA: Harvard University Press.

Thomson, Judith Jarvis. 1990. *The Realm of Rights*. Cambridge, MA: Harvard University Press.

Ullmann-Margalit, Edna. 1983. On presumption. *Journal of Philosophy*, 80: 143–63.

Uniform Law Commission (ULC). 2012. Uniform premarital and marital agreements act. Available at <https://www.uniformlaws.org/viewdocument/final-act-101?CommunityKey=2e456584-938e-4008-ba0c-bb6a1a544400&tab=librarydocuments>.

United Nations (UN). 1948. Universal Declaration of Human Rights. Available at <https://www.ohchr.org/en/udhr/documents/udhr_translations/eng.pdf>.

United Nations (UN). 1964. Convention on consent to marriage, minimum age for marriage and registration of marriages. Available at <https://www.ohchr.org/en/professionalinterest/pages/minimumageformarriage.aspx>.

United Nations (UN). 1966. International covenant on economic, social and cultural rights. Available at <https://www.ohchr.org/en/instruments-mechanisms/instruments/international-covenant-economic-social-and-cultural-rights>.

United Nations (UN). 1969. Vienna convention on the law of treaties. Available at: http://untreaty.un.org/ilc/texts/instruments/english/conventions/1_1_1969.pdf.

US Court of Appeals. 1986. *United States v. Dyer*, 784 F.2d 812 (7th Cir.).

US Court of Appeals. 2004. *United States v. Gray*, 369 F.3d 1024 (8th Cir.).

US Court of Appeals. 2011. *United States v. Plugh*, 648 F.3d 118 (2d Cir.).

US Department of Defense (US DoD). 2006. Department of Defense instruction regarding medical treatment of detainees. *American Journal of International Law*, 100: 945–8.

US Department of Health & Human Services et al. (US DHHS). 1978. The Common Rule, subpart C: additional DHHS protections pertaining to biomedical and behavioral research involving prisoners as subjects. *Code of Federal Regulations*, title 45, part 46. Reprinted in Emanuel et al. 2003, pp. 57–3.

US Department of Health & Human Services et al. (US DHHS). 1983. The Common Rule, subpart D: additional DHHS protections for children involved as subjects in research. *Code of Federal Regulations*, title 45, part 46. Reprinted in Emanuel et al. 2003, pp. 53–5.

US Department of Health & Human Services et al. (US DHHS). 1991. The Common Rule, subpart A: federal policy for the protection of human subjects. *Code of Federal Regulations*, title 45, part 46. Reprinted in Emanuel et al. 2003, pp. 39–48.

US Department of State. 2021. US Passport Application. Available at <https://eforms.state.gov/Forms/ds11.pdf>.

US Supreme Court. 1923. *Baltimore & Ohio Railroad Company v. United States*, 261 US 592.

US Supreme Court. 1966. *Miranda v. Arizona*, 384 US 436.

Valentine, M. Beth. 2018. Constructive 'consent': a problematic fiction. *Law and Philosophy*, 37: 499–521.

van den Haag, Ernest and John P. Conrad. 1983. *The Death Penalty: A Debate*. New York: Plebyn.

Van Der Veer, Daniel. 1979. Paternalism and subsequent consent. *Canadian Journal of Philosophy*, 9: 631–42.

Van Der Veer, Daniel. 1986. *Paternalistic Intervention*. Princeton, NJ: Princeton University Press.

Van Frassen, Bas. 1995. Belief and the problem of Ulysses and the Sirens. *Philosophical Studies*, 77: 7–37.

Waddams, S.M. 1976. Unconscionability in contracts. *Modern Law Review*, 39: 369–93.

Waldron, Jeremy. 1981. A right to do wrong. *Ethics*, 92: 21–39. Reprinted in Waldron 1993, pp. 63–87.

Waldron, Jeremy. 1988. When justice replaces affection: the need for rights. *Harvard Journal of Law and Public Policy*, 11: 625–47. Reprinted in Waldron 1993, pp. 370–91.

Waldron, Jeremy. 1993. *Liberal Rights*. Cambridge: Cambridge University Press.

Walker, Tom. 2012. Ulysses contracts in medicine. *Law & Philosophy*, 31: 77–98.

Warmke, Brandon. 2016. The normative significance of forgiveness. *Australasian Journal of Philosophy*, 94: 687–703.

Watson, Gary. 2004. Asserting and promising. *Philosophical Studies*, 117: 57–77.

Weale, Albert. 1978. Consent. *Political Studies*, 26: 65–77.

Weale, Albert. 1999. *Democracy*. Houndmills: Macmillan.

Wellman, Christopher Heath. 2012. The rights forfeiture theory of punishment. *Ethics*, 122: 371–93.

Wendler, D.S. 2006. Assent in paediatric research: theoretical and practical considerations. *Journal of Medical Ethics*, 32: 229–34.

Wertheimer, Alan. 1987. *Coercion*. Princeton, NJ: Princeton University Press.

Wertheimer, Alan. 1996. Consent and sexual relations. *Legal Theory*, 2: 89–112.

Wertheimer, Alan. 2000. What is consent? And is it important? *Buffalo Criminal Law Review*, 3: 557–83.

Wertheimer, Alan. 2001. Intoxicated consent and sexual relations. *Law & Philosophy*, 20: 373–401.

Wertheimer, Alan. 2003. *Consent to Sexual Relations*. Cambridge: Cambridge University Press.

Wertheimer, Alan. 2010. Consent to sexual relations. Pp. 195–220 in *The Ethics of Consent: Theory and Practice*, ed. Franklin Miller and Alan Wertheimer. New York: Oxford University Press.

Westen, Peter. 2004. *The Logic of Consent*. Burlington, VT: Ashgate.

Wiesing, U.; R.J. Jox; H.-J. Heſler; and G.D. Borasio. 2010. A new law on advance directives in Germany. *Journal of Medical Ethics*, 36: 779–83.

Wilkinson, T.M. 2012. Opt-out organ procurement and tacit consent. *Journal of Medical Ethics*, 38: 74–5.

Williams, Bernard. 1973. A critique of utilitarianism. Pp. 75–150 in J.J.C. Smart and Bernard Williams, *Utilitarianism, For and Against*. Cambridge: Cambridge University Press.

Williams, Bernard. 1981. *Moral Luck*. Cambridge: Cambridge University Press.

Williams, Elizabeth A. 2008. Gags, funnels and tubes: forced feeding of the insane and of suffragettes. *Endeavour*, 32 (4): 134–40.

Wispelaere, Jurgen De. 2012. Tacitly opting out of organ donation: too presumptuous after all? *Journal of Medical Ethics*, 38: 73–4.

Witmer-Rich, Jonathan. 2011. It's good to be autonomous: prospective consent, retrospective consent and the foundation of consent in the criminal law. *Criminal Law and Philosophy*, 5: 377–98.

Woodhouse, A.P.S., ed. 1938. *Puritanism and Liberty: Being the Army Debates (1547–9) from the Clarke Manuscripts with Supplementary Documents*. London: Dent.

Woozley, A.D. 1969. What is wrong with retrospective law? *Philosophical Quarterly*, 18: 40–53.

World Medical Association (WMA). 1948. Declaration of Geneva: The Physician's Pledge. Revised 2017. Available at <https://www.wma.net/policies-post/wma-declaration-of-geneva/>.

World Medical Association (WMA). 1949. International Code of Medical Ethics. Revised 2006. Available at <https://www.wma.net/policies-post/wma-international-code-of-medical-ethics/>.

World Medical Association (WMA). 1964. Declaration of Helsinki: Ethical Principles for Medical Research Involving Human Subjects. Revised 2013. Available at <https://www.wma.net/policies-post/wma-declaration-of-helsinki-ethical-principles-for-medical-research-involving-human-subjects/>. Reprinted in: *Journal of the American Medical Association*, 310 (2013): 2191–4; Emanuel et al. 2003, pp. 30–2.

World Medical Association (WMA). 1975. Declaration of Tokyo: Guidelines for Physicians Concerning Torture and other Cruel, Inhuman or Degrading Treatment or Punishment in Relation to Detention and Imprisonment. Revised 2016. Available at <https://www.wma.net/policies-post/wma-declaration-of-tokyo-guidelines-for-physicians-concerning-torture-and-other-cruel-inhuman-or-degrading-treatment-or-punishment-in-relation-to-detention-and-imprisonment/>.

World Medical Association (WMA). 1991. Declaration of Malta on Hunger Strikers. Revised 2017. Available at <https://www.wma.net/policies-post/wma-declaration-of-malta-on-hunger-strikers/>.

Wrigley, Anthony. 2007. Personal identity, autonomy and advance statements. *Journal of Applied Philosophy*, 24: 381–96.

Wyatt-Brown, Bertram. 1982. *Southern Honor: Ethics and Behavior in the Old South*. Oxford: Oxford University Press.

Zimmerman, David. 1981. Coercive wage offers. *Philosophy & Public Affairs*, 10: 121–45.

Zoglin, Richard. 2020. Why do none of Trump's jokes feel like jokes? *Washington Post*, 6 July; available at <https://www.washingtonpost.com/opinions/why-do-none-of-trumps-jokes-feel-like-jokes/2020/07/03/bdcc053a-bca1-11ea-bdaf-a129f921026f_story.html>.

Index

For the benefit of digital users, indexed terms that span two pages (e.g., 52–53) may, on occasion, appear on only one of those pages.